Oscar Dearest

PETER H. BROWN and JIM PINKSTON

"Oscar® Dearest

SIX DECADES OF SCANDAL, POLITICS
AND GREED BEHIND HOLLYWOOD'S
ACADEMY AWARDS 1927–1986

PERENNIAL LIBRARY

Harper & Row, Publishers, New York
Cambridge, Philadelphia, San Francisco, Washington
London, Mexico City, São Paulo, Singapore, Sydney

*This book is neither authorized nor endorsed by
the Academy of Motion Picture Arts and Sciences*

FIRST EDITION

Designer: Barbara DuPree Knowles

LIBRARY OF CONGRESS CATALOGING-IN-PUBLICATION DATA
Brown, Peter H.
Oscar® dearest.
Bibliography: p.
Includes index.
1. Academy awards (Moving-pictures) I. Pinkston, Jim. II. Title.
PN1993.92.B76 1987   791.43′079   86-45642
ISBN 0-06-096091-4 (pbk.)

87 88 89 90 91 MPC 10 9 8 7 6 5 4 3 2 1

Acknowledgments

Our passion for Hollywood in general, and the Oscars in particular, is long-standing and absolute. For giving us the chance to see a book come out of this lifelong passion, we are most grateful to Larry Ashmead, executive editor at Harper & Row, who convinced his editorial board to publish the kind of book we wanted to write.

And without Margaret Wimberger, our dedicated editor, whose patience and guidance inspired us to new levels of endurance, enthusiasm and, hopefully, accomplishment, there simply would have been no book.

To our agents, Bart Andrews and Sherry Robb, go our deepest appreciation for putting this book in the hands of the perfect publisher, and for shoring us up during the trying, sometimes painful, research process.

Credit must also be given to copyeditor William Reynolds, whose endless fact-checking helped to give the book a higher standard of accuracy.

That this book has been a labor of love from the beginning goes without saying. If we have succeeded, a large measure of our success is due to the many film industry people, and those on the periphery, whom we interviewed or who assisted in our research. We are most beholden to Valerie Allen, Julie Andrews, Hal Ashby, Mary Astor, Martin Baum, Bill Belcher, Peter Bogdonavich, Myron Brown, Pamela Brown, Frank Capra, Charles Champlin, Cher, Jeff Corey, Bob Crane, George Cukor, Philip Dunne, Blake Edwards, Joan Fontaine, Jet Fore, Carl Foreman, Gary Franklin, Dore Freeman, Lillian Gish, actress/director Lee Grant, film writer Lee Grant, Jack Haley Jr., Halston, Edith Head, Kim Hunter, Elois Jenssen, Howard W. Koch, Jerry Lazar, Irv Letofsky, John Lithgow, Sacheen Littlefeather, Bob Mackie, Dorothy Malone, Alice Marchak, Barbara Messing, Ann Miller, Vincente Minnelli, Meyer Mishkin, Pola Negri, Robert Osborne, Estelle Parsons, Marty Pasetta, Jackie Reach, Debbie Reynolds, Cliff Robertson, Buddy Rogers, Henry Rogers, Mark Rydell, George C. Scott, Gale Sondergaard, Rod Steiger, Howard Suber, Ron Talsky, Lana Turner, Trish van Devere, Marc Wanamaker, Orson Welles, Michael Westmore and Elaine Young.

For stills and other photographs, our thanks to the Margaret Herrick

viii Library at the Academy of Motion Picture Arts and Sciences, Associated Press/Wide World Photos, Back Lot Books and Stills, Bertil Unger, Bison Archives, Book City Collectibles, Eddie Brandt's Saturday Matinee, Bill Chapman's Picture Palace, Cinema Collectors, Edmunds Book Shop, Gary Franklin, Ken Hollywood, Hollywood Book and Poster Company, Long Photography, James Roark, Steve Smith, and UPI Telephotos.

Lastly, we wish to acknowledge the assistance of Linda Mehr, administrator of the Margaret Herrick Library, and her able staff: Steve Anderson, Sandra Archer, Scott Busby, Craig Campbell, Carol Cullen, Robert Cushman, Pat DeFazio, Stacy Endres, Sue England, Sam Gill, Tony Guzman, Diana Hrabowecki, Mona Huntzing, Kristine Krueger, Laura Kusler, Marlene Laskey, George Majewski, Jeffrey Mintz, Lisa Mosher, Susan Oka, Kathy Reesman, Tony Salome, Lucia Schultz, Warren Sherk, Leslie Skopp, Tony Slide, Richard Stermer, Patrick Stockstill, David Sugarman and Therese Trujillo. Their assistance is simply incalculable.

Contents

Foreword

May, 1986. Magazine publishing professionals had gathered in Los Angeles to honor achievements in their industry during the preceding year. Midway through the evening one publisher made his second trip to the podium to accept an award.

With a sly grin, he blurted to the audience, "You like me! You really like me!" The crowd roared.

The audience laughed because they recognized his remarks as the same words Sally Field had used more than a year earlier in accepting her second Oscar.

They laughed because they got the joke; they were pop culture savvy.

They laughed because almost everyone in America has an Oscar fantasy, and this man was willing to share his with the crowd.

They laughed at the absurdity of it all.

Well they might, too. Any ceremony that has opened with Teri Garr in an ersatz 1930s production number and closed with Elizabeth Taylor leading an all-star Bicentennial singalong, has left itself wide open to derisive laughs.

But the Oscars are also serious business. They mean big bucks to film distributors and theater owners, good press to a small army of reporters, and a camp ritual for a world-wide television audience.

For years the press has attributed the ceremony's appeal to its inherent glamor, but such critics have missed the point.

Sally Field's speech is much closer to the real reason. Her speech was lampooned by some as adolescent gushing, praised by others as a spontaneous expression of her excitement.

To everyone, however, the moment could hardly be anything but supremely human, and that's the key to Oscar's hold on the world's imagination. Whether by fluke or design, the Academy Awards ceremony, year after year, successfully bridges the gap between old world movie glamor and what is, fundamentally, human foible.

Television is too familiar and the stage too exotic for the stars of either to capture the imagination of the majority of the public. But movie stars, illuminated larger than life in the dark, in a medium that grew up with the century and is the closest we have come to a global language, are still glamorous, still vaguely ethereal.

That image is one that moviegoers everywhere want to hang on to. **xi**

But they also want to know that, but for the fickle magic of the camera (and the whimsical attention of the press), any one of them could be a movie star.

The Academy Awards are timeless reminders of this possibility. For more than fifty years, virtually every human emotion and experience has played a part in one ceremony or another.

The world has watched, outraged, as Judy Garland, Cary Grant, Greta Garbo and others were denied their industry's highest honor.

The world has watched, elated, as industry newcomers, people like Julie Andrews and Barbra Streisand, have shot straight to the top almost overnight.

The world watched while an aging Mary Pickford brushed away a tear while accepting an Oscar that was a simple "thank you" from her industry.

The world watched Barbara Stanwyck cry in memory of her friend William Holden, and it watched Charlie Chaplin cry at his industry's belated welcome home.

We were there to share Jane Fonda's elation at the long overdue honor for her father, and Liza Minnelli's triumph in the moment her mother never had.

At the Oscars, the world witnessed the sibling rivalry of Joan Fontaine and Olivia de Havilland, the father/son success of John and Walter Huston, and Elizabeth Taylor's bittersweet "Virginia Woolf" Oscar while husband Richard Burton went wanting.

Oscar hype has focused on the birth of Judy Garland's son, the near death of Elizabeth Taylor in the clutches of pneumonia, and Steven Spielberg's wounded ego.

At the Oscars, the industry forgave Ingrid Bergman for her indiscretions and Jane Fonda for her politics, and said goodbye to John Wayne and Susan Hayward.

Oscar winners have thanked mothers, fathers, sons, daughters, agents, directors, and psychiatrists. Shirley MacLaine thanked her spiritual guides; documentary filmmaker, Robert Epstein, thanked his partner in life.

The world gaped at Joanne Woodward's homemade frock, Barbra Streisand's see-through pajamas, Cher's Indian headdress, and Audrey Hepburn's flawless chic.

Yet amidst this super showcase of hype and glitter, the Oscars offer enough magic to remind audiences of the miracle of the movies. Anyone who doubts this need only remember the electrifying appearance of Katharine Hepburn in 1974.

All of these moments—bold and bright, poignant and ridiculous—the authors have endeavored to capture in a book that understands the fundamental appeal of the Academy Awards ritual, that pays tribute to its glamour, and that acknowledges what may be among the most human of foibles: our ceaseless interest in the Oscars.

Allan Halcrow

Oscar Dearest

The Oscars are absolutely the best institution in Hollywood.
—NORMA SHEARER, 1934

The Oscar is a cruel joke hatched up by a cruel town and handed out in a cruel ceremony.
—MARION DAVIES, 1943

Acting in films is not a goddamned horse race . . . and that's what makes the Academy Awards so very wrong.
—RICHARD BURTON, 1967

The Oscar is something to be feared . . . to be avoided because the town takes it too seriously, tries too hard to get it, thus ruining the real reason for making films. . . .
—GEORGE C. SCOTT, 1970

Hello, gorgeous.
—BARBRA STREISAND TO HER OSCAR, 1969

After I won the Oscar, my salary doubled, my friends tripled, my kids became more popular at school, the butcher made a pass at me, and my maid asked for a raise.
—SHIRLEY JONES, 1977

Of course, it's always wonderful to win the Oscar . . . everybody in the business wants one . . . if they say they don't, they're probably lying.
—INGRID BERGMAN, 1979

What does the Academy Award mean? I don't think it means much of anything.
—SALLY FIELD, 1980

It's a heartbreaker, that's certain. After that, I've nothing more to say about the Oscar. And I shouldn't have.
—ORSON WELLES, 1982

As long as they keep handing them out, I'll keep showing up to get them.
—SHIRLEY MACLAINE, 1984

. . . [the Oscar means] you like me—right now you like me!
—SALLY FIELD, 1984

It's real important to remember that we make films for artistic reasons and not to win a little gold statue.
—MARTIN SCORSESE, 1979

It's become real fashionable to scoff at the Oscar today, but those jesters would kill to win one.
—FRANK CAPRA, 1984

Prologue

The way I see it, there's only one place that does it right. Every year in Barcelona they give awards for poetry. The third prize is a silver rose. The second prize is a gold one. The first prize, the one for the best poem of all, is a real rose.

—PETER BOGDANOVICH

There's something desperate about it. It's even a bit coy; a scene too cute for words.

Dustin Hoffman has just descended from Hollywood's Valhalla with the 1979 Best Actor prize in his hands. He's just a knight with his Oscar, ready to take on the world. Because, two minutes earlier, Hoffman bought Hollywood—all of it, from the zircon hemline on Cher's dress to the last inch of cement in front of Grauman's Chinese Theater. Others stood in that same rarefied light of course. Sally Field, for instance; and Meryl Streep—but only for a few seconds.

Hollywood is still a chauvinistic empire: Man rules; the actor, *not* the actress. Hoffman has a fraction of time to himself, at the top of a billion-dollar hill. It's dizzy up there—a heady atmosphere that still has a hint of Gable and Bogie. And it's slippery—slick from the tracks of yesterday's kings on their way back down. Voight, Dreyfuss, Nicholson.

Plenty of time. It's not midnight yet. And Hoffman's won himself a few extra minutes by lustily dedicating his to all those nameless and faceless actors out in the smog. The ones who won't make it: quickly aging waiters and carhops smiling vainly at a town on the make. Hoffman tugged at his beautifully cut tuxedo. His mouth turned up at the corners in a little-boy smile. His friends hardly recognized it. But no matter; this wasn't a smile for intimates. It was a smile for Brazil, and Soho. A smile for the faceless fans in Kankakee, Illinois, and Midlothian, Texas.

Finally the last flashbulb has popped and even the gossip columnists are getting bored. Oscar in hand, Hoffman glides over to the ice lady of all Hollywood journalists, Rona Barrett, sits down next to her, and lowers his handsome head into her lap. "Well," he says, "the soap opera won." Rona's smile doesn't vary a millimeter.

She probably knows, as does everyone else in the room, that this is a new Dustin Hoffman; a "born again" Dustin Hoffman, not the same

One of a hundred lightweight Oscars is moved from the Academy to the Dorothy Chandler Pavilion for the Oscarcast. (© A.M.P.A.S.)

man of *Straw Dogs*, of *Papillon*, or even of *Lenny*. For he has crossed over into Hollywood's twilight zone—into the murky inner sanctum of the establishment. And if he later looks into the mirror and says "Hey, who's this guy?," he didn't show it that April night in 1980. Less than a decade earlier, Hoffman, still the angry young man of *The Graduate*, lashed out at the cruel realities of the Oscar rites.

Then he cried out, as if in pain, about the pointless, gross charade of the Academy Awards—an institution that honors the cotton candy of the box office instead of artistic integrity.

Well, Dustin Hoffman has some cotton candy of his own now. This year's winner. The world at large knows it as *Kramer vs. Kramer*, but the guys and dolls on Rodeo Drive know it as "Dustin's film"—many miles of celluloid that have carried him over the top. Only six months ago they sat in their Puccis and Guccis and chatted cattily about whether or not Dustin would be able to overcome a couple of weighty turkeys known as *Straight Time* and *Agatha*. Tomorrow they will all laugh smugly into their Perrier and chortle that they "knew it all along." Then they'll rush back to their sleek executive towers to call Dustin's agent. Perhaps, they coo, he could do a little *Kramer vs. Kramer* for them. They'd been planning to call him all along, of course. Isn't it funny about timing. This town is just one long coincidence.

The celebrity photographer Gary Franklin said it all in this portrait of a jubilant, arrogantly successful Dustin Hoffman the night he carted off the Best Actor prize in 1980 for Kramer vs. Kramer—*which also won for Best Picture, Best Director (Robert Benton), Best Supporting Actress (the magical Meryl Streep), and best original screenplay based on material from another medium (Robert Benton). Hoffman, the greatest Oscar baiter since George C. Scott, suddenly became the establishment pussycat, lapping up the cream that comes with an Oscar. "He held that thing so tight," Rona Barrett mused, "I thought he was using it as a scepter. But we didn't crown him. Or did we?" (© A.M.P.A.S.)*

Prologue

3

The same guys who whispered that he was through when *Lenny* bombed will now smile and wave boldly from their Alfas as Hoffman just continues jogging up the hill in Westwood. His boyish smile is back. He's 43, and this is Act 2.

Who can blame him for the momentary lapse? The Oscar ceremony is a pagan rite, after all; a night when the tribe comes out to bay at the moon and drink the waters of fame. The young ones come to nurse at the nipple of glamor; the old ones come to bathe in the golden light and reaffirm their manufactured identities. See, I'm still there—just look at the monitor if you don't believe it. The most realistic of them see it for what it is. Coming off the Oscar stage in the fifties, Joan Crawford heard a fellow star murmur, "You looked wonderful up there on the screen." Crawford pulled at her diamonds and hissed: "That's not me; that's Joan Crawford."

And so it was.

If there was anyone left in town who doubted the paganism of the Academy Awards, the last ten years have made converts out of them.

In 1974 there was Susan Hayward, almost carried onstage by a pair of strong arms, wearing a two-thousand-dollar dress and her old, gutsy smile. There was a pause before she started speaking, which sent a frozen dagger out into the heart of Hollywood. Everyone knew Susan Hayward was dying—bad news gets around Beverly Hills in less than an hour. Indeed, the world knew. The *National Enquirer* had dished up all the blunt details to eighty million readers. Up in a sterile medical tower on Sunset Boulevard two doctors and a nurse held their breath,

Such old-style glamour stars as Inger Stevens, left, and Shirley MacLaine—on the arm of a sartorially splendid Warren Beatty—turn out for the Oscars.

hoping that Hayward would make it those few last steps—her last in the soothing spotlight of mass love. One of them slammed his fist onto a steel counter and wondered at a world willing to put a girl that sick through a dog and pony show.

No sacrifice is too great for the voracious appetites of the one billion viewers out in the world television arena.

But when the Academy offered up Mary Pickford in 1976 there was no lower to go. As usual, they softened the blow with that balmy term, "special award." They promised no fuss, no invasion of privacy for filmdom's first superstar—a lady who had gracefully left public life. "A couple of people. One camera," they told the man who ran the vast Pickford empire.

Mary agreed. Four people, and they'd hardly be noticed in her living room. The day came, Mary Pickford descended from the distant upper reaches of Pickfair, the castle she'd shared with Douglas Fairbanks since movies were silent and they were king and queen. She rounded the corner into a blaze of light which blanked out the room's soft curtains. The network had squeezed about forty people in there—a restless, poking crowd. It would have frightened Streisand, let alone Pickford.

Still, she lifted her chin and broke into a fading Pollyanna grin. "Thank you so much," she said, tears forming at the edges of her eyes. On the Oscar show the boys in charge let this tape run its full, devastating course, tracing the camera over her Victorian face, capturing every year and every moment's emotion of that night written there.

Suddenly, the jig was up. It became clear that the Academy and its TV henchmen would root up any part or all of its ravaged past to win the ratings game—in much the same way that a dashing and handsome streaker materialized from the wings, in the 1974 ceremony.

Susan Hayward, in a hot red dress, holding aloft the Oscar she won for 1958's I Want to Live! *It had been a long haul to the top for the former Edythe Marrener, whose face first appeared among those screen-testing for the Scarlett O'Hara role in* Gone With The Wind. *Pushing her way through a series of exploitative film roles, Hayward finally got her teeth into a decent script in 1947 with* Smash-Up: The Story of a Woman. *Other nominations followed for* My Foolish Heart, With a Song in My Heart, *and* I'll Cry Tomorrow. *Then* I Want to Live! *The actress couldn't know on Oscar night that this would be the high point of her career. In usual fifties post-Oscar tradition, Hayward was pushed into one overblown production after another—all designed to cash in on her status as an Oscar winner. One of her last roles was in the tawdry* Valley of the Dolls, *where she fumed, to an equally obnoxious Patty Duke, "Get your butt outta my dressin' room."*
(© A.M.P.A.S.)

"Litle Mary," "Mary the Adored," "Mary the Queen of Hollywood," [Mary Pickford] poses ever so coyly with her Oscar. The photographer was the great George Hurrell, summoned to the royal presence to record the star's win for Coquette *(1928-1929). But Mary so coveted the award that she helped make it the object of greed it has become.* (© A.M.P.A.S.)

Mary Pickford receiving her special Oscar from Walter Mirisch on the 1976 Oscarcast. It was exploitative to be sure. It caused fellow Oscar winner Joan Fontaine to snap, "Well, at least I'll know ahead of time when I'm dying—they'll give me one of those honorary Oscars." But there were defenders—such as columnist Mike Royko, who said: "Many of those say they would rather remember her as she once was. Why? She's not dead. She may be old, but she is a living, breathing human being. She has thoughts and emotions, and, I'm sure, experiences happiness. That's what I thought I saw on her face when the camera came in close. There was even a tiny teardrop in her eye—a tear of joy." (© A.M.P.A.S.)

What's one more publicity stunt in the biggest Hollywood publicity stunt of them all—the Academy Awards?

Ratings translate into millions of viewers; millions of viewers translate into ticket buyers, who only mean money. Money, profits, movie grosses—this is the essence of Oscar.

Some say it wasn't always that way, a claim that's hard to judge. One thing's for sure, it was that way in 1948, when all the studios pulled their money out of the Oscar show after it became obvious that a British film, *Hamlet,* and a British actor, Laurence Olivier, were going to be the big winners. "Jeez," said some of the moguls. "We didn't go to *this* trouble to publicize foreign pictures."

The big boys weren't worrying about artistic integrity. They were worried about ticket sales.

There used to be a big glass case over at MGM which held the studio's Oscars—all stacked up neatly in a row, by movie and by year. Tour guides used to point out the case to tourists, quoting prices up and down the box-office scale. "Now, this here's the ten-million-dollar Oscar," they would say, pointing to the little gold man won by *Ben-Hur.* "And over here is the five-million-dollar Oscar for *An American in Paris.*"

Those tour guides aren't there anymore, and the Oscars have all been moved to the MGM Grand Hotel in Las Vegas—closer to the money.

Even more so today, ticket sales seem to be Oscar's overriding purpose. Only, inflation has hit. Boy, has it hit! Now they call them "the twenty-five-million-dollar Oscars." Some of them are worth a lot more than that. *One Flew over the Cuckoo's Nest,* the first film to win all top four Oscars since *It Happened One Night,* cashed in on its Academy Awards and added more than $50 million to its worldwide ticket sales. Video cassette sales have upped that by another 50 percent. The film would have made additional dough anyway. But it's hard to separate a movie's real attraction from Oscar hype. The studio bosses of today

might be mildly interested in what a film would do without *any* Oscar exposure, but they sure wouldn't want to risk finding out.

The result is inevitable and unfortunate: an Oscar that can create financial empires overnight will never be free of meddling and blatant attempts to buy or coerce the award out of the Academy's voters. The Academy adds to the problem by refusing to pump new membership blood into its branches, thereby failing to keep up with the vast artistic growth of the industry. Hollywood now has a central core of at least forty thousand actors, writers, cinematographers, and other artists and craftsmen. The Academy has four thousand seven hundred members, give or take a few. And only about 50 to 60 percent of those can be counted on to vote. Some put the figure as low as 40 percent. This means that the most important decision in the industry is made by only one-twentieth of that industry. And there is little chance that this will ever change.

A few of the wiser winners and nominees have seen through the desperation and avarice surrounding the Oscar.

Rosalind Russell, four times nominated and never a winner, came to view the city's barbaric rite with increasing dismay. "In 1942, I'd got my first Academy Award nomination for *My Sister Eileen*. Glad as I was about it, the honor put me under heavy pressure. It means too much to the studios to have their people win," said Russell in the seventies. "I still can't bear to think about the tension surrounding those races without breaking into a sweat."

Charles Champlin, executive arts editor of the *Los Angeles Times*, called the Oscar "the tail that wags the Academy." And it's true. Nobody truly cares that the Academy is at the forefront of the drive to restore and save old films, or that its archives now contain the largest single historic collection of stills, scripts, and movie clips—a library that has rescued many chapters of film history.

The crowds still gather, still wait with baited breath at a ceremony which brings out fewer and fewer superstars each year. As Oscar in the eighties has turned his back on stars in favor of "New York actors," most of the Best Actor and Actress nominees walk through the crowds unrecognized. For instance, F. Murray Abraham, Geraldine Page, William Hurt, Tom Hulce, and Ben Kingsley have swept in and out of the winner's circle with barely a whisper, while such nonwinners as Joan Collins, Diana Ross, Kevin Bacon, Sean Penn, and Jennifer Beals regularly bring down the house.

Likewise its research, scholarship programs, festivals, and technical publications get little or no media attention from the howling mob of reporters that storms the gates each year to report on the bacchanal crowning Hollywood's king and queen of the May.

Only a stalwart few have been able to resist the sweet screams of this Lorelei and her seductive promises of wealth, instant fame, and ego elixir.

Many have tried and failed—like Dustin Hoffman, who kicked out in rage at the Oscars when winning seemed hopeless to him, but came back to the fold when Oscar's honeyed words were whispered into his ears.

Two men stand above the pack—an almost forgotten screenwriter named Dudley Nichols and George C. Scott.

Nichols was first. He entered Academy history in 1936 by refusing to show up on Oscar night for his prize. (He'd already been told that he had won, for *The Informer*.) At that time the Academy was still being used by the studio establishment to halt the spread of labor unions. The three-thousand-member Screen Actors Guild, the five-hundred-member Screen Writers Guild, and the fledgling Screen Directors Guild had all asked their members, winners included, to boycott the ceremony.

Of the major winners, only Nichols and director John Ford, who also won for *The Informer*, stayed home. Bette Davis, Victor McLaglen, and others dutifully showed up to take their statues home.

Twenty-five years later, when even a Best Supporting Actor Oscar could add $2 million to a career, George C. Scott was caught up in the annual Oscar lust before he consulted his own conscience. Scott, already a legend on the stage, made his film debut in *The Hanging Tree* in 1959. Six months later Otto Preminger picked him to play the driven, vicious prosecuting attorney in *Anatomy of a Murder*.

Even up against co-stars Lee Remick, James Stewart, and Ben Gazzara, Scott walked away covered with glory. As his biographer, W. A. Harbison, said, "He never had to worry about getting a film once *Anatomy of a Murder* was released."

Hedda Hopper predicted an Oscar for him and he was easily nominated—along with Arthur O'Connell from the same film, Hugh Griffith in *Ben-Hur*, Robert Vaughn in *The Young Philadelphians*, and Ed Wynn in *The Diary of Anne Frank*.

Scott was the new face in town. He stood a good chance of winning. Friends said he wanted the Academy Award as much as he'd wanted anything in his career. Many newcomers to the factories of mediocrity —and Scott may have been one of them—are easily dazzled by the Oscar's golden light.

Years later, in a reflective moment, he told his wife, actress Trish Van Devere, that he had learned a valuable lesson on Oscar night, 1960. "He said he wanted it so badly that he became almost completely wrapped up in it. When he didn't win, he took a hard look, and came to believe it wasn't healthy to want something so much."

Van Devere, who became her husband's co-star in a half dozen films and on Broadway, said Scott first looked at himself and his own morbid fascination with the Oscar, and then at the larger picture.

Nineteen sixty was a good year to do it.

Old-style studio greed still had the Academy Awards in a vise. Whether the Oscar went to a good film or merely an expensive film was decided at the whim of potentates such as Darryl Zanuck, Hal Wallis, and Jack Warner. Nominations were easy to control; the finals were more difficult but still "buyable" in one way or another.

Nominations were decided by a slippery "sliding scale," by which Academy members gave five votes to their first choice, four votes to their second choice, and so on down to one vote for their fifth choice. The studios, viewing the Oscars in much the same way a college sorority views the election for homecoming queen, perfected a system that kept out many good films and included many, many turkeys. If you were a studio insider in 1960, you knew that you could put your guy first, and then list four completely hopeless choices as two through five. Your man got five votes instead of one.

MGM, the studio which founded the Academy, used the weighted scale beautifully in 1960. The men with keys to the executive washrooms played the system as if it were a fine violin. An MGM man who was truly loyal to his studio would list Charlton Heston, for *Ben-Hur*, as his first choice, perhaps followed by Rock Hudson for *Pillow Talk*, and Troy Donahue for *A Summer Place*. This clinched a nomination for Heston without bringing in a heavyweight to spar against him in the finals.

Of course, the system backfired occasionally, depending on an individual's definition of a silly performance. In 1960, Universal-International may have listed Doris Day tops for *Pillow Talk*, while over at MGM, "April fool" voters were putting her on *their* lists as a fairly hopeless choice. In any case, Doris Day was nominated for Best Actress on the flimsy strength of *Pillow Talk*.

Ben-Hur, a super-expensive chariot soap opera, went into the finals that year with more nominations than any film since *Gone With The Wind*. This headwind carried the film, Heston, Hugh Griffith, and director William Wyler to victory. In their respective races, the performances of Heston and Griffith were the weakest. Today, Heston's stint as the dashing charioteer is completely overshadowed by the work of his competitors that year: Laurence Harvey in *Room at the Top*, Jack Lemmon in *Some Like It Hot*, Paul Muni in *The Last Angry Man*, and James Stewart in *Anatomy of a Murder*.

George C. Scott wasn't aware of these cruel realities when he was nominated in 1960 for Best Supporting Actor in *Anatomy of a Murder*. Beaten by Hugh Griffith for *Ben-Hur*, he was so crushed when the winner was announced that he "vowed right then that such a small thing as a prize shouldn't make any difference."

"I came to see it as a fawning, dizzy 'meat contest' staged every spring. The process was not something I could live with comfortably."

He said all this and more regarding Oscar's barbarism two years later, when he was again nominated for Best Supporting Actor, for his performance in *The Hustler*. Scott told the Academy, by telegram, to take his name off the Oscar nomination lists. The Academy refused, stating tersely that it was "Mr. Scott's work and not Scott himself which was nominated."

Scott, in turn, informed the Academy that the campaigning by actors and their agents degraded the whole process. "It encourages the public to think that the award is more important to the actor than the work for which he was nominated," Scott told a writer for the *New York Times*. A close friend told the same writer: "He dislikes that whole Hollywood, back-patting atmosphere. For the Oscar, you have to throw a few cocktail parties yourself and get people to screenings so they can take a look

Oscar producer Howard W. Koch lost among the huge portraits of possible winners in the Dorothy Chandler Pavilion. The posters are arranged so that camera angles can be tested. Shown in this 1982 shot are blowups of, among others, James Coco, nominated Best Supporting Actor for Only When I Laugh, *and Frank Marshall, front right of Koch, producer of* Raiders of the Lost Ark.

at you and all that sort of thing." The friend said the Oscar façade went against Scott's own philosophy: "He told me that the Oscars were just a way for the motion-picture companies to make more money on the pictures and had little other value."

That year the actor was defeated by George Chakiris, whose musical performance in *West Side Story* brought down the house. But Scott finally got his point across to the Academy. (It usually takes more than a gallant gesture to get through to these crowned heads.) Despite his work in *Dr. Strangelove or: How I Learned to Stop Worrying and Love the Bomb*, *The Flim-Flam Man*, and *Petulia*, he wasn't knighted again by the swift Oscar sword until *Patton* burst onto the screen in 1970.

Scott had immersed himself in Patton's character; he ordered up old newsreels from World War II, running them dozens of times. His preparation showed in the film—the actor hid himself completely behind Patton's façade. There was no doubt that he'd be nominated for an Oscar. The question was: What would he do about it?

"Life isn't a race," Scott told the Associated Press. "It's a war of survival and there are many who get crippled and injured on the way. And because it's not a race, I don't consider myself in competition with my fellow actors for rewards or recognition. That is why I have rejected the nomination for playing Patton."

This furor secretly delighted the Academy voters, who like nothing better than to give an award occasionally to a maverick.

So they gave him the Best Actor prize (which still sits uncollected in Academy vaults). Many saw Scott's Oscar for *Patton* as a glorious sign that the Academy Awards, once and for all, were free of arbitrary favoritism.

So Scott decided to shut up about it. The year after *Patton*, when the Academy again nominated him for his work in *Hospital* (which many feel to be, along with *Hardcore*, his finest screen performance), he uttered not a single word about *Hospital*, the nomination, or the Academy. Therefore, his nomination and his loss created hardly a newsworthy whisper.

George C. Scott has seen nothing in Oscar's more recent history that would make him change his mind. "I fully expect that I'll never get another nomination," he said. "But if I did, I wouldn't talk about it."

His is the weariness adopted by many others tired of Hollywood's incessant worship of the dollar.

Liz Taylor, on the morning after receiving her second Oscar, for *Who's Afraid of Virginia Woolf?*, smiled tiredly and said, "It's nice to win, but the edge is certainly taken off because Richard [Burton] didn't win. And he *was* the best actor of the year" (also for *Who's Afraid of Virginia Woolf?*).

These dissenting voices have, however, been weak and few. The first half-century of the awards has wrapped the Oscar in a Wagnerian-like myth; the statue is truly "a golden idol," an international symbol of glamour and excellence.

An Oscar was the first thing shown to U.S. Army intelligence officers when they visited the home of Nazi actor Emil Jannings in Bavaria. Jannings, the first Best Actor winner, for *The Last Command* and *The Way of All Flesh*, had long before returned with his trophy to Germany, becoming powerful and wealthy as Hitler's "first actor."

Jannings, then fatally ill with cancer, invited international journalists and photographers to his home on the shores of Lake St. Wolfgang

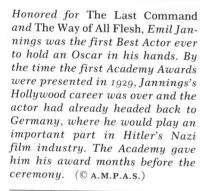

George C. Scott with field glasses trying to get a bead on the enemy in a snowy scene from Patton, *which won seven awards out of ten nominations. Scott refused to take the Oscar and wouldn't even reply to an official letter from the Academy asking what should be done with the orphaned award. "Choosing a best actor or even a best picture is a farce," he said publicly.*

Honored for The Last Command *and* The Way of All Flesh, *Emil Jannings was the first Best Actor ever to hold an Oscar in his hands. By the time the first Academy Awards were presented in 1929, Jannings's Hollywood career was over and the actor had already headed back to Germany, where he would play an important part in Hitler's Nazi film industry. The Academy gave him his award months before the ceremony.* (© A.M.P.A.S.)

and leaned on his Oscar for help. In halting English he explained, as would others, that he had been forced to "go along with Hitler or be sent to a concentration camp." With the Oscar near his fingertips, the heavy, aged actor said, "I've only made one propaganda film, *Ohm Krüger*—and that I did under pressure. When Goebbels first offered me the leading role in that anti-British picture, I refused. And he ordered it."

It would later come out that Jannings was not only popular but had been favored economically, being declared tax-exempt by Nazi Finance Minister Fritz Reinhardt.

And yet, the industry, and the world, didn't take the publicity stunt so seriously. And that's what the Oscars are: a gilded publicity stunt foisted on the planet.

Many of Oscar's earliest generation wonder how the award came to be taken so seriously. It didn't start that way.

To quote Cary Grant: "It was a private affair—no television, of course, no radio even—just a group of friends giving each other a party. Because, you know, there is something embarrassing about all these wealthy people publicly congratulating each other. When it all began, we kidded ourselves and said: 'All right, Freddie March,' we'd say, 'we know you're making a million dollars—now come on up and get your little medal for it.'"

By the late thirties it had veered out of control; Oscar was becoming a monster.

Alfred Hitchcock was so worried about an Oscar race in 1942 that he could not bear to attend the ceremony. He just paced up and down the silent hall of his Beverly Hills home.

"Turn on the radio!" he yelled to his wife. The first pearly-toned sounds of the orchestra began to waft through the house. But the director decided that made it worse. "No, no," he yelled, "turn it off."

He picked up a tennis racket and dashed out to his private court. One ball. Two. Then he was back in, stepping into his tuxedo. "Maybe if we just went on down."

His wife had finally had it: "For Chrissakes don't take it so seriously. Just remember, this is the group that gave an Oscar to Luise Rainer. Twice!"

That did it. A smile formed at the corners of his mouth. Supposedly, Hitchcock never mentioned the Oscar again. He never got one either. But he didn't care—or so he said.

In this same era, the early forties, mystery writer Raymond Chandler braved an Oscar ceremony and didn't come away unscathed.

"If you can go past those awful idiot faces on the bleachers outside the theater without a sense of the collapse of human intelligence; and if you can go out into the night and see half the police force of Los Angeles gathered to protect the golden ones from the mob in the free seats, but not from the awful moaning sound they give out, like destiny whistling through a hollow shell; if you can do these things and still feel the next morning that the picture business is worth the attention of one single, intelligent, artistic mind, then in the picture business you certainly belong because this sort of vulgarity, the very vulgarity from which the Oscars are made, is the inevitable price Hollywood exacts from each of its serfs."

Chandler wrote those words for a Los Angeles newspaper. The newspaper didn't dare print them. Finally, they found a home in the *Atlantic Monthly*, on the East Coast, safe from Oscar's revenge.

An Oscar in the family: Steven Bogart, three, hoists the statue his dad won the night before for The African Queen *(1951). Bogie and Bacall flank Stevie. (© A.M.P.A.S.)*

Is there hope for Oscar?

Probably not. Oscar's salvation may come only through laughter at the impossibility of even trying to choose a best film or a best performance, an apple over an orange. Can one truly say, for instance, that Geraldine Page's raw gutsiness in *The Trip to Bountiful* is artistically better than Meryl Streep's touch of genius in *Out of Africa*?

Humphrey Bogart was probably right when he suggested: "Let each of the five nominees do the soliloquy from *Hamlet* before an audience of voters."

Picture the scene as it would have been that year, when Bogie won for *The African Queen*. He would have competed against Montgomery Clift, Marlon Brando, Arthur Kennedy, and Fredric March. Incendiary!

"Of course," said Bogie, "I wouldn't have proposed that if Larry Olivier had been up."

CHAPTER ONE

Little Orphan Oscar

The Academy began its existence as a guild-busting company union dominated for many years by the massive resources of Metro-Goldwyn-Mayer.
—ANDREW SARRIS

D. W. Griffith looked ghastly. His skin was ashen; his stomach jutted out as a memorial to many boozy nights in two-bit bars. His hair was pillow-slip white, and his dinner jacket was not of the best cut.

They sent a limousine to get him—a Hollywood courtesy he hadn't known in more than a decade. At sixty-one the "Father of the Movies" was washed up—had been for ten years. His two greatest movies, *The Birth of a Nation* and *Intolerance*, had been made twenty years earlier. And twenty years is a lifetime in Hollywood. The studio bosses had closed the gates to him: Louis B. Mayer didn't even return his calls, while Cecil B. De Mille was conveniently "on location" when Griffith dropped by the Paramount lot.

His five hundred films wouldn't even buy him a bowl of soup in the Warner Bros. commissary. Hollywood only asks one question: What did you do last week? Last year is too far back in history and next year may never come. Has-beens like Griffith, John Gilbert, and producer Jesse Lasky, Sr.—no matter how great—have been treated like lepers. Failure, after all, can rub off, can't it?

But the limo that picked up Griffith late on the afternoon of March 5, 1936, was to drop him back into the arms of the Hollywood establishment. When the long, sleek car pulled up to the red carpet at the Biltmore Hotel, boy genius Irving Thalberg was there to greet him. So was the city's hottest new director, Frank Capra. And Walt Disney. Their dinner jackets were cut better than his; they had smooth tans from afternoons on private tennis courts. Diamond bracelets dripped from the arms of their wives. Their smiles said, Welcome home . . . why'd you stay away so long?

They greeted him like a retired Roman senator, coming in from his country villa for tribute. He was actually more like Banquo's ghost, more like emerging from the shadows and living death of unwanted retirement and seedy apartment-hotels.

One hopes Griffith didn't sense the forced warmth and icy chill that lay beneath the glassy smiles of the movie moguls. The Academy had no other choice but to pull Griffith out of the pasture in a last-minute publicity stunt designed to save the 1936 Oscars and, therefore, to save the collapsing Academy of Motion Picture Arts and Sciences, which was down to forty members and sinking fast.

Oscar was finally reaping the bitter harvest from almost ten years of misuse by Louis B. Mayer, Jack Warner, Joseph Schenck, and their cronies. These men, led by Mayer, founded the Academy to serve as a vast company union designed to keep all other unions, and therefore decent wages, out of Hollywood. By 1935 the name directors, actors, and writers had abandoned the Academy for the fairness and safety of their own guilds. When the moguls still clung to the Academy in its disguise as a company union, the movie stars blew the whistle on Oscar.

Paul Muni, James Cagney, and Gary Cooper, suddenly big men in the new Screen Actors Guild, sent out telegrams to fellow actors on March 3, two days before the Oscar ceremony. The messages, which differed according to the recipient, told virtually every name actor in Hollywood to boycott the Oscar ceremony. "It was either that or give the group some tacit recognition," said Cagney years later. "They were hoping that respect for the Oscar awards would help them keep the Academy in the labor business as a company guild."

D. W. Griffith, near the height of his power, in 1916, and on the set of Duel in the Sun *with Walter Huston.*

The "King and Queen of Holly-wood," Tyrone Power and Jeanette MacDonald, at their coronation (with crowns made and anointed in the Metro-Goldwyn-Mayer costume department). Power was making an MGM film at the time. Few took either of these two seriously—Power was too good-looking and MacDonald was told, firmly and politely, that she was Metro's reigning soprano, which did not include acting. As the Oscar men tried to wash their petticoats and regain their seriousness, the Academy Award choices were monopolized by heavy, theatrical performers such as Greer Garson and Robert Donat. In these contests Power's looks couldn't help him. He showed a rare virtuosity in Johnny Apollo, The Razor's Edge, and Nightmare Alley but his studio, Twentieth Century–Fox, kept cramming him into tights and Hussar costumes and forcing him to prance around such beauties as Linda Darnell and Loretta Young.

The studio bosses countered with telegrams of their own, politely ordering their artists to show up at the Oscar show. Or else! "It was like the iron fist in a velvet glove," said Jeanette MacDonald. "It's unnerving to ignore a telegram from your boss, Louis B. Mayer, telling you to show yourself at the Oscars."

But the guilds went management one better. A network of phone calls was initiated the very afternoon of the 1936 Oscar show: Jeanette MacDonald called Nelson Eddy; Joan Crawford called Harlow and Gable; Cagney called Blondell.

But before that, Frank Capra, new president of the Academy, had dropped his own bombshell. The Academy had suddenly found it in its collective little heart to give recognition at long last to D. W. Griffith.

"We had to do something," Capra said later. "The Academy was dying. And I was sure the upcoming Academy Awards banquet loomed dark and discouraging. So, to spur attendance, we countered the boycott by persuading Griffith to come out of his retired oblivion and accept a special statuette for his past achievements."

It worked, said Capra. "The boycott fizzled." Hardly! Capra was looking back at the thirties through rose-colored glasses. Bette Davis finally agreed to come (but probably because she knew she would win for *Dangerous*); Norma Shearer came on the arm of her husband, MGM production chief Irving Thalberg; Victor McLaglen came (to pick up his acting award for *The Informer*); but almost all the other name stars in Hollywood stayed home.

"It was so bad I didn't find but four people worth taking pictures of," said Darryl Warren, a photographer for three fan magazines. "I got a shot of Davis, but she looked like hell—and Shearer must have come in the back door. One thing we had, though—plenty of Frank Capra shots —plenty of 'em."

So D. W. Griffith became the first of a long parade of old and ailing directors and stars used by the Academy for one reason or another (usually to relieve Hollywood's conscience). They paraded him out like a thoroughbred horse with a lame leg.

"It was a moment I could hardly bear," said Oscar-winning scriptwriter Frances Marion, who had been discovered by Griffith before the end of World War I. "How had the industry honored this man who had contributed so much to all our lives? By presenting him with an Oscar for '*past* achievements.' No studio in the last fifteen years had given him a directorial job when he needed it financially—and what was more important to him—to preserve his dignity."

It was another low point for the Academy.

It's ironic that this charade was engineered by Frank Capra, one of the few men of feeling in the Hollywood hierarchy. He had said, after five years in Hollywood, "The city is brutal to has-beens. Those pushed off the top are rolled into the valley of oblivion. Often they are mired in degradation. I saw it all around me: D. W. Griffith, a forgotten man; Mack Sennett, walking unnoticed in the city where he had reigned as a King of Comedy; old stars pleading for jobs on the extras line. It's a stern warning."

Over the long haul, however, Capra was probably right about one thing—Griffith was the only man who still commanded enough respect in Hollywood to fill the vast empty tables of the Biltmore Bowl. The stars didn't come, the directors didn't come; but 1,200 of the movies' middle ranks showed up, paid for tickets, and got Oscar through one more year.

That was all Capra had hoped for. The day after the 1936 Oscar ceremony, he laid down the law to the Academy board. He slammed his fist on the board's oak table and ordered fellow officers to vote the Academy of Motion Picture Arts and Sciences *out* of the labor-union business. Nine shameful years were over for the Academy, years during which it had served, more or less, as a big-studio stool pigeon, stalling the winds of unionism, fair wages, and decent standards swirling around the movie industry—the fourth largest industry in America.

It had all started quietly (but not innocently) over Cuban cigars and Napoleon brandy in the "company" parlor of Louis B. Mayer's luxurious home. The year was 1927—before the Depression and on the eve of talking pictures. But not, as Mayer knew, before the unnerving labor movement gathering at the studio gates.

"Why shouldn't there be an organization of the creative elite of Hollywood?" asked Mayer, looking out over his badger nose at the headtops of two of his serfs, actor Conrad Nagel and director Fred Niblo. Mayer smiled inscrutably. And of course, the organization could serve as a convenient mediator and harmonizer in any disputes involving the crafts. Just how convenient would become apparent later. What Mayer left unsaid was that the members would be by invitation only—the cream of Hollywood actors, writers, directors, cinematographers, and, of course, the cream of Hollywood producers. But the cream of the crop by whose definition?

At first it was by Mayer's definition alone. He set out to form the Academy in his own image. And he succeeded, down to paying for the first dinner at the Ambassador Hotel, January 11, 1927. Why, that good soul even paid and supplied his own personal attorneys to draft the constitution and bylaws. (As hard as it is to believe now, the Academy Awards came only as an afterthought on the Academy's agenda, and were not even listed in a statement of aims adopted that night. It was an easy way to throw each of the creative groups a bone once a year, ensuring their goodwill during the labor squabbles.)

So thirty-six of Hollywood's "best people" came to Mayer's little gathering. And those people invited their friends, who invited *their* friends. . . . Soon there were 231 members, all organized into five branches: actors, directors, writers, technicians and producers.

"Those jerks in charge wanted it to seem like a labor union but to function as a company trust," said Zelda Cini, a correspondent in Hollywood for *Life* and *Time* during the '40s and '50s. "Then it would seem like everything was done kosher." In other words, they could freeze the guilds and labor unions out of Hollywood. The early Academy was so controlled by the bosses it was a wonder it survived.

"Everybody sat back and waited to see when the studios would call the Academy into action," said Cini, who wrote a history of the Academy for *Life*'s Golden Decade series.

It wasn't long. Four months after the Academy's organizational banquet of May 11, Louis B. Mayer came before it hat in hand. Things were going tough in the East, boys, real tough. The money men back east were out for blood. It was a bad rap, said Mayer. But those bankers just don't know how we do things out here in Tinseltown. They think we're irresponsible and wasteful. So just for the moment, perhaps a little 10 percent cut in everybody's wages would solve the problem temporarily. All the Academy had to do, according to Mayer and the producers, was to take up the proposal with the other branches.

The founders of the Academy, left to right and back to front: *Cedric Gibbons, J. A. Ball, Carey Wilson, George Cohen, Edwin Loeb, Fred Beetson, Frank Lloyd, Roy Pomeroy, John Stahl, Harry Rapf, Louis B. Mayer, Conrad Nagel, Mary Pickford, Douglas Fairbanks, Sr., Frank Woods, M. C. Levee, Joseph Schenck, and Fred Niblo.*

Mayer knew that these branches had already threatened to strike if the 10 percent cut was put into effect. To the great credit of the Academy, its leaders were not docile. They told Mayer to rescind the 10 percent slash. And the warning spread to the other studios.

Joan Crawford described Mayer as being "mad as hell" when he found out the organization he'd created in his image had somebody else's brain.

Okay, boys, no pay cut. The producers' branch of the Academy decided to officially withdraw the proposed cut at the Academy's July 28 banquet. And they worded their withdrawal so that the other branches were blamed for the "rampant extravagance and cost overruns of our industry."

Then the Academy quickly polished off an attempt by Actors Equity to organize in Hollywood. Why join that "eastern stage union" when you can get everything you want through the Academy? asked the producers. We'll even give you a contract.

And they did—the first contract of any kind between artists and producers. "Most actors were unconcerned as to which organization represented them as long as they had their way," wrote Murray Ross in *Stars and Strikes*. "If the Academy would help them, they saw no reason for clinging to Equity."

In the East, spokesmen for Equity claimed the Academy was a "company union" bound to cause trouble sooner or later. It was true. The producers' branch held the destinies of Academy members in an iron fist. "An examination of the Academy's first three years shows that a small number of influential 'foundation members' guided the Academy," wrote Ross. "The 'foundation members' were charter members and a select few who were elected to the inner circle. Other Academy members were not eligible for election to the board of directors and could not amend the bylaws."

Ross concluded: "The Academy was obviously never meant to be a thoroughly democratic organization."

The dictators who controlled the Academy gave just enough to make the actors happy. But not enough to lose their control. By 1932, the Academy of Motion Picture Arts and Sciences had become the perfect company union, presenting no danger at all to the studios while making it seem as if Hollywood workers actually had a functioning labor union. Even founding members of the Academy such as Douglas Fairbanks, Sr., wondered when reality would intervene and demolish the house of cards.

While these weighty matters consumed the time of the Academy's officers, a small committee was formed to find "some little way" of recognizing excellence in writing, acting, and directing. "Now mind you, we're not talking about anything grand," warned Louis B. Mayer to Academy organizer Conrad Nagel.

Nagel was given a budget of $500 to find some way to honor the industry's best and brightest. Louella Parsons had in mind a series of scrolls. "You know, like those things the city council hands out," she suggested to Nagel.

When Nagel suggested a banquet, Mayer's face turned red. "We're not going to spend that kind of money," he thundered.

"I considered it to be such a touchy subject that I appointed what I hoped would be a slow moving committee to 'think about' some sort of honorariums," Nagel said decades later. "I told them to take their time about it."

And time they took.

It wasn't until May, 1928, that the committee—including D. W. Griffith, actor Richard Barthelmess, and theater magnate Sid Grauman, among others—recommended a ball with awards in the form of statuettes to be offered for excellence.

By this time, Nagel's role as an uncomfortable "go-between"—walking a political tightrope between the studio oligarchs and the film community's rank and file—had been gratefully shifted to the broader shoulders of Douglas Fairbanks.

Fairbanks consulted his wife Mary Pickford, and the duo decreed it: the kingdom would have a ball with or without statuettes. (Louis B. Mayer still considered the statue proposal to be unduly costly.)

All of this took months and months. So the first Oscars (as they would be called) weren't presented until May 16, 1929.

There was little suspense and not a whole lot of glamor at that first banquet. After all, the winners had been announced in a press release three months earlier. Emil Jannings, winner of the Best Actor prize for *The Last Command* and *The Way of All Flesh,* was the first person to actually take an Oscar in his hands.

The winners were wined and dined on Jumbo Squab Perigeaux, Lobster Eugenie, Los Angeles Salad, Clear Terrapin and Fruit Supreme. (The winners had been selectively chosen by a panel of five, with no chance of a recount or a recanting. What those five decreed, stood.)

All of the films honored that night were silent ones—*Wings* was named Best Picture and a virtually unknown actress, Janet Gaynor,

OSCAR DEAREST

Norma Shearer took her Oscar over to the studio of photographer George Hurrell and had this promotional portrait taken. Then MGM used the photo to promote her next two films. The promotional abuse of Oscar was off and running. (© A.M.P.A.S.)

An unassuming young actress, Janet Gaynor, in the films for which she won the first Best Actress Oscar: Seventh Heaven *(left),* Street Angel *(center), and* Sunrise *(right). "It was just a little family affair at that time," Janet recalled. "We were just out having a good time, and I was happy to be honored by my 'friends.'"*

won for three silent screen performances: *Seventh Heaven, Street Angel,* and *Sunrise.*

"I remember it as being a quiet, warm experience," Gaynor said decades later. "Hollywood was just one big family then, and this was a bouquet—thrown to me, I think, because I was new and because they thought I had a certain freshness. It was nothing then like it is now. My agent didn't call me up the next day with an offer to double my salary; I didn't find a pile of scripts at my door. Photographers weren't camped on my front lawn. I just got up at 5:00 and drove off to the studio—as always."

The affair's master of ceremonies almost sounded embarrassed as he called up the winners. "This is all a bit like asking, 'Does this man play checkers better than that man plays chess.'"

Janet can be forgiven for playing down her early award. But a bushelful of the best roles *were* dropped at her feet, and she was one of the few who made a smooth transition to talkies. The Oscar was her buffer.

And the Hearst press made a great deal of it. Hoping to win an Oscar for his paramour, Marion Davies, William Randolph Hearst instructed Louella Parsons to gild the Oscar with all the Hollywood verbiage she could muster. Soon, Janet Gaynor and her Oscar were the fodder for hundreds of Sunday supplements. Oscar competition was off and running.

Within weeks, the true queens of Hollywood, Norma Shearer, Gloria Swanson, and Mary Pickford, decided they just *had* to have one. "I'm sure that Mary watched Janet mount the podium and thought, 'Gee, that would be fun, I'll have to get me one,'" said Robert Osborne, a major columnist for the *Hollywood Reporter.* "That's all it took. And, soon, the competition was cutthroat."

By that time the Academy was engulfed in a real drama. The Depression had finally hit the balmy shores of Hollywood in 1933, but it took a national bank holiday to make even a dent on film profits. Overnight, Paramount officially went bankrupt; movie financiers were ruined by bank failures across America. Only the earthquake of the same year made as big a dent in Beverly Hills.

Louis B. Mayer's gruff bark suddenly became a whine; the Warner

brothers admitted that they didn't know where their next $10 million was coming from; and Paramount's Adolph Zukor began eating at home instead of at his swanky club.

Mayer, one of the highest paid men in America, called together his fellow producers and said he had just the ticket. Boys, he said, we'll all just take a 50 percent cut in pay. He spread his chubby arms and offered to take the first official cut, pledging the thousands of others at MGM with a sweeping executive order. And you boys, he said, will get your studios to do the same. Presto! No Depression.

Mayer and the boys ran for their cars and headed east to the downtown Hollywood offices of the Academy of Motion Picture Arts and Sciences. They had all been saving the Academy for just such a situation anyway. The timing was perfect.

The fat cats explained to the Academy's board that a 50 percent cut for everybody—across the board—would surely be better than no paychecks at all. And that's what would happen if the Academy didn't act. And fast!

After all, weren't the big boys themselves taking pay cuts right along with the grips and the hairdressers? Sure they were. That's the spirit, Mayer told the Academy's officers.

Then somebody remembered just how much guys like Mayer and Jack Warner were taking home—and just how little everybody else took out of the pot. Mayer would still have $335,000 a year after his cut. Warner would have a little more. And Gable would still be stinking rich. But thousands earned $50 a week—even less; 75 percent of all actors (and there were thirty thousand of them, including free-lancers) pocketed less than $2,000 a year.

The Academy called a halt until it could work out a better formula. What say the cuts last only for eight weeks, with graduated reductions according to income? And what about exempting guys who make less than fifty bucks a week? The producers, in the glow of putting over their charade, answered a quick, "Sure." The Hollywood workers could choose between a waiver of half pay for eight weeks and giving up full salary for four weeks. The Academy demanded and received the right to audit all the studios' books so that the waivers could be canceled as soon as each studio recovered.

Then the waiver committee discovered that Samuel Goldwyn studios was solid enough to pay up in full. Go to hell, said Sam Goldwyn.

Murray Ross, in *Stars and Strikes,* wrote that these two actions were the first and probably the greatest blow to the Academy's prestige. When the dictators who ran the Academy said no, the Academy had nowhere to turn. Pierre Norman Sands, in a study of the Academy for the University of Southern California, expressed his belief that "the Academy only relied on a spirit of cooperation and lacked any enforcement mechanism." He also noted that the producers themselves may have scuttled the Academy's labor function in 1933. "It's quite possible that the unions themselves looked better to western management of the studios since they could be bargained with at arm's length rather than having their books opened up and audited by the Academy and therefore by their employees."

For the actors, the rat had eaten the cheese. The Screen Actors Guild was formed in October 1933. Within twelve months there were three thousand members. Soon to follow in 1933 were the Screen Writers Guild and the Screen Directors Guild, which was literally founded outside the Academy offices—on the steps. "We finally realized how the producers were using the Academy and us," said director King Vidor, a founding member of what became the Directors Guild of America. "What a lot of people didn't know was the fact that many producers and executives were subtracting the cuts from their employees' checks but not from their own."

Conrad Nagel, the actor Louis B. Mayer had handpicked to help found the Academy, resigned both as president and as a member, telling friends that he could not remain an officer of an organization that had been so basely used. Thousands followed his action. The Academy's membership was cut in half overnight.

Still, the producers insisted on using the organization. The labor guys in Washington, D.C., were busy all across America, drafting new codes and regulations for labor unions and employee groups. Mayer, Warner, and Thalberg cashed in on old debts and had the Academy of Motion Picture Arts and Sciences named the official studio-labor spokesman for the crucial hearings of the National Recovery Administration (a fancy way of describing total reorganization of labor).

Mayer and the other brass forced the Academy to forward the studios' demands to Washington, where they were incorporated into the new federal code. The studios asked for, and got, a code forcing all artists' agents to register and receive a license, a measure that would put the agents directly under the thumb of industry-wide political management. The studios asked for, and got, provisions limiting salaries of actors, directors, and writers (but no limits for executives). All these provisions were quickly written into the code, and the studio bosses sat back and waited to pull the rug out from under the artists.

They hadn't reckoned on Eddie Cantor. The singer with the banjo eyes wangled an invitation to spend Thanksgiving 1933 with President and Mrs. Franklin D. Roosevelt in Warm Springs, Georgia. Cantor, who was also the new president of the Screen Actors Guild, convinced Roosevelt, once and for all, that the Academy represented only the producers. At the last second, FDR got on the hotline to D.C. and stopped, by executive order, the anti-labor provisions of the code.

The executives were shocked into silence. Mayer had been so confident of victory that he scurried about Hollywood openly discussing the soothing balms of the salary-fixing board which would soon be put into effect.

Finally, it was too much even for the toadying Academy board members. They yelled for a halt and got the government to okay a series of producer-artist committees to draft a set of fair standards for the film industry. But Mayer and the others never got around to naming their delegates to the study groups. It was the last act in a pageant of bad faith: the Academy had played its last card.

Bosley Crowther, Louis B. Mayer's biographer, believed that Mayer had intended all along for the Academy to stave off the march of labor in Hollywood. "Finally, the Academy was exposed for what it was," wrote the *New York Times* film critic. "It was a 'company union' in a nice, refined, dignified way.

"Mayer's maneuvering during the 'bank holiday' period led to a spirit of rebellion toward the Academy that led to the genesis and strengthening of the guilds. Then there was the inevitable collapse of Mayer's company union."

Crowther blamed Mayer directly for the collapse of the Academy in

Eddie Cantor, president of the Screen Actors Guild, went all the way to the White House to keep Hollywood producers from turning the Academy into a labor union—a union which would have broken the back of SAG.

the mid-thirties. "Certainly Mayer's cute maneuver to raise the organization as a device for controlling actors and writers and his encouragement of it to play a hand in the obvious interests of the producers contributed to the end result. Mayer was often shortsighted and naïve."

And the Academy needn't look backward fondly at its founder. When Marie Dressler and Norma Shearer warned him that the back-stabbing might destroy the Oscar ceremony, he looked up glassy-eyed and said, "So what?" Still later, when his attorney warned him that he should give a nice chunk to the Academy for tax purposes (after all, Mayer had founded it), Mayer looked up and said, "Are you crazy?"

It was into this cauldron that Frank Capra dropped in 1935. For the next four years the story of the Academy Awards is Frank Capra's story. He saved them. Indeed, he was the first to really believe there was something worth saving.

Capra had been in and around Hollywood for twelve years before he finally acquired the right patina and pedigree to qualify for membership in the Academy. The son of an orange picker just off the boat from Sicily, he played the banjo in a Los Angeles honky-tonk, worked his way through the California Institute of Technology to become a chemical engineer, and sold stocks door to door before he bluffed his way into a job as a director. A San Francisco producer, in an unhinged moment, let him direct a one-reeler entitled *Fultah Fisher's Boarding House*. That was enough for Frank. He didn't know a *thing* about films. And it showed. So he went to work as a film cutter in a back-door Los Angeles sweat shop, jumping from there to being gag writer, then assistant director and on to full director status on Harry Langdon comedies. Harry Cohn hired him for Columbia Pictures, making him king of that lot within five years.

They called Columbia "the pauper" in those days—just a small-timer looking in at the show windows of the big boys: MGM, Paramount, Warner Bros. In 1930 Frank made *Ladies of Leisure*, a film which became an instant hit and made a star of Barbara Stanwyck.

The MGM brass got word that the movie was being sneak previewed in a neighborhood theater in distant San Bernardino, a city at the end of L.A.'s old red trolley line. Mayer sent up one of his yes men with a round-trip ticket and one order: find out if this movie's any good, and if it is, find out if we can hire that Capra guy away from Columbia. The answer to the former was yes. But it was no dice on Capra. Cohn had him sewn up for a decade.

This should have been flattering for the new director in town. But Capra had caught the near-fatal Oscar mania. He told Stanwyck he'd get one for himself, get one for Harry Cohn, and one for her. Ordinarily he would have had a good chance since, to quote gossip columnist Louella Parsons, "Everybody—and I mean *everybody*—is talking about Frank Capra and his film." The day nominations were announced Capra sent an office boy out in a limo to get *Daily Variety*, which reported the minute-by-minute news of Hollywood to a captive audience. Capra paced back and forth on the Columbia sound stage. "I hope to hell he gets nominated," said Cohn. "Otherwise we'll never get any work out of him." The page finally made it back from Sunset Boulevard, and Capra knew from the look on his face that he hadn't been nominated. "But I thought Stanwyck would get a nomination for sure," said the director. "It opened my eyes immediately to the truth about the Oscars.

"That was the disadvantage of working at Columbia—nobody there could get the Oscar. It galled my ego. The major studios had the votes. I had my 'freedom,' so to speak, but all the honors went to those who worked for the big, establishment studios."

Capra threw down his copy of *Variety* and became a celluloid crusader, jousting after his personal "Holy Grail"—the Oscar. Only four others would match the ferocity of his Oscar campaigns: Irving Thalberg, seeking a second Oscar for his wife, Norma Shearer; William Randolph Hearst, trying to get even a nomination for his mistress, Marion Davies; John Wayne, seeking to bag the award for his epic, *The Alamo;* and David O. Selznick, who was obsessed with a second Oscar for his wife, Jennifer Jones.

The Academy was especially vulnerable, Capra deduced, because of the perverse control of the organization by eight or ten bosses. So be it: stick them in their Achilles' heel. The director used his considerable writing techniques to attack the Academy in a letter to the Academy directors that exploded with fury. "The Academy is unfair to the creativity of the films." Next Capra whispered in Harry Cohn's ear that the men in control of the Oscar were robbing the executive of his due. At first, Cohn told him to forget it. "Capra, don't worry about those awards —they only give them to that arty junk."

Capra knew Cohn's weak spot: cash. And he used it. "Harry, they may give Oscars for 'arty junk' but a bunch of Oscars can add a million bucks to the ticket sales." Cohn's face brightened immediately. He was on the phone to Academy member Jack Warner the next day.

It's easy to imagine the panic Capra's letter caused in the founders' circle of the Academy, which in 1930 was frazzled by the toils of being a labor union and an awards monitor at the same time.

A special-delivery letter reached Capra's front door a couple of weeks later. It was from MGM director and Academy founder Fred Niblo.

Director Frank Capra saved the Academy and Oscar during his four-year term as the organization's president. In the thirties, the studio moguls tried to guillotine the Academy, and the unions tried to kill it because of its ties with the major studios. Capra became known as Oscar's own "Henry Kissinger."

"The Board of Governors cordially invites you to Academy membership." This was better than Capra had dared to hope for. Usually, one Academy member nominates another, and a long process of screening and voting follows. Capra was being invited to join by the entire board—voted, sealed, and delivered. A week later he found himself a "unanimous nominee" for the Academy of Motion Picture Arts and Sciences board of directors. His letter had really hit the Oscar people where they hurt; they could not afford one more public slap at their dubious integrity.

Once inside, Capra found the final voting to be quite kosher. It was the nomination process that was rotten. Then, as now, the nomination process favored box-office hits over artistic achievements, gave emotion the edge over acting ability, and was dominated by cliques within the branches.

"By secret vote each branch selected five nominees for their respective Oscar," Capra said. "For example, only directors who were Academy members voted to select the 'best' five directors. The trick was to get nominated by the clique of major studio directors who had achieved membership. And those brahmins were not about to doff their caps to the 'untouchables' of Poverty Row."

He decided he'd have to direct at least one picture for a big studio, such as MGM, to get his first nomination. "Making good pictures was not good enough—unless you had the correct pedigree." Harry Cohn got his enemy Louis Mayer to hire Capra for a film, but the director turned out to be too innovative for MGM. Mayer bounced him back like an India rubber ball. Back to square one.

Why not make one of those super-real "Depression era" films as King Vidor had done in *The Crowd*, which received two nominations in 1927/28? Thus, in 1932, came Capra's *American Madness*, one of the first films to grapple directly with the fear and panic of the Depression. To rescue his film from the turgid pace of realistic melodramas, Capra stayed in the editing lab for a month, creating a new form of fast cutting from one bit of action to the other. "I speeded up the pace of the scenes to about one-third of a normal scene. If a scene played normally in sixty seconds, I increased the actors' pace until it played in forty seconds. When *American Madness* opened, there was a sense of urgency, a new interest, at work. The audience loved it."

Here, surely, was an Oscar for Capra. The Hollywood critics quickly killed his chances. They didn't like it. "They said it was not 'Academy material.' Although critical appraisals were light reading for the public, they were gospels for highbrow Academy voters," said Capra. (This is still true today. Films that are panned by Sheila Benson of the *Los Angeles Times*, Stephen Farber of *Los Angeles* magazine, and TV critic Gary Franklin stand little chance of taking home the big awards. In fact, Franklin's acid and highly personalized telereviews make him, some say, the most influential critic in filmland, winning him a contract with L.A.'s KABC-TV for $350,000 per year. When Franklin gave *Runaway Train*'s Jon Voight a "ten plus" on the Franklin scale, he set in motion a sweeping campaign which earned the actor a questionable nomination for Best Actor.)

Capra decided to make "the artiest film of them all. How about miscegenation. That ought to get 'em." The film was *The Bitter Tea of General Yen* (1933), about the gothic affair between a Chinese warlord and an American missionary (played by Stanwyck, Capra's preferred actress). The finished film was of rare quality and, according to Euro-

pean directors, was thirty years ahead of its time. Not everyone agreed. Certainly not the Academy, which passed over it completely.

"There was and is a mystique about Academy voters that confounds trends, predictions, and logic," said Capra. "But those who grabbed off the little statuettes didn't give a hang how they got them. They just knew an Oscar tripled their salaries and zoomed them to world fame. Salary increases didn't whet my appetite. But world fame—wow!"

There was only one more road open to the director—corn. Oscar voters loved maudlin emotion and belly laughs more than the gold on their statues. Capra had just the formula: a Damon Runyon story about an "Apple Annie" (May Robson) who becomes a "lady for a day." So let's just call it that, said Capra: *Lady for a Day*. Tears and sappy dialogue worked. The film was nominated in four categories, including Best Picture and Best Director.

In his own words, Capra became impossible to live with. "I kept telling myself that I would win 'four awards.' No other picture had ever won four awards. I would set a record. Hot damn! I wrote and threw away dozens of acceptance speeches. I ordered my first tuxedo. Rented a plush home in Beverly Hills. All to be 'seen' by the few hundred Oscar voters." (To everyone's chagrin, these things are still done today.)

He went to the Oscars with his speech tucked carefully into the pocket of his six-hundred-dollar tux.

Things started going wrong ten minutes into the ceremony. The writing award went to RKO's *Little Women*. Then Will Rogers came out with the sealed envelope for best achievement by a director. Rogers's honeyed words described the profession of directing. Then he opened the card: "Well, well, well, what do you know. I've watched this young man come up from the bottom—and I mean the bottom."

Frank Capra stirred in his seat. It was he. It had to be he. Nobody else had worked up from the sawdust floor of a honky-tonk. At last, at last . . . it was his turn. Rogers drawled out his words, "It couldn't happen to a nicer guy. . . . Come on up and get it—Frank."

Capra's table exploded, and Capra rose slowly with dignity, as befitted Hollywood's newly knighted. It was a long way up to the podium. Capra dodged around Norma Shearer, bumped into Robert Taylor, squeezed by Ginger Rogers, and headed toward the spotlight—which was searching through the dark to find the winner. "Right here." Capra waved. "Right over here." All those people in the dark were confused, but the man on the spot was not. The lighting director already knew who'd won, had gotten the word when he came in to work. He located the Fox table and threw the glare onto the Best Director of 1933: Frank Lloyd.

"I stood petrified in the dark, in utter disbelief," said Capra. " 'Down in front!' somebody yelled, and I began the longest, saddest, most shattering walk of my life. I wanted to crawl under the rug. All my friends at the table were crying." Capra's humiliation was complete. "I decided that if they ever did give me one, I wouldn't be there to accept. Not me . . . never again."

He didn't keep his pledge. A year later the Oscar voters did give his film *It Happened One Night* all four of the major Oscars (Best Picture; Best Actor, Clark Gable; Best Actress, Claudette Colbert; and . . . Best Director). At the end of the year the members turned to him in a last-ditch attempt to save the fast-sinking Academy. They elected him president.

"It was a dubious honor," Capra said. "I say 'dubious' because it would mean presiding at a deathwatch." The Academy had become the favorite whipping boy of Hollywood; its membership was down from six hundred to forty; its officers were dedicated but discouraged; its staff was reduced to one loyal, underpaid executive secretary, Margaret Herrick, who was the Academy's alter ego; the major source of Academy funding, help from the big studios, had been swiftly curtailed once the brass could no longer "use" the organization as a guild buster. With few dollars in its treasury, and fewer in sight, the odds were ten-to-one the Academy would fold and Oscar would become a collector's item.

The Academy was also under siege by the guilds representing actors, directors, and writers. "The producing companies did everything short of asking for the National Guard to prevent guild organizations," said Capra. "Then the talent guilds decided to wreck the Academy in order to deny the studios the promotional value of the Oscars. Oddly enough, the short-sighted company heads couldn't have cared less—the Academy had failed them as an instrument of salary cuts so they [the studios] withdrew their memberships and financial support. The organization was beached—left in the care of a very few staunch Academy-oriented visionaries dedicated to the cultural recognition and preservation that has become the Academy's strong card."

How few? Capra says that only seventeen people were left as truly active members. "The recognition should go to them. Nobody else helped.

"I don't think most people knew how close we came to dissolving," Capra said. "Board members had to put up their own money to pay the people who made the Oscars, and I had to do some fancy pleading for cash to pay the phone bill and buy stationery. Then I had to plead with the officers of the talent guilds to allow me to mail Academy ballots to their guild members."

It took four long years, but it worked. By 1939, new blood had begun to flood in. Then came the war; it was the cavalry to the rescue. Nobody had time for Oscar politics during World War II; the studio bosses, however, decided to put their dough back in to support the Oscar shows, which were fast becoming the best publicity stunt in Hollywood history. The Oscars were once again smiled on by Mayer, Warner, and the other money gods; all was right in the Academy's world.

The truce was, sadly, a false one. The studios would make one last attempt to sink the Oscars—this time in the guise of patriotism.

It started with Laurence Olivier, a man Hollywood had turned down on his first two go-rounds. Olivier, as handsome as the dawn, was brought back to America in 1933 to star with Garbo in *Queen Christina*, after his first three Hollywood films failed two years earlier. He barely got inside the gates when Garbo, apparently trying to save her lover John Gilbert's career, said she would not make the film with Olivier; it had to be Gilbert or nobody. It was a bitter blow to the British actor, who once again fled back to England as a reject.

Sam Goldwyn, however, had seen his tests for the MGM picture and decided, the same day, to cast Olivier as Heathcliff in *Wuthering Heights*. When the actor strode onto the screen in his suffocatingly snug riding habit, there were sighs from lady moviegoers around the world. He was rushed into a dizzying list of movies—*Rebecca, Pride and Prejudice, That Hamilton Woman*, and *The 49th Parallel*. On a second trip to Hollywood in 1938, Vivien Leigh, his lover but not yet his wife, tagged along; agent Myron Selznick saw her and took her to his brother David, who signed her up as Scarlett O'Hara. The lovers were suddenly the hottest stars on both sides of the Atlantic.

A year later Britain was engulfed in war, and Olivier talked himself into a flying commission in the Fleet Air Arm of the Royal Navy for the duration. Hollywood forgot him. When he mustered out of the air corps, he immersed himself in his first love, Shakespeare. They say he produced the monumental *Henry V* on a budget so tight it wouldn't have paid for a decent newsreel in expensive Hollywood. One thing was certain: the ad budget was zero, and the film opened to no fanfare in Los Angeles. Ticket buyers came in trickles; David O. Selznick dropped by for a matinee and found the theater playing to half a dozen patrons.

Backfence gossip in movieland fixed that. Gossip columnist Hedda Hopper once referred to the movie capital as the "biggest small town in the world." For instance: One day Joan Crawford rushed into the sprawling Los Angeles Farmers Market at noon and ran out with an armful of kiwi fruit. "A friend wrote me from Paris—telling me that a paste from this mixed with egg whites and ice water took off wrinkles and frownies in five minutes," said Crawford to Jeanette MacDonald. The movies' top soprano had dropped in at the market to pick up a gift —a fact she quickly forgot as she drove out with the last of the kiwi fruit. By late afternoon the fruit sellers in the open-air shops had been driven nearly mad with calls for kiwi. Telegrams were sent to Mexico ordering bushels of the seedy little pods. By then it was too late; Crawford had tried it, scraped it off her face, and phoned a couple of friends to say: "That junk didn't do one goddamned thing. And today I could have used it."

A brooding Sir Laurence Olivier in Wuthering Heights, *the 1939 film which should have put the British master on the road to a major American film career. While he was making the film, his soon-to-be wife wandered over to MGM to pass the time away and was chosen to play Scarlett O'Hara in* Gone with the Wind, *just as he was dropped from his Samuel Goldwyn contract. He found himself up for a Best Actor Oscar the same fateful night* Gone With The Wind *swept the Oscars. And Sir Larry was beaten—not by Clark Gable as he expected, but by a fellow Brit, Robert Donat, for* Goodbye, Mr. Chips.

It was this network that turned Olivier's *Henry V* into a sleeper. The movie folk went in theater parties, ordered private screenings, and filled gossip columns with descriptions of the actor. As a result, the film was nominated for Best Picture of 1946, Best Actor, artistic decoration, music, etc., etc.

The studio bosses were horrified. The British were coming, and threatened to engulf their cozy little relationship with the Oscar. The Oscar voters, lured to the theater to see one British film, started shopping around for others. British acting, British costumes, British cinematography, and British accents were Oscar-vogue. *Brief Encounter, The Seventh Veil,* and *Caesar and Cleopatra* were all nominated in one category or another. Louis B. Mayer fumed, and other studio bosses talked as if the British nominations were outright treason!

The Academy pulled an emergency rabbit out of the hat. Laurence Olivier, they decided, would receive a "special" Oscar, lauding him for his guts. (Who else would film a dull Shakespeare historical play when *The Jolson Story, The Yearling,* and other nice themes were around for the picking?) A Special Award it was, and Olivier could just keep his sticky English fingers off the regulation Oscars. The British got only three minor awards—the special-effects prize for *Blithe Spirit;* the writing (original screenplay) Oscar, given to *The Seventh Veil;* and the writing (original story) statue, to *Vacation from Marriage.* That was that.

But 1947 was worse. *Great Expectations,* a film by David Lean, was nominated for five Oscars, including Best Picture. This time the fat cats couldn't dismiss it as a tribute to William Shakespeare; this film could have been made right there in Hollywood. To top it off, some normally patriotic American directors like George Cukor and King Vidor were spreading it around town that David Lean was a pretty fair director—fair enough for them to give him a personal nomination for Best Director.

The disease was catching. The Academy had nominated an Italian film, *Shoeshine,* for best screenplay; a French film, *A Cage of Nightingales,* for original story; a British film, *Odd Man Out,* for editing; and still another British film, *Black Narcissus,* for color cinematography and art direction. W. R. Wilkerson, who, as publisher of the *Hollywood Reporter,* was the unofficial voice of the studios, warned that America had helped Europeans with the war but didn't need to help them get "our Oscars." (This time foreign films won four Academy Awards, becoming a growing menace to the studios.)

Nineteen forty-eight brought down the house! Months before the first Oscar balloting, Laurence Olivier's *Hamlet* opened to wildly enthusiastic crowds in New York and, later, in Hollywood. This time everyone was going to see the British film. The men at the top set their chins grimly and realized that gossip was already giving the Best Picture and Best Actor awards to Olivier. J. Arthur Rank's ballet film, *The Red Shoes,* opened a couple of weeks later and was also being talked of as an Oscar-caliber movie.

Before Christmas 1948, angry executives from the "big five"—Warner Bros., Paramount, MGM, Twentieth Century-Fox, and RKO—flew to New York and called a joint emergency session, the first time the five studios had met since the labor crises of the thirties. The big five had Oscar on a short leash, and they knew it. Since 1939 the studios had subsidized the Oscar ceremony as an international publicity event.

They'd given $87,000 in 1947, and had already agreed to pay $57,000 in 1948.

Never in their wildest dreams had the studios expected to pay the costs of an Oscar ceremony which honored a Limey film.

Academy president Jean Hersholt, renowned as Dr. Paul Christian in the long-running radio series and in several movies, had known on December 16 that the studios were threatening to pull out. But, he said later, he figured the studios would "come around" as Oscar time neared. The industry simply swept the controversy under the rug until the night of the Academy Awards, March 24, 1949, when Hersholt told a national radio audience of the pullout. He added that the studios were out to wreck the Academy.

Caught off guard, the big five claimed the Oscars won by *Hamlet* had nothing to do with their withdrawal of the life-giving dough. "We just didn't want it to seem as if there were conflicts between us—the studios —and the awards," said a spokesman for the brass. It was just a bizarre coincidence that the pullout came in a year that honored a British film. Give us a break, boys, the execs said to the press. And many Hollywood journalists bought the explanation. Several even ran mild retractions saying that "British films had nothing to do with it."

At a joint press conference, Nicholas Schenck of MGM, Barney Balaban of Paramount, Spyros Skouras of Fox, Major Albert Warner of Warners, and Ned Depinet of RKO issued a statement so sweet it could have melted in their mouths: "We intend to continue our moral support of the idea of making awards of merit for superior achievements in motion pictures. We shall continue our financial support of the original function of the Academy of Motion Picture Arts and Sciences. But we shall no longer pay the costs of this ceremony."

Somehow they also managed to say, "The step is not a commercial one. In fact it is in the interest of 'less commercialization.' Remember the companies as companies were never members of the Academy. That is as it should be." The last paragraph of their statement, however, betrayed their full intention: "The artistic standards of our industry are *not* dependent on this annual competition. There are, in fact, many awards by many groups for which the creative talent of our industry could strive."

Now there, Academy! Take that and stuff it down *Hamlet*'s throat.

Back in Tinseltown, the *Hollywood Reporter* trumpeted that the voting in the 1946 Oscars might not have been quite up to snuff and, therefore, highly traitorous.

The *Reporter* said flatly that the accounting firm counting the ballots should hand the ballots back to the Academy board for a public recount. "We have yet to run across a single voter who favored *Hamlet*," said the *Reporter*. "From ANY WAY you look at it, *Hamlet* was not the best picture of the year, and the Academy voting, which gave it the top honor, was not as a direct result of the voters (IF THEY VOTED THAT WAY) preferring it to our own-made top pictures, but was rather a vote against the studios that pay them."

Hersholt's address at the Awards ceremony turned Hollywood Boulevard into a political hotbed. The Academy president said a spokesman for the studios told him, "We don't want the Academy standards foisted on us; we want to make commercial pictures unhampered by considerations of artistic excellence."

At a press conference the morning after, Hersholt said Columbia,

Universal-International, and Republic had withdrawn not just Oscar-show funds but "all funds including money for operation and research."

Eddie Mannix, a former carnival bouncer who rose to the top of the MGM corporate ladder, answered Hersholt by saying, "In America it is still not a disgrace to be in a business that makes money. It isn't a crime. We're going to continue making the kind of pictures the public wants and will pay for."

Columbia's Harry Cohn was ready to count Oscar out: "It looks to us as if the Academy Awards is going to fold. This studio will therefore reserve judgment as to any future plans for financial support. Maybe the Academy has far outlived its usefulness."

As the dust settled it was only too clear why the bosses had ripped open the Academy's gut. New financial studies of Oscar-winning pictures from 1945 to 1947 showed that an Oscar for Best Picture added an extra gross of two milion smackers a year.

Emmet Lavery, a noted screenwriter and Academy governor, penned the best post-mortem in *The Saturday Review:* "So we come now, in the twenty-first year of the Academy's existence, to the parting of the ways between the major Hollywood studios and the Academy." It was, in his view, a happy parting. He expressed surprise only that it did not happen sooner—preferably at the Academy's very beginning. And, he pointed out, this did not mean the end of the Academy, but, on the contrary, an expansion and development on an independent level. Finally, the annual awards could be seen as the free choice of the 1,800 Academy members. "At the ripe old age of twenty-one, Oscar has shown that he is free to vote as he pleases."

As usual, the studios were speaking out of both sides of their mouths. They took back their marbles, but they retained their votes. (And the Oscar for Best Picture did not go to another foreign film for fourteen years).

Time magazine called him "Little Orphan Oscar." And that he was, for a sticky couple of years. Radio commercials, increased dues, and a fund drive tided the Oscar ceremony over until 1952, a year in which the Academy recovered from twenty-five years of money problems in one fell swoop.

Television rode in like the Lone Ranger. Television—the archenemy of the movies, the unmentionable, the devil in video clothes. The money men at RCA had watched the 1951 ceremony with greedy eyes. What they saw was a veritable Aladdin's lamp of movie stars appearing, and at no charge—Marlene, Marilyn, Elizabeth Taylor, Helen Hayes, Fred Astaire, Gene Kelly, Martin and Lewis. The guys from RCA knew that TV was going begging for superstars; Hollywood had forbidden them to even breathe a line on network TV. Oh, maybe a line or two on a talk show. But nothing more.

What if RCA and its stepchild NBC picked up more stars than there were in the heavens on one show—and free at that? They went to the Academy and laid it on the line: a hundred thousand bucks for your Oscar show, and we'll do most of the work.

In 1952 the studios, who had set the Oscars adrift, watched the Academy Awards sail forever from their control. Millions stayed home from the movies to watch the Academy's show. (Later, Academy officers revealed that there would have been no Oscar ceremony that night if NBC hadn't come to the rescue.)

The television era was on; the Academy Awards were suddenly the property of the world. Ladies in Paris saw how Grace Kelly did her hair; movie buffs in Lincoln, Nebraska, got their first look at Cecil B. De Mille; Audrey Hepburn's bangs became an international rage. And the Oscar was suddenly worth millions of dollars to a winning picture or, more importantly, to a triumphant actor. And it was TV that finally freed the Academy from its bondage to the studios. Starting with $100,000 in 1952, network and advertising money rolled in until it reached the millions, with the Oscars being broadcast to three hundred countries.

In 1986, the People's Republic of China was among the countries viewing the ceremonies for the first time (via twenty-four-hour tape delay), bringing the total worldwide audience to more than a billion.

Oscar began demonstrating real box office power—frightening box office power—six years ago. In 1980, three hundred million people saw Dustin Hoffman take home the prize as Best Actor. Since Hoffman's film, *Kramer vs. Kramer*, was named Best Picture and copped a passel of other awards, Oscar proved to be worth a cool $25 million to the film. In the last six years the monetary power of the Academy Awards has reached awesome proportions. Industry economists put the value of a major Oscar at a million dollars in 1965; now a nomination alone is worth that, to a picture or to a star. In 1979, after Olivia Newton-John appeared on the Oscar stage to sing the nominated song "Hopelessly Devoted to You" (from *Grease*), record stores across America and in England and France, particularly in France, couldn't get enough copies of the soundtrack to meet the demand.

Oscar began turning from gold to platinum in the early seventies. William Friedkin, director of the Oscar-winning *The French Connection* (1971), believes the award added "at least $5 million to that picture's gross income. If a movie wins several Oscars—big ones—then the payoff is doubled." "There's no money in getting an Oscar per se," said Ernest Borgnine, Oscar winner for *Marty* (1955), "but in time you may be offered a million dollars in parts."

A prime example of this Oscar upmanship is Gene Hackman, who took Best Actor Oscar for *The French Connection*. Hackman's fee per picture jumped from $200,000 to $500,000 after he won the honor. And his fee had previously reached the six-figure level after his Oscar-nominated role in *Bonnie and Clyde* (1967). But it remained for Tom Conti, a 1983 Best Actor nominee for *Reuben, Reuben*, to set new standards for audacity: his per-picture price of $100,000 zoomed to $1 million in less than a year.

Hollywood's bankers watched the Oscar-winning films of the early seventies reap massive money harvests in the months following the ceremony. And their busy little minds came up with a better mousetrap, specifically designed to maneuver the post-Oscar box office. It started with *One Flew over the Cuckoo's Nest*, the Best Picture of 1975. Three weeks before the Oscars, United Artists, which distributed the Jack Nicholson–Louise Fletcher film, took a straw poll in Hollywood and deduced that the film would be an easy winner. UA had released the film in a big blast toward the end of 1975, taking in major holiday ticket sales, and then pulled the movie in during midwinter. Then the movie won all four of the major Academy Awards—the first film to do so since *It Happened One Night* in 1934. The morning after the ceremony, United Artists booked the film into a thousand theaters in America, Canada, and Great Britain. Film writer Gregg Kilday wrote that the movie's total of five Oscars probably added $43 million to its take. Forty-three million dollars! And this was not a coincidence. Universal announced that the Best Picture award added $30 million in profits for their 1973 winner, *The Sting*. And before the 1977 ceremony, United Artists and MGM got their heads together and paired two Oscar-caliber movies, *Network* and *Rocky*. The duo divided most of the big Oscars for 1976, and after the awards, the films opened as a double bill in nine hundred theaters—pulling in a total of $20 million in eight weeks. Naturally, this puts great pressure on the studios to get their films nominated and bag at least one Oscar. The ad line "Oscar-winning film" has become a cure for what ails the box office of the eighties. (In 1979 when Paramount was stuck with the turkey *Star Trek—The Motion Picture* and Walt Disney was carrying the disaster *The Black Hole,* the publicists at both factories stumbled over each other trying to get nominations for the films—*any* nominations. Each film did get a nomination for Best Visual Effects—and both lost.)

Actually, Twentieth Century–Fox learned that even the most dismal film could get a Best Picture nomination if it paid enough and if the studio kept repeating all over town, "This film is Oscar-class; this film is Oscar-class; this film . . ." The tactic won Best Picture nods for *Cleopatra* (1963), *The Sand Pebbles* (1966), *Doctor Dolittle* (1967), and *Hello, Dolly!* (1969), all pictures that probably shouldn't have been in the top ten, much less the top five.

"This means some pictures *have* to get an Oscar to make it in the marketplace," said a publicist for Paramount. "That's a dangerous situation. When a film has to win in order to make back its cost, some of us will have to do everything short of killing to get them."

CHAPTER TWO

Oscar's Uncrowned King

He's too successful. He's too young; his genius is too great. They'll never give him the gold. —CLINT EASTWOOD, 1985

Steven Spielberg's eyes misted as he looked out over his kingdom with a princely nod of the head.

He held a block of gold aloft as if it were a scepter.

Below the dais sat his consort, a Hollywood princess of the rarest sort —Amy Irving. Her eyes, also, had filled. And the gaze she gave her lord and master was alive with rapture.

His court sat supplicant at a circle of tables—Spielberg-anointed directors and heir apparents, such as Joe Dante (the wizard of *Gremlins*), Robert Zemeckis (Spielberg's hand-picked director of *Back to the Future*), and Barry Levinson (the genius behind *Diner,* and a Spielbergian convert).

But the adulation rippled far beyond this Arthurian court, out through the minds and imaginations of a thousand Hollywood directors —most of them the city's busiest. The men with the custom-tailored tuxes and celluloid-honed brains were all there to worship a celluloid god, a kingmaker, the most successful filmmaker in the seventy-year history of the world's most powerful and lucrative art form.

The venerated Directors Guild of America—eight thousand strong— had just handed Steven Spielberg its highest honor, the Best Director prize for 1985. And this was taken as a sure sign that Steven's film, *The Color Purple*, would soon take home the Academy Award as Best Picture of the year: only twice in the last forty years had the DGA winner been different from the Academy honoree.

The room had rocked with approval as Steven bounded up to the podium, a veritable Rocky Balboa, grabbed the hunk of gold in his fist, and said emotionally, "If some of you were trying to make a statement with this—thank God for you!" A score of TV cameras zoomed in on Spielberg, with his "body by Jake," his José Ebert hairstyle, and his tuxedo by Universal pictures. The prince had been vindicated. Knighthood was reaffirmed, and all was right in the celluloid heavens.

Little explanation was needed. TV audiences around the world understood Steven's "thank God for you!" Translated simply, it meant,

"Thank God, DGA. You understand my genius. The poor old Academy does not!"

It had been just a month since the August, infirm, nepotistic directors' branch of the Academy (all 230 of them) had denied an Oscar nomination to the man who had created *E.T.*, *Raiders of the Lost Ark*, and *Close Encounters of the Third Kind*. And that decision by a bunch of old men, still led by many who had once made silent films, had stunned the world as much as it had flattened Hollywood.

Steven Spielberg had entered the Oscar derby in December as a white-hot "can't miss." Not only had he abandoned the hokum of outer space for the real world of the Old South, he had brought Alice Walker's racial classic *The Color Purple* to the screen after ten other directors had failed.

The *New York Post* was so certain of the director's eventual triumph that it trumpeted in December: "The only thing left for Spielberg to do is decide which tux to wear as he picks up his Oscar."

Then came that black day in February, unleashing a scandal which hit the Academy with a fury it hadn't seen since it was the slavish tool of the studios in the early thirties. (Indeed, only Bette Davis's failure to receive a nomination in 1934 for *Of Human Bondage* had created such unhappiness with the Oscar system—both within the Academy and without.)

There was such a hurricane of ill will and dissent that the two obvious and overriding reasons for Spielberg's snub (as it will forever be called) were all but ignored. In retrospect, however, they seem all too obvious.

First, Steven Spielberg's growing wealth, arrogance, autonomy, and sensitivity set him up for a fall.

Second, the Academy's directors' branch had become an undeniable anachronism, an exclusive "college of Cardinals," dominated by a generation of men whose careers were fading when Technicolor came in.

Had Spielberg been less arrogant or the directors less strident, this greatest of all Academy scandals would never have erupted in the first place. At no other time in Oscar's history would it have been possible to give a film eleven nominations and its director no recognition at all.

On Oscar night, many of the nation's entertainment press corps were secretly rooting for Spielberg's film to win as seventy-nine-year-old John Huston opened the Best Picture envelope and handed it to Billy Wilder, who read the Academy's choice.

If Steven had managed to pull that Oscar out of the hat, it might have been the best entertainment story in a decade. On the East Coast, NBC staffers for "Today" had already assembled a collection of film clips which showed Steven in action on the sets of *E.T.*, *1941*, and *The Color Purple*. It was the same across America, as the world held its breath. "When that last envelope was opened, the words coming out of my mouth in a desperate chant were '*Color Purple . . . Color Purple . . . Color Purple!*' " recalled *Los Angeles Times* film writer Jack Mathews. "I didn't like the movie, but its win would have made a great story. Snubbed for a Best Director nomination; snubbed in ten previous categories; then, on a sentimental crest for Steven Spielberg, to pull out the Big One in the last act."

Mathews said the *Times* was well prepared "to tell *that* story as well. I even overheard an editor verbally composing a headline for it: *Africa —6, Purple—Won.*" (The *Times* had run the following headline the day

Steven Spielberg, Hollywood's latter-day "autocrat," on the set of Raiders of the Lost Ark, *which added to Spielberg's Oscar bids with nominations for Best Picture and Best Director. But* Raiders *lost out to the turgid drama and rambling artistry of* Chariots of Fire, *and Warren Beatty grabbed Oscar's brass ring for directing* Reds. *Better luck next time, Spielberg fans declared as the world waited for* E.T.

after the nominations were announced: OUT OF AFRICA—11; COLOR PURPLE—11; SPIELBERG—0.)

"But, no," lamented Mathews. "It was *Out of Africa* one more time. Its total of seven Oscars wasn't as monotonous as the nine-Oscar sweep of *Gandhi* (eyelids grow heavy at the very mention of that) in 1982. But try to write about them."

Steven Spielberg had been a self-created mogul for years when the cracks began to appear in his rosy, "aw, shucks" façade. But nothing so much as the horrific events of a July 1982 night revealed the traces of a man of straw underneath.

John Landis was directing the Spielberg-produced *Twilight Zone: The Movie*, when allegedly sloppy stunt work sent the blades of a chopper slicing through three actors—two children and the popular character actor Vic Morrow.

Landis took the fall as studio representatives assured an anxious world that the Sir Galahad of *E.T.* was nowhere near the location at the time; nor, they said later, did he know of what were called "hellish and almost impossible shooting conditions."

Then, following a year of trouble, Spielberg and George Lucas jetted into town to put their hands and feet into cement on the hallowed

ground of Mann's Chinese Theater to celebrate the opening of *Indiana Jones and the Temple of Doom*, which Steven had directed and George had produced. The press, much of the live television world, and a thousand fans were cooling their heels as Tinseltown's richest twosome refused to leave their private jet until a police escort arrived to whisk their persimmon-colored limo from Burbank Airport to downtown Hollywood. "Sorry," said one Paramount official. "But all the cops were temporarily used up during Walter Mondale's campaign stopover."

When Steven finally did arrive, he coyly ducked most of the serious questions thrown at him in favor of announcing that his were the first sneaker-shod feet to be placed in the consecrated forecourt of the Chinese Theater. "What about the blatant violence and brutality in your latest film?" screamed one telecaster about *Indiana Jones*. "See ya' later," Steven said cheerily.

Photos of Spielberg and Lucas decorated the world's newspapers the following day in a profusion which silently affirmed that the real superstars of this generation are no longer actors but producer-directors.

Days later magazines proclaimed Spielberg the "True King of Hollywood." As if this weren't bad enough, the suddenly-married Amy Irving Spielberg exclaimed giddily, "Here I am with the Prince of Hollywood. I guess that makes *me* the Princess."

Almost from that moment, Spielberg courted arrogance and flirted with ego as if they had suddenly become his closest friends: *Los Angeles* magazine named him one of the fifty richest men in California; he became a megaproducer on television to such an extent that the *L.A. Times* ran his likeness on a *Calendar* magazine cover with the question: "Is Television Ready for This Man?"; and, as if to add hemlock to the nectar of narcissism, the Spielberg court took the keys to a palace built especially for them in a corner of the Universal studios lot.

This palace of stone, rare marble, scented wood, and movieland gilt was the nail in the coffin of Steven's lost nomination. At least, for the mostly anonymous members of the Academy's directors' branch (with incomes of mostly *five* figures).

Not since Rudolph Valentino had a sheik's assignation suite added to the Paramount lot had such a rarefied domicile graced a studio. And its value (estimated to be between $4 million and $5 million by some and as "little" as $2 million by others) has no precedent.

Construction on Casa Spielberg is believed to have begun sometime in early 1984, when *E.T.* was still pouring massive millions into the coffers of Universal Pictures. The only signs of building at that time were small construction roads which veered into the corner of the lot from almost directly behind the *Psycho* house built by Alfred Hitchcock. Intrepid reporters who inquired about the royalist masonry rising behind dusty foothills were told that "future set construction" was under way.

At about the same time, Steven (listed by some sources as being worth $100 million personally) told *Newsweek* that he was proud of his unassuming lifestyle in the Hollywood hills. "I don't live on the Hollywood Riviera with seven women feeding me while I sit in the sun with a reflector under my chin." He then guided the reporter through a homey domicile that reflected the mellow sixties rather than the frantic eighties. "I come home each night and watch TV until I fall asleep, and I'm proud of that . . . proud that I wake up early the next morning and go to work early. I have to do it that way since I bring all my private terrors and fantasies to my films."

But this same man—a child of Phoenix, Arizona's suburbia—didn't bat an eyelash about accepting the adobe Versailles, which boasts a forty-seat movie theater (complete with a professional candy counter and popcorn machine), a video arcade, and outdoor spas which could draw admiring gasps from Jackie O. Navajo rugs at $5,000 a pop, Santa Fe Indian vases with "don't ask" price tags, and more than $80,000 worth of neon lighting complete the castle that Steven built.

Truthfully, however, it serves as headquarters for the obsessive, ever-expanding production network through which Spielberg is taking over more and more of Hollywood, as his tentacled protégés worm their way into the production inner sanctums of Paramount, Warner Bros., Universal, Metro-Goldwyn-Mayer, United Artists, and now NBC, which is committed to taking on heady Spielberg products for at least a half-decade into the future: the largest advance financial guarantee in TV history was reportedly promised by the network to obtain the director's "Amazing Stories" teleseries.

It has been estimated that by the end of 1987, more than $2 billion in tickets will have been sold to films directed, produced, or directed *and* produced by Spielberg. Just a few examples: *E.T.*, $400 million gross, 133 million tickets sold; *Jaws*, $228 million gross, 76 million tickets sold; *Raiders of the Lost Ark*, $230 million, 68 million; *Indiana Jones*, $191 million, 64 million; *Back to the Future*, $165 million, 55 million; *Close Encounters*, $146 million, 48 million; *Gremlins*, $138 million,

Actress Amy Irving (Mrs. Steven Spielberg), whose coy remarks about her husband didn't help his chances for an Oscar. On one occasion she added to the legend of arrogance growing up around Spielberg by saying, "Here I am with 'the Prince of Hollywood.' I guess that makes me the princess."

46 million; *The Color Purple*, $100 million, 34 million; *Poltergeist*, $65 million, 22 million.

Statistics like these are bound to both confuse and enrage the majority in the Academy's directors' branch, whose combined credits read like the late-show listing in *TV Guide*. In *their* day only directors like Alfred Hitchcock, Michael Curtiz, and George Cukor even had office suites. And Cukor, king of women's films, admitted before he died that MGM "stuck me in a glorified closet which had served as the bath suite of Norma Shearer's dressing room, and Victor Fleming [director of *Gone With The Wind*] was in a rebuilt sound truck."

The great producer-director princes such as Spielberg, Lucas, Stallone, John Hughes (*The Breakfast Club*), Michael Douglas (*Romancing the Stone*), Walter Hill (*48 Hours*), Ivan Reitman (*Ghostbusters* and *Legal Eagles*), and Sydney Pollack (*The Way We Were, Tootsie,* and *Out of Africa*) would have found scant haven in the old Hollywood, where front offices dictated and stars were second-in-command. It must be hard even for such stars as Meryl Streep and Fonda to grasp the fact that directors such as Spielberg and Bogdanovich *are* the stars of their own films.

"To tell you the truth, it burns my guts," said Henry Hathaway, one of Hollywood's most durable directors, in a rare interview before his death in 1984. "A director is like a painter. In a painting it's the skill and workmanship which stands out—not the painter. A director should work the same way. A director belongs *behind* the camera. In an Errol Flynn film, Errol was the star, not Michael Curtiz."

But when Spielberg begins a picture, from the moment he appears on the scene, *he* is the star. For instance, when he took *Close Encounters of the Third Kind* on location in Alabama, photographers stampeded to the set. Richard Dreyfuss and Teri Garr remained virtually unnoticed in the public relations fracas which exploded around the closed set. One photographer from the *Miami Herald* even signed on as an extra to catch a shot of Spielberg on a derrick, high above a crowd scene.

Such events have burdened Spielberg with a mantle of personal fame perhaps unequaled since Cecil B. De Mille—who also went Oscarless.

When *Indiana Jones and the Temple of Doom* opened, it was Steven, not Harrison Ford, who put his tennis-shod footprints in the cement at Mann's Chinese Theater.

Actors who work with the king of the wunderkinds have described his growing love of power as "amiable arrogance."

But arrogance it is—whatever the form, and it hacked away at his chances for the Oscar.

The fury of the anti-Academy reaction blowing up around *The Color Purple* scandal was but the sorrowful end of the road in a Spielberg backlash which had seen its ugliest hour in 1983, when the aging Academy voters threw out a bloated bouquet of Oscars to an endless, tedious, unexperimental movie, *Gandhi,* by an equally old-fashioned director, Richard Attenborough. That biography, which is close to unwatchable by entertainment standards, produced a tidal wave, swamping Spielberg's masterpiece, *E.T.—The Extra-Terrestrial.* When the last Oscar was announced that year, the sighs of youngsters the world over must have been audible, as the film which most pleased them in this decade was shut out of any of the major awards.

It was that same septuagenarian group of voters who, the same year, tossed a Best Picture nomination to the baffling *Missing* and passed up *An Officer and a Gentleman, Sophie's Choice,* and the youth-oriented masterpiece, *Diner.*

And while there was no Best Actor/Actress honor possible for the engaging *E.T.* puppet, strong supporting players Drew Barrymore and Henry Thomas were passed by so that a hammy Charles Durning could clasp his fist about another Oscar nomination certificate for the dreadful *Best Little Whorehouse in Texas* and so that the shrieking Teri Garr (an old-guard overactress if there ever was one) could sit among the Best Supporting Actress nominees for her performance in *Tootsie.*

It was almost a foregone conclusion that *E.T.* could not beat the self-important, bedsore-producing *Gandhi* for Best Picture, but such dewy-eyed Academy members as George Lucas hoped against hope that Spielberg would capture a Best Director prize anyway (as Warren Beatty had done the year before—with *Reds*—despite another trying Best Picture, *Chariots of Fire*).

The youngsters hadn't counted on Richard Attenborough's allure for the directors' branch. Ah! Here was a director they could understand. After appearing in an endless list of tedious war films, Attenborough groped his way up, becoming a director of equally tedious but oh-so-British epics such as *Young Winston* (did we really want to live *every* minute of Churchill's first twenty-two years?) and *A Bridge Too Far* (which took you to the Bridge at Remagen and left you lying in the mud, where thousands of good actors ran about with guns too loud and voices too inaudible for the mikes to pick up.) The old men of the branch must have been thrilled to see silent films on the screen again.

So, when Attenborough (now called, so cutely, "Sir Dickie") made *Gandhi*'s life into a posturing Technicolor slide show (the kind that Mom and Dad used to bore the neighbors with), here was an Oscar made in heaven.

Not just a few small boys (who sneaked downstairs to watch the Oscars) cried into their pillows for that intergalactic man of peace, E.T.

"Now here's the man who was cheated out of his Oscar last night—Steven Spielberg," said a television newscaster the next day.

Spielberg had already foreseen his fate in a blinding burst of future sight. "If the Academy decides to give me an Oscar someday, I'll be glad to accept it," he told the same news reporter. "But I don't think it will be for a film that I really care about. *E.T.* is my favorite movie, although it's not my best-directed movie—that's *Close Encounters of the Third Kind.*"

He reflected for a further moment. "There's always a backlash against anything that makes more than $50 million in film rentals, and history (like *Gandhi*) is always more weighty than popcorn."

Spielberg was, perhaps, blindly seeking an excuse for his costly Oscar defeats.

Actually, the Academy is schizophrenic in its attitude toward box-office power. For instance, they chose the massively successful *Rocky* over *Network* in 1977. And, in 1953, they picked the financial giant, *The Greatest Show on Earth* over *High Noon, Moulin Rouge,* and *The Quiet Man.*

In the eighties high-toned epics came into fashion again, causing *Gandhi* and *Chariots of Fire* to win over barrelfuls of box-office giants. Critics lavishly praised these unworthy epics for this sudden outbreak of good taste.

The Academy's rebuff of *The Color Purple* was, therefore, even more astounding than has been depicted. With Alice Walker's novel Spielberg had stumbled onto a real fantasy—a woman's story of racism and cruelty. It took Spielberg almost two years to talk Warner Bros. into letting him and co-producer Quincy Jones make the movie and, even then, the man who is paid $1.8 million just to direct, co-produced and directed the film for the basic minimum allowed by the Directors Guild, $40,000.

Steven was certainly on the right track.

Then he did the inexcusable: he signed on master comedienne Whoopi Goldberg as his heroine and set out to make the film "entertaining." Now, we were all taught by Sir Dickie and by *Chariots of Fire* that entertainment makes a message picture too bearable—too damned bloody watchable.

So the old men of the directors' branch blanched in their overstuffed seats.

When the smash hit song "Miss Celie's Blues" erupted from the mouth of one of the film's central characters, Spielberg's Oscar probably felt its feet just beginning to crumble. The day after the film opened, the director uttered the unwisest words of all. He said modestly to a Cable News Network reporter that he thought *The Color Purple* was of Oscar caliber.

That did it! As we all know, only the four-thousand-odd voters (and many are *odd*) of the Academy of Motion Picture Arts and Sciences can tell with any degree of certainty if a film is of "Oscar caliber." They are the only ones who can assure us that Cher's portrayal of Rusty Dennis in *Mask* was below muster, while Jessica Lange's sobbing, lip-synching performance as Patsy Cline in *Sweet Dreams* was of the highest order. And it is only they who can tell us, absolutely and adroitly, that Judd Nelson and Emilio Estevez in *The Breakfast Club* and Eric Stoltz in *Mask* were inferior, while the posturing, slobbering Eric Roberts was just right in *Runaway Train*.

From The Color Purple, *three powerful stars*, left to right: *the stand-up comic, Whoopi Goldberg, the film's star; Oprah Winfrey, who was discovered on a talk show; and Margaret "Shug" Avery, who got her first major job from Spielberg.*

Four days before the nominations were announced, Spielberg hedged his bets by saying, "Of course, it means a lot to win anything, being recognized for your work. Anyone who denies that isn't speaking from the heart. An Oscar would be wonderful. But it's not the last goal for me."

When Steven's name was missing from the directors' nominations, even the tabloids took notice of the scandal—certainly a first for them. STEVEN SPIELBERG SNUBBED BY JEALOUS COLLEAGUES, trumpeted *The Star*. And the Los Angeles *Herald-Examiner* (not a fan of the Spielberg film) stated succinctly: "If a movie has eleven nominations, someone has to be responsible."

These voices couldn't have been more correct. Other chroniclers of the entertainment scene echoed these sentiments. Commenting on the burden of guilt building up within the Academy's membership, columnist and entertainment reporter Robert Osborne, who wrote the official history of the Academy the year of its fiftieth anniversary, said, "You could even feel it that very night, the night of the Oscars."

The irreverent TV reporter Gary Franklin believes that *The Color Purple* won its eleven nominations because the Academy voters "saw it as a way to salve the Hollywood conscience. Those nominations paid lip service to racial harmony. Just take a look around and you will see that the film industry is highly racist. There are no black directors to speak of—certainly none in the forefront. There is no black power in the ivory towers of the studio system. So instead of doing something constructive about gaining a balance for black artists, the Academy tossed them a bone—eleven nominations to a very flawed film." Franklin is the highly respected renegade entertainment critic for KABC in Los Angeles and is now as powerful as Rona Barrett was in her day.

Co-producer and composer Quincy Jones flatly called the Academy's failure to award even a single Oscar to the film an example of the "racism that is rampant in this industry. I believe that film was shut out in the final voting because of sociological problems within the Academy and the film industry. If that same story of brutality and individual triumph over it had been made with a white cast in a white setting, it would have won Best Picture and a number of other Oscars."

In most of the interviews conducted on the "Spielberg Scandal," the word *envy* was used invariably in many contexts. Mark Rydell, director of *The Rose* and *On Golden Pond*, said that envy led to a misunderstanding of the film and its rejection by Oscar voters. "In my opinion, you must judge a director on how well he achieves his objectives. Steven Spielberg set out to make an entertaining, uplifting film from Alice Walker's novel, and he succeeded."

Gary Franklin agreed: "There are so many reasons people vote a certain way in the Academy and one of them is to vote *for* a film or director because you are *against* somebody like Spielberg. There are real hates within that organization; real cases of people voting against other people. I think the Spielberg matter may have been the classic example of that."

Spielberg may be arrogant, wealthy, and successful, and *The Color Purple* may be flawed; but the flaws in the directors' branch of the Academy are far more egregious.

Of its 230 members (membership goes up and down every three months), more than 78 percent are over fifty-five (about 70 percent are over sixty). Almost one-fourth are over seventy—with some checking in at over eighty. About 45 percent of them have not made a film in the last ten years, while 20 percent have not made a film in the last twenty years. At the other end of those sad statistics, only five members of the branch are under thirty and only twenty are under forty.

To make a bad situation worse, some of the finest directing forces in the medium today are members of the branches in which they made their entrance in the film world: Stallone, Redford, Alda, Beatty, Poitier, and Cassavetes are all in the actors' branch and, therefore, are ineligible to vote in the nominating process for directors. And although some have tried, like Peter Fonda, it is not easy to switch, and has not been accomplished to date. Ron Howard wisely waited until he had established himself as a director before joining the Academy—as a member of the directors' branch. Paul Newman, chosen to receive a Lifetime Achievement Award in 1986, produced and directed *Rachel, Rachel*, one of the five Best Picture nominees for 1968. The film also received nominations in three other major categories—Best Actress (Joanne Woodward), Best Supporting Actress (Estelle Parsons), and Best Screenplay—Based on Material from Another Medium (Stewart Stern). Although he won the New York Film Critics Award for direction that year, Newman received no nomination from the Academy's directors' branch.

As it turned out, 1968 marked the first time that the winner of the Directors Guild Award (Anthony Harvey for *The Lion in Winter*) did not coincide with the Academy's Best Director (Carol Reed for *Oliver!*).

Capping it all is the fact that the *real* leadership of the directors' branch—the men most likely to vote and to influence others—are still from the era of the great studio system, a time that was a low ebb for the Academy. They are men like Andrew Marton, André de Toth, Paul Landres, Ronald Neame, Vincent Sherman, Arthur Lubin, and George Sidney.

"I have a feeling that this 'old guard' is the most likely to vote regularly," said Charles Champlin of the *Los Angeles Times*. "I'm not saying that there is anything wrong with that. But it does tend to place the votes of the newer, far busier members askew."

Champlin once estimated that less than 60 percent of the Academy membership votes in the very best years. Former Academy president Howard W. Koch, a major producer in his own right, said he believes that 40 percent would be considered a good voter turnout. "Not that we will ever know," said Koch. "But I believe that. This means that one or two votes either way can determine a nomination . . . a very important thing to be determined by such a small number."

The authors of this book conducted an anonymous survey of the directors' branch through a questionnaire mailed to 190 members (the rest could not be located).

Although only 10 percent returned their completed survey sheets, the results indicated that those members of the branch did not give a single vote to nominate Spielberg for Best Director of *The Color Purple* nor to nominate Peter Bogdanovich as Best Director of *Mask*. And most often they gave as their reason, "Neither film was good enough."

But several of those responding openly admitted their envy of the world's most successful director of all time—financially speaking, of course. One participant, when asked why, in his opinion, Steven Spielberg was ignored in the nomination process, responded that it probably had to do with the need of those who have not shined so brightly to deprive him, for as long as possible, of the one thing he doesn't have for doing what he does bigger and better and more successfully than everyone else. He confessed that he loves, admires, and respects Steven Spielberg, yet wishes he would disappear, all in that same rush of emotion. For as long as Spielberg is there to measure oneself against, it's difficult not to feel oneself coming up short.

Occasionally, the outcome of the Oscar director's derby ends in bursts of unsportsmanlike conduct, and often from strange quarters. When Michael Cimino took home that prize for the 1978 Oscar-winning film, *The Deer Hunter,* he was chastised publicly by Jon Voight (Best Actor for the competitive *Coming Home),* who said, "Our film had the best director in the business, Hal Ashby. Cimino doesn't hold a candle to him."

Three years later a very ungrateful David Puttnam, producer of the much-Oscared *Chariots of Fire,* fired some low blows at the victorious Warren Beatty, who had nudged out *Fire's* Hugh Hudson for the auteur prize. "His modest little six-million-dollar picture was named Best Picture," sneered columnist Marilyn Beck. "So you'd think he would be satisfied. Right? Wrong." Puttnam singed the columnist's ears with this statement: "Hugh Hudson [*Chariots of Fire* director] is without a doubt a better director than Warren Beatty is or he ever will be. And Steven Spielberg [up for *Raiders of the Lost Ark]* is better—and also Louis Malle [up for *Atlantic City].*

Then Puttnam leaned down close to Beck with fangs a-showing and

Sydney Pollack, who won two Oscars for producing and directing Out of Africa, *which defeated Spielberg's* The Color Purple. *Many Oscar watchers believe Pollack would have beaten Spielberg had Spielberg been nominated for Best Director. Pollack had been overlooked for his* The Way We Were, Three Days of the Condor, *and* Tootsie. *"It was destined to be his year,"* concluded columnist Robert Osborne.

anger in his eyes: "You know why Beatty got that Oscar—the Academy was simply acknowledging the fact that a gorgeous actor, a pretty boy, could raise $50 million to make that picture . . . that lumbering picture [*Reds*]."

"Oh my, oh my!" said a Los Angeles *Herald-Examiner* columnist. "Such an ugly burst of envy. That man must be green all over by now."

In 1986, in the aftermath of the Spielberg shutout, critics across America called for a reorganization of the directors' branch which would include a judicial use of old-age Drano to clean out the clouded thinking behind the selection of such an important award. "Anyone who says that envy to a great degree didn't badly affect Spielberg's chances would be crazy," speculated Peter Bogdanovich, "but don't look for any changes in the near future. They just will not be forthcoming."

The *Hollywood Reporter*'s Martin Grove was furious about the "Scandal Spielberg" and publicly entered the fracas by calling for an "in-house" investigation of the Academy's directors' branch. He devoted an entire column to it, blasting the archaic voting procedures of the fifty-nine-year-old institution.

Among other things, he said: "Can it be that a filmmaker whose picture is deemed worthy of eleven nominations, including Best Picture and three for acting, is not deserving of a Best Directing nomination? When one considers that neither Whoopi Goldberg nor Oprah Winfrey had previously acted in theatrical films and are now being honored, respectively, with Best Actress and Best Supporting Actress nominations for their work in *Purple,* can it be that the director who nurtured their performances is not, himself, worthy of a nomination for his efforts?

"These are questions that the Academy should be held accountable for answering. If the Academy genuinely wants to restore the confidence of not just the industry but moviegoers around the world in the validity of its Oscars, it should lose no time in addressing itself to this issue.

"It should appoint a blue-ribbon panel to examine the balloting by the directors' branch and to see if, for example, there was any organized effort to dissuade voters from nominating Spielberg. Did any branch officials seek to influence the voting? Among the prime movers of the directors' branch, are there any with whom Spielberg has had major business differences in the past?"

The issue of economics alone must have brought about a maelstrom of jealousy: In the decade since he burst upon the Hollywood landscape with *Jaws* (1975), wunderkind Steven Spielberg has produced and/or directed an incredible body of work that has earned, in addition to $1.6 billion in the U.S. alone, an incredible fifty Oscar nominations, and twelve of the golden statuettes.

During the summer of 1982, he had three blockbusters in release at the same time: *E.T.—The Extra-Terrestrial, Raiders of the Lost Ark,* and *Poltergeist*. In fact, during much of June and July, these films were taking in a combined total of $1 million a day at box offices throughout the land. Overseas coin had yet to be reckoned with.

This certainly makes Steven Spielberg Oscar's "uncrowned king." And it looks as if he may have to play Napoleon: he may have to crown himself.

CHAPTER THREE

Secret Ballot

As of 1931, if I, a director for a minor-league studio, wanted to win an Oscar, making good films was not good enough. —FRANK CAPRA

Joan Blondell was fighting mad. Her cheeks flushed under her makeup, and her platinum hair waved in the wind like a flag. "They did it again! They did it again!" she yelled across the Warner Bros. lot, aiming her voice at anyone willing to listen.

She had been in the middle of a musical number from *Stage Struck* being directed by tap-mad genius Busby Berkeley when the master called a coffee break, and Blondell ran to a newsstand near the front gate. It was February 1935. "They delivered the *Citizen* yet?" she asked. "Just got here," said the paper seller, sailing a copy through the air to her outstretched arms. Blondell scanned the front page, searching for a report on the Academy Awards nominations. "Those bastards. What the hell do you have to do to get nominated anyway?" Back on the set, she waved the front page before co-star Dick Powell's face. "They passed Bette up again. Not a mention—not for Bette or the movie." Powell reached for her hand and said, "Don't take it so hard. You know as well as I do that the Oscar business is all politics. Bette will understand."

And Bette Davis, Joan Blondell's pal, *did* understand. And more! She knew damn well why her incredible performance in *Of Human Bondage* hadn't won an Oscar nomination. Hadn't Jack Warner ordered her not to appear in the Somerset Maugham classic—a decision he had rescinded only to shut Bette up? "Nobody in their right mind would want to play that vicious bitch," warned the boss of Warner Bros. "You'll live to regret it."

As it turned out, the only thing she regretted about the movie was the Academy Awards scandal which surrounded it. It sure wasn't the first time Oscar had overlooked the best Hollywood had to offer. King Vidor's 1928 triumph, *The Crowd*—considered to be one of the best two or three pictures of the twenties—didn't even rate a Best Picture nomination. And in 1930 the Academy handed Norma Shearer an Oscar for her limp-wristed role in *The Divorcée*, passing over Greta Garbo in *Anna Christie* and Gloria Swanson in *The Trespasser*.

PRICE, WATERHO[USE]

(Official Board of Tell[ers])

Twelfth Annual ACADEMY AW[ARDS]

OFFICIAL

Nomination Ba[llot]

Award for the BEST PICTURE of the [Year]

VOTE FOR TEN PICTURES IN THE ORDER OF YOU[R PREFER-]
ENCE; that is, put the title of the production which is your f[irst choice]
[o]n the first line, your second choice on the second line, and so [on]
[fo]r TEN. Write titles only.

[FIRST] CHOICE _Mr. Smith Goes to Wash[ington]_
[SE]COND CHOICE _Young Mr. Lincoln_
[ ] CHOICE _Of Mice and Men_
[ ] CHOICE _The Beachcomber_
[ ]OICE _Bachelor Mother_
[ ]HOICE _Gone With the Wind_
[ ]OICE _Great Man Votes_
[ ] _Backdoor to Heaven_

[ ] for Ballot of Your Own Branc[h]

[Fill] Out and Return them Both Toda[y]

[POLLS] CLOSE WEDNESDAY, FEBRUARY [ ]

OFFICIAL

Nomination

Ballot

The Time is short VOTE Today!

ACTING Awards. Vote for FIVE CHOICES in each classification, in t[he]
order of your preference. Refer to Reminder List before voting. Leads are eligible on[ly]
for the general Best Performance Awards. Those marked in the Reminder List by [a]
check ✓ are considered Leads. If you wish, you can nominate any supporting playe[r]
for both the Supporting Award and the general Best Performance Award.

ACTOR Nominations for "the best performance by an actor."

FIRST choice _Robert Donat_ (Name of actor) in _Goodbye Mr. Chips_ (Title of picture)
SECOND choice _Henry Fonda_ in _Young Mr. Lincoln_
THIRD choice _Gene Lockhart_ in _Blackmail_
FOURTH choice _James Stewart_ in _Mr. Smith Goes to Washi[ngton]_
FIFTH choice _Charles Coburn_ in _Made For Each Other_

ACTRESS Nominations for "the best performance by an actress."

FIRST choice _Jane Bryan_ (Name of actress) in _We Are Not Alone_ (Title of picture)
SECOND choice _Bette Davis_ in _Dark Victory_
THIRD choice _Betty Field_ in _Of Mice and Men_
FOURTH choice _Elsa Lanchester_ in _The Beachcomber_
FIFTH choice _Vivian Leigh_ in _Gone With the Wind_

Supporting Actor Nominations for "the best performance by an actor in a supporting role."

FIRST choice _Gene Lockhart_ (Name of actor) in _Blackmail_ (Title of picture)
SECOND choice _Charles Coburn_ in _Made For Each Other_
THIRD choice _J. Edward Bromberg_ in _Hollywood Cavalcade_
FOURTH choice _Roman Bohnen_ in _Of Mice and Men_
FIFTH choice _____ in _____

Supporting Actress Nominations for "the best performance by an actress in a supporting role."

FIRST choice _Jane Bryan_ (Name of actress) in _We are Not Alone_ (Title of picture)
SECOND choice _Hattie McDaniel_ in _Gone With the Wind_
THIRD choice _Betty Field_ in _Of Mice and Men_
FOURTH choice _Elsa Lanchester_ in _The Beachcomber_
FIFTH choice _____ in _____

Turn Page for Your Ballot on Best Picture!

This time, though, the Academy had gone too far. Nobody in Hollywood, unless he was deaf and dumb, could have overlooked Bette's performance in *Of Human Bondage*. It opened at New York's Radio City Music Hall on June 28, 1934. The reaction was violent; people cheered and clapped when the final credits were shown, and some eastern critics called Davis the best actress, so far, of the talkies. Nobody disagreed. It was common knowledge in Hollywood that the actress had gone through hell to win the part and had given so much of herself during filming that superstars fought with each other to get tickets to the sneak previews. Bette was finally given permission only when Jack Warner found out he could make a bundle by loaning her out at an inflated fee to RKO to play Mildred. "Go on, hang yourself!" Warner said to the actress before dismissing her.

Bette just jutted out her New England chin, took home her copy of the Somerset Maugham novel, and began trying, painstakingly, to master a Cockney accent. She even hired a transplanted Englishwoman to help her. The lady moved into Bette's house, slept on the couch, and began her coaching.

A rare copy of a 1939 Oscar ballot shows the choices available to voters and the complexity of the nomination process. (© A.M.P.A.S.)

A young Bette Davis and Leslie Howard in 1934's Of Human Bondage, *a brutally frank film which wowed Hollywood and the rest of America with its brilliance and unleashed a storm of bitterness when Bette was passed up in the nomination process. Offering evidence of her acting range in the character she played, evolving from fiery bitch to dying heroine, Bette's performance was certainly the best of the year—one of the best of the decade. But politics within the Academy froze her out in a scandal which almost destroyed the Academy Awards.*

"For eight weeks. Morning, noon, and night, I was at it," said Davis. "I even answered the phone with it. And naturally, I drove the family mad, but it was worth it when I found that I had mastered the accent well enough to win the praise of the British cast."

The performance was so stunning that those directors who could get permission dropped by the RKO lot to see the daily rushes. The critical success of the film should have only strengthened the actress's chance to win the Oscar.

When the Academy failed to nominate her, almost everyone in Hollywood screamed "foul!" It was time, everyone decided, to take a good, hard look at the Oscar ballot box. Who in his right mind would nominate Claudette Colbert (in her fine, but lightweight, bit in *It Happened One Night*), Grace Moore (an opera singer who hit the high notes but little else in *One Night of Love*), and Norma Shearer (for shedding tears and holding a hankie in *The Barretts of Wimpole Street*) and *not* Bette Davis in *Of Human Bondage*? It was even harder to take because the Academy had the option of expanding the list from three to five if performances warranted, and, in fact, did expand the Best Actress list to six nominees in 1935.

There was no way around it. Bette Davis had been passed over on purpose. It was only the latest—but the worst—sign of the political rot eating at the soul of the seven-year-old Academy of Motion Picture Arts and Sciences.

The conspiracy against Bette Davis, however, started at Warner Bros. Jack and Harry Warner, both founders of the Academy, made it known that *they* were not supporting Bette Davis for the Oscar in an RKO film! The implication was clear: the Academy members working for Warners should not support her either. "My bosses certainly didn't help by sending instructions to all their personnel to vote for somebody else. So naturally, it worked!" Davis remarked with understandable bitterness some years later.

And over at RKO, which had managed to get only two dozen nominations (few of them major) in the first seven years of the Oscar, the bosses were only lukewarm toward Davis. She was not, after all, under contract to RKO. And an Oscar to her would only succeed in making the Warner brothers wealthier at their expense.

The Oscar slighted Bette Davis and *Of Human Bondage* for other reasons as well. In 1934 Oscar was held by his privates, so to speak, in the grip of a few big studios: Paramount, United Artists, and Metro-Goldwyn-Mayer—particularly Metro-Goldwyn-Mayer. Eleven of the founders were now from MGM, and that studio had taken the hog's share of nominations and Oscars since 1927 (155 nominations and 33 Oscars in the first seven years—twice as many as Warner Bros., three times as many as RKO, and four times as many as Columbia).

Louis B. Mayer's personal Oscar power was even more insidious. During the first several years, he apparently had an almost royal veto over some of the ballot decisions. (And "ballot" is too kind a word for the first seven years of Oscar decisions.) It was Mayer, and Mayer alone, who kept King Vidor's monumental *The Crowd* from being nominated in 1928. The MGM film, the first to deal realistically with the bleakness of lower-middle-class life, was a classic when it was released. Mayer made it clear to the handpicked nominating committee that he wished them to "bypass MGM to avoid appearance of a conflict of interest." It was all right, he said, to nominate King Vidor for Best

Director. The other nominees were Frank Borzage, a studio-popular director for *Seventh Heaven;* and a now forgotten man, Herbert Brenon, for a now forgotten film, *Sorrell and Son.* The decision that was made in the finals remains clouded in mystery. Who decided on Borzage over Vidor? The Academy historians say the Oscars were decided by an impartial panel.

"Well, that's a crock," said Joan Crawford, when she was reminiscing in the sixties. "The committee only formalized decisions that were already made by a few key producers. You've got to remember, the Academy, then at least, was only an extension of the 'executive suite.' "

King Vidor also told it differently: "At the start the voting was done by five people only—a situation which fortunately didn't last very long. The first year Sid Grauman, Mary Pickford, Douglas Fairbanks, Sr., and Louis B. Mayer voted for everybody. I figured I had a good chance to win. My film *The Crowd* had gotten spectacular reviews, and Mayer himself had produced it. After an all-night voting session Sid Grauman called me at 6:00 A.M. and told me he'd held out for my work in *The Crowd* until daybreak."

"Well?" asked Vidor. There was a pause on the other end of the line. "Your problem, Vidor, was Mayer. He wouldn't vote for it because it wasn't a big money-maker for MGM." Vidor hung up the phone in disgust. "Even then money mattered—though [the Oscar] didn't earn an extra million dollars like it does now."

Joan Blondell, an actress who averaged twenty films a year in the Warner Bros. factory, braved the wrath of studio boss Jack Warner and led the drive to gain a nomination for Bette Davis as Mildred in Of Human Bondage. When Joan brought her fiancé Dick Powell, with all his box-office clout, into the fracas, it sent shock waves through Warner Bros.—ending at the desk of Jack Warner. Warner, in turn, ordered the Academy to liberalize the selection process.

"I'm a great admirer of the Academy," recalled Vidor, who never got a regular Oscar—though the late director amassed a body of work that places him among the top twenty directors in U.S. films. "But it was nearly ruined by tampering from the big studio men who founded it."

Hollywood directors screamed like Paddy's pig over Vidor's Oscar loss, so the Academy dropped the cozy little committees that decided the winners during the first two years and opened up the final voting to include all Academy members. But not before the bosses made sure that Mary Pickford got an Oscar for *Coquette* and MGM took home a Best Picture award for its choppy, though for its day financially successful, *Broadway Melody*. Pickford's Oscar was, to be fair, a "career Oscar" for her twenty years of monumental contributions as the movies' first superstar. She earned it, but it was to set a precedent for the Oscars that continues today. The Academy gives awards again and again, not for the best performance of the year but for years of fine duty under fire.

James Murray and Eleanor Boardman (Mrs. King Vidor) despair over their lower-middle-class life when Murray loses his job as a night clerk. The film was The Crowd, *and it was a stunner—the first Hollywood film to truly delve into social realism. In addition, with its ominous overtones, somber photography, and strident script, it predicted the coming Depression. Director King Vidor always called it his masterpiece. Coming in* 1928, The Crowd *should have been the major contender for the first Oscars. But Louis B. Mayer called Vidor in to explain the facts of life —Oscar-style. "These awards are going to be passed around," said Mayer. "So you, the film, and the actors will not be nominated. It will be MGM's turn next year with* Broadway Melody." *Before his death Vidor told the authors: "The Oscars began their history on that 'fixed outcome basis.' I knew right then that integrity was at stake. I have never changed my mind."*

Bette Davis was robbed of her Oscar nomination for *Of Human Bondage* by a thoroughly emasculated Academy. The old "committee system" had been disbanded, and the full membership of each branch selected the nominees. But hundreds of writers, scores of directors, and virtually thousands of actors had deserted the Academy in unhappiness and downright hatred over the misuse of the organization by the studio moguls. Perhaps history will never know how few voters decided the Oscars during the thirties. One thing is certain: the process was ruled by the producers and studio bosses when Capra took over as president of a fast-vanishing Academy in 1935. He maintained that the full membership numbered "fewer than" fifty.

Producer Walter Wanger, who succeeded Capra as Academy president in the early forties, claimed several times that the membership was forty or below.

The voters were a veritable Hollywood handful, that's certain. Capra said he had to beg the members of the Screen Actors Guild, the Screen Directors Guild, and the Screen Writers Guild. "At that time, any support of the Academy, even voting, was taboo."

Studio politics, pure and simple, cost Davis the nomination and, probably, the Oscar. It had happened before and it would happen again. (But it could never happen now because the voting membership is so much larger.)

Still, the "Bette Davis Affair" scared the hell out of the Academy. Bette's friends and admirers, including Joan Blondell and Dick Powell, stirred Hollywood gossip (always the city's greatest force) to create general outrage in the acting community. Mayer and the rest of the bosses took the bait. On February 15, 1935, the Academy announced that write-ins would be permitted in the voting for the 1934 Oscars. But this was only a grudging gesture. Claudette Colbert won, followed by Norma Shearer and Grace Moore. "I suppose there was no chance for any part of the process to be fair because everybody quit the Academy," said Joan Blondell. "But when they left Bette out, we all began taking a closer look and decided: 'Hey, something's rotten in Beverly Hills.' "

The scandal marked the end of an era for Oscar. Six years of tea-party voting were finally over. Marie Dressler, an early winner, described the syndrome as "cream and sugar with my Oscar, please." The year Mary Pickford won, virtually all the voters had been guests in her palace, Pickfair, at least once. In Norma Shearer's case, her husband, MGM production chief Irving Thalberg, delivered the executive vote; most of the other voters had been guests at Irving and Norma's wedding.

"This is not to say that these early awards didn't hit right on target," said writer Frances Marion, another early winner. "I think it had more heart to it then."

As president, Capra immediately opened up the ballot box—extending voting power to all the guilds, including actors, directors, and extras. Thus, there were 14,000 potential voters. "But we still had to beg the guilds to let their people vote. Many, many people felt the voting was a tacit support of the Academy and that support of the Academy was anti-labor."

Capra's plan helped. But not Capra, nor Wanger, nor even Bette Davis (Academy president briefly in 1941) could successfully cure the Oscars of their near-fatal domination by the big studios. The ballot box was the tender issue in the beginning and it remained such until the late sixties when Academy president Gregory Peck finally began weeding out many aged voters.

Academy voters have littered almost sixty years of film history with the carcasses of creative giants who have gone Oscarless in the name of box-office success and big-studio politics. Bad voting was the issue in 1935; it was the issue in 1945. It was the issue in 1970 and in 1985. Oscar's history is characterized as much by the movies and performances it slighted as by the ones it honored.

It was Oscar voters who passed up Greta Garbo and handed sob sister Luise Rainer two of the little gold men. It was Oscar voters who named the mawkish musical *Oliver!* Best Picture while failing to nominate *2001: A Space Odyssey* and *Easy Rider* (two films that were listed by *Time* magazine and the *New York Times* as best of the decade).

Academy members gave Elizabeth Taylor an Oscar for *Butterfield 8*, one of her worst movies, but did not nominate her for *A Place In the Sun*, one of her best. They named *The Greatest Show on Earth* Best Picture over *High Noon*, *Moulin Rouge*, and *The Quiet Man* (while failing to nominate *Singin' in the Rain*, *Come Back, Little Sheba*, *The Bad and the Beautiful*, or *Viva Zapata!* in the same year).

For 1939 they nominated Mickey Rooney for *Babes in Arms* and not Henry Fonda in *Young Mr. Lincoln*. For 1943 they nominated Mickey Rooney for *The Human Comedy* and not Henry Fonda in *The Ox-Bow Incident*. For 1955 they nominated Spencer Tracy in *Bad Day at Black Rock* and not Henry Fonda in *Mister Roberts*.

The example of Henry Fonda is particularly important because it demolishes the Academy's greatest defense against its incessant critics. The men and women who have apologized for the Oscar in speeches, articles, and books always say that the Oscar adheres to one golden rule: Oscars are not always given, so say the apologists, to the actor or actress who gives "the best performance of the year"; but, so they say, the Oscars *do* even out the odds by honoring actors or actresses who have consistently given a career full of fine performances. But what about Greta Garbo or Irene Dunne or Cary Grant or Myrna Loy, who has never even been nominated?

Henry Fonda is perhaps the prime example. His Oscar nomination and subsequent win as Best Actor of 1981 for *On Golden Pond* came after forty-six years of turning in one good performance after another, including his brilliant Oscar-nominated performance as Tom Joad in 1940's *The Grapes of Wrath*. His Oscar-caliber roles through the years have included *Jezebel*, *Jesse James*, *Drums Along the Mohawk*, *Chad Hanna*, *The Male Animal*, *The Big Street*, *My Darling Clementine*, *The Fugitive*, *War and Peace*, *Twelve Angry Men*, *The Wrong Man*, *Advise and Consent*, and *Once Upon a Time in the West*. The Oscar bosses have said that Fonda's numbers just didn't come up right—his best roles were always during years of bountiful male performances. That's not true, of course. When 1957's *Twelve Angry Men* was nominated for Best Picture, the voters opted for Marlon Brando in *Sayonara*, Alec Guinness in *The Bridge on the River Kwai*, Anthony Franciosa in *A Hatful of Rain*, Charles Laughton in *Witness for the Prosecution*, and Anthony Quinn in *Wild Is the Wind*. Only Guinness's performance was as good as or better than Fonda's.

Other Academy big talkers were quick to say that "Hank knows the score; it doesn't really affect him; he knows about the politics."

The Academy passed up Fonda so many times that it became an inside joke. In a delicious bit of irony, Billy Wilder cast Fonda as a president of the Academy offering a long overdue Oscar to an aging movie star in 1979's *Fedora*. Unfortunately, Fonda wasn't on screen long enough to bag a nomination for Best Supporting Actor—but the thought was there.

The domination of the Academy by the studios seemed just another example of the quaint and madcap way Hollywood did things. "Oh, you know how it is out there," said Elsa Maxwell, discussing the Oscars with the Duchess of Windsor. "They just play dress-up once a year. It's not to be taken seriously."

Then came 1941, when the Academy passed up *Citizen Kane*, by everybody's estimate one of the ten best films ever made. "It's just a good thing that *Birth of a Nation* didn't have to face these voters," said writer Dalton Trumbo. "They'd have given it an honorable mention for cinematography and tossed Lillian Gish a bouquet for Best Supporting Actress."

Then television, the infidel, forever ended any quaintness the Oscars may have possessed. People turned on their TV sets and quit going to the movies. It happened overnight. In 1948 the films had one of their best years ever. In 1950 they had one of their worst. The Hollywood bosses were grabbing at straws, pulling things out of the hat—3-D and Smell-O-Vision, CinemaScope and VistaVision—to get people back to the ticket windows.

Overnight, the Oscar became a deadly serious matter. The fat men in the front offices had discovered an amazing thing in 1948. A special box-office study showed that *The Best Years of Our Lives* and *Gentlemen's Agreement* both earned about $2 million extra after they won the Best Picture Oscar. Louis B. Mayer and others thought it was a whim of the times, at first. But subsequently, a Dow Jones study published in *Fortune* magazine proved that both films had virtually finished their normal box-office runs by Oscar time. The Oscars, said the Dow Jones men, caused the films to "make two million extra—each!" Thus ended, forever, Oscar's virgin objectivity.

From that day forward, Oscar had a cash value. And Oscar is nice for a lot of other reasons, too. But agents, public relations men, executives,

The soft tones of a California sunset treated Oscar kindly in 1967 on its thirty-eighth anniversary, when Liz Taylor and Paul Scofield took home the top acting prizes. It was to be the last year of the dinosaurs, and unsettling winds were blowing through the audiences— both out in America and inside the Santa Monica Civic Auditorium, where the ceremonies were held. A couple of years later Academy bylaws were changed, stipulating that a third of the board of governors be either under thirty-five or have been members for five years or less. The results of this infusion of youth began to show up quickly. Jane Fonda's win for Klute *could never have happened during the old era.* (© A.M.P.A.S.)

and the national theater chains—particularly the chains—see it as money in the bank. This era is far from over. What else can explain the defeat of *Network* by the sappy *Rocky* in 1977? (And *Rocky* was surely the weakest picture of the five, the others being *All the President's Men*, *Bound for Glory*, and *Taxi Driver*. *Marathon Man*, *The Shootist*, and Ingmar Bergman's *Face to Face* weren't even nominated.) Or the overblown, overproduced, tedious *Gandhi* winning over the highly entertaining, technically superb *E.T.—The Extra-Terrestrial* in 1983? (Other nominated films that year were *Missing*, *Tootsie*, and *The Verdict*, any one of which would have been a better choice than *Gandhi*. Productions that were locked out of a Best Picture nomination were *Sophie's Choice*, *Victor/Victoria*, *Diner*, *The World According to Garp*, *An Officer and a Gentleman*, *Frances*, *Poltergeist*, *The Road Warrior* and *Das Boot*—most of which were superior to the Indian epic.)

The use of Oscar as a blank check was already an institution by the time the first true critics of the awards appeared on the national scene. Until the fifties, most of the movie press accepted the Academy's decisions as being of unassailable virtue.

Then, the first true critic wasn't a Hollywood reporter but a writer of mysteries—Raymond Chandler, author of *The Big Sleep*, *Farewell, My Lovely*, and many others. "It isn't that the awards never go to fine achievements as that those fine achievements are not rewarded as such. They are rewarded as fine achievements at the box office," Chandler wrote in *The Nation*. "They are not decided by the use of whatever artistic and critical wisdom Hollywood may happen to possess. Instead, they are ballyhooed, pushed, yelled, screamed, and in every way propagandized into the consciousness of the voters so incessantly in the weeks before the final balloting that everything except the golden aura of the box office is forgotten."

Chandler, writing in the late forties, came to many of the same conclusions that other critics would reach in the eighties—namely, that the voters normally do not heavily attend the movies they vote on, and the percentage of the Academy that actually votes is never higher than 60 or sometimes 70 percent and is often less than 50 percent. (Former Academy president Howard W. Koch says it may be as low as 40 percent.)

Studio bosses will deny this even now. "Why, studios can't control votes," Darryl Zanuck used to say. "It's a *secret* ballot, for Chrissakes." True, how true. But to quote Joan Crawford, "You'd have to be some ninny to vote against the studio that has your contract or that produces your pictures. Your future depends on theirs—so to speak. And if an Oscar means a better future, then so be it."

The Hollywood brass has talked out of the other side of its mouth when outraged by an occasional show of Oscar impartiality. Most notably, execs yelled when the Academy chose a British production—Laurence Olivier's monumental *Hamlet*—as Best Picture of 1948, with Olivier named Best Actor. And it was a picture that wasn't even being distributed by a Hollywood company. (It won two other awards.) And, don't this beat all, a second limey pic, *The Red Shoes*, was also up for Best Picture in place of perfectly good red-white-and-blue efforts like *I Remember Mama* and *The Luck of the Irish*, for God's sake.

This seemed so fishy that the bosses bad-mouthed the Oscar-voting process, which they had always defended like the Statue of Liberty. W. R. Wilkerson, publisher of the *Hollywood Reporter* and the media voice for the studios that fed his paper with ads, said right out that the ballot box must have been stuffed. "It's a mystery to us as to who actually did cast a vote for *Hamlet*," said Wilkerson in his front-page column, "Trade Views." (It was no secret that Wilkerson spoke for the studio establishment.) Wilkerson figured out that, according to his convoluted arithmetic, *Hamlet* would have to have gotten 317 votes to win the Oscar. "Where are the 317 that voted for *Hamlet*? Can you find them? We can't!"

A day later Wilkerson wrote: "We wonder what would have happened in the balloting for the Best Picture of the year had *Hamlet* been made in one of our own Hollywood studios. Our guess is that it would never have been voted Best Picture if it were Hollywood made" (hinting that the studios would hardly have let it get that far).

He concluded: "Have we a bunch of goofs among our Academy voters, who, like many of those New York critics, kid themselves into believing that Britain is capable of making better pictures than Hollywood? Now really!"

Wilkerson decided to let the matter drop with a warning: "If they can't honor American pictures then perhaps they've outlived their usefulness." The Academy voters took the hint. Not until 1963 did the Best Picture award go to a foreign-made film, *Lawrence of Arabia*.

The studios decided early that the Academy Awards ceremony was a glorified publicity stunt, the ultimate public relations tool in a city ruled by flaks. Publicists, in fact, have their own Academy branch, whose membership has ranged from 150 in the fifties to 218 today. The men and women who run the Oscar campaigns are a part of Oscar's inner sanctum. They are privy to the secrets of voting, have representation on the Academy's board, and are on the receiving end of the largesse from Oscar campaigns competing against their own. The Oscar brass has never been able to adequately justify the existence of the P.R. branch—or for that matter, the branches of executives and administrators. The Academy gives no Oscar for the Best Ad in a Technicolor Medium or The Finest Cold Cuts and Champagne Supper for Voters. Likewise, there's no Oscar for Best Use of the Executive Washroom or Most Creative Hype Memo from a Studio President. If there is a hint of shameful conflict of interest within the Academy, then it's probably to be found in these three branches—administrators, executives, and public relations executives. Every other branch—ranging from acting to art directors—gives awards to the supposed best of their branches. The branches for executives and administrators are actually holdovers from the twenties and thirties, when the Academy was still a pseudo company union. And there are 490 of them—one eighth of the Academy's total membership of about 4,000. "And these members *vote*," said former *Los Angeles Times* columnist Joyce Haber, author of *The Users* and other caustic books about Hollywood. "A lot of those other branches get very apathetic and scattered. The executives and the flaks all have something to gain—or to lose—in the sweepstakes."

As for the acting and other artistic and crafts branches, they're a different breed of political cat. They are biased toward big box-office pictures, usually honor age over youth (no matter how deserving), and some of the branches, particularly editing and cinematography, are locked into voting patterns that are thirty years old. Since each artistic branch nominates its fellows (the actors nominate the five best actors, the musicians nominate for the music awards, and so on), all of the

Oscar mistakes and preposterous awards start here. This procedure puts an awesome amount of power in a very few hands.

The nominations themselves can well mean the difference between profit and loss for a film that's failing at the box office. To quote *Los Angeles Times* entertainment editor Charles Champlin, "Nominations alone can mean additional playing dates for a film, possibly more favorable rental terms," plus more business and longer runs. In the early spring of 1978, for instance, a ballet film, *The Turning Point*, was laying embarrassing eggs throughout suburban America. Then the Oscar people gave it a whole bushelful of nominations, including Best Picture, Best Actress (both Anne Bancroft and Shirley MacLaine), plus a supporting pick for sexy ballet star Mikhail Baryshnikov. As a result, those little matchbox theaters in America's shopping centers drew moderate crowds through the final Oscar ceremony. Analysts of the National Association of Theater Owners say that five or more nominations for a movie can often do as much for profits as a final victory. A Best Picture nomination with a couple of acting nods thrown in will get a movie priceless exposure on the Oscar show, with its more than one billion viewers. In 1980, for instance, film clips from Bette Midler's *The Rose* (which wasn't even nominated for Best Picture) pushed the six-month-old film back into the top ten box-office list and sent the soundtrack album to the top of the *Billboard* chart.

It's the nomination process that's criminal—outdated, prejudiced, careless, and backward.

The long road to the Oscar starts the first week in January, when the Academy members receive a list of eligible films—which includes, more or less, every new feature film that played for fifteen days in Los Angeles. All the members vote for Best Picture nominees, but all the other five finalists are determined by the branches concerned.

Before that, most branches pick a quarter-final list of ten nominees. The hundred or so directors of photography in the Academy's cinematography branch are in full control of the lists of ten and the later lists of five. A hundred, or fewer, is only a handful in the hotbed of jealousy, hypocrisy, and spite that is Hollywood. But most Oscar watchers say the preliminary voter turnout ranges from 40 percent to 60 percent. Therefore, a place on the list of five cinematography nominees is undoubtedly determined by four or five votes either way.

The hundred-member cinematography branch is perhaps the prime example of the Oscar's internal rottenness. Year after year, decade after decade, the men behind the camera have worshiped at the altar of the box office and studio bosses. They have repeatedly honored nonsense (such as *Cleopatra* in 1964) and have frozen out innovation (such as the work on *Tom Jones* the same year). Because cinematography is probably the most essential of the movie arts, its branch's old-fashioned voting patterns and outright favoritism beg for a much closer look.

Charles Champlin, who has been publicly monitoring the nomination process for twenty-five years, took just such a look at the ten cinematography final lists for 1967 and came away annoyed. He found that Twentieth Century–Fox, pushing the disastrous *Doctor Dolittle*, and Paramount, pushing the so-so *Barefoot in the Park*, may have been responsible for freezing out some dazzling examples of photography.

Apparently, Fox let it slip that *Doctor Dolittle* was to be the choice of the studio's cinematographers in the Academy. So the inane movie musical about animals made it into the ten while the trend-setting photography for another Fox film, *Two for the Road*, was offered up as a sacrificial lamb. Across town, Paramount's flaks wined and dined Oscar's cinematographer voters, bagging a top-ten spot for their film *Barefoot in the Park*, freezing out *Far From the Madding Crowd*, *Accident*, and *Cool Hand Luke*.

"The omissions, some of them, are worrisome. So is the cumulative suspicion that cost is a plus consideration," wrote Champlin. "Look at the case of *Camelot*, which took five nominations, including art decoration, set decoration, and cinematography. And this is a film," said the critic, "whose principal disappointments were visual."

But Champlin's public warnings fell on deaf ears in the photo world. A year later, the cinematographers ignored the innovative photography of *2001: A Space Odyssey*, *Rosemary's Baby*, *Rachel, Rachel*, and *Faces* in order to nominate the pedestrian work on *Oliver!*, *Funny Girl*, *Ice Station Zebra*, and the lead-weight disaster *Star!* The one nominee with inventive work, *Romeo and Juliet*, fortunately took the Oscar.

Champlin again unfurled angry newsprint. "Among the movies not, I repeat *not*, nominated for cinematography were *The Charge of the Light Brigade*, *Petulia*, *The Thomas Crown Affair*, *The Fox*, and *Hell in the Pacific*. But *Star!*, lavish and unimaginative throughout, was nominated."

"The Academy membership is probably less and less a fully accurate reflection of the fast-changing industry and even less of the moviegoing public," Champlin wrote. "What emerges still smacks less often of a pinpointing of excellence than of local pride, sentiment, correction of past oversights, consolation, retribution, study of the grosses, and an orientation toward what *was* rather than what is."

Public embarrassment, however, has not fazed the elderly voice of the Oscar cinematographers (who mirror voters in such branches as editing and music as well). There are dozens of examples. One is a case of the photo establishment against one young maverick photographer. His name is Gordon Willis, a camera wizard who burst on the movie scene in an incendiary display in 1971. The film was *Klute*, the moody study of a New York hooker played by Jane Fonda. Willis used light and dark like a modern Rembrandt to paint the screen. His camera panned across Fonda, in half shadow, as she unzipped her dress, and his images exposed the soul of her character. The stills—frozen from the film —are achingly beautiful.

The Oscar cinematographers had a tough time excluding Willis from their nominations. In fact, they had to nominate one man twice, in a move that leaves little doubt about their bias. The double nominee was Robert Surtees, sixty-four, nominated for *The Last Picture Show* and *Summer of '42*. Other nominees were the cinematically boring *Nicholas and Alexandra*, *The French Connection*, a stunner, and the so-so *Fiddler on the Roof*, which took the Oscar.

Then came *The Godfather*. Paramount began preview showings of Francis Ford Coppola's masterpiece far ahead of the Oscar votes. The jaded critics, artists, and movie bigwigs walked out of the previews stunned—by the performances, the emotion, and by the raw, jagged style in which the movie was filmed. Willis used dazzling light and deepest shadow to penetrate the gothic world of crime, religion, great love, and basest evil. The trip his camera made across Brando's face exposed ridges and craters of personality unequaled in film history. Director François Truffaut said cinematography would "never be quite the same." Not since Gregg Toland's work on *Citizen Kane* in 1941 had film photography moved into such experimental depths.

Critics predicted a cinematography nomination and, probably, the Oscar.

They hadn't reckoned with the Oscar's creaky cameramen. They froze Willis out again, nominating an incredible list: *Butterflies Are Free,* "*1776,*" *The Poseidon Adventure, Cabaret,* and *Travels with My Aunt.* A common saying in Hollywood around Oscar time is, "Don't take it personal." But sometimes it is personal. Not until his brilliantly innovative work on Woody Allen's *Zelig* in 1983 did Gordon Willis grudgingly get an Oscar nomination from the Academy cinematographers' branch. His previous work was on view in such critically acclaimed box-office bonanzas as *The Godfather Part II, Paper Chase, All the President's Men, Annie Hall,* and *Manhattan,* all of which went begging in the photography category when Oscar-nomination time rolled around. In order to bypass Willis for *Annie Hall,* the voters had to nominate Fred J. Koenekamp for *Islands in the Stream* and William A. Fraker for *Looking for Mr. Goodbar.* But Willis was a young and relatively new cinematographer, who also happens to be black (ah-ha!), and none of the artists nominated in 1978 (the year of *Annie Hall*) was younger than forty-seven. One was seventy-one, one sixty-five, and another fifty-three.

"Taste is undoubtedly a factor here," said Champlin. "Willis' work, like the work of a young Caleb Deschanel [*The Black Stallion, Being There,* and *More American Graffiti*], tends to be poetic, dark, and moody, far removed from the clean, well-lighted style that was the norm in an earlier age when some of the branch's voters did their best work. Deschanel, in all events, was also snubbed by the cinematographers this year [1979]." (Note: Deschanel was nominated, but lost to others, for *The Right Stuff* in 1984 and *The Natural* in 1985.)

The cliquish cameramen have excluded many excellent nominees by their insistence on voting for themselves. Only eighteen of the eighty-eight cinematographers nominated in the last twenty years were not members of the approximately one-hundred-member Academy branch. Of those eighteen, twelve were foreign.

"The controversies in some of the nomination processes suggest to me that Oscar's health would be improved by making several more of the nominations Academy-wide," Champlin continued. "The argument, of course, is that it takes an editor to know editing. Some of us would endorse this view more wholeheartedly if the excellent Dede Allen in New York [*Bonnie and Clyde, Dog Day Afternoon, Rachel, Rachel, Alice's Restaurant, Little Big Man,* and *Night Moves*] had even been nominated. But she hasn't been." (Note: In 1982 Dede Allen received her first, and so far only, Oscar nomination, for *Reds.* Predictably, she lost, to Michael Kahn and *Raiders of the Lost Ark.*)

Charles Champlin's renewed pleas for more open voting were made just before the Oscar ceremony in 1980. And it is only the latest chapter in what has been his twenty-five-year, painstaking crusade. His analyses of voting processes have amounted to more than a thousand newspaper inches since 1968. His force has already been felt in improved procedures for foreign film and music voting. One former Academy president expressed his belief that "Academy members listen to Champlin because his reports on the Oscar race tell 'all sides' of the issue. You know those radical ones—Andrew Sarris of the *Village Voice* and

Aljean Harmetz of the *New York Times*—are only interested in ripping us apart."

Champlin's strongest words were written in February 1980: "Putting the nominations on an Academy-wide basis would get rid of the inbreeding and infighting. It would make the Academy Awards a popularity contest, but they are anyway. And the 4,512 voters are, after all, men and women who make their living from motion pictures and know a jump cut from a slow dissolve and sunlight from shadow.

"This is a transfusion," says Champlin, "that might save Oscar from hardening of the arteries—a frequent complaint in gents of his generation."

The critic was being kind. Academy-wide voting for nominations would, in plainer terms, take the nominations out of the hands of the executives, the flaks, and, sad but true, out of the hands of artists somewhat past their prime.

The money men who head the conglomerates such as Gulf & Western, MCA, and Coca-Cola learned long ago to coerce, cajole, and even buy the votes of the cliques within the branches.

It's not easy to buy votes now, and the cliques have cracked a little—*Annie Hall* would never have taken the 1977 Oscar otherwise. But voting by box office is far from dead: witness the defeat of *All the President's Men* and *Network* by *Rocky*. (We can consider ourselves lucky that super-fists Sylvester Stallone didn't take the acting prize from the incomparable Peter Finch.)

As few as ten years ago, Oscar voting practices were pretty much "the worthless, grotesque circus" that Dustin Hoffman described. The huge studios, particularly Twentieth Century–Fox, could still force dreadful but expensive films down the throats of Oscar voters.

Oscar bigwigs like former president Fay Kanin have just shrugged. "Hey, why bring up the past? That's behind us. Isn't it?" Well, no. It isn't. With Oscar, nothing is over. The old voting patterns come back as frequently as Shirley MacLaine. And the Academy is adamant about the glamor and the rightness of its decisions. Luise Rainer *was* the best actress of 1936, the Academy tells us again and again. *Patton was* the best picture of 1970, they tell us. We may know, down in our artistic psyches, that Garbo was better than Rainer and *M*A*S*H* was certainly finer than its militaristic competitor. But then the Oscar show comes on with its drivel about the old days, and the world once again has reason to believe erroneously that *How Green Was My Valley* was a better movie than *Citizen Kane* or that winner Yul Brynner was a better actor than non-winner Montgomery Clift.

Ten years ago it was so bad even the gossip columnists were yelling. Joyce Haber, then the lady with the nastiest pen, said the worst thing about Oscar voters was that "they don't even see the films; they rely on ads in the trade papers." But almost as bad, said Haber, was the voter turnout. "You'd have to describe it as 'pitiful.' I know one producer who lives abroad, and his doctor, a specialist, but not in films, fills in his nomination and voting ballots every year. I know a producer who lives in Beverly Hills and has his college-graduate son do the job for him. And I just had dinner with a Broadway star, who is also a sometime movie actress and a member of the Academy. She admitted to me that she had not seen *any* movies. She'd been on tour, don't you know. She kept asking me how to vote," said Haber in a mock scandalized tone. "I refused to add to the problem. Suddenly, she looked at me and said,

'I'm going to vote for Paul Newman and *Butch Cassidy* because I think he's so-o-o handsome.' " Haber didn't find any of this cute. "These people are serious. I have to ask, 'Did *Butch Cassidy* get a Best Picture nomination because of Paul Newman's beautiful baby-blue eyes?' "

The same era brought Andrew Sarris, the eastern critic, to the coast, and he found even less to cheer about than Haber. "It is a matter of conjecture, to be sure, but I find myself annually depressed by the strong suspicion that few of the [then] three thousand members of the Academy see as many as a dozen films a year." His suspicions appeared in the *Village Voice*, so the Oscar brass just shoved their hands in their Sy Devore suit coats and drawled, "Well, you know that type of paper." (Ironically, the workup for Universal's Oscar campaign for *Airport* indicated that only 46 percent of Academy members could be expected to see more than two of the nominated films. The studio direct-mailed *Airport* propaganda to the stay-at-homes, gaining the flyby a nomination over *Ryan's Daughter*, *Little Big Man*, *Women in Love*, and *The Great White Hope*.)

"It seems likely that a huge number of ballots are cast for pictures and performances purely on hearsay," said Sarris. Then he quoted Academy president Walter Mirisch: "As an Academy we also seek excellence in judging the work of our peers." Sarris answered, "Peers, schmeers. Have you guys and dolls seen many movies this year? I doubt it."

Voting by hearsay and prejudice is still a part of the Academy. In 1979 tap dancer Ann Miller told an interviewer, "My friends all say they don't know how they're going to vote this year. Why, just look at the sloppy appearance of those actresses, Jill Clayburgh, Jane Fonda, Ellen Burstyn, etc. There's no glamor left. I don't even think I'll vote."

In 1970 the Academy voted with its stomach. Free food, free booze, and enough gifts to gag Nero lured Oscar voters into silk-lined traps. Gorged on food, dazed by advertising, laden with free record albums and desk sets, the electors lined up in mobs to vote for the turgid *Anne of the Thousand Days*, the disastrous *Hello, Dolly!*, and a foreign film, *Z*, which pigged in far more than its share of nominations. Critics started yelling, "What the hell happened?" The normally timid *Entertainment World*, a British film journal, asked, "How did *Anne of the Thousand Days* win ten nominations and *Midnight Cowboy* only seven? It's incomprehensible." And Aljean Harmetz of the *New York Times* said, frankly, "The fact that *Anne of the Thousand Days* received ten nominations and *Hello, Dolly!* tied *Midnight Cowboy*—including a Best Picture nomination for both—had more to do with beef stroganoff and imported champagne and three-inch prime ribs than with any quality in the films."

Caterers imported from Paris prepared a buffet table for those who attended the free showing Universal held for Oscar voters in the winter of 1969–1970. (The food alone cost thirty-five dollars per person, according to Universal sources.) And thirty-five screenings were held— many of them exclusively for the Academy's nominating branches. The cinematographers were ushered onto the Universal lot for a cocktail hour and buffet supper before the 8:30 P.M. showing. Suntanned ushers, wearing silk tights and velvet doublets, handed the voters high-priced propaganda about *Anne of the Thousand Days* and guided them to the buffet room. The tables were sagging under the weight of the food: cocktails, seven hot appetizers, cold roast beef, cold ham, chicken breasts Hawaiian, beef stroganoff, imported rice, fresh fruit salad (with out-of-season fruits costing up to $3.95 a pound), cheeses, and French pastries. The next day the voters who showed up received a special-delivery letter from Universal, thanking them for coming and offering still more propaganda about the Richard Burton–Genevieve Bujold movie (whose stars were both nominated). "We cultivated the hell out of the artistic branches," said a public relations spokesman for Universal. "And, boy, did it work." *Anne of the Thousand Days*, a creaky movie that might as well have been made in the thirties, got an entirely undeserved bouquet of nominations. All of the artisans who were wined and dined by the studio, with the exception of directors and editors, included the film in their lists of five nominees.

Twentieth Century–Fox had to try harder. The greedy studio brass had a twenty-five-million-dollar lemon on their hands, the ungodly *Hello, Dolly!* "We decided that lavish advertising would do no good for this one; the whole town was already gossiping about how bad it was," said a Fox publicity man. "We decided to blow the budget on prime ribs from Kansas City and imported champagne. Then we had the showings. The branch voters then saw the movie through champagne-colored glasses."

Hello, Dolly! *was perhaps nominated as a salute to Hollywood's well-endowed taste buds since Twentieth Century–Fox shunned traditional Oscar campaigning and spent megabucks on fancy buffet dinners. "The technique of unlimited liquor and prime rib au jus had worked so well for Fox in* 1967 *when* Doctor Dolittle *was nominated for Best Picture," wrote Aljean Harmetz in the New York Times. "It was all so silly," remembered one film editor. "All the editors standing around and knowing they'd been bought."*

The cinematographers can be excused for this one; *Hello, Dolly!* had several seconds worth of fine camerawork during the movie's opening titles. What it did *not* have was good editing. In fact, it had miserable editing. Its scenes jerked from one to another like a rusty trolley car, and musical numbers bumped into each other on the screen. But it's simply amazing what good drink and a fine table will do. The editors saw to it that *Hello, Dolly!* was nominated. "It was all so silly," said one editor, "all of us editors standing around the party tables—knowing we'd been bought."

There were, of course, examples of very fine editing that year— *Downhill Racer, The Wild Bunch, The Gypsy Moths,* and *Easy Rider,* to name a few. But what could the poor editors do? After they had given away places to *Hello, Dolly!*, they had to at least nominate the better-known films *Midnight Cowboy, They Shoot Horses, Don't They?,* and *Z,* an Algerian film that had the most expensive campaign of all. After these and *The Secret of Santa Vittoria,* there was no more room.

The big losers that winter were *Easy Rider* and Sam Peckinpah's *The Wild Bunch.* Nobody today looks twice at *Hello, Dolly!* or *Anne of the Thousand Days. Easy Rider* and *The Wild Bunch* are not only revived, they are part of the regular curriculum at many film schools. Peckinpah's people knew immediately that the nominations were a poor call. "I don't understand why two drinks and a bad hors d'oeuvre should make a difference in your critical judgment," said Joel Reisner, Peckinpah's principal assistant.

The Wild Bunch might have had a chance, but its studio, Warner Bros., refused to plug the film in any way. "In December of 1969 Warner Brothers told me that the grosses of *The Wild Bunch* didn't justify extra ad costs," Reisner said. "The studio probably didn't believe Sam Peckinpah would get nominated no matter what they did. The Oscars are merely a popularity contest, and Sam has fired an awful lot of people over the years. Warners also knew *The Wild Bunch* was an unfriendly, unpopular film." (As Aljean Harmetz pointed out, the film was so far outside the establishment that only five of the hundred-and-fifty member Academy's editors' branch showed up for the screening.)

The bored, disinterested Oscar voters are primed and waiting for fresh winds of hype. Last year's hype won't do. Or last week's, for that matter. The 2,800 voters (and the voter turnout is never higher than 60 percent of the full membership) exist in a rarefied atmosphere. Paperweights, posters, toys, and books flood through the mail—to Kathryn Grayson's house on the grounds of the Riviera Country Club, to John Travolta's sprawling spread in Santa Barbara, to Ginger Rogers's ranch in the foothills of Oregon.

The studios, agents, and flaks spent about $7.5 million during the three months of Oscar campaigning in 1980. That's $2,500 per voter, if most of the Academy members—by some miracle—happened to vote. The grand pageants are carefully staged. Take Bette Midler's bid for a Best Actress nomination.

The ballyhoo started in November 1979—months before the final vote. Fox, which made her film, *The Rose,* let the word get around that Midler was "sensational" portraying a Janis Joplin–like rock singer in her rise and fall. Then the previews began, with the first screening set for a Tuesday.

Tuesday morning: Beverly Hills and Hollywood had been covered with Bette's image. Black-and-red posters (with Midler screaming a

song in front of a vivid red rose) blanketed the city. On Sunset Boulevard, Bette had risen above the Strip like a cardboard phoenix with sixteen-foot arms spread to enfold the voters on their way to work—Alan Ladd, Jr., heading for a meeting at Warner Bros., Jane Fonda driving in to her Sunset Boulevard bank, Connie Stevens going to an exercise class.

Car radios suddenly swelled with lullabies in the Bette Midler voice: the film's soundtrack album had been released that morning, not so coincidentally. (Members of the musicians' branch received soundtrack albums in the mail.)

Tuesday night came! The parade of Rolls-Royces lined up at Twentieth Century–Fox was flagged through the VIP gate into a parking lot with ample spaces—an unheard-of luxury in the city of cars. But a necessary one. Nothing must jangle the nerves of the Oscar voters on their way to see the film debut of "The Divine Miss M."

A bleached-blond secretary somehow crammed into Jordache jeans checked off the names of those entering the Fox screening theater,

Bette Midler in Mark Rydell's The Rose (1979), *which repackaged the rock superstar as an Oscar-caliber actress. Her home run the first time out echoed the triumphs of Julie Andrews in* Mary Poppins *and Diana Ross in* Lady Sings the Blues. *Unfortunately, Hollywood's reaction to such quick Oscar jackpots is often nearsighted and paranoid. "You should see the worthless scripts I've been offered since* The Rose," *Midler told TV host Phil Donahue. And Ross said, "Scores of offers appeared that would have had me playing Billie Holiday over and over again." In the case of Julie Andrews, Fox built such musical dinosaur films for her that she was caught in a big-budget prison.*

which is just off Peyton Place Square—still intact from the television series of the sixties. No inch of film would roll until the last voter was ushered to his red velvet seat.

Finally the theater darkened, and Bette's voice began a rock-'n'-roll cry. For the next two hours not a sound was heard as one of the most dismal films of the seventies unfolded on the screen. Not one hand clapped as the film ended and the titles ran off. But no matter—the hype had been planted so firmly in the minds of the voters that Bette Midler would make the list of nominees with flying colors.

The whole process runs so smoothly and is done so quickly that nobody really notices; the idea that Bette Midler is a great actress has seeped into Hollywood's creative consciousness.

Often, it's not money but moxie that outfoxes all other contenders. That's what got the Algerian film Z, which in 1970 became the second foreign-language film to be nominated for Best Picture in the Academy's history. (The first was France's *Grand Illusion* in 1939.) And Z was nominated for five Oscars—each one of them due to the wizardry of free-lance P.R. man Max Bercutt, who was hired by the film's distributor to get Z as many nominations as the traffic would bear. The five Oscar bids probably added $5 million to the grosses of the movie in this country alone.

Bercutt told Aljean Harmetz that he had to fight two biases to get the film nominated. "Academy members nominate first out of loyalty to their studios or connections. Second, they nominate out of loyalty to the 'Hollywood product.' "

Bercutt had seen the system from the inside, and that was a plus. He was publicity director for Warner Bros. during the sixties, one of its golden epochs.

The first target of the campaign for Z was the ever-present corps of Oscar voters in the ranks of the retired—at least five hundred actors, artists, and executives who had served their time and had been turned out to celluloid pasture. "These people haven't worked in five to ten years. But these old-timers are very important. They're the keepers of the bees of Hollywood's past. This was the toughest target. How could I get them to vote for a film with subtitles? I decided that the answer was to show them the film and to try to instill in their minds that it is the greatest picture in ten years."

The P.R. man took a new print home with him. "Those voters don't go out much, so I took the print to their houses. I screened it for twenty people or for one person. I told them that a nomination for Z would make the Academy look important worldwide."

The voters also had soundtrack recordings delivered to their front doors two weeks later. (All nominations had already been released and Z wasn't named as a nominee for best score.) "It was great advertising with the great big Z on the cover. I hoped that enough members would play the album, like it, and say, 'Poor film, why didn't it get a nomination?' Then they'd vote for it in one of the other categories," explained a publicist.

Hollywood's gossip mill caught on quickly that Z was getting special treatment. Other studios and public relations men began telephone campaigns asking the voters to "vote Hollywood—vote against Z."

But they were too late. Z got a Best Picture nomination, shutting out the Hollywood products *They Shoot Horses, Don't They?* and Peter Fonda and Dennis Hopper's *Easy Rider*.

It goes without saying that Oscar hype wouldn't be worth manufacturing if the economic stakes weren't so high. Still, the harm done is not major. Some quite dreadful films get nominated. (Some even win: *The Greatest Show on Earth, Oliver!*) Some quite wonderful films aren't even mentioned for Best Picture: *Papillon, Singin' in the Rain.*

But once or twice a decade a studio's greedy-minded Oscar campaigning turns dark and nasty, and occasionally the quest for an Oscar crushes some good guys under. This happened in 1973, when Warner Bros. was trying to get an Oscar for Linda Blair, the fourteen-year-old star of *The Exorcist.*

The Exorcist had a bizarre and difficult birth. Billy Friedkin, who had already won an Oscar for directing *The French Connection*, was only thirty-one when he began directing William Peter Blatty's story of demonic possession. It took two years out of his life and aged him, he said, five years. First, Friedkin tested five hundred young girls to cast the lead, finally picking an incredibly gifted girl, Linda Blair, who was then twelve. Almost from the first day of filming, a demon or demons stalked the production. Things disappeared from the set; a fire of mysterious origin roared through a set that had taken five months to build; a character actor playing a motion-picture director who is murdered by the demonic child dropped dead a week after his movie death scene. "There were even some strange images that showed up on film," said Friedkin. "These were things that were unplanned—double exposures on Linda's face."

But the film came in only a million or two over budget—hardly anything in the inflated overruns of the seventies. Friedkin delivered the film to Warner Bros.—and all hell broke loose. The limited-engagement openings in New York and Los Angeles broke every box-office record. The film brought in $100 million in the first six months. A hundred million dollars! And this was before *Jaws* or *Star Wars.* In eight months both *The Sound of Music* and *Gone With The Wind* were toppled from first and second place in the list of all-time box-office champions. Every studio in town was into devil worship. And agents were signing up sinister-looking kids by the handful.

A hit of that magnitude does strange things to studio executives. First they look over their shoulders, wondering if it's real. They then try to guard the goose that laid the golden egg. Warners had two geese: Billy Friedkin and Linda Blair, a bit of a star to be protected, nurtured, and gently shoved into one vehicle after another. In Linda's case she was rushed from *Airport 1975* to *Exorcist II: The Heretic*, to *Hard Ride to Rantan*, and, in 1979, to *Roller Boogie.*

To protect and nurture Miss Blair, *The Exorcist*'s producers and Warner Bros. apparently decided to get her an Oscar at all cost. I mean, my Gawd, here's a twelve-year-old girl who spoke in the voice of the devil, played the full erotic range from nymphet to ancient whore, and whose voice, said a critic, had "the timbre of Orson Welles, the depth of the Vatican choir, and the range of the Royal Shakespeare Company." Isn't that amazing? asked the Warner Bros. press corps. Isn't that amazing? Why, not even Patty Duke . . .

The Academy's voters, also shaking their heads and clucking in amazement, quickly nominated Linda Blair for best actress in a supporting role. "Her voice leaves scratches on your soul," said *Paris Match.* "Incomparable," said the *Times* of London.

Warners just basked in the afterglow of Linda Blair. Not even Tatum

68 O'Neal, with her incredible debut in *Paper Moon*, could give her a race. The Oscar, everybody decided, was hers.

But Linda Blair's voice would come back to haunt them all—Hollywood, Billy Friedkin, and Warner Bros. Because it wasn't Linda Blair's voice at all. It was the voice of Mercedes McCambridge, a former Oscar winner with vocal cords like Gideon's trumpet. And Mercedes McCambridge, some of the big guys decided, would just have to be sacrificed in the quest for Oscar gold. After all, Friedkin was her pal. She'd understand. Case closed.

It might have ended that way. And Linda Blair might have taken home her Oscar, however undeservedly. Worse things have happened in the name of Oscar.

Mercedes McCambridge had no official credit on the release print. She had none on the posters, the advertisements, or on the jacket of the record album—on which her voice was undoubtedly the main drawing card.

But one of Hollywood's veteran journalists got the drift of a particularly nasty rumor about the denial of McCambridge's contribution to *The Exorcist*. So Charles Higham, writer for the *New York Times, Los Angeles* magazine, and the *Directors Guild Magazine,* picked up the

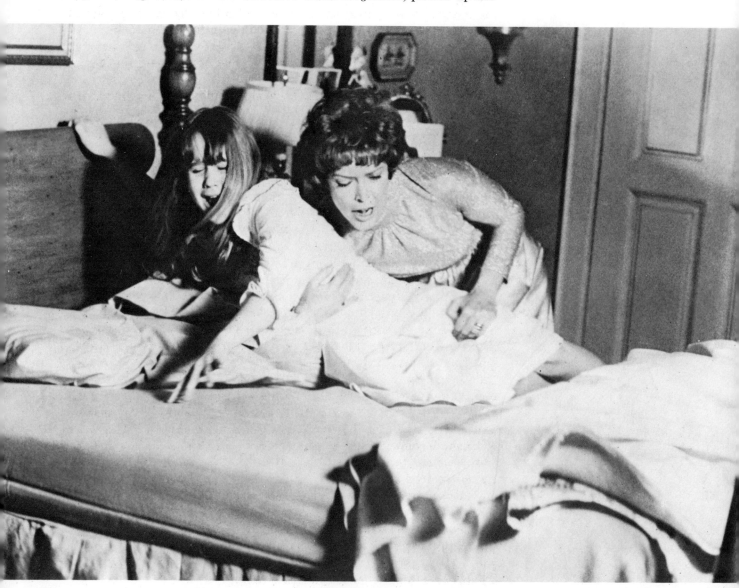

phone and gave her a ring. He found a story of horrific, but typical, Hollywood greed. McCambridge poured out the story in anger and hurt, her words tumbling one over the other as they had on *The Exorcist* soundtrack.

"I gave the most difficult performance of my life," she said. "Warners didn't give me a single credit on the picture or in the advertising." (A frightening thing in a town where an actor is only as good as his last credit.) "Even the man who supplied the jewels got a credit. I cried. Billy Friedkin promised me a special credit—'And Mercedes Mc-Cambridge' it was supposed to say. Doing that soundtrack was a terrible experience. I didn't just do the voice; I did all the demon's sounds. That wheezing, for instance. My chronic bronchitis helped with that. I did it on one microphone; then on another, elevating it a bit; then on a third and fourth, two tones higher each time. The wailing just before the demon is driven out, that's the keening sound I once heard at a wake in Ireland. I used moaning cries I had used when playing Lady Macbeth for Orson Welles. For the groaning sounds, I pulled a scarf around my neck, tight, and almost strangled."

McCambridge, who became a radio actress when she was still in college, won the Best Supporting Actress Oscar for her first film, *All the King's Men* (1949). Orson Welles called her "the world's greatest radio actress," and she was nominated again for her work in *Giant* (1956). When the word got out about her predicament there was immediate outrage, to such an extent that some Academy officers began investigating the legality of giving an Oscar to actors whose contribution is solely audio. "We don't know if that could even happen, but it's obvious, we're going to think about it," an Academy spokesman told the *Los Angeles Times*.

The actress, in interviews, described the job as one of the toughest, mentally, she ever faced: "I had to imagine the incredible, bottomless agony of a lost soul. I drew on memory for that. I've been an alcoholic, saved by A.A., and I've seen people in state hospitals, vegetables in straitjackets, the hopeless, abysmal, bottomless groaning and screaming. I used imitations of those hellish cries. Who better than I would know how the devil feels? I'm out of hell; he's there forever.

"And when I spoke the scene in which the little girl spits out green vomit, when I made the sounds of violent expectoration, I swallowed eighteen raw eggs along with a pulpy apple. Sometimes I was so exhausted and my circulation so sluggish, I couldn't drive home."

Higham acknowledged that his stories probably "cost Linda Blair the Oscar." But in Oscar's double-dealing history that is something to be proud of.

If he needed any reassurance, he got it while attending a press party honoring Linda Blair's birthday. It was at Chasen's, an exclusive Beverly Hills restaurant. Higham had just settled down when a flak from Warner Bros. pushed his way up to him, waving the proofs of Higham's story on McCambridge and her experience with *The Exorcist*. "What's your idea in writing a piece like this?" asked the man from the executive suite. Higham, an acute observer of Hollywood greed in his books on Katharine Hepburn, Cecil B. De Mille, Bette Davis, and others, looked up calmly and asked, "What was your idea in smuggling the proofs out of the paper before their removal was authorized?"

Linda Blair did not win the Oscar. It went to Tatum O'Neal. And *her* whole performance was up there on the screen while Linda remained a puppet given life by McCambridge's voice.

Linda Blair and Ellen Burstyn in a scene from The Exorcist. *Linda's double-threat performance as the sweet young girl with the demon-possessed flip side easily gained the fourteen-year-old a nomination for Best Supporting Actress. Flaks at Warner Bros. quickly began figuring the box-office draw of an Oscar for Linda and went wild with greed. To ensure its success, the studio carefully erased the identity of a potent though secret ingredient in her performance—the "voice" of the devil—furnished magnificently by former Oscar winner Mercedes McCambridge.*

The shabby Oscar plotting involved in *The Exorcist* is hardly surprising. More surprising was the failure of the mass media to really pick up on the scandal. Day in and day out, year after year, more than seven hundred reporters—from as nearby as Long Beach to as far away as Calcutta—spend part of their year covering the Academy of Motion Picture Arts and Sciences. (Eight hundred members of the press were accredited to cover an Oscar ceremony in the seventies.) Fewer than ten of them do any objective reporting on the Oscars—primarily Lee Grant and Charles Champlin.

A study of more than seven thousand articles on the Academy Awards—all published in the last eight years—showed that only fifty articles portrayed many sides of the Oscar story. Twenty-five of those were by Champlin, with the others divided among fewer than ten reporters, among them Andrew Sarris, Aljean Harmetz, Rex Reed, and an insider, Peter Bogdanovich. The rest of the press swallows the Oscar decisions as if they were handed down by Moses on stone tablets.

And this is why a turkey of a film like *Oliver!* can be named best picture of the year without worldwide laughter.

Actors chase after Oscars in a race so intense that hope turns into paranoia and dreams are crushed by the force of gluttony. Veterans of the British stage will open shopping centers to get one, grown men cry over just a nomination, and some of the classiest actors in town find themselves behaving like freshman cheerleaders at the season's first pep rally.

Scores of writers have tried to capture this hysteria on paper with fair-to-middling results. Neil Simon didn't quite get it right in *California Suite* and lord knows Russell Rouse's *The Oscar* failed to illuminate. Journalists haven't fared much better.

Why did The Exorcist *lose to a lesser work? Critics asked the question then and it seems more pressing as the years have passed. Though* The Sting, *which won, was formidable competition, William Friedkin pioneered a genre—the big-budget gothic horror picture—with his landmark film. "I think that many voters were worried that the subject matter might reflect poorly on American films as a whole," said Rona Barrett. "People just did not want the movie to be a representative of Hollywood." But the McCambridge Affair drove the nail into the coffin. Here Mercedes is pictured with John Ireland in* All the King's Men.

But in 1983 journalist Jerry Lazar and Oscar-nominated actor John Lithgow collaborated in a unique project which graphically depicted one actor's descent into the Academy Awards' cauldron of pressure and insecurity. Lazar cashed in on an early hunch that Lithgow would be nominated as Best Supporting Actor for his portrayal of the transsexual Roberta Muldoon in *The World According to Garp*, and followed the actor from his first pangs of expectation to his dashed hopes when Louis Gossett, Jr., took home the Oscar for *An Officer and a Gentleman*. Lazar even convinced Lithgow to keep a diary—a keepsake of his feelings and longings as the drama played out in public. The journalist had a hunch that Lithgow was sensitive and articulate enough to describe the internal process in an honest and direct manner. And he was right. In tandem (Lithgow called Lazar his "Boswell"), they produced a fifty-thousand-word depiction of one Oscar race that reads as if the events were filmed.

The very first day the two men met, Lithgow complained to Lazar, "I think about the Oscars constantly. I want to put it out of my mind, but people won't let me. Even Mary's [his wife's] friends say corny stuff to me like, 'See you at the Dorothy Chandler!' " Several minutes later, however, he complained that, more than an Oscar, he wanted a job. "I've only worked thirteen days since June 28," he said as the two sat in an open-air market on January 4.

Later, Lazar handed him the diary. John gave the journalist free access to both his personal and professional life. Some of the completed diary was printed in the June 1983 issue of *California* magazine. But thousands of words remained on the print-shop floor.

The day the Golden Globe nominations were announced, Lithgow confided to his diary: "I wasn't in the group. This is all to the good, more evidence that I will definitely *not* be nominated for an Oscar. Why waste more time thinking about it. . . . But I do notice myself reminding people that those foreigners named Pia Zadora the 'most promising new star' last year."

By mid-January, though, Lithgow had broken down and hired a publicist—something he had promised himself he definitely would not do. Luckily, his choice was Neil Konigsberg, the K of PMK Public Relations, one of Hollywood's hottest. Konigsberg consistently weaned Lithgow from the highs and lows of one Oscar race and into a carefully guided plan of "career publicity." Again and again Konigsberg would tell his client: "There is life after the Oscars." Nevertheless, it was a wrenching experience when the actor had to borrow $10,000 from a bank—half to put down on a new car and half to pay the up-front fee of the publicist.

Konigsberg was able to put his finger in the leaking dike, preventing the drowning of Warner Bros., which realized that *The World According to Garp* wasn't going to earn major Oscar gold. When Lithgow flew to New York to receive the New York Film Critics award, for instance, the studio argued that, since *Garp* was no longer in release, the actor could do little for the film. Konigsberg persisted and pried $500 from the Warner Bros. coffers.

The actor told his diary in late January, "Neil is proving himself very effective and efficient. So it's no surprise that his bill for the coming month appeared punctually in the mail this morning. It's very, very expensive. Forget, for example, the second car."

By mid-February, just before the Oscar nominations were announced, the actor had jumped onto the bandwagon. When a packet of press clippings arrived from the PMK offices in New York, Lithgow tore it open before an amazed Lazar and bragged, "I'm in the lead. I stole the f---ing show."

The day before the nominations were announced Lithgow was viewing the Oscars more warily. He was back in New York and had wangled a brief extra visit with his son Ian, who was living with his ex-wife. "Two brief nights with Ian only made it sadder for me to leave him again. I had a hurried and distressing visit with a gravely ill and very close friend. All of this against the gloomy slushy backdrop of NYC. Who had time to think about the Oscars? At the moment I feel like I need a good infusion. A little glory fix to pull me out of a rotten mood. I begin to see the awards as brightly colored decals that we stick onto our drab and humdrum lives."

The actor spent nomination eve tossing through a troubled nightmare in which he visualized the Oscar ceremony as a lavish political convention with actors receiving votes candidate by candidate. But he was nominated, and basked in the glow of that first burst of publicity.

On March 7, the results of *People* magazine's Best Supporting Actor poll were announced. Lithgow had guessed correctly that Gossett won—as he would win the Oscar. And John? He finished last.

But the Oscar nomination brought its share of in-town attention. Warner's suddenly decided to run five center spreads in both *Daily Variety* and the *Hollywood Reporter* to tout Lithgow and Glenn Close (for Best Supporting Actress in the same film) in campaigns which cost $52,000, or slightly more than either received for *Garp*.

By March 20, most of John's hopes had been dashed in a paranoid attack: "I talked to a lot of people," he told his wife, "and I'm convinced that I'm not going to win. Everyone said, 'We haven't seen you in *Garp*, but we've heard a lot of good things about it.' "

In this purgatory between the nominations and the big night, Lazar ran in flanking movements around Lithgow. For instance, he huddled with Lithgow's agent, Rick Nicita, at Harry's Bar to find out what economic clout the nomination had. (Lithgow had just been cast as the disapproving preacher in the Kevin Bacon starrer, *Footloose*.)

"John's still as talented. The nomination is just a recognition of reality—it doesn't change reality." The agent explained that he had tried to get an escalator clause added to the *Footloose* pact which would have gotten more money if Lithgow won. "They responded by saying that if they had money to give, they'd give it now."

With two weeks to go, Nicita cagily summed up Lithgow's chances: "I would say at this point that John has a very good shot. But I have trouble thinking that the Academy, which is very conservative, could get behind a picture that's as intellectual as *Garp*."

On Sunday, March 13, the TV show "Entertainment This Week" and Amen Wardy, Newport Beach clothiers, hatched a publicity stunt and offered Lithgow a thousand-dollar tux in exchange for allowing himself to be filmed during the fitting. "I feel like my whoredom has reached its apotheosis," Lithgow joked with Lazar.

Despite all his humor, despite all his intellectualizing over the pep-club aura of the Academy Awards, Lithgow was seduced again and again into seriousness. After an interview two days before the Oscarcast, he caught sight of a *Dramalogue* magazine cover with Lou Gossett's face on the cover. Storm clouds transformed his face. "Don't forget, John," warned Konigsberg, "no matter what happens at the Oscars, life goes on. The sun will rise the next morning."

Lithgow looked at his feet: "You mean I should have brought glass slippers."

During the last few hours before the ceremony, Lithgow analyzed the mirage that grows from a nomination: "An Oscar nomination is a splendid thing. It fills you up with helium; you feel that your life has been elevated forever. And then something very real happens to you. In my case, close friends lost their baby four days after the nomination. Dealing with the split between the way the Oscar nomination makes you feel your life should really be and the fact that your life remains the same can get you awfully depressed."

Lazar analyzed the effect of the Oscar hype on John's wife, Mary, a UCLA professor: "It's an odd combination, actor and professor, and the Oscar hoopla has accentuated the differences in the professions. 'His glories are of the moment,' she acknowledges. 'My career is on a different schedule. All this publicity John's gotten—I love it, I think it's great, but it's distracted me so that I resent it sometimes. I'd like to just go back and do my work. I'm used to being around people who care about me and what I have to talk about. Ever since the nomination, I've felt, 'Give me my John back!'' "

John Lithgow, whose success in The World According to Garp *plunged him into the hellish grappling with sudden fame known as "Oscaritis," here adjusting the hundred-and-fifty-dollar bow tie of his thousand-dollar tuxedo the night he was nominated for Best Supporting Actor. "My whoredom has reached its apotheosis," he quipped about the free evening dress. It was furnished in return for a promotional video of the actor being fitted at a Newport Beach men's-wear emporium.*

Later, Lithgow looked back on his first Oscar nomination (he was nominated again the next year for Best Supporting Actor in *Terms of Endearment*) as a learning experience of major importance to his film career. "I needed a publicist," he admitted. "I only realized later that I was being bombarded by reporters who had no particular concern for me or my career."

He also admitted that the second Oscar nomination put him in the ranks of the "hot, hot actors—whether or not you win. My salary took quantum jumps with each subsequent role from *Footloose* to *Terms of Endearment* to *Buckaroo Bonzai* to *The Manhattan Project*. This is all connected with the Oscar nominations—we may as well be honest about it. I was paid $50,000 for *Garp* and now I make half a million. It may not be much compared to Robert Redford, but I consider myself well paid. That's a *lot* of money."

Lazar believes such a candid examination of Oscar's prowess was possible only because of Lithgow's "incredible sensitivity, sense of humor, and willingness to be studied."

Later, John Lithgow received this letter:

Dear John,

Although I will not condemn you forever to be Roberta Muldoon, I will always see your face when I think of her. . . . If I had some Oscars to give, please know I'd give them to you. . . .

Fondly,
John Irving
[*Author of* The World According to Garp]

CHAPTER FOUR

Naked at the Feast

Remember, Barbra, it's the choicest fruit that the birds always pick at. . . .
—BETTE DAVIS TO BARBRA STREISAND
JANUARY 1984

Yentl couldn't make it as a man, wasn't happy as a woman, and couldn't even read the right books.

She loved a man she couldn't have, was the wrong sex to be a rabbi, and lived in the wrong century.

Yentl wasn't allowed to kiss Mandy Patinkin but almost had to make love to Amy Irving!

All things considered, 1984 was a bad year for her—she couldn't even get nominated for an Oscar. A Golden Globe, yes. An Oscar? Out of the question.

In the long, long list of unnominated performances, productions, and feats of direction, Barbra Streisand's *Yentl* stands as a beacon symbolizing the folly and the unintentional hilarity of the Academy Awards.

By passing over Streisand, the Oscar voters went a long way toward writing their own slow but perhaps eventual epitaph as world-respected judges of artistic achievement. The Academy's sins of omission are legion, of course, but the Streisand shutout was done unashamedly before a stunned international film community.

In order to keep Streisand's labor of love out of the top five Best Film nominees, Oscar voters had to turn to Britain's super-boring backstage epic, *The Dresser,* and Philip Kaufman's mind-bogglingly lethargic study of outer space, *The Right Stuff.* To bar her from the Best Actress ranks, they had to reach far down the ladder to siphon up Julie Walter's so-so histrionics in a light-headed comedy, *Educating Rita.*

Yet Amy Irving's lukewarm supporting work in *Yentl* brought her a Best Supporting Actress nomination—the only major nomination the film garnered.

What are film historians supposed to deduce from this: that Barbra Streisand can't act but Amy Irving can? that she can't direct but Peter Yates, nominated for *The Dresser,* is one of the best? Can it possibly be that Mandy Patinkin's subtle earnest lover in *Yentl* wasn't quite up to snuff, while the drunken, careening pratfalls of Michael Caine *(Edu-*

cating Rita) and Albert Finney *(The Dresser)* were just too marvelous for words?

"I guarantee you that if I, a man, had made *Yentl*, I would have gotten the Oscar," said KABC-TV's outspoken film critic, Gary Franklin. "Barbra wants to do good work, consistently good work; and that's very dangerous in this town."

In trying to analyze the Oscar balloting, Andrew Sarris of the *Village Voice* may have hit upon the key: "Amy Irving's nomination is one of the imponderables. Can it be that the people who say 'no' to Streisand just might say 'yes' to Amy Irving so they can say 'no, no, a thousand times no' to Barbra?"

As the furor gathered electricity in the hectic weeks between the nomination announcements and the night of the awards, Oscar's dark underbelly of fear and envy seemed exposed to the sun for the first time

Barbra Streisand's soulful eyes—so evocative of her 1985 film Yentl—*failed to impress the Academy's chauvinistic, hardhearted voters. Despite the ecstatic response to the film from the public, and from the New York (and most other) film critics, Oscar bids were denied the film and its actress-director. The entire "Yentl Incident" left the Academy with its integrity in doubt. "If I (a man) had made that film, I would have won Best Director, Best Actor, and the film would have won," said KABC-TV film critic Gary Franklin.*

in years. It preceded the "Spielberg Affair" by two years, slicing a hole in Oscar's armor which revealed, at long last, that the Academy Awards may, after all, be little more than overgrown elections for prom queen or biased straw ballots to choose the captain of a high-school football team.

Did they snub her on purpose? "Yes," said KABC's Franklin; "yes," said Rex Reed; "it appears so," echoed the *Los Angeles Times*.

As the sun set over the opulent Dorothy Chandler Pavilion, the biggest story in town was not the film which took home the Oscar, *Terms of Endearment*, but the tale of backstage bigotry, greed, and sexism which kept *Yentl* from receiving a single one of the top four nominations.

Stars arriving at the glittering event passed beneath a sign which proclaimed AN OSCAR FOR *YENTL*, THE LOST CAUSE. With an added footnote: "Best Director's Nominees—1927 to Present: Men, 273; Women, 1," the lone woman directorial nominee being Lina Wertmuller for *Seven Beauties* (1976).

Though Barbra shrank from the controversy with a few ladylike protests to handpicked reporters, a story of heartbreak seemed to leak through the walls of her mansion. In an almost tearful conversation with the *Hollywood Reporter*'s Robert Osborne, the actress-director struck back at those who labeled her "Barbra the Terrible." "I've always been embarrassed by the label of 'superstar,'" she confided to Osborne. "I really believe the audience knows the truth."

As soon as "Barbra the Great" became "Barbra the Shunned," Hollywood seers began stumbling around for reasons. Others inaugurated a Greek chorus of mourning which hasn't dimmed to this day. "I voted for her as Best Actress and for Best Director," snapped Shelley Winters. "And I don't know anyone who didn't."

Actress turned director Lee Grant, who herself had been cheated out of a Best Director nomination for *Tell Me a Riddle* in 1980, said that the loss of the nomination paled beside Streisand's accomplishments as a director: "What is important is that she keeps on making films," said Grant. "She really kicked in the door for women with this one."

But it was sexism which shut the door with a bang on Barbra's Oscar chances. "We are still very, very primitive male chauvinists in Hollywood," said character actor Nehemiah Persoff. "If Warren Beatty or Robert Redford had done this film, the Academy would be worshiping either of them again. But Barbra is a woman—not allowed into this elect society."

An apt analogy. It was terribly meanspirited of the Oscar people to toss Redford and Beatty statuettes for their tentative steps as auteurs while denying even a nod to Barbra. ("At least one would have been nice—Best Director or Best Actress," said a Streisand confidant. "We weren't greedy.")

Others chalked up the shutout to Barbra's on-going sixteen-year quest to make the movie. "I had just finished *Funny Girl*," Barbra said of her ordeal. "And I called up my agent and said, 'I have got my next film—*Yentl!*' I was twenty-five at the time. And before the cameras started turning on this movie I was celebrating my fortieth brithday."

Thus it was equally meanspirited of the Academy to deny an Oscar bid for her enduring vision while giving the whole ball of wax the previous year to that potboiling clunker *Gandhi*, which Richard Attenborough had been carrying around in his tweedy pockets for twenty years.

"I got turned down and turned down and turned down," said Barbra. "There are certain people in this town—in this business—who still get pleasure from saying, 'Guess who I turned down today?—Barbra Streisand!' "

It was a spate of nasty rumors, however, which may have sealed the tomb on *Yentl*'s Oscar pretentions.

After the rough filming was all but complete, Barbra moved from Czechoslovakia, where the location work had been done, to a London film studio—where Steven Spielberg just happened to be doing editing and postproduction work on *Indiana Jones and the Temple of Doom*.

Suddenly there were whispers of strange and devious doings out there in the dark. Ah-hah! Wasn't that Steven Spielberg sneaking into Barbra's cozy cutting room? It was, it was, and paparazzi got it all on film. The tabloids immediately called it "the romance of the decade," and the Hollywood film artisans bethought themselves a plot. So, Steve is in there helping Barbra out, the thinking went. No wonder they say her film is good.

And where there was one goblin, why not three? Soon rumor had it that George Lucas, in London to see rough cuts of *Indiana Jones*, and Sydney Pollack, on the isle to work on preproduction for *Out of Africa*, were in there just working like beavers in Barbra's lab.

The cutthroats of gossip failed to get a rise out of Barbra; but they did raise the ire of Spielberg. "I looked at the rough cuts with her because she's a friend. We *do* things like that in this industry," he snapped at a British reporter. "She listens very carefully to everything you have to say—then does it her own way. I couldn't have improved on her movie if I had tried."

Barbra then quoted Steven at a New York press conference. She said that she had shown *Yentl* to both Lucas and Spielberg, then added: "They are my peers. Spielberg showed his *Raiders of the Lost Ark* to Martin Scorsese. Does that mean Scorsese helped edit the film? I hate tooting my own horn but after Steven saw *Yentl*, he said, 'I wish I could tell you how to fix your picture, but I can't. It's terrific. It's the best film I have seen since *Citizen Kane*.' " (This is exactly the kind of statement which costs a nominee Oscar votes. Artists are supposed to be humble, don't you know. It says so right in your voting handbook.)

Spielberg himself said, "*Yentl* is so good it makes me think of what I face in directing *The Color Purple*. Barbra is so good with people, I wonder if I can be as well. It's frightening for me to take on this kind of film." (Talk about foreshadowing! Spielberg couldn't have known that the Academy's guillotine voting style would soon have his head in the artistic basket.)

When the dust finally settled on *Yentl*'s poignant quest for an Oscar, it seemed that publicity and Streisand's own superstardom had turned the voters cold. You just aren't allowed to be self-sufficient: an actress, a singer, a director, a songwriter—all rolled up in one. Add a minor controversy to that and there goes your Oscar. After all, when you still have the likes of Ann Miller, Kathryn Grayson, Henny Backus (the actress [?] wife of actor Jim Backus, who is the voice of Mr. Magoo), Monica Lewis, Patti Andrews (as in Maxene, LaVerne, and . . .), you have to be very careful to sidestep even the merest hint of impropriety.

This was surely the knife in the heart of another landmark film— *Mask*, which, two years later, was all but barred from the nominee ranks because of an ill wind of publicity which blew up around it.

The film was conceived by the brass at Universal, who fashioned a beautiful script around the true story of a boy turned into a modern-day "Elephant Man" by a disfiguring disease (craniodiaphyseal dysplasia).

To package a "can't fail" deal, Universal's Renaissance man, Frank Price, handpicked Peter Bogdanovich to direct and Cher, with her newly unleashed acting talents, to star.

Bogdanovich and Price then scoured the ranks of Hollywood's new talent crop before selecting a fairly unknown twenty-one-year-old, Eric Stoltz, to play the heart and soul of Rocky Dennis, who triumphed over adversity to find hope in his own destiny.

The things Oscars are made of, right?

More nominations and Oscars have gone out for portrayals of triumph over disease and crippling than for any others—Eleanor Parker, John Hurt, Susan Hayward, and dozens more are proof positive.

With *Mask*, trouble began on the first day of shooting. Peter Bogdanovich had bolted out of a four-year hiatus from film to bury himself and his troubles in *Mask*. He had just emerged from the shadows of infamy after the public airing of his love affair with *Playboy*-centerfold-turned-starlet Dorothy Stratten.

The director had promised himself a comedy to break his deathly vigil until a producer coerced him into reading the script. "From the moment I read it, I felt it was inevitable that I do this film. Because the first play Dorothy Stratten had ever seen was *The Elephant Man*. She was absolutely bowled over by it. Shortly after she saw it, she went to the store and bought some books about John Merrick. While I had some problem looking at the photographs, she did not. I couldn't understand her interest until she was killed and I saw the play myself. I realized then that extraordinary beauty sets you apart as much as extraordinary grotesquerie. I believed that *Mask* was showing Dorothy's flip side."

The filming began under this heavy weight, which, some would say, inspired Bogdanovich to show a humanity he hadn't revealed since his breakthrough film, *The Last Picture Show*.

But everyone, particularly Cher, believed that Eric Stoltz was the glue which held the picture together.

And the role did not come easily to him.

"I was excited the first time I heard about it," Stoltz told interviewers. "It just sounded kind of magical—Peter Bogdanovich and Cher."

Eric, along with about seven others, read for Peter a number of times. But he tried a trick of his own: he came to the final reading wearing a pair of pantyhose over his head with holes cut out for the eyes and mouth. "There were a lot of executives in the room, and I don't think they knew exactly how to respond," he recalled.

The role was his the next day.

Frank Price had already called in Michael Westmore, scion of the fabled wizards of makeup, the Westmores, to the huge, black Universal tower and asked him to work enough magic to transform the handsome Eric Stoltz into Rocky Dennis.

"I only want to do this if we can do it in color and make it lifelike," said Price.

Westmore then disappeared into his laboratory to experiment with rubber, plastic, and fiber, searching for a way to simulate the grotesque mask of bone which so disfigured Rocky Dennis. He made more than a score of trial runs on his son, Michael, before finding the solution.

He eventually used three types of foam rubber and a latex covering to simulate skin. Westmore bored into the thick, semihard foam to create a series of honeycombs allowing Stoltz to use his facial muscles to move more than thirty outer sections of the "mask," which was so crucial to the artistic success of the final film.

"I worked with Eric for weeks helping him learn how to use his own buried face to show emotion on the surface of the covering. And I slowly watched this kid do brilliant things—with the mask, with his eyes, and with his voice," said Westmore.

It took three hours to seal Eric into the layers, which were applied in sections and then covered with the latex. Stoltz then toiled for seven weeks inside a smothering casing of rubber and plaster. "It was the most difficult thing I have ever asked a man to do," Bogdanovich recalled. "It was pure hell. We took a skin-surface temperature reading on Stoltz's face and it reached a hundred degrees. Plus he gave that incredibly sensitive performance. I don't see how they could have failed to nominate him."

Cher agreed: "When I came out onstage Oscar night to present the Best Supporting Actor Oscar, it broke my heart to read off those names, knowing that Eric wasn't included. He gave, in my opinion, the best supporting performance of the year."

Despite these belated but kind words, the political infighting between Bogdanovich and Universal and the public barbs which flew between the director and Cher had already helped cheat Eric of the nomination he would have probably received under normal conditions.

Cher told dozens of reporters that her own "best scenes were left by Bogdanovich on the cutting-room floor. That's where my finest moments ended up."

The actress's snipes coincided precisely with Peter's major tussle

FOR YOUR CONSIDERATION

GOLDEN GLOBE NOMINEE
BEST SUPPORTING ACTOR

ERIC STOLTZ

BEST SUPPORTING ACTOR

with the top-heavy Universal executive corps over control of the final print and the slicing of Bruce Springsteen's music from the film's score.

Bogdanovich: "Some of the best scenes *were* cut. Cher was right about that. We're only talking about six to eight minutes. But they were crucial moments; crucial in that they showed the humanity of Rocky, Rusty, and their milieu. As for the Springsteen music, not only had Rocky himself used it as an anthem—it was needed to express the passage of time and to show Rocky's emotional coming of age."

Cher sniped back that Bogdanovich could have had Springsteen's music if the musician had insisted on it, and he could have worked harder to win Bruce's support. "If Bruce had wanted those songs in the film, Columbia Records would have approved. It's as simple as that."

Peter countered: "If Cher would have stood behind me and fought for the Springsteen music and the lost footage, I think we would have won. Furthermore, if she had just taken no sides at all, I think she would have been nominated, Eric would have been nominated, the film would have been nominated, and *I* would have been nominated."

The trouble was—nobody shut up.

Universal carped at Peter. Cher carped at her director. And Eric fled from the glare of publicity to remain an amorphic figure whose visage simply faded away by Oscar time.

As if Stoltz's loss of a nomination weren't enough, Steven Spielberg fired him from another Universal picture, *Back to the Future*, in a gesture that seemed to say "You're just not good enough, kid!" and tightened the hangman's noose around the young actor's neck.

TV's top brat, Michael J. Fox, had been the first choice of producer Spielberg and director Robert Zemeckis. No dice, said the producers of Fox's TV series, "Family Ties."

So the studio, which had used Eric in *The Wild Party*, signed him for the part. Six weeks into filming, Spielberg dashed from the screening room and told the world that he "wasn't getting quite the quality I wanted."

Stoltz was fired the next day.

If he wasn't good enough for the flighty *Back to the Future*, then how on earth could he be trusted with an Academy Award? And he wasn't.

Spielberg apologized, after the damage was done. "It was the toughest call I ever had to make. After all, four million dollars went down the drain. Eric Stoltz is a remarkable young actor in the same league with Sean Penn and Emilio Estevez. I should have gone with my hunch and delayed the film until we could get Michael J. Fox."

Of all *Mask*'s lost Oscar glory, Cher's dashed hopes caught the fancy of the media. But Cher herself promptly dismissed her loss of a nomination.

"I was flying to New York at the time the nominations were announced," she said. "When I opened the door to my hotel room, it was filled with flowers and piles of messages informing me that I hadn't been nominated. That hotel looked like a funeral parlor. But I didn't mourn or talk it over with *anybody* but my agent."

"The boat had sailed."

This, of course, was the same Cher who, several months earlier, had trumpeted: "The one scene Peter keeps talking about—the scene that was cut—was *my* scene. If I can live with it—so should he. He was just amazed that the studio people were screwing with his work. So I basically said, 'You screwed with my work, now *they* are screwing with my

When it became clear that Universal wasn't going to mount an ad campaign for young Eric Stoltz for Best Supporting Actor in Peter Bogdanovich's Mask *(1985), friends of the actor (including, apparently, Cher and Beverly D'Angelo) raised the money to run this ad, which graphically depicts the range Stoltz showed in* Mask. *But Universal was too busy working for Klaus Maria Brandauer's understated work in* Out of Africa, *and Stoltz was lost in the shuffle. "You can forget Streisand, Cher, and Spielberg," quipped columnist Robert Osborne. "Eric Stoltz was the real shutout."*

Hollywood finally found something that Cher could do—act! After a stint in a Robert Altman film, Come Back to the Five and Dime, Jimmy Dean, *Mike Nichols cast the rock queen in* Silkwood *to play opposite Meryl Streep as a decidedly unglamorous lesbian who may have killed Silkwood. "When I saw the film previewed, everybody laughed when my name came on the screen," she recalled. "But nobody was laughing at the end." The film gave her a nomination and prepared the way for her real chance in* Mask.

work.' It's like being a slave and having someone sell you. One master is as good as the next when you are a slave." When she put on her newly fitted actress hat, however, Cher slyly admitted that *Mask* had been a wonderful experience.

Bogdanovich has depicted *Mask*'s lost Oscar dreams as just another archetypal Academy Awards story: fortunes changed within the Universal hierarchy (and *Mask* had been conceived by the "wrong person"); Peter the Great made waves; Universal had to put its Oscar hopes on the thirty-five-million-dollar *Out of Africa*, which *needed* the box-office power of those little gold statuettes; Eric Stoltz was fired from *Back to the Future;* six precious minutes ended up in the deep, dark vaults of Universal City; and Cher talked and talked and talked.

Cher: "But basically, whenever there's any sign of trouble connected with a film—any film—its Oscar chances are lessened."

One indication that Oscar's hems are showing, that he's out of step with the times, that he's marching to the wrong drummer, is the good fortune that rained down on the unnominated three in the wake of their Oscar shutout. Peter was offered four films at once and became, to quote him, "hotter than I've ever been"; a bouquet of scripts were tossed on Cher's doorstep; and Stoltz was hired for two major films—*The Emerald* and *The Children's Crusade.*

So who needs that statue?

While Eric, Cher, and Peter can survive fine without Oscar's help, there have been enough oversights in the last five years to account for considerable mourning.

For starters, the Academy has skipped over an entire genre—and the spanking new stars who go along with it. When John Belushi and the gang made *National Lampoon's Animal House* in 1978, none of those involved could have known that an entirely new genre had been born, a genre that started with rough-and-tumble humor and advanced to the biting satire of *The Breakfast Club* and the soft, bittersweet humor of *Splash.*

The creative forces involved in *Animal House*—director John Landis and writer Harold Ramis—didn't care that they had built Hollywood a newer, comic mousetrap. They only wanted to make a funny movie. The film's far raunchier stepchild, *Porky's,* carried that success one step further by pouring $230 million in pure gold into the coffers of Twentieth Century–Fox, which had budgeted the movie at $3.9 million.

Hollywood's first Brat Pack—James Dean, left, Sal Mineo, and Natalie Wood, totaled five nominations among them, but it was hard going. The Academy made them grow up first: Natalie had to make it into adulthood for her first Oscar bid, in Splendor in the Grass; *Dean got his nod for* Giant; *Sal Mineo had to become a villain in* Rebel Without a Cause *to gain recognition.*

But it was the second generation which honed much of the broadness, and introduced subtle direction and fine acting—only to find that even more money fell from a very youthful sky. With the 1982 film *Diner*, the 1983 movie *Splash*, and 1985's *Breakfast Club*, the genre entered the big time. These movies have two things in common which Oscar voters simply cannot deal with: humor and *very young* talent. To date, these "coming-of-age" films have garnered very few major nominations; with the exception of a best song nod here and there (such as "Footloose"), writing nominations for *Splash* and *Diner*, and editing and cinematography nominations for *Flashdance*, there has only been grudging recognition of special effects (such as the pyrotechnics of *Ghostbusters*); and one or two others.

The Academy was caught by surprise by a bankable treasure trove of post-teenage talent. Known not always so affectionately as the "Brat Pack," these juveniles lit up the screen with the color Hollywood loves most: green (as in money).

Despite their ability to sell tickets, not one member of that group has been nominated. But there have been plenty of chances. For instance, almost the entire male membership of the Pack was incendiary in *The Outsiders* and *Rumble Fish,* a pair of Francis Coppola films in the mold of *Rebel Without a Cause*. Those names now light up marquees across America: Tom Cruise, Emilio Estevez, Sean Penn, Rob Lowe, Matt Dillon, and Mickey Rourke.

But it is *Diner* that is now considered *the* classic in the coming-of-age genre. Rourke and fellow Packers Kevin Bacon and Steve Guttenberg were considered by many to be shoo-ins for Oscar-nominated gold for 1982. Guttenberg even sweetened the pot with one of the most vig-

The stodgy Oscar voters—more than 60 percent of whom are over sixty—have no idea how to deal with the brilliance of Hollywood's new Brat Pack. Although the Pack comprises dozens of performers, not one of them has been recognized by the Academy. From St. Elmo's Fire *(1985), here are, left to right, Packers Andrew McCarthy, Emilio Estevez, Judd Nelson, Rob Lowe, Mare Winningham, Demi Moore, and Ally Sheedy. "Maybe they were just all so good, the Oscar people were confused," said critic Gene Siskel. "Hollywood is often decked by really fine acting."*

orous ad campaigns in recent memory. But all it earned him was a place on the Oscar presenters' list. Rourke has also been conspicuously absent from the nominees list despite heavyweight acting in *The Pope of Greenwich Village* and *Body Heat*.

It was with *The Breakfast Club*, however, that the Academy's anti-youth bias was fully apparent. That 1985 film about five high schoolers locked in a library unleashed a fury of acting by Judd Nelson, Ally Sheedy, Anthony Michael Hall, Molly Ringwald, and Emilio Estevez which, at first glance, seemed too obvious to ignore. But ignored it was, even by its own studio, Universal—a studio too busy fishing for *Out of Africa* Oscars to notice the kids on the front doorstep. The ad campaigns the studio ran for the film included full-page spreads which listed all the actors in a single list buried in photos and verbiage. That type of ad has always been pig Latin to Oscar voters—many of whom are in the Motion Picture Country Retirement Home. When something is new, or even the least bit trendy, the voters have to be pounded over the head with praise for their sagacity.

One of the head Brat Packers, Sean Penn, has delivered three electric performances, in *Taps*, *The Falcon and the Snowman*, and *Racing with the Moon*, but only attracted serious industry attention when he married Brat Princess Madonna.

"It's hard for these kids to be noticed," said director Bogdanovich. "They just don't have front-office priority at the studios."

Ah, if Emilio Estevez were only seventy, or Ally Sheedy were British, or if any one of them would suffer a life-threatening accident. Then, maybe, the nominations would come pouring in.

CHAPTER FIVE

Winners and Losers

Having been forced by its own celebrity to take itself seriously, Oscar's trouble is that it now takes itself too seriously. The voting rules and bylaws are now longer than the U.S. Constitution and harder to understand. Occasionally the bylaws seem intended to function like protective tariffs, keeping out imports and modernist tendencies. —CHARLES CHAMPLIN, 1980

April 14, 1980. A line of black limousines glistens in the smog and is hopelessly snarled at a downtown off ramp of the Hollywood Freeway.

The Cadillacs are backed up for blocks, stalled in a gaunt and otherwise deserted canyon of concrete. The bankers in vested suits and the secretaries in Gloria Vanderbilt jeans have all disappeared into the suburban maze.

Here in downtown Los Angeles there's hardly a sound—the occasional hacking cough of a derelict wino, an army of cleaning ladies chattering in Spanish, a far-off siren.

The engines of the limos purr in unison. A sandy-haired transient looks out from his bed of newspapers and raises a bottle of Tokay wine toward the cars. "Have a nice day!" he yells. The chauffeurs don't turn their heads; they can't hear him, encased as they are in an air-conditioned, perfumed world. In the backseats all sign of life is safely hidden behind glass of midnight blue. Sometimes a window or two will roll down, revealing the flash of a Halston gown or the sensuous fabric of a Calvin Klein dinner jacket.

The line of sleek cars stretches up an asphalt hill and ends at a blaze of strobe lights on the concrete terrace of the Los Angeles Music Center, an icy and impersonal monument to pretentious architecture. A fleet of helicopters with banks of video cameras hovers overhead, shooting down on the crowd. Chauffeurs click their heels, jerk open the doors, and the Hollywood of today spills out in a garish puddle of plastic chic.

Two old women in dirty sweaters and ripped polyester pants barely glance up from the standing ashtrays they are clawing at for used cigarettes. One shrugs; the other stares ahead. Up above their heads soars the sign that explains it all: WELCOME, it says, TO THE FIFTY-SECOND ANNUAL ACADEMY AWARDS.

The Oscars. They now play out their story of envy and greed in a palace of cement, surrounded by the empty skyscrapers and dirty streets of downtown Los Angeles—only five miles from the Hollywood Roosevelt Hotel, where they started, but light-years away in time and style.

Many of the superstars now drive anonymous family cars to the Oscars, park them down in the bowels of the earth, and then ride the elevator up to the auditorium. Some of them even come in car pools: from far away in the San Fernando Valley, or from the stucco-and-swimming-pool forests out in Orange County. Because this is where the so-called New Hollywood lives.

It's all sedate, a shopping-mall sort of thing. When the show starts, the doors are shut and locked, returning the city to its sterile quiet. Even the applause seems muffled.

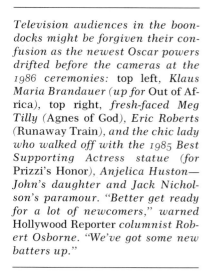

Television audiences in the boondocks might be forgiven their confusion as the newest Oscar powers drifted before the cameras at the 1986 ceremonies: top left, *Klaus Maria Brandauer (up for* Out of Africa), top right, *fresh-faced Meg Tilly (*Agnes of God*), Eric Roberts (*Runaway Train*), and the chic lady who walked off with the 1985 Best Supporting Actress statue (for* Prizzi's Honor), *Anjelica Huston—John's daughter and Jack Nicholson's paramour. "Better get ready for a lot of newcomers," warned* Hollywood Reporter *columnist Robert Osborne. "We've got some new batters up."*

But this severe setting is uniquely appropriate to the Oscars of the seventies and eighties—an era that has finally swept clear the baroque ghosts of Hollywood past and ushered in the New Hollywood, a kingdom ruled by Jane Fonda's generation. It's a world where a director (such as Steven Spielberg or George Lucas) or a super exec (such as Alan Ladd, Jr., or Richard Zanuck) is more likely to be a celebrity than the actors who work for him.

And it's an era of machines and grotesque novelties: the biggest stars at the 1978 Oscars were a whining robot (R2D2) and a golden tin man with a stutter (C-3PO).

Approaching their sixth decade, the Academy Awards more closely resemble the annual banquet of Chrysler-Plymouth dealers than the gathering of movie royalty they are supposed to be. Most of the men in finely cut dinner jackets are glorified accountants, and the movie reporters backstage ask the winners questions about camera angles or the intricacies of scripting.

There's an up-front honesty about the Oscars now that would have been impossible in the old Hollywood. For instance, Jane Fonda, when asked about her Oscar chances in 1980, shook her head decisively. "No, I think Sally Field will win—she gave the best performance."

There have also been brave changes in the ceremony itself. In 1980, when the acting nominations were announced, the traditional scenes of each performance were deleted, replaced by clips showing the entire panorama of an actor's career. The bits of film with Al Pacino, for example, traced his work from *The Godfather* to *Dog Day Afternoon*, concluding with 1979's . . . *And Justice for All.* A subtle change on the surface, but a clear sign that the Academy is finally facing up to the unfortunate reality of its voting patterns: an actor is almost always rewarded for his total career rather than for any single performance.

Even the style brought by an irreverent Robin Williams has given the awards a new objectivity and a sense of humor about Oscar's highly dubious past. And in a sense, the Academy of Motion Picture Arts and Sciences is haunted by its past; it has to gracefully live with the fact that it never gave Garbo a 'real' Oscar, or Cary Grant, or Alfred Hitchcock. What else can it do but joke about a Best Picture list that honored *Mrs. Miniver* and *The Greatest Show on Earth* but not *Citizen Kane* or *A Streetcar Named Desire?*

Everyone involved is now comfortable with the reality that Oscar's story *is* the story of Hollywood—its pitiless avarice, its fatal disregard for the integrity of its actors, and its shameless worship of the box-office receipts.

When they passed out the first statuettes at the Hollywood Roosevelt Hotel on May 19, 1929, Hollywood was still in the high noon of its gothic period. Gloria Swanson came to the Oscars in a chauffeured car whose puce tones matched the embroidery on her gown; Harlow was still a featured player; and the voters couldn't decide whether they should allow talkies into the competition.

The first Best Actress was Janet Gaynor, a girl all the Academy members knew personally, and the Best Actor was Emil Jannings, a man none of them knew and who had already fled back to Germany in fear of sound cameras.

But Oscar's deadly flaw had already appeared. These were awards given *by* the establishment *to* the establishment, and it was the *way* you played the game, not how well you played it, which won you an Oscar. An actress turning in a truly bad performance (such as Norma

Why didn't Alfred Hitchcock win an Oscar? Hitchcock's first American film, Rebecca, *easily took the Best Picture award, but John Ford was named Best Director for* The Grapes of Wrath. *Hitch wasn't nominated again until* 1945, *for the breakthrough film,* Lifeboat, *in which all the action took place in a cramped rescue boat. Perhaps that film was just* too *dazzling: Oscar voters tossed the Best Director prize to Leo McCarey for the heavyhanded and maudlin* Going My Way *(which also, inexplicably, won an Oscar for Bing Crosby). Later, Billy Wilder's direction of* The Apartment *bested Hitchcock's masterpiece,* Psycho, *which wasn't even nominated for Best Picture.*

Shearer in *The Divorcee*) walked off with the gold because she towed the line. A maverick (such as Ruth Chatterton) could give the finest performance in years (such as her work in *Dodsworth*) and remain UnOscared. If an actor, no matter how fine, refused to play the studio game, then just don't nominate him. What can folks say about that? Not much—and Louis B. Mayer and the boys knew it.

Oscar's history is littered with the skeletons of those frozen out by the establishment before round one: Marilyn Monroe, George Raft, Alan Ladd, Errol Flynn, and the most haunting of them all—John Barrymore.

John Barrymore was probably the best screen actor of the early thirties—certainly he was the best actor in 1932, when his work in *Grand Hotel, Bill of Divorcement,* and *The Mad Genius* was on the screen. Greta Garbo, after working with Barrymore on *Grand Hotel* for only one day, called the cast together, took Barrymore's hand, kissed it, and said, "It's such a great pleasure to work with so perfect an artist."

But in the Victorian parlors of the Hollywood Hills, Barrymore had two counts against him. First, he was the great offscreen lover of the twenties. Rudolph Valentino and Ramon Novarro got the girls on the set, but Barrymore took them into his own, real bed. The studio bosses, most of them great lechers, fumed at Barrymore's easy conquests. And second, he refused to play by the rules—drank too much, snickered at Hollywood's pretensions, and spurned the invitations to its dull week-end parties.

Louis B. Mayer and others soothed any feelings of shame they may have had by nodding and agreeing that Barrymore wouldn't be all that interested in the Oscar anyway; he'd already possessed all the adulation of Broadway and London. But Barrymore wanted an Oscar—desperately. Frances Marion was only one of many who sensed "his hurt, his denials, the shame of becoming an object of ridicule. But most of all, there was his frustration at never once being recognized as a great artist in Hollywood circles. He always insisted he would toss that 'phony Oscar' into the ocean if he won it," said Marion. "But that was only a small boy whistling into the dark—he really wanted an Oscar above any honor he had ever received."

One of the most shameful examples of the Academy's prejudice was its neglect of John Barrymore (here in full fancy dress for Arsène Lupin)— a neglect born of envy. Arguably the best artist of the early talkies, Barrymore laughed on the outside at his exclusion from Oscar's ranks. But he sobbed once in the presence of Gene Fowler over being snubbed for Bill of Divorcement.

Garbo! *Here shown with lover, on-screen and off, John Gilbert in* Flesh and the Devil *(1926). Most critics and members of the public consider her the greatest actress ever to appear in films. Twice the New York Film Critics—by all standards a more impartial jury than the Oscar voters—named her Best Actress; in 1935 for* Anna Karenina *and in 1937 for* Camille. *The Academy didn't even nominate her for the first, and gave the Oscar to Luise Rainer in 1937. Much later the Academy trotted out one of those "honorary" Oscars for the nonattending Garbo. The Academy's rejection of Garbo is proof enough that the awards, during the early decades, were not given by peers; they were awards given by and to movie politicians. Garbo's peers—when they were actually consulted—gave her unanimous recognition: in 1950* Daily Variety *polled two hundred veterans of the movie industry, and Garbo was named Best Silent Actress, Best Sound Actress, and Best All-Around Actress.*

Just before Barrymore died, he told his biographer, Gene Fowler, that he had spent sleepless nights puzzling over his failure to get even a nomination. "You know, Gene, I think they were afraid I'd come into the banquet drunk, embarrassing myself and them. But I wouldn't have, you know."

The establishment, particularly Mayer, also shut John Gilbert out in the cold. A matinee lover of the late silent period, Gilbert barely hung on to his career after his disastrous talking debut, *His Glorious Night*. His fortunes and the quality of his films dropped each year. But Garbo made a last-ditch attempt to save him in her film *Queen Christina*. In it, he was good enough to attract attention from both the New York and London critics. A brave coterie of Gilbert's cronies, with help from Joan Crawford, approached Mayer about getting John an Oscar nomination. "Mayer just laughed at us," one of the group said later. "He'd already counted Gilbert out."

Mayer was a person whose whims could be imposed on the Academy: if he didn't want an MGM player nominated, no force in Hollywood could override his veto. For that matter, the head of any major studio had the same veto power in the first decade. "They all got together and passed those awards around—you were either on the list or off it; it didn't matter how good you were," said Joan Crawford—long after she'd won her hard-fought Oscar in 1946 for *Mildred Pierce*.

This fact alone accounts for decades full of so-so Oscar winners that clutter up Academy history. A generation of Oscar holders bagged their awards for moderately good service for the home studio. The Oscars held by Ginger Rogers, Loretta Young, Bing Crosby, Luise Rainer, Norma Shearer, and Marie Dressler are best excused by those conditions. (Have you ever tried to watch *Kitty Foyle* or *The Divorcée*?)

Hollywood mavericks didn't begin taking home the gold statues in any number until George C. Scott and Jane Fonda broke the spell in 1971 and 1972, respectively.

The forty years before that are crowded with oversights—not the least of which were Alan Ladd and Marilyn Monroe. Some may think Monroe won an Oscar because of her legendary status: the decades following her death have seen her elevated to hallowed places on every critic's list of good performances. But during her lifetime her artistic status was somewhat fuzzy. And she was the latest in a long line of comediennes and bombshells, including Mae West and Jean Harlow, who didn't get nominated. On the other hand, everyone in Hollywood knew she wanted—and felt she would get—a nomination for the 1956 film *Bus Stop*.

Her work in the film was praised universally by the critics. And the gossip factory in Hollywood buzzed with stories of her painstaking study of the tragicomic Cherie. The first day on the set, Monroe threw out the costumes designed for her and, to replace them, drove to used-clothing stores in the run-down parts of Los Angeles. Her director, Joshua Logan, fed the gossip columns with a steady stream of praise.

But when the nominations were announced the afternoon of February 18, she found her exclusion from the list heartrending. "She was bitterly disappointed when she heard about the list," said gossip columnist Sheilah Graham. "The two things she wanted most during that era —an Oscar and a baby—were just to escape her grasp. To her, it meant they felt she 'wasn't good enough.' "

Although Monroe's increasing temperament and unreliability were working against her, it was studio politics that ultimately doomed her chance for an Oscar nomination for *Bus Stop*. Her studio, Twentieth

George Cukor and Marilyn Monroe —a delicate balance but dynamite when it worked. Privately, Cukor said that Marilyn deserved an Oscar—if they gave them for comedy. Marilyn's home studio, fattened from her box-office success, ensured her exclusion from the nominees for Bus Stop *(1956) by deliberately throwing their votes to Deborah Kerr for* The King and I. *Then, after her brilliant work in Billy Wilder's* Some Like It Hot *(1959), Fox executives hinted to their Oscar voters that since* Some Like It Hot *was a United Artists film, it would be better to slight Marilyn again. Sheila Graham would later depict Marilyn's heartache over her failure to gain a nomination.*

Century–Fox, put on a massive campaign to get a nomination for Deborah Kerr in *The King and I,* which was an expensive picture and needed all the help it could get from the Oscars. Fox let word get to their own employees that Kerr was to get the nomination—*not* Marilyn. A good indication of the fury with which the studio campaigned is evident in the ease with which Yul Brynner won the Best Actor prize for *The King and I*—over Kirk Douglas (*Lust for Life*), James Dean (*Giant*), Laurence Olivier (*Richard III*), and Rock Hudson (*Giant*). Hedda Hopper, rooting for Dean, said that a shaved head "is a strange reason for giving somebody an Oscar."

Alan Ladd, another casualty of the studio system, was neither temperamental nor unreliable. He had already turned in several Oscar-caliber performances (including his work in *The Blue Dahlia*) by the time he got his once-in-a-lifetime part, Shane. In 1954 the Academy voters rated the film highly, giving it nominations for Best Picture, Best Director (George Stevens), and two Best Supporting Actor bids, Brandon de Wilde, a juvenile, and the film's heavy, Jack Palance. But the voters turned a cold shoulder to Ladd, who was the strongest acting force in the film. Ladd's wife, Sue Carrol, a former silent star who had become an agent, used her considerable influence in Hollywood's drawing rooms to launch a grass-roots campaign.

She forgot about Paramount's undeniable clout with the Academy, and Paramount was a studio scorned. Ladd, long under contract there, had decided to free-lance. It was an unwritten law that a star, once off the payroll, was immediately jettisoned, and denied the considerable fringe benefits of a studio contract—including publicity and help in the

93

Oscar sweepstakes. Paramount, therefore, gave all its votes to contractee William Holden, who won for the studio's *Stalag 17*. There was certainly room for Ladd on the acting list for 1953; his performance in *Shane* far outshone Richard Burton's in the biblical extravaganza *The Robe*, and Marlon Brando's in the toga tragedy *Julius Caesar*.

Since Hollywood from 1920 until 1960 was a dictatorship of moguls, all Oscar voting patterns were subject to change at the drop of a memo. Which means there were no true patterns or trends in a half century of Oscar balloting.

Some seasons maudlin emotion ruled. It was surely that, and nothing else, that got Liz Taylor her first Academy Award for the miserable *Butterfield 8* in 1961. The week voting started in March of that year, Hollywood tabloids carried the headline LIZ DYING. And she was, given up for gone in a London hospital. Her second-by-second battle for life dominated the front pages right up until the last voting day, when the headlines crowed, LIZ RALLIES. The most jaded Oscar voter would have needed a heart of lead to withstand the publicity from Taylor's brush with death. In February, Taylor, who'd stolen Eddie Fisher from the town darling, Debbie Reynolds, hadn't had a prayer to win the Oscar. By late March, her victory was a foregone conclusion. "Hell, I even voted for her," said Debbie years later. Any of the four actresses up against Liz should have won it over her: Greer Garson in *Sunrise at Campobello*, Shirley MacLaine in *The Apartment*, Deborah Kerr in *The Sundowners*, or Melina Mercouri in *Never on Sunday*.

Greatly to her credit, Taylor said then, and repeated it hundreds of times, "I won the Oscar because I almost died—pure and simple." The irony of it is that she had deserved the Oscar the previous year for *Suddenly Last Summer* or even the year before that for *Cat on a Hot Tin Roof*.

Even emotion, however, will go only so far. It didn't do Judy Garland a bit of good when she was up for Best Actress in 1954's *A Star Is Born*. Garland had been driven out of MGM four years earlier after an all-too-public battle with booze, pills, and her own neuroses. At one point she was literally thrown off the lot. Less than eighteen months later, Garland had clawed her way back up, a comeback culminating in a new deal husband Sid Luft got for her at Warner Bros.—four films in four years, starting with *A Star Is Born*. The filming was a long one, punctuated by temperament and Judy's yo-yo weight problems. But when director George Cukor called it a wrap he viewed the final rough cut, and pronounced the film a masterpiece. Jack Warner didn't think so. First he cut about an hour from Cukor's footage, substituting a lavish production number which was eventually called "Born in a Trunk." Both Judy and Cukor hated the result.

But the reception by critics and the public at large was thunderous, hoisting Garland easily into a Best Actress nomination, along with Dorothy Dandridge for *Carmen Jones*, Audrey Hepburn for *Sabrina*, Grace Kelly for *The Country Girl*, and Jane Wyman for *Magnificent Obsession*.

Rumor in Tinseltown predicted Garland was an easy victor. The producers of the Oscar show (and many Academy officers) were so certain she would win that a bank of cameras were jammed into her room at the Los Angeles hospital where she had had a baby several days earlier. There was a letdown and bizarre quiet after the envelope was opened and Grace Kelly was named Best Actress.

Alan Ladd in Shane.

Liz Taylor and Eddie Fisher at Academy banquet the year she won for Butterfield 8.

Judy Garland never won an Oscar —that's legend. But in 1939's The Wizard of Oz, *she won a "toy" statue for her work on the yellow brick road gang. MGM had chances to nominate Judy for* Meet Me in St. Louis *and* The Clock, *but the front office vetoed it. Her next and only other chance came in 1955 when she was nominated for her comeback in* A Star Is Born. *Opposite, left to right, Judy Garland, Greer Garson, and Jane Wyman all show signs of age at the disastrous 1955 nominations party. This was the year that Hollywood tried to televise the nominations as well as the finals—an idea which was quickly dropped when the TV audience failed to turn up. The nominations just didn't have the "horse race" atmosphere so beloved by the American public.*

Several things probably happened to the headwind Garland had when she entered the race. Warner Bros. politely let it be known that they weren't officially backing her; the Garland deal had collapsed under the weight of the expensive musical. And Paramount campaigned heavily for Kelly. Rumor has persisted that the Kelly-Garland race was the closest that didn't end in a tie. Hedda Hopper, who had pried bits and pieces from accountants in earlier races, always said that Kelly beat Garland by seven votes. "And you know where those seven votes were, don't you? They belonged to those bastards in the front office at MGM."

Occasionally the Oscar is awarded to expiate guilt. It was surely that which threw the award to Ingrid Bergman for her role in the 1956 film *Anastasia*. The Swedish star had been hounded by both the press and the Hollywood establishment after she left her dentist husband and daughter in 1949 and moved to Italy with her lover, Roberto Rossellini, whom she later married. The whole incident might never have happened if her first Hollywood boss, David O. Selznick, hadn't shaped an image for her that fell somewhere between Joan of Lorraine, whom she played (often), and the Virgin of the Roses, a role planned for her in a film that was never made. But she continued to be pilloried to such an extent that she began fighting back with a series of interviews of her own, in Rome.

"Leave me alone," she told a particularly obnoxious group of report-

Judy Garland singing "The Man That Got Away" from A Star Is Born.

A triumphant Liza Minnelli serenades a mute line of Oscars in 1973 —almost twenty years after her mother, Judy Garland, had been robbed of her own Oscar by the inferior performance of Grace Kelly in The Country Girl.

ers at the Rome airport. "The details of my private life are between me and Rossellini and not between me and the world."

Then the Fifties dawned—bringing with it a more relaxed code of social and moral modes. Divorce became more rampant and the young movie-going audience was far more tolerant than its counterpart in the moralistic Forties.

A gang of newspaper feature and gossip columnists welcomed Ingrid back to the fold when she flew to Hollywood and embarked on her first American film in years, *Anastasia*.

Soon everybody perceived the silliness of Bergman's censure. Finally, the furor of her "Rossellini years" waned in an epidemic of good humor. Thus the Oscar for *Anastasia*.

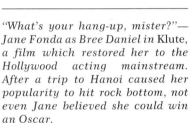

"What's your hang-up, mister?"—Jane Fonda as Bree Daniel in Klute, *a film which restored her to the Hollywood acting mainstream. After a trip to Hanoi caused her popularity to hit rock bottom, not even Jane believed she could win an Oscar.*

Later Jane Fonda rode a wave of "we forgive you" sentiment to earn her first Oscar in 1972 for *Klute*. For voters with memories of "Hanoi Jane" on their minds, this was some concession. By then the Academy had embraced the perverse form of radical chic which had also flooded high society of the period. It suddenly became "in" to put down the Academy and to embrace outrageous causes. It had worked for George C. Scott. He decried his nomination for 1970's *Patton*, and refused the Oscar he won so handily. (It's still in the Academy vaults.) The voters took this rejection on the chin and nominated him the very next year for *Hospital*. Similarly, after Brando refused to accept his *Godfather* award by sending an Indian in his place, the now miniskirted and blue-jeaned voters tossed him a nomination for his tawdry sex play in *The Last Tango in Paris*.

Fonda's Oscar for *Klute* was tinged with the same anti-establishment

Jane Fonda speaks passionately at a UCLA peace rally in 1970, fanning the flames of controversy which swirled around her and threatened her once promising career. "It will take a miracle to get her back into this business," said Henry Fonda to a Rolling Stone *reporter. Nevertheless, Jane's austere manner of dress and wildly cut hair created a fashion which began to erode some of the glamor so necessary for success at the end of Hollywood's annual trek to the fountains which feed it—the Oscar fans themselves.*

aura. The actress told Charles Champlin that her post-Oscar benefits virtually rebuilt her sagging career. She was offered more than forty key film roles in the three years after *Klute*. And this led her directly to the 1978 triumph, *Coming Home*.

The awards to Fonda and Voight are viewed by many as a definite sign of Oscar's newly found maturity. Fonda had fought the Hollywood establishment for six years to launch this withering picture of life after the Vietnam War.

In the past, the voters had reluctantly given awards to projects that were made "in spite of" the film establishment. Only a decade earlier the voters had given a Best Actor Oscar to Cliff Robertson for his performance in *Charly*, a property he had been forced to buy himself and carry from bank to bank seeking financing. The voters tossed him the Oscar almost as a grudging trophy. But they sure as hell weren't going to do him any other favors. His parts thereafter have been few and unimaginative.

These erratic patterns have made, and continue to make, the Oscar voting seem like an overblown election for class favorite, at worst, and a contest for the "most likely to succeed," at best.

Some members of the Hollywood elite say openly that the roll call of the Oscarless has become more exclusive and illustrious than the winners' circle itself.

Vivien Leigh accepting her Oscar during a live radio broadcast. Her victory for Gone With The Wind *(1939) had been a sure thing—rumors had it that she took in 93 percent of the vote from her opponents: Greer Garson for* Goodbye, Mr. Chips *(Hedda Hopper reported that Garson received but ten votes); Bette Davis for* Dark Victory *(twenty-two votes, sniffed Hedda); Irene Dunne for* Love Affair *("too few to even count"); and Greta Garbo for* Ninotchka *("a handful"). Hedda knew of what she spoke: she and her assistants called "every" voter the day before the awards were revealed.*
(© A.M.P.A.S.)

Just the cream of "the unawarded," as Burgess Meredith calls them, includes:

Barbara Stanwyck, Greta Garbo, John Garfield, <u>Paul Newman</u>, Rosalind Russell, Charles Boyer, Leslie Howard, Merle Oberon, Edward G. Robinson, Franchot Tone, Montgomery Clift, Marlene Dietrich, Fred Astaire, Peter Sellers, James Mason, Kirk Douglas, Danny Kaye, Peter O'Toole, Richard Burton, Robert Mitchum, Cary Grant, Irene Dunne, Liv Ullmann, Tyrone Power, Tony Curtis, Charles Bickford, Claude Rains, Natalie Wood, James Dean, Angela Lansbury, Albert Finney, Kim Stanley, Thelma Ritter, Agnes Moorehead, Myrna Loy, William Powell, Alan Alda, Ann-Margret, <u>Michael Caine,</u> Al Pacino, Marsha Mason, Burgess Meredith, Jane Alexander, Gena Rowlands, Jeff Bridges, Lana Turner, Piper Laurie, Rip Torn, Judy Garland, and Glenn Close.

The Oscar people looked a second time when Ingrid Bergman took a third Oscar, for her supporting role in the 1974 film, *Murder on the Orient Express*. Holding the statue upside down, the actress recognized another nominee, Valentina Cortese, "who should have won for *Day for Night*."

Oscar's winners and losers all mill about after the rite, congratulating and consoling each other and showing "casting grin no. 19" as if they had never really been competing with each other. But after the last waltz at the Academy Board of Governors' Ball, the losers dash home to call their agents, their psychiatrists, and their mothers to question why they lost this most desirable of all the earth's prizes.

The Oscar race occasionally becomes vicious; as was the case when David Ward saw his Oscar (for writing *The Sting*) tarnish before his eyes only months after he carted it home.

On October 14, 1974, Steve Shagan, a screenwriter whose script for *Save the Tiger* had lost to Ward's, wrote Academy president Walter Mirisch suggesting that Ward's Oscar be pulled back to the Academy's bosom because the winner had been guilty of plagiarism.

It seems that Shagan, Ward's major competition, had read an article in a trade paper about a lawsuit filed by an aging southern professor, who claimed that *The Sting* had been taken, part and parcel, from a book he had written in the forties.

Shagan immediately demanded that the Academy conduct an investigation into the matter—which, in turn, started a forest fire of rumors throughout the film community. David Ward, who had been the writer of the hour on the 1974 Oscar stage, was suddenly David the shunned. He shrank from both the publicity and its handmaiden—professional jealousy.

Universal Pictures, producers of *The Sting,* was so badly frightened by the southern professor's claims that it settled out of court—even though David Ward offered proof that he had used only statistics and facts from that 1949 book and six other nonfiction texts on con men and swindlers. Then the studio graciously presented Ward with a bill for $600,000, a sum which was eventually paid by *Sting* producer Michael Phillips; actors Robert Redford and Paul Newman; the film's director, George Roy Hill; and a handful of others.

In the meantime, Ward retreated to his canyon hideaway, saw his first marriage disintegrate, and carried around Xerox copies of *The Big Con* in his car in case he was called upon to prove his innocence.

For the most part, Ward remained undefended until February 1982, when journalist Mike Greco set out to prove the writer's innocence through an in depth article in the *Los Angeles Times*'s *Calendar* magazine.

Greco discovered that the same *facts* were available in half a dozen other books. "I found nothing of a factual nature about con men that was used in *The Sting* that could not have come from any of these other books. I also examined nine other books about con men and con games and none of these books—including the work in question—included any of the plot elements that make *The Sting* work dramatically. And none of these studies suggest a story which also 'cons' the audience. There are also no dramatic characters such as Hooker, Gondorff, Linnigan, or Salino; nor any subplots such as those Ward used . . . or . . ."

In any event, Greco amply proved Ward's innocence and exposed an all too apparent case of dollar-green Oscar envy. But Shagan has protested and protested and protested that this isn't so.

"We [himself and two prominent screenwriters nominated that same year] decided to bring the matter to the attention of the Academy because we felt the integrity of the writers' branch was in jeopardy."

Horrors! That the collective Oscar pensmen should be the least bit besmirched—those same wise men who have nominated such clunkers as *Designing Woman*, *Operation Petticoat* and *Pillow Talk*.

Ward, the winner, said that Shagan, the loser, bad-mouthed him all over town about the alleged plagiarized script. "Every time someone would ask me if I ripped off *The Sting*, Shagan's name would be invoked as an authority on the affair."

Shagan again protested: "I'm not into attacking fellow writers. David Ward won the Oscar. God bless him. I wish him well."

But Greco discovered that Shagan apparently told writer Stephen Farber in 1979 that "the Academy didn't want to make waves by revoking Ward's Oscar. They felt it would undermine their image if people knew that the Academy gave its award for best original screenplay for an act of plagiarism."

Farber's article, published in *New West* magazine, only added poison to the dart which had struck Ward's Oscar. "I was at a party shortly after that article appeared, and overheard someone telling an amused group of listeners, 'All David Ward needed to write *The Sting* was a Xerox machine.' I stopped going to parties," the beleaguered writer complained.

Jealousy permeates the Oscar game like gas rising from the decaying murk of a Florida swamp; there is simply so much at stake. And character assassination often follows in the wake of victory.

Since Shagan lost the Oscar to Ward, he apparently took the offensive (though he denies this). He would have achieved precious little. Had the Academy pulled Ward's Oscar, it would have brought Shagan no closer to ownership of a statuette. The Academy Awards aren't like Miss America where the runner-up claims the cape and crown to reign instead. In any case, it seems likely that Shagan's tedious script for *Save the Tiger* would probably have placed fourth or fifth behind those for *American Graffiti*, *A Touch of Class*, and *Cries and Whispers*.

If the David Ward-Steve Shagan affair proves anything at all, it's that the Academy Award is seen by some as something almost worth killing for; or at least worth ruining another man's reputation and artistic stability.

CHAPTER SIX

Oh, This Old Thing!

Shirley MacLaine looked down at her five-thousand-dollar dress and thought: "What if I win and have to get the Oscar in this old thing." It was 1960 and she lost.

Two handsome chauffeurs leaned down, opened the wide limousine door, and grasped two supremely elegant hands, hands freshly manicured for a cool $250 on Rodeo Drive.

The fingers traveled up the well-muscled arms of the attendants, who were, in reality, more like footmen. Then one gorgeous leg slid out of the car, encased in a pounded leather-and-satin boot which reached midway up the perfectly proportioned limb.

There was a flash of thigh as the potentate inside bent her head gracefully and emerged into the glare of laser lights and the delicate shading of the pink California sun.

The crowd gasped and then roared in delight as one of the campest film stars since Gloria Swanson began a lithe walk down the red carpet of fame and adoration, leading to the glass-and-concrete palace which is the setting for the Academy Awards.

Cher had long been known for the personal style and the kitsch of her Oscar clothes. But this year was different: she had been cheated out of a nomination in her landmark performance as Rusty Dennis in *Mask*, so she had decided to make a statement by arriving as a punk acid queen.

From the tops of her multi-thousand-dollar boots to the very tips of her hackle-feather headdress, the former Cher Bono (once the bottom half of a magical rock team) was encased in a black confection of beads, hand-woven satin from India, jet crystals from Africa's Gold Coast, and earrings which resembled nothing so much as the great waterfall at the ruins of Machu Picchu.

Above her soared a headdress of rare hackle feathers (eight hundred of them) and velvet that caught the afternoon breezes, causing it to sparkle and undulate as if it were virtually bearing the princess to a sacrifice on the top of a pyramid.

Cher, now an actress to reckon with, had chucked thespianism for this one night to present an image which was one part Ming the Merciless, one part burlesque stripper, and one part fashion queen. As she slowly walked out on the Oscar stage to present the award to the Best Supporting Actor (who turned out to be old-timer Don Ameche), sex literally dripped from her arms, breasts, and shoulders. Mae West would have loved the moment.

Once ensconced behind the podium, she waited for the shock to subside before saying: "As you can see, I have received and read my Academy brochure on how to dress as a *serious* actress."

Poor Don Ameche took his Oscar from the black visage beside him, and almost visibly shied away—an unusual reaction from a man who more than once had starred opposite Carmen Miranda.

The outfit, with its sizzling effect on the star's elegant frame, was easily the sartorial highlight of an evening where shoulder-padded monster dresses careened about the stage; where Jane Fonda looked as if she had been wrapped in a sequined Ace bandage; and where Sally Field gave the impression of Gidget wearing a dress which was too old for her. It hardly needs to be said that Best Actress Geraldine Page's late "bag lady" gown (which caused her to look a bit like the Pillsbury Dough Boy in drag) was but the latest super-frump getup in a decade of inelegantly dressed Oscar winners.

"To hell with it; they didn't nominate me—so f. . . it, let's have fun," Cher told couturier Bob Mackie. So half a dozen seamstresses fashioned this twelve-thousand-dollar gown in which she presented the 1985 Best Supporting Actor award to veteran actor Don Ameche. The voters passed Cher over for Mask yet nominated the ubiquitous Anne Bancroft for her overacted nun in Agnes of God. "I wanted them all to see that I still have it at forty," she later mused.
(© A.M.P.A.S.)

The months of planning and execution which went into Cher's twelve-thousand-dollar "gown-to-lose-in" are far more typical of the sartorial norm in an evening where each thread and each bugle bead is meant for world consumption. (Joanne Woodward once cried when she had to accept her Oscar in a homemade dress, and Tom Cruise was chastised by an agent because the pants he wore to present an Oscar weren't tight enough.)

The moment Cher realized that she had lost an Oscar nomination (in favor of a hammy, dated, stagy performance by Anne Bancroft trying in vain to play a nun in *Agnes of God*), she called super-designer Bob Mackie to huddle with her in a New York penthouse. (Oscar watchers agree that Bancroft *took* Cher's nomination. Hers was the weakest performance of all the nominees.)

Mackie arrived to find a Cher who was hell-bent-for-leather determined to throw the Academy's massive affront back in its face. Even before Mackie sat down with his fabric samples and sketch pad, Cher barked at him: "They didn't nominate me this year so f—it . . . to hell with it! Let's have a good time."

Mackie, who almost single-handedly created the American Indian princess look which put Cher on the fashion map, understood perfectly what his client was saying: "She said it in fun to make sure I understood it wasn't a serious fashion statement. All of my circle of designers are friends of hers," said Mackie. "And we all felt she was kind of robbed this year by not being nominated. So I decided to give it a good ride."

Later, almost as an afterthought, Cher telephoned Mackie to give him a bittersweet message. "You know, I'm going to be forty this year," she said. "Shouldn't I show them that I still have it—that I still have the look of Cher from the early days?" she asked the designer.

"No doubt about it," he said.

"In the earlier days, she burst on the world with that glamorous Indian look with the loincloth and the bare midriff. It was kind of her signature mark in the early seventies."

So Mackie had two basic messages: Cher wanted to sling her allure at the gray-faced men, and for the most part, nondescript women who had turned their backs on her greatest work. And she wanted to show off the legs, the waist, the shoulders, and that endless midriff which had said volumes over the decades.

Cher had been asked to be a presenter in January, and work on the black gown and headdress began in February, during the week Cher was frozen out of the Oscar derby. This gave Mackie about five weeks, and he was going to need it. Leather was shipped in from Spain, beads from the Third World, and just the tiniest, choicest cuts of chiffon and satin to billow about those legs.

But the success of the whole thing rested on hackle feathers—rare spurts of plumage from feisty French roosters, themselves the rarest of farmyard fowl. The needs of that headdress went far further than that tall order. Normal hackle feathers are a puny five to six inches long—fine for most of the world. But impossible for Cher. Her Oscar crown demanded hackles of eight to nine inches—hackles to tower above her head and point to the rafters at the Los Angeles Music Center, where the Oscarcast is held.

So the hunt was on. Bob Mackie's operatives in provincial France trooped through legions of farm yards as they chased the necessary roosters across one-fourth of Europe. Like the plumage of egrets and the fast-running ostrich, hackles can be harvested without killing the birds, allowing them to produce more for a later day. The trick is catching them. "We about denuded Europe of prime hackles," Mackie chuckled. "But we got what we wanted."

Hackles in hand, Mackie constructed a Queen Elizabeth I foundation of velvet and stiffened sailcloth, with spines of plastic to hold it all aloft. Then each elegant hackle was hand-inserted into little synthetic quill holders—all of them angled to spurt the hackle fountain in a score of directions from the headdress. "Must have taken two weeks to put them all in," recalled one of Mackie's workmen. "Somebody said it was just like assembling a Rose Parade float."

Meanwhile, work on the boots, and the beaded chain mail of jets which barely—just barely—draped the actress's breasts proceeded in a handful of workshops in Los Angeles. Once assembled, Cher took one look at it and whooped victoriously.

Fashion gives women Oscar contenders a second language—a language denied to the penguin-suited men. They can say what they want through the magic of fabric, thread, and glitter.

And this language has rarely gone unused.

For instance, two years before *Mask*, when Cher was nominated as Best Supporting Actress for *Silkwood*, she huddled with Mackie and emerged with a true "serious actress gown" of understated chiffon and silk punctuated by crystal beads.

And gowns have played a true and enduring part in the Oscar cavalcade from the very earliest days when Mary Pickford ordered her Oscar gown from Paris the same week she started work on *Coquette*, the role she had decided would win the Oscar for her. They had a considerable luxury of time in those early days, when an actress of Pickford's stature used politics to guarantee the Oscar the minute she signed for the film. (Indeed, she told her friend Dorothy Gish that she wouldn't even have made *Coquette* if she hadn't wanted—some would have said *needed*—an Academy Award for her mantelpiece.)

Greer Garson, second from left, and Teresa Wright, far right, with their Best Actress and Best Supporting Actress awards for Mrs. Miniver *(1942). Oscarcasts during World War II were brimming with patriotism; also shown here are Van Heflin, left, Best Supporting Actor for* Johnny Eager, *in his army captain's uniform, and James Cagney, Best Actor for the patriotic* Yankee Doodle Dandy. *The Oscars themselves were gilded wood as the Academy did its part for the war effort. They were replaced by real Oscars in 1946.* (© A.M.P.A.S.)

For the sake of politics, Tyrone Power arrives at the 1938 Academy Awards with Norma Shearer, his co-star in Marie Antoinette. *Miss Shearer was up for Best Actress. The entrance, however, was just a glamorous façade. Ty bolted from Norma's side as soon as the house lights dimmed, and took off for a Palm Springs vacation with his wife, Annabella.*

Norma Shearer's Academy Award gown, created by MGM couturier Adrian, was one of the dresses in her winning film, *The Divorcée.* "That way," she explained to him, "people will see me holding the Oscar in the very same dress I wore in the film and will say—how very appropriate, how very, very appropriate."

It was television, however, which sealed fashion's overriding importance to the Oscar ceremony. With millions of people watching the movement of each pleat, the size of each abdomen, and the shape of each neck, panic and fear ruled each decision.

When Sally Field was up for *Norma Rae,* she came to Bob Mackie in a troubled state. "She was nervous," Mackie said. "But she wanted to prove to the audience that she sure as hell didn't look like Norma Rae. So we had a great, long meeting. I remember that she was trying not to look too serious (so serious it would look like she expected the Oscar), and neither did she want to look the grande dame."

They finally agreed on a chiffon suit with a beaded Hawaiian blouse. "It was very visually exciting," said Mackie. "And I thought it described Sally's essence to a T."

"There are so many ifs, ands, and maybes about it all," Mackie said. "It can be hell. They don't want to look like they just *knew* they would win; they don't want to look as if they are trying too hard; they don't want to look as if they are taking it all too lightly. Some kind of fashion balance has to be struck."

It can become very gothic and even silly, however—with touches of Norma Desmond, Clara Bow, and even *Whatever Happened to Baby Jane?*

Diana Ross will probably always hold the record for trying the hardest to look like a movie star the year she was nominated for the 1972 film *Lady Sings the Blues.* She jetted out to the West Coast to give Bob

Fashion maverick Lauren Hutton awash in crepe, satin, and costly Belgian lace (not to mention a king's ransom in diamonds), becoming the only major star to wear a hat to a recent ceremony. (They had been staples in the late thirties.)

As if to gild the lily, Zsa Zsa Gabor wrapped herself in a fifteen-thousand-dollar Givenchy gown complete with Marie of Rumania's rubies to attend the 1978 Oscar Board of Governors' Ball on the arm of Efrem Zimbalist, Jr. "There are some of us who still know how to celebrate Hollywood's biggest night," she spewed at a New Wave newspaper reporter.

Mackie an order for not one but two dresses. He provided a white silk pantsuit with a beaded vest for her to present an Oscar and a black beaded dress covered with black rosebuds in which to graciously receive her Academy Award.

That may have been tempting the fates: Diana never needed that basic black.

As with everything else about the Oscars, the fashion race begins early—at about the exact moment the nominations are announced.

It's an undeniable fact that Beverly Hills's swank Rodeo Drive has two big seasons: Christmas and Oscar month. At Giorgio's of Beverly Hills, the demand for formal gowns doubles during the weeks before the awards. "They come in looking not necessarily for an expensive dress, but for one that makes a grand entrance," says Fred Hayman, owner of Giorgio's. "We know our customers will want something special for the awards, so we often buy one-of-a-kind gowns."

The men gravitate to Jerry Magnin's on Rodeo Drive, where fully 30 percent of the tuxedos on display are hand-cut by the dozens of tailors who cater to the film industry.

The *real* stars of the evening, then, are the costly designer originals commented on by fashion reporters around the world in the next morning's newspapers. But during Oscar's first twenty-five years, fashion made little or no impact on the world because of the untelevised, little-photographed ceremonies. Winners collected their statuettes in an odd assortment of garb which ranged from the plain suits worn by Bette

Davis and Claudette Colbert to the elaborate film costumes favored by Norma Shearer and Mary Pickford.

In 1935 Colbert was forced to accept an Oscar wearing a wool traveling suit. She had been so certain that Norma Shearer would win that she was boarding a train for New York when her name was read as the honoree for *It Happened One Night*. A special police escort was sent to fetch her while the train was held at Union Station. Colbert's acceptance speech was one of the most practical: "I could say a lot more, but a cab is waiting so I'll just say thank you."

From the first televised show in 1953 to the present, appearance has ruled. And for the first sixteen televised years, designer Edith Head ran the whole fashion show and had the right of approval over gowns worn by presenters and winners.

"It wasn't as autocratic as it sounds," said Head in a 1979 interview. "Because the television censors were so strict, I was appointed guardian of hemlines and bodices. I sat in a little booth right at the entrance to the stage to check each outfit." For emergencies, Head, winner of eight Oscars for Best Costume Design, kept a kit of silk roses, shawls, and velvet wraparound skirts to drape across immodest stars.

"We had a crew backstage to keep stars from slipping by with irregular attire. I had three seamstresses, a prop man with a spray to dim the diamonds, and a large box of cleavage covers. These last were the most important. We couldn't trust the stars who were to go onstage. After I approved their gowns, some would push up their cleavages just before going on."

In one instance Edith Head's eagle eye failed, leading directly to the collapse of an Oscar dress code. The year was 1966, when miniskirts were just starting to dominate international fashion. Julie Christie, almost certain to win Best Actress honors for *Darling*, was also starring in *Doctor Zhivago*. The Academy flew her from London to Los Angeles to be a presenter. Christie, refusing Head's help in fashioning a gown,

Claudette Colbert in the gray traveling suit she wore to accept her Best Actress Oscar for It Happened One Night. *Supposedly unaware of her win, she had been ready to board a train for New York when she was pulled off and hustled to the ceremony by a desperate Oscar organizer. This story seems somewhat unlikely since in 1935 the winners were known weeks in advance. But it's the story Claudette tells. More likely, she simply didn't think it a big deal until she was hauled off the train.* (© A.M.P.A.S.)

Bette Davis and Spencer Tracy: the essence of Oscar glamor, thirties-style. Her fashion designer (Collette) must have raided every egret's nest in Europe to make the crushed velvet dress into a stunner. Davis recalled that in those days "the studio started working on its nominees slightly after dawn—continuing into our limos headed for the Oscars." Davis was taking home her second Oscar, for 1938's Jezebel, *and Tracy clutched his second, for* Boys Town. (© A.M.P.A.S.)

Julie Christie in a panorama of moods as she accepts her Best Actress Oscar for Darling *in 1966. To accept her Best Actress prize, she showed up in mini-length gold pajamas from Carnaby Street—the very year the Academy had officially banned minis. Julie managed to sneak past Oscar costumer Edith Head and break the rule—opening a floodgate.* (© A.M.P.A.S.)

said, "I've brought a little something over from Britain." When Christie dashed by the official booth, Head looked at the demure neckline and nodded instant approval—without realizing that the booth, designed well before miniskirts, allowed Head to see only from the top of Christie's thighs up.

As the actress swept onstage there was an audible gasp of admiration for the mini she'd bought off the rack at a London boutique. Head peered around the curtain and whispered, "Oh my God!"

"It was the end of an era when stars spent months planning their gowns," Head once said in regret. "I remember one year when elegance still reigned and Joan Crawford, a super-perfectionist, had me design the same dress for her in both white and black. Each cost three thousand dollars." Crawford was worried about the actress who was presenting an award right before the one she would present—a rival, Deborah Kerr, who had officially informed the Academy that she would be wearing white. "I don't trust her," Crawford told Head. "I think she might change at the last minute." The inevitable happened: Kerr showed up in white. "Joan switched to the black gown and was the hit of the evening," Head recalled.

In 1955 an innocent rosebud stuck in the blond hair of an Oscar winner brought the fashion world to its feet.

"I had designed a dress for Grace Kelly that was just perfect," Head said. "Her hairstyle, a pageboy, was equally perfect."

As the actress passed Head's perch on her way to present an award, the designer noticed that Kelly's golden tresses were losing their curl and slipping down her neck. Head grabbed a rose from her own ensemble and slid it into Kelly's hair. A hairpin was added, and the future princess swept onstage. The Grace Kelly chignon was born. The style, complete with rosebud, was copied by women around the world.

Joan Crawford, her husband Douglas Fairbanks, Jr., and director Frank Lloyd, three members of Hollywood's royalty arriving at the 1930 Oscars. The Academy Awards were a family affair in those days. They didn't even call the award Oscar then, and it had no effect on the box office—not that anyone could tell.

Award-winning costume designer Edith Head. (© A.M.P.A.S.)

For that appearance, Head had designed one of the most expensive Oscar ensembles ever: Kelly's ice-blue silk gown. The material alone cost $4,000 because the rare color could be achieved only by dyeing individual threads before the fabric was specially woven in Paris.

The story of Grace Kelly's twelve-thousand-dollar Oscar gown revealed the interwoven stitches of greed, glamour, and sartorial arrogance of gothic Hollywood. As early as December 1954, when *The Country Girl* had been in release for only a few weeks, the Paramount executive corps decided that Grace would not only win an Oscar but that she would receive it packaged as a sort of intergalactic Barbie doll to be admired the world over.

"She will be in blue champagne!" said Edith Head. "The silk will match the bag and gloves. The pearls will be only the most select 'ivory globes' from the Indian Ocean, and the beaded bag will be fashioned from more than four thousand mother-of-pearl beads from the coast of Kenya."

With this terse yet baroque edict, Edith set in motion a queen's ransom of weavers, cobblers, pearl divers, and goldsmiths which would have pleased Marie Antoinette.

Starting in February, Grace stood for twelve fittings as Edith's drapers cut and shaped the silk into a cascade which perfectly matched the willowy elegance of Grace Kelly.

On the way to the ceremony, Edith rode through the streets of Los Angeles in Cecil B. De Mille's own limousine with Grace at her side. "Even then I was stitching seed pearls inside the folds of the dress," Edith recalled. "All day we had been in a dither over the champagne silk slippers—which were too small and had to be stretched by a leather expert in downtown Los Angeles. But it was all worth it. I'll never forget the gasps that greeted her arrival at the Pantages Theater."

"I designed [the dress] to swirl lightly about her as she glided up to get that Oscar," Edith recalled. "There was never the slightest doubt in my mind that she *would* get it. I just wanted to make sure she looked like a million dollars as she gave that acceptance speech" (also carefully crafted, but never used, by the Paramount bank of staff screenwriters).

A ten-thousand-dollar Halston that Liz Taylor wore to the 1972 Oscars was the recent record holder. (Cher's $12,000 Bob Mackie gown for the 1986 Oscarcast now holds the record for the eighties.) The gown was created as a showcase for the one-and-a-half-million-dollar diamond Richard Burton had recently given her. (Three security guards surrounded Taylor during the ceremony and party afterward.)

The gowns thought to be among the most expensive at the 1984 ceremony were Joan Collins's three-thousand-dollar confection highlighted by red, white, and black bugle beads, and Dyan Cannon's fourteen-hundred-dollar black-and-white silk dress—both created by Ron Talsky, official designer for the 1984 ceremony and Oscar fashion's chicest man of the hour.

Since the advent of television, two Oscar ensembles have garnered the most press attention: Barbra Streisand's black see-through pajamas in 1969 and Joanne Woodward's homemade frock in 1958.

Woodward accepted the Best Actress award for *The Three Faces of Eve* in a dress she had made herself on an old sewing machine. "I thought Liz Taylor would walk off with the award for *Raintree County,* so I didn't invest a lot of money in the dress. I was convinced nobody would see it."

The almost-nude look of Streisand's harem outfit in 1969 was an illusion. The star wore a multilayered pantsuit selected by the producer of the Oscar show, Howard W. Koch. "Barbra took all the heat for that," Koch recalled. "But it was my fault. She came to me with three outfits. Close up, the black one looked dazzling. But I hadn't counted on the lights from a TV camera that made the fabric appear invisible."

The panic Howard saw on Barbra's face when she ran to him for last-minute advice spoke volumes about how insecure the actress was over her own image. "We shut down production of *On A Clear Day You Can See Forever* early so Barbra could get ready for the ceremony," Koch, the film's producer, recalled.

The actress grabbed Koch's arm and virtually dragged him back to her dressing room, where she paraded three outfits before him.

"The first one was a sort of tailored black-and-white dress—I remember it very well. It had a collar and yards of heavy material."

"It makes you look like Old Mother Hubbard," said the producer. "Chuck it."

Her second choice was no better. "I don't even remember that one. But it seemed to detract from Barbra's own allure."

The splendid Streisand derrière the night she accepted her Oscar for Funny Girl. *This see-through onstage look was soon all the rage. Within weeks Janis Joplin appeared equally undressed before a crowd in San Francisco and Twiggy was seen in a West End revue wearing a carbon copy of Streisand's glittery pajamas.* (© A.M.P.A.S.)

"Forget it," advised Koch.

The Great Streisand slumped onto a divan—a lady bereft of fashion on what was to be the most important night of her life.

The luminous eyes lowered and the Chinese Ming fingernails rapped noisily against each other. She sighed deeply before a gleam appeared in her eyes.

"Well, I have one other thing, Mr. Koch," she said. "But you may not like it."

"Put it on," Koch ordered.

Several calculated minutes later Streisand coyly reentered the room in a billowing getup which defied description. Yvonne De Carlo, queen of the harem pictures, would have loved it. It began with a coat of gauzelike material which swirled around Streisand's figure like transparent crepe paper gone wild. It was gathered ever so cutely at the wrists and ankles, apparently to prevent the gossamer tucks from coming loose in the blasts of conditioned air which wafted through the Oscar-night audience.

Since Barbra's dressing room was murky and Koch's eyes were tired, he failed to notice that the outer coating of the dress—if it could correctly be called a dress—disappeared when struck by light. Koch could, however, see the tucked bikini pants and chiffon bra which shielded the star from complete nudity.

The actress twirled before him in her dressing room and shook her straight-cropped hair.

"That's what I call an Oscar outfit," Koch said, propelling his star from the set toward the limo for a date with an Academy statuette.

"When it turned transparent, I wasn't affronted," Koch remembered. "It was a great moment. I defy anyone who watched to forget."

The psychedelic late sixties eroded the glamour so critical to Oscar's survival as an international event. Shapeless tie-dyed monstrosities, plastic jewelry, and garish prints dominated. Inger Stevens arrived one year decked out in vinyl, and Fonda accepted her Oscar for *Klute* in a Mao pantsuit.

When TV ratings plummeted, the Academy outlawed fluorescent colors and wild prints, hoping to return the show to its more traditional formality. This panicked the stars, who scrambled for a way to dress mod while bowing to Oscar's conservatism.

Enter two designers: Bob Mackie, whose glitzy costumes for Cher and Carol Burnett had set the industry on its ear, and Ron Talsky. Mackie studied past Oscar broadcasts and tested fabrics during fully lighted onstage run-throughs. He determined that the special requirements of looking fabulous while alighting from a limo or bounding up a moving stage required one-of-a-kind gowns. By 1975 Mackie was *the* Oscar designer, creating seventeen of the twenty-five superstar gowns that year.

Talsky began his rise with one very special dress, an Oscar gown that also ignited a love affair between the handsome costumer and the beautiful Raquel Welch. Talsky explained: "Raquel had her heart set on wearing a carefully draped print dress in 1971 despite the Academy's ban." So he created a subtle sheath. "I suddenly was 'in' after the next day's fashion columns. And that one dress began a long, romantic affair between Raquel and me—a marvelous fringe benefit." (Though the affair is over, Talsky and Welch have remained friends.)

Mackie and Talsky ushered in the era of sequins, beads, and the

Presenter Raquel Welch in the dress that launched a blazing love affair. In 1971 Raquel just couldn't seem to find the dazzlingly proper gown for the Oscarcast, and a friend told her to try a new guy on the Oscar block, Ron Talsky. She did, and took him along as her escort as well. They fell into each other's lives, arms, and residences for an enduring affair which pumped up the gossip columns for years. "It was the best fringe benefit I ever got from my service as an Oscar designer," Talsky later quipped.

super-dressy look. One exception was the 1977 awards ceremony, which emerged as perhaps the dowdiest show in history. The Academy had surrendered control of the show to the difficult, autocratic director William Friedkin, who decreed that everyone would wear black and white. He also sent a curt directive to the presenters that said: "No sequins, no beads, no rhinestones." Mackie immediately resigned as the show's official fashion designer. Then Friedkin went one step further: he told all the actresses they must bring their gowns to him for personal approval. Many, like Jane Fonda, refused. "It's none of his business what I wear," she snapped before showing up in a muted, beige gown. Ellen Burstyn, Best Actress winner for *Alice Doesn't Live Here Anymore*, brought three dresses to Friedkin. The director disapproved of them all. Burstyn stormed off, and when she reported the night of the show, the actress was wearing an oversize man's tuxedo. She fumed at Friedkin. "You wanted black and white, no sequins, and you got it."

In 1979 the Academy began offering free gowns to the presenters if they would agree to place themselves in the hands of the show's official costumer. Kim Novak was the first to accept the Academy's offer—with smashing results. She had been in retirement for five years when she agreed to be a presenter. Talsky, serving as Oscar costumer for the first time, approached the legendary superstar with some timidity. Novak

A picture worth a thousand words: Oscar and Kim Novak as she came out of retirement for the 1979 awards. Novak had summoned designer Ron Talsky to her northern California hideaway and huddled with him before a bank of mirrors. She took his hand. "This has to be the most fabulous dress of my career. I'm coming out of retirement with this appearance." She then gave the designer a series of precise measurements. "But Miss Novak," said the embarrassed Talsky. "You are a bit larger than that right now." "Never mind," said Kim, "I'll fit into the dress on Oscar night." "And she did," said Talsky, "with a bit to spare."
(© A.M.P.A.S.)

took Talsky's hand and said, "This has to be the best dress you've ever designed because it's going to signal my return to Hollywood." He created a bias-cut satin number that hugged every curve of Novak's body. When Talsky was fitting the final pattern, Novak instructed him to cut the dress far smaller than her size. "Don't worry," she assured him, "I'll lose the fourteen pounds."

"It was only two weeks until the Oscars, but she lost that and a bit more," he says.

Not all couturiers are as pliant as Bob Mackie when it comes to meeting Oscar's sartorial needs. For example, Halston—designer for Jackie Kennedy, Marisa Berenson, and Liza Minnelli. Ann Miller asked him to do a special "comeback dress" for her appearance with Mickey Rooney at the 1980 Academy Awards ceremony. "I've got to look good after six years on the road with *Sugar Babies*," Ann told the New York fashion prince. Halston instantly decided to draw on Ann Miller's status as the "sequin queen" during her tenure in MGM musicals. He ordered sequined blue fabric of the kind MGM costumers used to fashion her scanty dance costumes in such films as *Kiss Me Kate* and *Lovely to Look At*.

When she showed up for the first fitting Halston told her: "I've got something simple but elegant planned, but I'd like to make one quick suggestion: please get rid of that antiquated hairstyle." Ann took one look at the glitzy, clinging gown being fitted and reluctantly agreed.

Ann Miller in her four-thousand-dollar Halston with Mickey Rooney at the 1980 Oscarcast. A bright Egyptian blue, the gown had been commissioned by Ann. "I want to show some of that old 'MGM flash,'" she told Halston. Seamstresses sewed more than ten thousand beads onto the dress in swirls that caught the spotlight dazzlingly. Ann and Mickey were then appearing together in the boffo stage show Sugar Babies *and were introduced by Johnny Carson as "two of the movies' greatest natural assets."*

Bogie and Joan Crawford arriving at Romanoff's for the 1954 nominations telecast.

Then she shot back at him: "You know I've got to be quite careful because I'm afraid that my hair might be more famous than I am."

Halston has remained so blasé about the Oscarcasts that he has turned down repeated requests from Hollywood's high and mighty, such as Oscar winners Geraldine Page and Anjelica Huston—both rejected by the couturier in 1986. "I just didn't have time," he pleaded a bit unconvincingly. Could it be that he didn't wish to see the corpulent Gerry Page clomping up the fabled stairway with a Halston flapping about her like an Arabian tent?

But he has never turned down Liz Taylor—even when in 1976 she summoned him to the coast to craft a gown for her to wear in the Oscar finale.

"Liz had originally asked for the dress weeks before the Oscarcast," Halston recalled. "And I said, 'Come out to New York and we'll see what we can do.' I just don't flit about the country just to make one dress—no matter how big the star." Then Liz called Halston late one night at home. "Please, please come out here and do that dress," she pleaded. "I really need it desperately."

So Halston made an exception and flew to the coast, staying in a Beverly Hills Hotel bungalow not far from Liz's own. The creation he crafted—a clinging, red-sequined confection—brought down the Oscar house in the final minutes of the show. And Halston got one unexpected fringe benefit: he became Liz's date for the show.

As the glitter has faded on Oscar's coattails, crowd pleasers have become rarer and rarer. But here are two: Young Timothy Hutton arrives to collect his Best Supporting Actor Oscar for Ordinary People *in a tux by Ralph Lauren. Farrah Fawcett drew gasps in a metalic dress which seemed to be poured across her body. Farrah almost stayed home that night after the L.A.* Times *questioned her appropriateness as a presenter. "We need you; we need your glamor," producer Howard W.Koch pleaded. Miss Fawcett was wooed back.*

CHAPTER SEVEN

Milking the Oscar Tree

What's all this fuss over John Wayne's Oscar ads? People have been buying Oscars for at least twenty-five years. —HEDDA HOPPER, 1960

John Wayne was mighty satisfied as he picked up the afternoon papers on February 27, 1961. A broad grin spread across his face. *The Alamo,* his mediocre tribute to American freedom, had been nominated for seven Academy Awards, including the big one: Best Picture of 1960.

Hollywood hadn't wanted the picture made in the first place. But "the big guy" (that's what they called Wayne in those days) had bullied, shoved, and pleaded until several studio financiers gave him the go-ahead. Even then, Wayne had to pour his entire fortune, almost a million dollars, into his opus about Jim Bowie, Davy Crockett (played by Wayne), and other Texas heroes.

Filmed in 65-mm. and patriot-color, *The Alamo* opened to reviews that could only be described as "lukewarm," by Wayne fans, or derisive, by more honest moviegoers. The Duke had directed the film himself, so the Hollywood elite said polite things, such as, "It seems like the work of a veteran director, not a newcomer," and "We knew he had it in him."

The voices weren't strong enough for Wayne; somewhere along the line he began to feel that Hollywood owed him an Oscar for *The Alamo.* He had, after all, dreamed of making his personal celluloid testimony for more than a decade. So it galled him when Tinseltown's artistic elite called it a "nice little picture," nice but pale compared to the other masterpieces made in 1960—*Psycho, Inherit the Wind, Exodus,* and *Spartacus* among them.

Those movies were all part of the town's incessant "Oscar talk." *The Alamo* was not. Wayne decided that the situation was not only unfair, it was downright unpatriotic. Jetting in from Rome, he faced down some reporters at the airport and barked: "This isn't the first time the Alamo has been the underdog. We need defenders today just as they did one hundred twenty-five years ago." But reporters were growing tired of Wayne's blind encomiums of his picture, and he received a wave of bad press.

Hollywood folks just weren't getting the message, so Wayne picked **119**

up the phone and called super-publicist Russell Birdwell, the man who had created the hysteria over David O. Selznick's *Gone With The Wind* (largely by publicizing the search for someone to play Scarlett O'Hara). Birdwell was never a man to rate the artistic value of any of the movies he hyped, and Wayne gave him enough money to exceed even the high costs of past Oscar campaigns.

The publicist already knew that an Oscar nomination and perhaps even the Oscar itself could be bought. Who should know better than the publicists? Out of an Academy membership of about 2,000 in 1960, more than 200 were publicists and executives representing large public relations companies.

"A few hundred votes, and sometimes as few as twenty-five or fifty, one way or the other, could determine the winner," said Henry Rogers, co-founder of Rogers and Cowan Public Relations and a veteran of dozens of successful Oscar campaigns. "The Academy Awards are more of a popularity contest than a talent contest," said Rogers. "Whether Hol-

John Wayne and company on location for The Alamo *in Brackettville, Texas. Many Texans and thousands of vacationers from other states turned out to watch one of the great legends direct a film. What they found was a man of large humor acting very little like a director and much like the guy next door. It was sad, therefore, when the Oscar campaign made a laughingstock of this achievement. A great fear seems to be abroad during Oscar time—a fear that says advertise or perish.*

lywood likes to face up to it or not, the voter casts his ballot emotionally, and not critically. Unable to decide which performance he feels is best, he allows his emotions to take over—he has no choice."

John Wayne and Russell Birdwell decided to work these emotions up to a fever pitch. They started with a press release, the likes of which had never been seen before—even in Hollywood. It ran 183 pages, positively dripped with sugary adjectives, and depicted Wayne as the George Washington of films, storming the celluloid heights for God and country.

Then came the ads—hundreds of them. Every day Hollywood opened up the trade papers to find new ads, full-page and with fist-sized headlines.

The ad campaign didn't stop with asking the Oscar voters to consider *The Alamo*. It soon acquired a bullying tone. And the message was simple: If you don't vote for *The Alamo*, you're not patriotic.

Hollywood commentators, used to such drivel, kept silent at first. But it finally got too bad—even for them. "The implication is unmistakable," said Dick Williams, entertainment editor of the *Los Angeles Mirror*. "Oscar voters are being appealed to on a patriotic basis. The impression is left that one's proud sense of Americanism may be suspected if one does not vote for *The Alamo*."

He made a public appeal, asking Wayne to stop. "Obviously," said Williams, "one can be the most ardent of American patriots and still think *The Alamo* was a mediocre movie."

John Wayne was just waiting for this signal. He assaulted the Oscar beachhead as if it were Iwo Jima. The ads were doubled and became even stronger. OSCAR WILL MAKE UP HIS OWN MIND, read one headline. One ad, which ran for several days, personally attacked Williams, depicting him as a scandal-sheet writer.

Williams figured the cost of *"The Alamo* Campaign" at "over $75,000 and probably as much as $150,000." Some Academy officers were insulted; but many more were not. Because it worked. Bringing in seven nominations, *The Alamo* was listed as one of the five Best Picture nominees along with *The Apartment, Elmer Gantry, Sons and Lovers,* and *The Sundowners.* Edged out by the blatant campaign were *Psycho, Sunrise at Campobello, Never on Sunday, Inherit the Wind, Dark at the Top of the Stairs, Exodus,* and *Spartacus.*

To this day, the Wayne-Birdwell campaign remains the low point of the Oscar derby. And if Wayne's own Oscar campaign was deplorable, one of his stars, Chill Wills, made it much worse. Wills had been in Hollywood since 1935, playing his down-home, corn-pone character in film after film. He decided *The Alamo* was his chance. His personal Oscar campaign even outdid Wayne's, culminating in a double-truck ad listing by name hundreds of Academy voters. "Win, lose, or draw," said the ad, "you're all my cousins and I love you all." Groucho Marx replied with his own ad: "Dear Chill, I am delighted to be your cousin, but I voted for Sal Mineo."

Then Wills decided to call on God. In an ad, under a picture of the entire *Alamo* cast, Wills wrote, "We of *The Alamo* cast are praying—harder than the real Texans prayed for their lives at the Alamo—for Chill Wills to win the Oscar . . . Cousin Chill's acting was great. Your Alamo Cousins."

John Wayne, finally waking up to the excess he had helped create, took out a personal ad in the *Hollywood Reporter* and *Variety*. The

"It's up to Oscar": This ad, which ran during the shameless Oscar campaigning of 1961, brought loud guffaws from the tables in Beverly Hills's bistros, since it capped a year-long campaign to gain an Oscar nomination for John Wayne's overlong, overblown film The Alamo. *But the advertising worked and the film took home a bushel basket of Oscar nominations. There is some evidence that the campaign may not have been necessary. The Wayne-directed movie was generally respected for his deft handling of the colossal battle scene.*

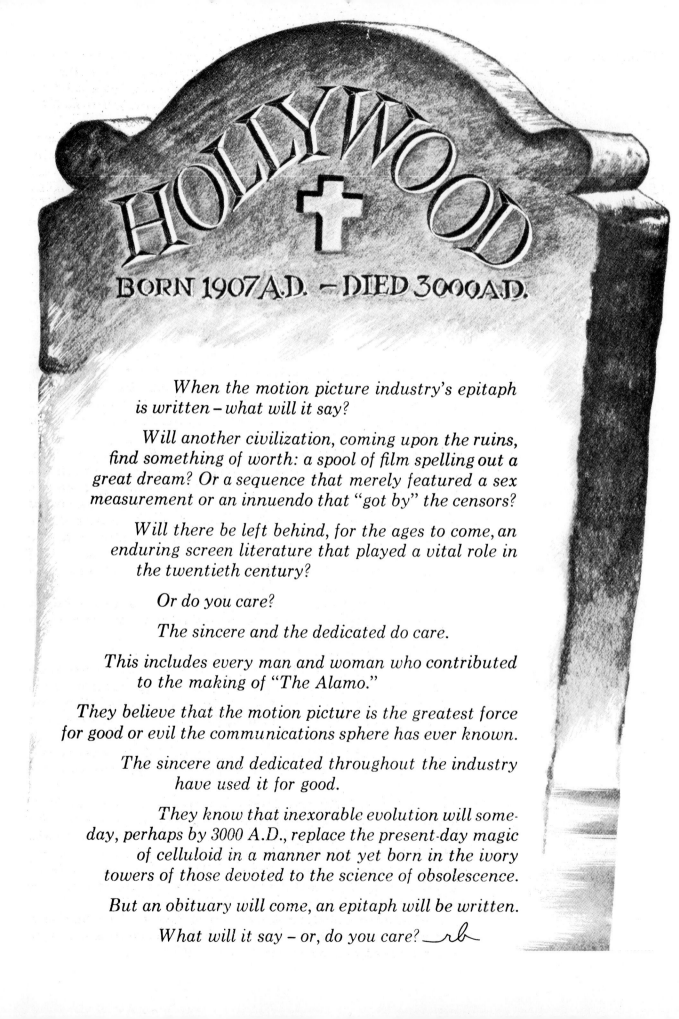

HOLLYWOOD ✝

BORN 1907 A.D. — DIED 3000 A.D.

When the motion picture industry's epitaph is written – what will it say?

Will another civilization, coming upon the ruins, find something of worth: a spool of film spelling out a great dream? Or a sequence that merely featured a sex measurement or an innuendo that "got by" the censors?

Will there be left behind, for the ages to come, an enduring screen literature that played a vital role in the twentieth century?

Or do you care?

The sincere and the dedicated do care.

This includes every man and woman who contributed to the making of "The Alamo."

They believe that the motion picture is the greatest force for good or evil the communications sphere has ever known.

The sincere and dedicated throughout the industry have used it for good.

They know that inexorable evolution will some-day, perhaps by 3000 A.D., replace the present-day magic of celluloid in a manner not yet born in the ivory towers of those devoted to the science of obsolescence.

But an obituary will come, an epitaph will be written.

What will it say – or, do you care?

actor admitted that the campaign had gone too far, concluding: 'No one in the Batjac organization [Wayne's producing company] or in the Russell Birdwell office has been a party to [Mr. Wills'] trade paper advertising. I refrain from using stronger language because I'm sure his intentions were not as bad as his taste."

In *Shooting Star*, Maurice Zolotow, Wayne's principal biographer, expressed his belief that Wayne was exhausted and pursued by demons after *The Alamo* experience. "He had gone through a terrible and lengthy journey to get to the place where, finally, the film was up for the Oscar. He was physically and mentally at the end of his tether. He was overwhelmed by debts and everything he owned was mortgaged for the money he had raised to make the film."

This campaign was excessive but was certainly not an isolated example. For thirty years Hollywood press agents, studio executives, and overly zealous agents had been tastelessly beating drums to bag both nominations and Oscars. In 1956 Jennifer Jones was nominated for *Love Is a Many-Splendored Thing* thanks to trade-paper ads specially printed in gold ink; Cecil B. De Mille's cartoonlike *The Greatest Show on Earth* stole the Oscar in 1953 from *High Noon* after a campaign as noisy as a circus parade; and a golden-worded bit of ballyhoo enabled Lee Marvin's *Cat Ballou* cowboy to take the 1965 Best Actor award away from Rod Steiger (*The Pawnbroker*), Richard Burton (*The Spy Who Came In from the Cold*), Laurence Olivier (*Othello*), and Oskar Werner (*Ship of Fools*).

A similar splash by MGM in 1951 got a Best Picture Oscar for *An American in Paris*, Vincente Minnelli's frothy ballet film, which was charming but not truly the best film of the year. That campaign created more injustice than most because the musical beat out *A Place in the Sun*, *A Streetcar Named Desire*, *Quo Vadis*, and *Decision Before Dawn*. (Because of MGM's intense prenomination campaign for *Quo Vadis* and *An American in Paris*, those lightweights aced out *Death of a Salesman*, *The African Queen*, *Detective Story*, and Hitchcock's *Strangers on a Train*.)

The Academy gets its back up about all this politicking every three or four years and fights back by announcing that the Oscar race is totally unconnected with the massive ad wars.

If only this were true.

Sadly, ruthless Oscar politics are as much a part of the process as the gold statue itself. Joan Crawford once said, "He who barks loudest in the Oscar race gets scratched first and best. Some very talented performers have refused to dirty their hands. And those actors were out in the cold while much inferior actors made the golden circle."

And Crawford should know. She waged not only the most famous campaign for an Oscar; she and her publicist, Henry Rogers, wrote the book on buying one.

The year was 1945, and Crawford's career was on the line. Since 1925, she had been at the top of filmdom's heap, first as the veritable image of the Jazz Age, then as the hard-luck shopgirl-who-makes-good of the thirties, and finally as the successor to Greta Garbo and Claudette Colbert at the pinnacle of glamour. She'd married and divorced Douglas Fairbanks, Jr., Franchot Tone and Philip Terry. In 1940 she was the fourth highest paid woman in America.

She had all the laurel leaves of Hollywood success. All but the Oscar. And the fact that she had never even won a nomination was starting to gnaw at the edges of her career.

This ridiculous tombstone, predicting the death of Hollywood, appeared in the Hollywood Reporter *as part of an ad package intimating that even God considered this film* (The Alamo) *the best ever made. But Wayne and his publicist, Russell Birdwell, didn't stop with the trade papers. They issued a two-hundred-page press release and strung a banner across Sunset Boulevard that read, "This Is the Most Important Motion Picture Ever Made. It's Timeless. It Will Run Forever."*

One night, after she read that her arch-rival Norma Shearer had been nominated for the fifth time, she turned to her daughter Christina and began spitting out her frustration. "It doesn't matter how brilliant an actor's performance is. The awards are a dole—a reward to the studios rather than a fair vote. If a star had won the award the year before, no one at the same studio has a chance."

She knew what she was talking about; for several years Joan Crawford was not only a member of the Academy, but as the daughter-in-law of Academy founders and officers Douglas Fairbanks, Sr. and Mary Pickford, was privy to the intimate machinations of the organization.

Crawford finally resigned from the Academy to protest the studio system's grabbing control of the nomination process. Nobody denied that she had reason to be angry at the Academy and her studio. For twenty years she had been getting only cast-off roles rejected by Mrs. Irving Thalberg and Greta Garbo, who was treated with kid gloves by everyone at Metro. Even when she sparkled in a role, as she did in *Grand Hotel*, MGM invariably threw its weight behind Shearer, Garbo, or Marie Dressler.

There's no doubt that the studio could have gotten her a nomination and probably an Oscar had it wanted to. By 1935 the Academy of Motion Picture Arts and Sciences had a membership of around forty (depending on which officer you quote), and the big men associated with the organization frequently made their wishes known since financing of the awards came largely from the studios.

Then the roof caved in on most of MGM's big stars, making talk of Oscars a frivolity. Garbo and Shearer suddenly found their pictures turning into flops, and Joan Crawford—along with Marlene Dietrich, Katharine Hepburn, and Mae West—was labeled by the exhibitors as "box office poison."

Crawford felt she had one last chance at MGM. She needed strong parts, not the parade of shopgirls she'd done for the past five years. She needed to abandon her furs, her wide-eyed, high-fashion look. "I need something I can get my teeth into," she told her friend Dore Freeman, then in charge of the MGM still department. "But I don't know if I'll get it."

Crawford was making a fashion-program picture called *Mannequin* when she got word that MGM had bought Clare Boothe Luce's study of female bitchiness, *The Women*. Shearer, Rosalind Russell, and Joan Fontaine were already cast, and the rest of the parts had been penciled in.

"I want to play Crystal," said Crawford after assaulting Louis B. Mayer in his office.

"Why, Joan?" asked Mayer. "The woman is crude, unredeemed."

"But," said Crawford, jutting out her chin in defiance, "it's the best part in the picture. And I can do it."

Mayer made Crawford audition for director George Cukor, who took her. It was to be the last stand in the fifteen-year Shearer-Crawford feud.

Joan and Rosalind Russell stole the picture, and Crawford traded her chit from that film for a chance to play a disfigured beauty in *A Woman's Face*. A year later, however, she found herself back in the rut. "I want out of my contract," she told Mayer. "Now!" After a long fight, the boss agreed to let Crawford go, telling friends that he felt her career would crumble without MGM's protection.

A month later Jack Warner grabbed her for a fee of $100,000 a picture. But Joan had tasted, finally, success as an actress, and not just any script would do. "Joan realized," said Dore Freeman, "that this was a comeback for her. What she did would make the difference. She would sink or swim on the strength of one picture."

She could find no script good enough for two years, which is a long time for a film star to be offscreen. Then she read the script of James M. Cain's *Mildred Pierce*. "This is it," she told Jack Warner. "This is the right role." Warner heaved a sigh of relief. Bette Davis had turned it down, so Crawford's decision solved two problems at once.

Mildred Pierce was only a week into production when producer Jerry Wald saw something special in the daily rushes. He smelled an Oscar in the making. He called publicist Henry Rogers, Crawford's press agent, and the Oscar hype of all Oscar hypes was born.

"Why don't you start a campaign for Joan to win the Oscar?" asked Wald.

"But, Jerry, the picture's just starting."

"So what?" asked Wald, who told Rogers to call Hedda Hopper and feed her a column item about Joan's performance in the film. It worked.

Two days later, readers across America, but most importantly those in Hollywood, woke up to this from Hedda: "Insiders say that Joan Crawford is delivering such a terrific performance in *Mildred Pierce* that she's a cinch for the Academy Award." That night Wald went to a Beverly Hills party and had his own item fed back to him. Producer Hal

Joan Crawford in Mildred Pierce
(1945), *which won her an Oscar.*

Wallis sidled up to Wald: "Hey, Jerry it looks like Crawford's going to win the Oscar. I don't know where I heard it; I must have read it somewhere."

Henry Rogers, who has been called the Henry Kissinger of Hollywood publicists, decided to launch a full-blown Oscar campaign, which he described in *Walking the Tightrope: Confessions of a Public Relations Man*, a rare and truthful look at the inner workings of movie publicity. He went out to Joan's dressing room at Warners and broke the campaign to her bit by bit, saying, "I wish I could take credit for this. But it's Jerry's idea. I want your approval to start a campaign right here and now to get people in the industry thinking in advance that you're going to win the Oscar."

Crawford, in full *Mildred Pierce* makeup, raised one eyebrow. "Go ahead, I'm listening."

"If Hedda ran the kind of item she did this morning, I'm sure I can get other columnists to jump on the Joan Crawford bandwagon. Joan, you know as well as I do that members of the Academy vote emotionally. People in our business can be well influenced by what they read and what they hear. Word of mouth has a tremendous advantage. This town is indignant over the way you were treated at MGM. You've cultivated the press all these years, and they love you."

Crawford was silent. She lit a cigarette, and shook her head. "I'm worried about one thing. It could kick back and I could become the laughingstock if it ever got out that Joan Crawford's press agent was plugging her for an Academy Award."

Rogers pulled out a draft of his plan, with all the techniques centered on secrecy and the necessity for all the publicity breaks to seem spontaneous. She reluctantly gave the go-ahead. "It sounds good. But I don't think it can work. I've never been well liked in this business. I've given performances before that I thought deserved Academy consideration, but I never had a chance. People in Hollywood don't like me, and they've never regarded me as a good actress."

Six months after the innocent little sentence in Hopper's column, Rogers's plan was having an effect on Warner Bros. itself. Jack Warner, picking up vibes from Rogers's journalistic whispers, told assistants that *Mildred Pierce* "is going to be a much more important picture than we originally thought."

There were lines at the box office when the film opened in Los Angeles and New York. The next day Warner ordered the studio to go all out for the Academy Awards, starting a series of ads unprecedented in the eighteen-year history of the Academy Awards. Rogers thought Crawford would win; so did Jack Warner and, ironically, Louis B. Mayer.

Only Crawford herself had doubts.

The day of the awards, Crawford called Rogers. "I can't do it, Henry. I'm so frightened, I know I'm going to lose. They won't vote for me."

"Nonsense," said Rogers. "They love a comeback story. You're going to win. I can feel it."

The actress only shook her head. Then Wald called her. He didn't have to say much. After all, he'd taken a chance on her when nobody else would, casting her in *Mildred Pierce* against the advice of Warner executives and even the film's director, Michael Curtiz.

"I'll try," she said. "I'll try." Her dress was laid out, her hair done. But Crawford was forty then, which is the breaking point for most Hollywood stars, and insecurity took over. Her iron will failed her for the first time; the years and the disappointments had gotten to her. She faltered in late afternoon when her temperature soared to 104 and her doctor ordered her to bed.

Crawford's good friend and biographer, Bob Thomas of the Associated Press, wrote about that night thirty years later. "She deserved the prize, she realized. But would they give it to her?" But by God, she had showed them! While her arch-rivals at MGM, Norma Shearer, Greta Garbo, and Jeannette MacDonald, had vanished from the screen, Joan had returned in triumph. She had dangerously absented herself from the world's theaters for two years, an eternity in the life of a star. It was an arduous time, during which the lack of income and a calamitous third marriage had depleted her savings. She waited and waited, and found *Mildred Pierce*."

At about nine Crawford curled up in her bed, in a Parisian robe and gown. So certain of victory was Henry Rogers that he had brought carefully chosen photographers to the house; the radio had been turned on for an hour.

Finally, Charles Boyer, onstage at Grauman's Chinese Theater, announced the nominees: Ingrid Bergman in *The Bells of St. Mary's*, Joan Crawford in *Mildred Pierce*, Greer Garson in *The Valley of Decision*, Jennifer Jones in *Love Letters*, and Gene Tierney in *Leave Her to Heaven*.

When Crawford's name was read as the winner, her eyes turned moist for only a second. Everyone turned as she looked up and said: "This is the greatest moment of my life."

And no one doubted that she meant it.

A triumphant Joan Crawford takes her Oscar for Mildred Pierce *shortly after midnight. Crawford's bedside was attended by reporters and photographers. Over the years, the rumor grew that Crawford had been perfectly well that night. The truth is that she had a temperature of 104 as she reclined in bed, listening to the Oscar show on the radio. The temperature subsided the moment her name was called—"Take your Oscar and go to bed, Joan." But the evening wasn't totally without artifice: her nightgown and wrap were designed by Helen Rose, and a trio of makeup men and hairdressers had worked over her face and hair before she let the photographers in.* (© A.M.P.A.S.)

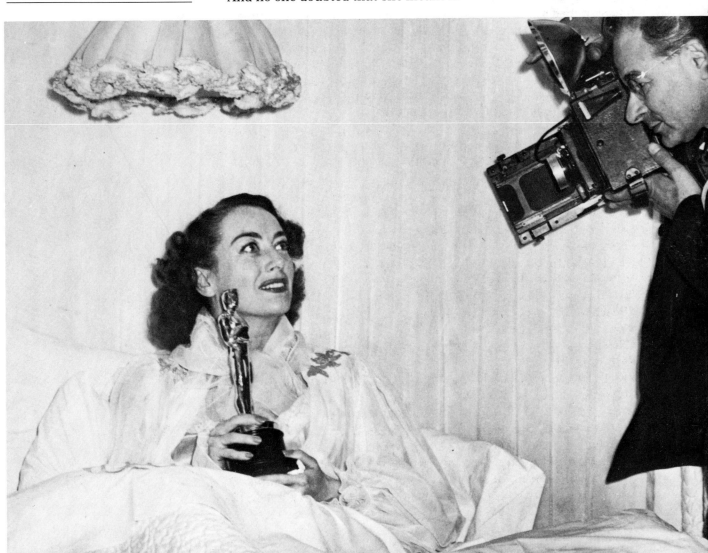

Crawford's daughter Christina stayed up with her for a while after everyone else left: "She sat holding her Oscar [Curtiz had brought it to her], turning him around to view from every angle. Then we walked down the stairs together, and she placed him all alone in a special niche at the bottom of the staircase. Mother stepped back to admire him. Turning to me she said with a note of sarcasm: 'I said I wouldn't be there, but I never thought it would turn out like this.' "

The next morning a thousand telegrams were delivered to Joan's house, with flowers arriving all day. But perhaps the one telegram that meant the most came from her old boss, Louis B. Mayer. And Crawford knew *he* meant it. He had told his secretary and publicist, Howard Strickling, that he had voted for Joan, not MGM's Greer Garson. "Why?" asked his secretary. Mayer turned his head away. "Because she deserved it."

That story ended happily, and as Rogers polished his Oscar touch through the next decade, there were many successes (such as his subtle campaign that helped win 1946's Best Actress Oscar for Olivia de Havilland in *To Each His Own*) and some keen disappointments.

One of his failures is almost as legendary as his triumph for Joan Crawford.

"I was convinced that a publicity campaign, conceived and executed by the Henry Rogers publicity organization, could result in an Academy Award for my client," Rogers wrote in *Walking the Tightrope*. "Who would be the next person I would touch with my magic wand?"

The star this time was Rosalind Russell, an actress as universally liked as Crawford was disliked. Russell had been nominated before, but her producer husband, Frederick Brisson, thought she would never have a better chance than with *Mourning Becomes Electra*, a boring, turgid rendering of Eugene O'Neill's masterpiece.

Rogers went to Brisson, asking him, without Russell's knowledge, if he could do for her what he had done so beautifully for Crawford and de Havilland. There would be a bonus if Russell got nominated and a large bonus if she won. (Some say it was more than $10,000. In any case, it was enough to cause Russell to throw up when she lost to Loretta Young.)

Rogers tried everything. He bossed fraternities into naming Russell actress of the year, convinced a Las Vegas expert to issue odds on all the candidates with Russell the six-to-five favorite, and carefully fed the Hollywood rumor mill. So successful was Rogers that *Variety*'s annual poll of 25 percent of the Academy voters showed that Russell had no competition.

Brisson booked a table at the Mocambo for dozens of celebrants. And Rogers told his wife to go ahead and spend the $5,000 for new living room furniture, which she did.

As the world knows, it was Loretta Young who said, as she accepted the statuette, "At long last!"

Roz Russell broke her beads; she had automatically risen to get her Oscar. Thank God for the dark—nobody really noticed.

Rogers got healthily drunk at the Mocambo, remembering only later that even he had gone to sleep during a showing of *Mourning Becomes Electra*.

The stories behind Joan Crawford's award and behind *The Alamo* nominations are the happy side of the story. Far more venal are the recurrent drives by big studios to gain Oscar nominations for films that

Roz Russell, ever Oscarless, and costar Robert Montgomery in Fast and Loose *(1939).*

they, and almost everyone else, know are not of Academy Award caliber. The publicity stunts (and they rate no higher a title than that) achieve their goal year after year in a rotten tradition which stretches back to Oscar's first decade.

Every time this issue rears its head at Oscar time, the Academy issues sanctimonious denials. In 1980, for instance, Academy president Fay Kanin told CBS reporter Steve Edwards, "I seriously doubt that ad campaigns have any effect on voting. At least I hope not."

Hard evidence through the years makes such denials seem ridiculous.

The track record of Twentieth Century–Fox alone during the last twenty years is proof enough. Time and again that studio has succeeded in hoisting dismal but expensive films into the Academy's golden five. Each time it happens several excellent films are frozen out. For example, in 1964 Fox's *Cleopatra* was nominated for Best Picture at the expense of *Hud* and *Irma La Douce*. Three years later, it was *The Sand Pebbles*, from the same studio, sacrificing *Blow-up*, *Morgan!*, and *The Professionals*. And in 1969 a Fox spending spree managed to squeeze the disastrous *Hello, Dolly!* into the five Best Picture nominations in a year that shamefully shut out Peter Fonda's *Easy Rider*, *They Shoot Horses, Don't They?*, *The Prime of Miss Jean Brodie*, *Bob & Carol & Ted & Alice*, *Goodbye, Columbus*, and *The Sterile Cuckoo*.

The classic case of the "Twentieth Touch," however, was the vehement campaign they waged for *Doctor Dolittle,* a 1967 film that even the boys in Fox's back rooms knew was a disaster. "The sixteen-million-dollar turkey," they called it.

The "*Doctor Dolittle* Oscar Caper" is special because Twentieth Century–Fox got caught with its votes down. A brilliant writer named John Gregory Dunne was taken to the studio's corporate bosom to paint the studio in golden tones.

Studio bosses had no way of knowing they had taken an asp to their collective breasts.

Dunne followed the movie from its first edited frame to its last bought vote, then put it all together in a volume called *The Studio,* which is now a text in some film schools. The book revealed the studio's dishonest reaction to a bad picture so thoroughly that to this day many Hollywood executives go into a cold sweat for fear it could happen again. Public relations men describe their careers as "before Dunne" and "after Dunne," the latter resembling Joseph Goebbels's PR plan for Hitler.

The journalist hadn't dug too far before he uncovered the fine hand of Rogers and Cowan—the same publicity firm that ran Crawford's campaign. And their hand showed up first in a splashy but highly inconsequential announcement in the *Hollywood Reporter* that another R&C client, Bobby Darin, was going to unveil the *Doctor Dolittle* songs at a Red Cross gala for Princess Grace.

Rex Harrison could have "talked to the animals" in Doctor Dolittle *(1967) by turning in his performance on the telephone. The super-expensive musical was a dismal product from its first chimp to last yak. And there's no doubt that Twentieth Century–Fox knew it. Still, Fox played the Oscar game as well as Harrison played his role, gaining the film a handful of important nominations: for its ho-hum cinematography, its mediocre art and set decoration, its grating sound, and even for Best Picture. The victory spoke well for the finesse of Fox P.R. men who coaxed, wined, and dined a shoddy product into Hollywood's golden circle.*

Dunne was such a hail-fellow-well-met that he found himself on a plane aimed at Minneapolis, the site of *Doctor Dolittle*'s sneak preview. Across the aisle was Warren Cowan, Rogers's partner in the P.R. firm. "The picture, as befitted its $16 million budget, was scheduled to be the studio's major contender in the Academy Award race," wrote Dunne, who sneaked a look at the early master plan for *Dolittle*'s publicity. On the list was a plan to manufacture and distribute (free) Pushmi-Pullyu cuff links and tie clasps. (*Doctor Dolittle* disappeared so quickly that it's hard to remember, but the Pushmi-Pullyu, we believe, was a singing-dancing llama that duetted with the film's star, Rex Harrison.) The studio's strategy also included plans for wax figures in Madame Tussaud's Wax Museum in London and a *"Doctor Dolittle* Day" at thousands of schools across America, which would apparently free the students to see Rex and Pushmi.

The people who haplessly wandered into the *Doctor Dolittle* preview in Minnesota didn't exactly groan as the film wound through the projector. But none of them wandered out singing the Pushmi-Pullyu song either. The reaction was not much better at a preview in San Francisco.

Bosley Crowther and other New York critics finally poised their pointed quills and scrawled reviews in blood. "The youngsters should enjoy it and the intermission was thoughtfully inserted at just about the right place," wrote Crowther in the *New York Times*.

Time warned that "size and a big budget are no substitutes for originality or charm." And even the trade paper *Daily Variety*, which to quote Dunne, "depends on advertising from the studios," said, "the pic suffers from a vacillating concept in script, direction, and acting."

This in no way dampened Fox's campaign to buy the Oscar nomination.

Dunne got this down in black and white. Texts of memos from studio publicist Jack Hirschberg stated, "The following has been decided regarding our Academy Award campaign for *Doctor Dolittle*. Each screening will be preceded by champagne or cocktails and a buffet dinner in the studio commissary. *Doctor Dolittle* is the studio's prime target for Academy Award consideration."

Hirschberg then provided a breakdown of the Academy branches, organizing the showings to accommodate all of them.

"The studio's Academy Award exploitation plan for *Doctor Dolittle* was highly successful," wrote Dunne. "Despite mediocre reviews and lukewarm box-office returns, the picture garnered nine nominations and won two Oscars."

Again, what was *Doctor Dolittle*'s gain was the Academy's loss—in prestige and objectivity. To get *Dolittle* nominated, the Academy had to overlook *In Cold Blood, Cool Hand Luke, Two for the Road, Barefoot in the Park, The Dirty Dozen, The Whisperers,* and *Thoroughly Modern Millie.*

This tradition continued into the seventies, although big-budget films suddenly went out of Oscar fashion in 1978. In 1975, *The Towering Inferno* took a Best Picture nomination away from *Alice Doesn't Live Here Anymore* and *A Woman Under the Influence*. The next year, *Jaws* made it into the golden circle instead of *Shampoo*.

The communications explosion in Hollywood has given the big producers and publicists more toys. Pay-TV reaches an estimated 90 percent of the Academy's eligible voters. And movies that have been made available to pay-TV (such as *Breaking Away*) have fared better than average in preliminary voting because then even the preview for a nominated movie can be an important trump card. Theta Cable shows those trailers fifteen or more times a day to provide almost subliminal advertising which goes directly to Oscar voters. (The trailers for Bette Midler's *The Rose* ran so often that several of those scenes must still be engraved on the Academy's collective psyche.)

Some of the campaigns become so dangerously crude that they backfire entirely.

In 1961 Montgomery Clift's overt advertising undoubtedly cost the troubled actor his final chance for an Oscar. Not only did the ads capitalize on *Judgment at Nuremberg,* they tried to make hay from Clift's ill and depressed appearance. Since all Hollywood knew how sick he was, the implication was "Vote for Clift now—it's your last chance." Obviously, not enough did, and George Chakiris walked off with the Best Supporting Actor Oscar for *West Side Story.*

Joan Crawford said it best: "Why suddenly expect the process to be fair—it didn't even start out that way."

Today's neurotic, disrespectful, sullen Oscar contenders often shun the very publicity which might bring them the award they so eagerly seek. They hide, disappearing into the European continent or pleading ever-so-busy schedules—all to avoid those public confrontations which are manna to the fans and the P.R. machine.

Sometimes even studios with a crop of Oscar films despair, admitting that they can do little or nothing to promote their current Oscar contenders. In 1982, Paramount couldn't produce a single star from any of the three films they had in the final voting. "Everybody in the western world wants to interview Warren Beatty and Diane Keaton about *Reds,*" said Paramount's publicist, Marcy Bolotin. "But *we* can't even get in touch with them."

The studio also got nowhere with Harrison Ford and Steven Spielberg of *Raiders of the Lost Ark.* And the stars of the film Paramount pushed the hardest, *Atlantic City,* made it clear from the beginning that they would grant no interviews. Susan Sarandon pleaded a "full schedule," and Burt Lancaster barked severely: "I don't do that anymore." Nor did the studio have any luck with James Cagney, Elizabeth McGovern, Howard E. Rollins, Jr., and Mary Steenburgen of *Ragtime,* which, though not up for Best Picture, did have eight nominations.

Over at Fox, where executives thought *On Golden Pond* would be a sure-fire winner as Best Picture, Henry Fonda was too ill for a publicity tour; Katharine Hepburn gave her usual "no," politely but firmly, and Jane Fonda hired Hollywood's hefty P.R. "no" woman to shoo reporters off her tail.

But over at Warners, publicists were able to produce the entire cast, the producer, and the director of the dark-horse film, *Chariots of Fire.* (What part this openness had to do with the film's victory will never be known.)

Many stars put their P.R. hirelings through hell after turning them loose on Oscar's yellow brick road. When Jill Clayburgh wanted an Oscar for her work in the 1978 film *An Unmarried Woman,* she hired an old friend, Norman Twain, a New York theatrical producer who instantly announced that "the difference between winning and losing is in the neighborhood of fifty votes."

Twain based his campaign on the fact that Clayburgh was at that very moment starring in his own production of David Rabe's play *In the Boom Boom Room* at the Long Beach Theater Festival.

The intrepid producer stubbornly refused to let Clayburgh appear on the crucial "Tonight" show because "they couldn't tell us who the host was going to be, and Jill could have been on with a *juggler*."

After doing everything but staging a three-ring circus, Twain declared on "A.M. Los Angeles" that "there's no one, no one *thing* that is going to win for her other than her performance. I won't lobby or throw her into a cauldron of publicity. She's much, much bigger than that."

The same year, Hollywood publicist Robert Levinson won a Best Actor nomination for Gary Busey in *The Buddy Holly Story* through a clever mixture of hype and down-key publicity. "I knew when I saw the rushes that Gary had a good shot at the nomination," Levinson said. First, he had to lure the shy Busey from his haunts in Redondo Beach and into the limelight of Hollywood.

Levinson convinced Columbia Pictures to open *The Buddy Holly Story* in Dallas, where, coincidentally Busey, appearing in full Buddy Holly regalia with the late singer's guitar, opened the official Buddy Holly Park in Lubbock, Texas.

The publicist zeroed in on the Hollywood Foreign Press Association, which hands out the well-publicized but highly suspect Golden Globes. (The honors are voted on by an equally suspicious flock of seventy-six international reporters, many of whom lack credentials and true print affiliations). Busey got his Golden Globe nomination and a passel of publicity ending with a full interview and a cover on *Rolling Stone* magazine.

He also wangled an *US* magazine cover and a stint as guest host on "Saturday Night Live." Alas, Gary won the adulation but lost the Oscar

Gary Busey, Best Actor nominee for The Buddy Holly Story *(1978), at the Oscars.*

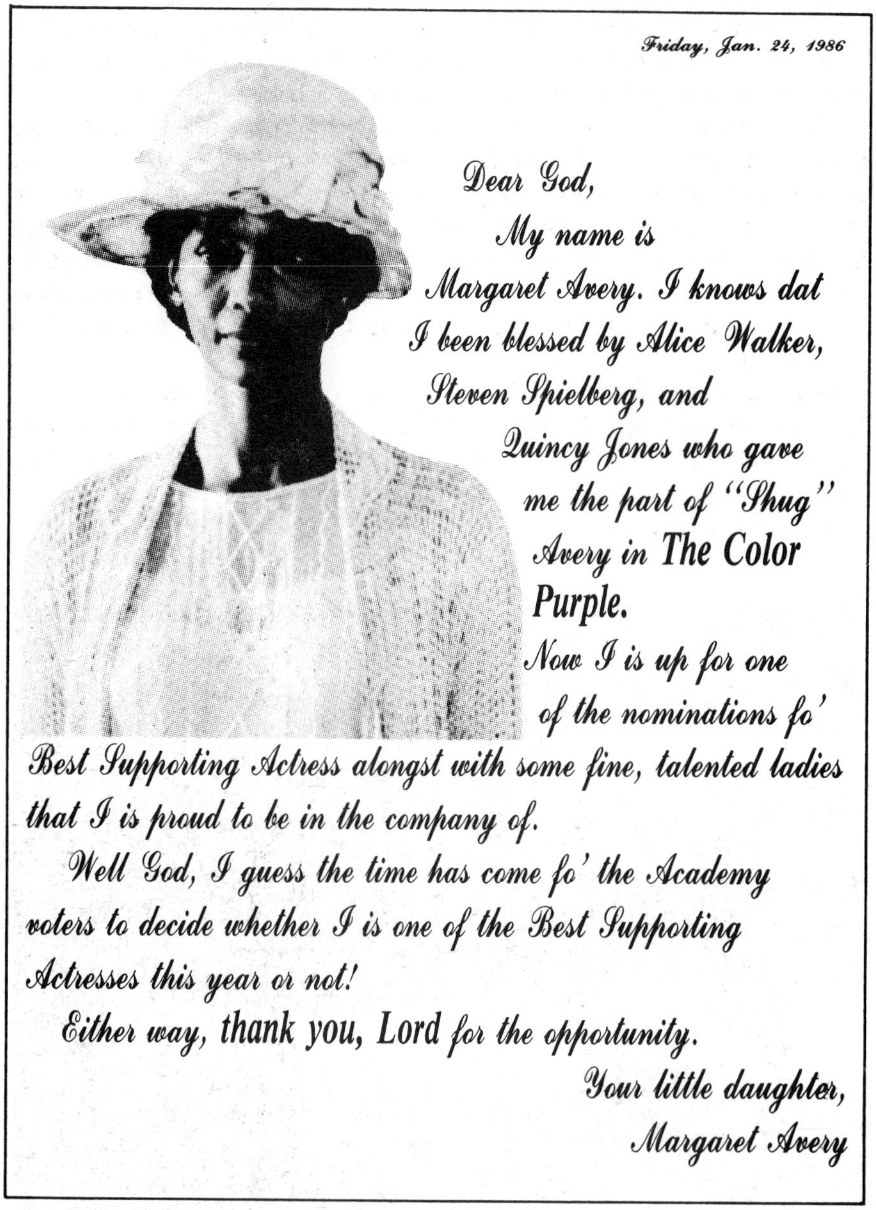

Friday, Jan. 24, 1986

Dear God,
My name is
Margaret Avery. I knows dat
I been blessed by Alice Walker,
Steven Spielberg, and
Quincy Jones who gave
me the part of "Shug"
Avery in **The Color Purple.**
Now I is up for one
of the nominations fo'
Best Supporting Actress alongst with some fine, talented ladies
that I is proud to be in the company of.
Well God, I guess the time has come fo' the Academy
voters to decide whether I is one of the Best Supporting
Actresses this year or not!
Either way, **thank you, Lord** for the opportunity.
Your little daughter,
Margaret Avery

Dear God indeed! Margaret Avery's embarrassing prayer to God—perhaps seeking intercession in the Oscar race for 1985—has to be one of the lowest points in an already shameful downpour of flakery which erupts each year.

to Jon Voight, who portrayed a crippled Vietnam veteran in *Coming Home.*

The Oscar advertising campaigns are becoming more costly and more resplendent each year. Where a simple, dignified ad used to suffice, the studios now mount baroque, bloated armadas of hype which often include complete, fold-out posters printed in Switzerland at costs approaching $100,000. In 1986, for instance, Cannon Films promoted its ridiculous *Fool for Love* with a slick cardboard insert so elegant and bulked up, that the trade papers, in which it appeared, couldn't fit in Hollywood mailboxes.

Ashley Boone, president of marketing at Columbia, estimated that each studio spent "at least" $400,000 to tout the five Best Picture contenders of 1983—a cool $2 million spread evenly among *The Big Chill, The Dresser, The Right Stuff, Tender Mercies,* and *Terms of Endearment.*

A year later Orion Pictures spent more than $600,000 on *Amadeus* and reaped eleven nominations, while Warner Bros. took out more ads for Clint Eastwood as Best Actor in *Tightrope* (seven in *Daily Variety* alone) than any other performer received and came up empty-handed. The Hollywood tough guy was bested by Albert Finney for *Under the Volcano*, who didn't get the benefit of a single ad.

(Spokesmen at Warner Bros. said "in greatest secrecy" that Eastwood's contract with the studio *"demands"* that a major advertising campaign be mounted for any picture in which he appears. "More and more actors are requesting Academy Award support as a requirement in their contracts," said a Paramount executive. "And even if they don't set those conditions, if Tom Selleck can get ads for Best Actor in *Runaway*, how do you tell Charles Durning he doesn't get one for *Mass Appeal?*")

In 1985, the biggest spenders were *Places in the Heart* with forty-five full-page ads and *Amadeus* with fifty full pages. In the nomination process alone, *The Natural* boasted twenty-one full pages and *Birdy* twenty.

Greystoke: The Legend of Tarzan, Lord of the Apes received the most lavish publicity of any movie that same year when Warner Bros.

Cannon Films spewed forth an avalanche of advertising and public relations tricks to win Jon Voight a Best Actor nomination for Runaway Train *(1985). It is believed to have been the costliest campaign in Oscar history, with a reputed price tag of $500,000, including ads, press junkets, and massive giveaways. And the sheer force of it worked. Voight got a nod for his greasy protrayal on a train and in a movie which went nowhere.*

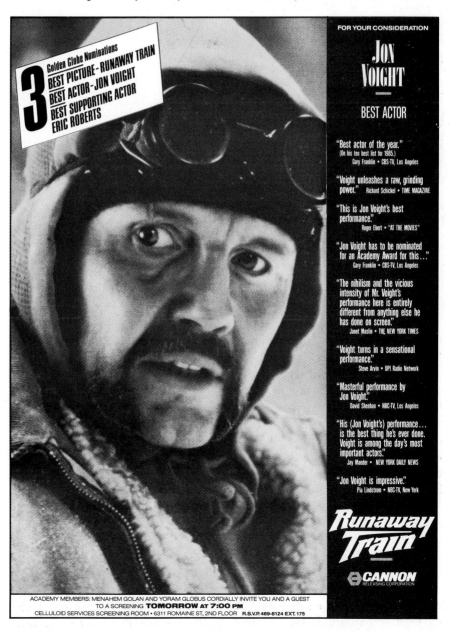

136 ran a twenty-eight page, full-color insert in *Daily Variety* on January 8, at an estimated cost of $110,000. It consisted mostly of color pictures from the film, preceded by a page suggesting nominations for everything from best technicals to best primate makeup. In the end it was nominated for three Oscars—Best Supporting Actor (Ralph Richardson), Best Screenplay Based on Material from Another Medium and Best Makeup. It won no Oscars.

A similar "lost cause" was *Ghostbusters,* the biggest hit of 1984, for which Columbia launched a massive campaign, including fifteen full pages in both *Daily Variety* and the *Hollywood Reporter.* The breakdown included three for director Ivan Reitman, two for star Bill Murray, three for co-stars Dan Aykroyd and Harold Ramis, one for actress Sigourney Weaver, three for the screenplay by Aykroyd and Ramis, and one for the movie's score. The film earned only two nominations—for visual effects and for the title song.

To show how silly it all becomes: in 1985 Tri-Star Pictures ran ten pages seeking nominations for a sci-fi film, *Runaway;* four pages for

FOR YOUR CONSIDERATION
BEST ACTOR
DON JOHNSON

"Don Johnson is so intensely outstanding . . . This is really a terrifically talented actor."
David Sheehan, KNBC-TV

"Johnson proves his dynamic dramatic talent in 'Cease Fire' painting a cogent and powerful portrait."
Judith Crist, WOR-TV

"Strong leading performance . . . affecting enough to suggest that Johnson's new renown has at least as much to do with authentic acting talent as with good looks."
Janet Maslin, New York Times

"Above all, 'Cease Fire' proves that Don Johnson is more than just another pretty cop. He's a real actor after all!"
Rex Reed, N.Y. Post

"The film has a wonderful opportunity for Don Johnson to stretch his talent. Perhaps now his popularity will help draw audiences to a worthy film deserving of their attention."
Kevin Thomas, Los Angeles Times

" 'Cease Fire' is certain to profoundly affect anyone who sees it, not the least for Don Johnson's Academy-caliber performance."
Candice Russell, Ft. Lauderdale Sun Sentinel

CEASE FIRE

E.L.F. Productions and Double Helix Films present CEASE FIRE • DON JOHNSON • LISA BLOUNT • ROBERT F. LYONS • RICHARD CHAVES and CHRIS NOEL as Wendy Associate Producers RICHARD STYLES and RALPH R. CLEMENTE • Executive Producers ED FERNANDEZ and GEORGE FERNANDEZ • Produced by WILLIAM GREFÉ Written by GEORGE FERNANDEZ based on his play "Vietnam Trilogy" • Directed by DAVID NUTTER • Released by Cineworld Enterprises Corporation

ACADEMY MEMBERS: SCREENING TOMORROW, JANUARY 15 AT 8 P.M., HITCHCOCK THEATER, UNIVERSAL STUDIOS

To illustrate how far Hollywood film companies will go in the name of Oscar, one has only to view such ads as this one for Don Johnson in a thoroughly dreadful film, Cease Fire. *The movie was made a long time before Johnson's international popularity in "Miami Vice." Fortunately, the strategy didn't work.*

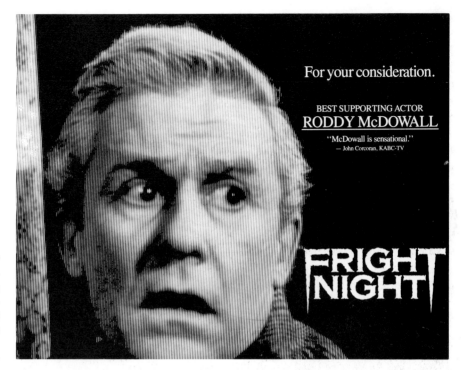

For your consideration.

BEST SUPPORTING ACTOR
RODDY McDOWALL

"McDowall is sensational."
— John Corcoran, KABC-TV

FRIGHT NIGHT

Not all campaigns work, no matter the actor or the dough spent. Such was the case with Roddy Mc-Dowall's Oscar try for 1985's Fright Night. *Nothing can overcome a simply dreadful film.*

The Muppets Take Manhattan, which managed an original song score nomination; and three pages for *Supergirl.*

In 1986 Universal spent a whopping $500 per Academy voter in its drive to win Oscars for seven films, including *Out of Africa, Back to the Future, Mask,* and *The Breakfast Club.*

The competition for a place on the presenters list is equally ferocious . . . a key spot in front of those one billion TV viewers can overhaul a career—make a star out of a newcomer or revive the fame of a fading star.

For instance, George Burns wangled an Oscar appearance for a young chorus girl who worked in his Vegas act. She was only in view for three minutes, but it made her an instant star. Her name is Ann-Margret. Similarly, it created an entirely new career for John Schneider —from the *Dukes of Hazzard* cast. He was offered a slot to sing and dance in a production number built around the song from *Ragtime.* He came out in a $1,500 tux, sang the song in a Frank Sinatra style and waltzed with a ballerina borrowed from the New York City Ballet. Summer stock offers poured in the next morning.

A presenter's slot can also be a balm for a lost nomination . . . Steve Guttenberg, an up-and-coming star, waged a valiant campaign to get a nomination for his work in *Diner* in 1982. When it failed, he was asked to present a key Oscar. His appearance resulted in offers for two new parts on the spot, including the male lead in *Cocoon.*

The presenters tradition had remained a matter for Hollywood politicians until 1980, when a young investigative reporter, Andrew Epstein, completely dissected the stars handing out the Oscars, asking them, "How did you get the job? and why?" His conclusions, published in the *Los Angeles Times* the day before the Oscars, created havoc and panic backstage the following night. Some stars discussed in the article called the *Times,* threatening not to show up for the ceremony if retractions were not printed. Epstein's facts, however, held up, and everyone, some of them pouting, made their grand entrances.

Howard W. Koch, again producer of the show, told Epstein, "Every

press agent, manager, and agent I know calls me. Some with good ideas, others to promote someone with a picture opening just to get the exposure." Jack Haley, Jr., a frequent producer of the show, said, "You're on your own to cast the show, but I'm constantly besieged by publicists and agents. I've been constantly amazed by some of those they pitched. I'd have thought that some of those people were dead by now."

Sometimes the network carrying the show foists TV stars of their more troubled shows onto the presenters list. The most blatant example was Robert Blake, whom ABC asked Koch to put on the show. Blake was then starring in that network's "Baretta."

"I got a call from someone at ABC," Koch told Epstein. "He said, 'Look, I've never asked you for a favor. . . .' On show day, he [Blake] shows up with a beard and a dirty pair of sneakers. The person from ABC assured me that everything would be okay by the time of the show. That night, he comes in with a big eccentric tuxedo and smoking a big cigar."

Epstein looked a bit deeper and uncovered a bit of Oscarcast nepotism: Presenter Patrick Wayne, for instance, was hosting a syndicated TV show being produced by Marty Pasetta, director of the Academy Awards show that year. "Nobody is going to believe us," said Koch. "But it was my idea to put Patrick on the show, not Marty's. I was in Marty's office one day, saw a picture of Patrick, and thought it would be a good idea to use him. People want to see John Wayne's son. They want to see the son of a great actor."

And one pair of presenters, Robert Hays and Kristy McNichol, were starring in Koch productions.

The most infamous "presenter scandal" occurred in 1973, when the Academy, with much fanfare, announced that Olympic swim champ Mark Spitz would present one of the major awards that year.

The news flashed around the world. A London newspaper doctored one of Spitz's old swim photographs, showing the Olympic swimmer in his quite brief tank trunks holding an Oscar over his head. The caption read, "And now for the best performance by a swimmer doing the breaststroke . . ."

The decision to have Mark Spitz hand out an Oscar ranks as one of the most blatant examples of misuse of the Oscar show in Academy history. At that time, Spitz had retired from the chlorine and was living the life of a budding movie and TV star in a swank apartment in Marina del Rey. The dashing water baby had just signed a contract with Norman Brokaw, a wizard of cash and hype employed by the world's largest talent agency, William Morris. The *Los Angeles Times* commented that Spitz was "being merchandised like a chunk of plastic livestock." The water boy had recently signed a multi-million-dollar contract with Schick. And a Mark Spitz poster, showing him grinning in ever-so-tiny briefs and selling like hotcakes, guaranteed Spitz fifteen cents for each copy sold. Brokaw told *Sports Illustrated* that his soggy client would make TV specials and, eventually, movies, "when the suitable vehicle comes along." It only stood to reason that an appearance on the Oscar show would remind Hollywood (and the rest of the world) that a male Esther Williams was ripe for the picking.

This time, it didn't work. Spitz had already shown up as a lightweight on a TV variety show; his wooden, arrogant manner earned him national derision. And the Academy was bombarded by the public with protests over his pending appearance. Art Sarno, longtime publicist for

By 1975 Mark Spitz's motion-picture and television career was a national joke. For instance, Bea Arthur, television's Maude, built a show around the line: "And Mark Spitz will drink a glass of milk on this very stage." He had been paid to be a spokesman for the dairy industry. "The Carol Burnett Show" spoofed the water baby by having Lyle Waggoner in a couple of ounces of tank suit appearing on a talk show with his own dairy case. But in 1974 Spitz was still raw enough for the powerful William Morris Agency to wangle him an invitation to present one of the Oscars—a showcase bound to help agents find the swimmer a movie role. It was announced to Hollywood on February 13, 1974—and retracted only a day later after an industry-wide uproar. It was one thing for Mickey Mouse to hand out an Oscar or, more recently, for Miss Piggy and R2D2 to serve as presenters. They, after all, were movie stars—however artificial. Bowing out, Spitz told the Hollywood Reporter, "I think the honor of being a presenter should be reserved for those who have contributed to the motion-picture industry." Ah. . . if only it were.

the Academy Awards, recalled that an equally powerful fuss was made by people within the film industry. What's he have to do with movies? asked the industry. And Spitz was forced to stroke his way back to the pool.

On February 15, 1973, he publicly withdrew in special written statements to the *Los Angeles Times,* the *Hollywood Reporter,* and *Daily Variety.* Spitz said, "I told the Academy the honor of being a presenter should be reserved for people who have contributed to the motion-picture industry."

Still, William Morris, even in the face of the evidence, continued to claim that Spitz *did* make an appearance on the March 1973 Academy Awards. A spokesman, Brokaw, told Andrew Epstein: "Uproar? I don't recall an uproar. Mark appeared on the show. I remember this because Mark didn't have a tuxedo—he had plenty of swimsuits, though—and we went to a tailor that Howard Koch recommended."

A search of the videotapes of the Oscarcast shows no appearance by Mark Spitz.

But maybe, like streaker Robert Opel's appearance, Spitz's was just too brief to notice.

CHAPTER EIGHT

Hush, Hush, Sweet Oscar

The real show is backstage and out there in the audience. It's written on the faces of the losers, in the hearts of the winners, and told in whispers behind perfumed hands. —DOROTHY KILGALLEN, 1963

The young usher blushed through his deep tan and tried to smile. "Uh, ma'am, the show's already started. You can't go in now."

The raven-haired lady in buckskin and beads stared right through him and sized up the door keeping her from the orchestra seating for the 1973 Oscar show. She grabbed her turquoise necklace and shifted nervously from one moccasin to another.

The costumed intruder turned to her companion, who was dressed to the Beverly Hills nines. "Let's try the other door."

They glided noiselessly over the two-inch carpet at the Los Angeles Music Center and stormed a second wall of doors. The six-foot traffic cop on guard hooked his thumbs in the top of his skin-tight pants and looked down at the Indian. He opened his mouth to bark, but the Indian's companion beat him to it.

"Brando!" she said. "We're here for Marlon Brando."

"Oh, wow!" said the cop. "Wow!" He almost saluted and led the pair to a side door. They ducked down a slight hall, opened a second, smaller door. This time they just flashed their tickets and whispered, "Brando."

"You'll have to wait until the next break," said another usher, who dropped his programs and burst into a run, heading for Oscar's inner sanctum behind the golden curtain.

The usher grabbed the arm of a sweating assistant director and gasped, "Brando's being represented by an Indian."

"So what?" said the A.D., thinking that Brando's first wife was, after all, a former Indian movie star—Anna Kashfi.

But the usher, second-guessing him, said, "No, I mean an American Indian—you know: in moccasins, beads, leather." The assistant director's arrogant grin contorted into an expression of almost sheer terror.

He began elbowing his way through America's most famous backstage scene. Past Raquel, past Liv, past Charlton. Finally he found him —Howard W. Koch, Oscar producer for the Academy of Motion Picture Arts and Sciences, and for a night, the most powerful man in Hollywood.

"Uh, Mr. Koch," stuttered the A.D., "there's an Indian here representing Marlon Brando."

Howard Koch threw his fists up to his face in frustration. This, he thought, is too much, as his mind whirred over the Academy's rough sailing through recent political controversy, a history made unavoidable with Jane Fonda a winner and Vanessa Redgrave a multiple nominee.

"I quickly called a powwow offstage," said Koch. "We considered everything. We even considered arresting her on the grounds that seats are nontransferable"—a move that might have been disastrous because stars and nominees have sent proxies since the awards began.

Koch tugged at the satin lapels on his coat and decided to risk the ordeal: he had to confront her. "Might as well learn the worst now," he told a confederate as he slipped out into the darkened auditorium.

Onstage, Julie Andrews and director George Stevens were presenting the Best Director award to Bob Fosse for *Cabaret*. Koch's first words were drowned out by screams from the film's stars, Liza Minnelli and Joel Grey, in nearby seats. The Oscar chief's face was as blank as Buster Keaton's as he stood before his adversary.

She had a good figure, looked lovely, and seemed to be composed. Five thousand dollars worth of New Mexican turquoise was on her neck, her white buckskin had been rock-hammered in Canada, and she had made her leather thong headdress herself.

"I am Howard Koch," said the flustered official.

"And I am Sacheen Littlefeather," said the dark-haired beauty.

"You can't read *that*," he said, pointing to the sheaf of papers in Miss Littlefeather's hand. "We're running late. You just can't read it."

Sacheen lowered her eyelids. "If Marlon should win, I *am* going to read it."

"If you try to read that, I'll cut you off the air," he repeated as the Oscar show quickly moved toward its climax.

"Okay! Okay!" said the Indian maiden. "I won't read it." Koch headed backstage while Sacheen Littlefeather and the beautiful girl with her, Brando's secretary, Alice Marchak, were seated next to Brando's pal James Caan.

Caan leaned over and grabbed Alice's hand. "He's gonna win, Alice, he's gonna win!"

The lights dimmed at that second. Roger Moore and Liv Ullmann walked to stage center and read the list of Best Actor nominees as clips from the performances rolled onto the screen: "Marlon Brando, for *The Godfather;* Michael Caine, for *Sleuth;* Laurence Olivier, for *Sleuth;* Peter O'Toole, for *The Ruling Class;* and Paul Winfield, for *Sounder*."

There was the usual breathless pause as Hollywood and three hundred million people around the world waited to crown Hollywood's "King for a Day."

"The winner is . . . Marl—" There was a mighty roar because this was a comeback. And Hollywood, above all other things, loves a comeback. Sacheen Littlefeather moved from the protective darkness into the Oscar spotlight, and the audience began to buzz with rumor and speculation. She held up her hand as Roger Moore tried to give her the Oscar and blushed as he realized she would not take it. Then she declined for Marlon Brando in her own halting words, explaining that Brando was protesting the treatment of Indians—by America generally, and by the movies specifically. The silence was deafening as Sacheen Littlefeather drifted offstage and was mobbed by the press.

Koch sighed, partly in relief. It was, he thought, not as bad as it could have been. Visions of Marlon's typed, three-page speech danced in his head. Anyway, the show was almost over and he was off the hook.

But not the Academy. And not Brando. For a year the Battle of "Little Big Oscar" raged in Hollywood and the rest of the country. Brando was pilloried by conservative critics; turned into a hero by liberal critics; and alternately loved, hated, and suspected by the powers that be in Hollywood.

Rona Barrett screamed "Coward!" over network television, explaining later in a full-page ad in a trade paper that her real concern was for the very survival of the Academy, and expressing her fear that "what Marlon Brando did this year could signal the death of Oscar as we know him."

The international media turned this symbolic act into a charade, a circus for mass consumption, wherein a lovely Indian girl turned down an Oscar and then disappeared into the night—to vanish without a trace. And those responsible for the furor which followed lost sight of the girl, the actor, and the somewhat elegant gesture and depicted them as rapacious opportunists out to make a splash at the expense of poor ol' Oscar.

The truth, however, was far different, and simpler than even the kindest gossip columnist might have imagined. It involved a chance meeting between a world-famous director and a girl on a San Francisco hilltop, an unhurried and secret friendship between a superstar and the naïve Indian, and a rushed encounter with infamy which was almost an afterthought.

Sacheen Littlefeather's personal story, told here for the first time, is graphic enough proof of what Oscar and the garrulous press at its bronze heels can do to one brief minute of time by freezing it, giving it international importance, and distorting it to revive the grimy stars which are deteriorating on Hollywood Boulevard.

A chance meeting between director Francis Ford Coppola and Sacheen Littlefeather began it all. The occasion was one of those friendly protests which, before they went out of style, raised conservatives' hackles.

"I went up to Mr. Coppola and told him that I read he was interested in Native Americans," recalled Sacheen. "I said I'd written a letter to Marlon [Brando (himself of Native American blood)] and had a photo to send with it. We chatted for a few minutes, he gave me an address, and we turned toward other conversations."

Sacheen mailed the letter, enclosing the photo, and forgot about it as the months drifted by.

"Months and months down the line, I was working at a San Francisco radio station. It was five P.M. I was ready to go home, exhausted. I was about to leave when the phone rang."

"Is this Sacheen Littlefeather? I have a person-to-person call," said the operator.

"Yes," said Sacheen, mystified.

Then she recognized the voice and sat down slowly in her chair.

"Do you know who this is?" asked Brando, whose voice still gravels as it did in *Streetcar Named Desire* and *The Wild Ones*.

"Of course," answered Sacheen.

There was a pause, perhaps motivated by her tone—matter-of-fact and slightly unimpressed.

"I'm Francis Coppola's friend," Brando added, as if that were necessary.

"Well, you certainly took long enough," she replied.

They both dissolved into laughter, which faded into a conversation lasting for hours. The superstar, who had three years earlier named his second daughter Cheyenne, spoke of his concern for the troubles of Native Americans.

A firm but informal friendship began on the phone that day.

Meanwhile, Sacheen became increasingly active in Indian causes and *The Godfather* was released, putting Brando back on top. A series of Sacheen-Brando letters began. When Sacheen was invited to appear before the Federal Communications Commission, which was looking into the misportrayal of Indians in films and on TV, she reached out to him for advice. He hosted her at his Bel Air home, where he offered counsel, and she became acquainted with the superstar. (Though they were both in the same house, Brando would still call her room through a private phone network so they could talk for hours.)

Brando never asked for anything in return—until the afternoon of March 26, 1973.

"I'd like you to do me a favor," Brando said over the phone to Sacheen in San Francisco. "Can you do it?"

"Anything within reason," she answered.

He explained he was up for an Oscar for *The Godfather* and then said in quiet tones: "I want you to represent me—to appear in my place at the Academy Awards."

Although stunned, Sacheen murmured, "Sure, yes . . . if you want me to—yes!"

Then Brando warned her about the vicious press and the almost inhuman celebrity which is drawn to the Oscars. "Are you willing to be lied about; to have things distorted about you; to have people say anything about you that they want and to be helpless before them?"

"I don't know exactly what you mean," Sacheen said. "But if that goes along with the territory, then yes, I'll accept the responsibility."

("I was not a famous person, and didn't know the type of fame he was talking about," Sacheen recalled later, with a trace of bitterness. "Perhaps I was naïve about saying yes. But I trusted him. We were friends.")

"Fine," said Brando. "I'll have my secretary arrange for everything."

But hours drifted by, and it was late afternoon. Still no official word from Brando.

She called him back. He told her to get a ticket to Los Angeles and they discussed what she would wear the next night.

"I have no evening gown," she said. "But I do have an antique buckskin I wear to powwows and ceremonials."

"Fine," he answered.

Sacheen rushed into her bedroom to pack, taking the antique, 1903 ceremonial gown from its protective carton and folding it carefully into a suitcase.

Two hours later she was sitting in Brando's Bel Air living room. She was directed to her rooms only to find Brando and his son Christian making up the guest bed—Brando himself!

"He came back in when I was ready for bed and tucked me in, like a father or a tribal elder. He said good-night quietly—almost in a whisper—turned out the light, closed the door, and walked out. If he had acted in any other way, I would have been terrified. I was still so much in awe of him."

Tuesday morning, the day of the Oscars, Sacheen rose early, had fruit and tea for breakfast, and waited—becoming increasingly edgy—for Brando to summon her to his study. "I would catch glimpses of him as he moved through the rooms in another wing of the house," she said.

"Late in the afternoon he called her in: "I want you to refuse the Oscar if I win," he told her. To Sacheen, Brando seemed absolutely certain he *would* win.

"Alice Marchak will go with you," he said succinctly before directing her to the dining room for dinner.

Silence settled on the house as the rest of the town took to its limos and furs for the pagan communion at the Music Center.

At 7:00 P.M. as the curtain went up on the Oscarcast, Brando began dictating an elongated, blustery statement about the treatment of Native Americans by Hollywood. He droned on . . . and on . . . and on as the sun began to set on a hushed Beverly Hills—still as Christmas morning in Oscar's honor.

Alice Marchak, already gowned and coiffed, was summoned to the presence and handed a tape to transcribe. "I have never seen anyone type so fast," Sacheen recalled. "It was getting later and later."

Suddenly Alice realized there was no limo to carry them to the Music Center. She rushed out into the enclosed garden, where Brando's teenage nephew Marty was practicing his guitar. "Marty, are you busy?" Marchak asked. Within minutes Marty and a friend were in the front seat and Alice and Sacheen in the back in a car speeding toward downtown Los Angeles.

Incredibly, none of the four had been to the arts complex before. "Alice began shouting directions about where we should be," Sacheen said. "But we found it by sheer luck."

It was a quarter to nine when the car moved past the first bank of the private cop corps guarding the precious horde inside. "This was a show which was set to end at nine," said Sacheen later, her voice still reflecting the panic she felt that night.

And it was only minutes later when the official collision between her and Howard Koch occurred. "He scared me," Sacheen said. "Even though I promised not to read the statement and promised not to speak longer than a minute, I could still see that he didn't trust me. But I had no choice but to go into that frightening hall and fulfill a promise I had made. There *was* no other choice."

The rest of the story was played out in full view of the world: that night marked the first time the Oscarcast was relayed by satellite, to forty other countries.

"When the envelope was opened by Roger Moore and handed to Liv Ullmann, even I could feel that silence in the huge crowd. Marlon Brando's name was read, and my heart sank.

"Onstage Roger Moore tried to hand me this Oscar, and I held up my hand in a gesture that was to make me famous around the world. But at that second, I was frightened and trying hard to concentrate on what I had to say."

A few words into her rejection speech, Sacheen heard wave after wave of hate washing over her. "You could hear the boos and the hissing. But then the tide seemed to change and I heard just as many people say, 'Let her speak! Let her speak!'

"That audience was split and I could feel it."

Tears rolled down her cheeks as she fought for control. Finally, she let her gaze rest on Liza Minnelli's startled face and took it word by word for the sixty seconds.

Then she was off, rushed by security men to the press arena.

The rest swam by her in a daze. Before she knew it, she was back in San Francisco for a few brief private moments—the very few left before the maelstrom of controversy raged around her and made her the target of media hatred, public scrutiny, and the subject of a massive FBI investigation.

The furor in Hollywood died the minute producers realized they couldn't make a film about it. Sacheen drifted into Oscar's past. And Brando reported to the set of *The Missouri Breaks*, for which he would collect $1.3 million and a percentage of the profits.

It was quite another matter in the headquarters of the Academy of Motion Picture Arts and Sciences in Beverly Hills. There, Academy prexy Daniel Taradash called an emergency board meeting to discuss what insiders called a cure for Oscar's misuse as a public soapbox. "I don't know what we can do," Taradash told the *Los Angeles Times*.

She called herself Sacheen Little-feather—Indian princess for a night at the Academy Awards in 1973. Here a puzzled Roger Moore and a slightly abashed Liv Ullmann get a sign from Littlefeather that she will not accept Marlon Brando's Oscar for The Godfather. *(© A.M.P.A.S.)*

"We don't know if anything will work, but we have to look at the use of the Oscar lectern as a platform."

One thing was sure: there was no going back. Brando's political coup had worked. Hate mail against Brando was not massive enough to hurt him, the Oscars, or *The Godfather.* So Oscar big chiefs like Charlton Heston and Gregory Peck simply girded their loins and waited for successive waves of politics to wash through the seventies and into the eighties.

"You might as well cancel the Oscars if you're going to muffle the winners," said Koch to a friend. "We'll have to bank on the good faith of most winners."

But Oscar's new role as a soapbox opened a Pandora's box of troubles that are certain to continue as long as the ceremonies last.

Brando's grand gesture of refusing Oscars began almost innocently. The actor had already rejected the Golden Globe and the Reuters News Agency World Film Favorite prize when he was nominated for the Oscar. He sent the same telegram to each of the organizations: "There is a singular lack of honor in this country today—what with the government's change of its citizens into objects of use, its imperialistic and warlike intrusion into foreign countries and the killing of not only their inhabitants but also indirectly of our own people, its treatment of the Indians and the Blacks, the assault on the press, the rape of the ideals which were the foundation of this country. I respectfully ask you to understand that to accept an honor, however well intentioned, is to subtract from the meager amount left. Therefore, to simplify things, I hereby decline any nomination and deny anyone representing me."

The wire got scant attention from the press and much of that was distorted. Joyce Haber wrote, "Brando, who won the Reuters Poll for World Film Favorite, presumably sent a wire to that agency using such foul language that it could not be read on the air." This type of reporting quickly convinced Brando that he would either have to turn down the Oscar in person or send someone he could trust.

The Academy virtually bombarded Alice Marchak with letters and phone calls asking if Brando would come. Over at Paramount, which produced *The Godfather*, the brass became increasingly jumpy as the rumor mill predicted the star would be a hands-down winner. Paramount threw up its hands and publicly announced that Robert Evans, its handsome production chief, would collect Brando's Oscar.

Somewhere in the South Seas Brando decided otherwise. He jetted into Los Angeles the day before the ceremony and asked Marchak to meet him at his house. "I want you to go to the Awards—with Sacheen," he said, sending his secretary running to the phone.

"I remembered we didn't have tickets," said Marchak. "So I called Mr. Koch's office at Paramount and asked him to send two tickets to Brando's house."

Since Hollywood is still the smallest back-fence town in America, the news spread like wildfire. Brando was coming to the Academy Awards —In Person! The wire services sent out the item as a bulletin, and newscasters in the East led off their broadcasts with the announcement.

Many Oscar watchers were primed for a theatrical event; one even thought the Academy had staged Brando's last-minute change of heart to build ratings for the show and, in turn, advertising dollars—their biggest source of revenue (about $1.7 million). After the show, however, some critics, notably Charles Champlin, despaired of Oscar's future.

Champlin, whose moderate voice has brought winds of change to the Academy, stated, "Brando was arguing in absentia that attention must be paid, and he took the occasion of a very promotional evening. The question is whether the gesture, in all its arrogant sincerity, succeeds in dramatizing or in trivializing the problem."

Then the columnist threw an offhanded compliment to Brando: "Say what you will about him, he's an electrifying nonpresence as well as an electrifying presence."

Hollywood and the Oscars bolted off to new winners, new hatreds, new prejudices. In less than a whispered second, Vanessa Redgrave would play Academy Award villainess; then Michael Cimino and his ultraviolent *Deer Hunter;* then the polished arrogance of Dustin Hoffman; then . . .

But for Sacheen Littlefeather, the Oscar ordeal was only beginning. "I felt used up before the plane even landed back in San Francisco," she said. "I had no idea of the trouble in store for me."

First, a national tabloid questioned her birthright as an American Indian. A relentless reporter produced a birth certificate which purportedly proved that Sacheen—Marie Cruz—was the daughter of a Filipino and a white woman. "I know that there was some confusion about my racial identity," she said. "When I was born, and some clerical worker got my father, William Manuel Cruz, mixed up with a Filipino named Cruz—also an expectant father. Since my father was deaf and couldn't speak, he was unaware of what happened to my birth certificate. And, later, when my mother learned of it, it became a family joke."

(Ironically, Sacheen's mother had filed an amendment to her daughter's birth certificate at the Salinas, California, public records offices. A clerk forgot to transfer that notation to the copies which were made available to the press, and Sacheen's mother had to file again after the Oscar furor in 1973. That correction is now a part of public record.)

Then there was a raging national controversy over Sacheen's name. "I had always been called Sacheen by my family, though my name of record was Marie. As for 'Littlefeather,' that came about during the protest and occupation of Alcatraz Island when I wore a small eagle feather in my headband. That name stuck, appealed to me, flattered me. So I adopted it."

The semiregular employment Sacheen obtained in films and TV evaporated after the Oscar ceremony. "There were too many questions," she said. "I was suddenly considered unhirable . . . there would be trouble if I was hired. I traced these rumors to their sources and realized I was on some kind of blacklist.

"Shortly after this, Barbara Walker, a close friend and producer of one of the Billy Jack movies I had made, called me from Los Angeles very upset and told me that two FBI men with badges had come to her home one morning to question her about me. She was frightened, and so was I."

Sacheen became paranoid. Soon she saw traces of the FBI in all areas of her life—culminating in the public revelation that, for years, an Indian activist whom she trusted and who was important in her life, had been an FBI infiltrator in the American Indian movement. "I realized how serious this was. I *was* under investigation, and there was nothing I could do about it."

The nightmare reached its zenith on a dark night in 1974 when she was fired at by men in a car who sped away. The stress piled upon her increasingly until she retreated into a private shell from which she only recently began to emerge.

"You ask if I felt exploited by Mr. Brando," she said. "I felt exploited . . . period! By everything and everyone. I don't think that Mr. Brando meant to exploit me or hurt me in any way. It just happened that I was exploited in a cruel and vicious way by the media."

If Academy honchos thought the Marlon-Sacheen *cause célèbre* had earned them a deserved respite from controversy, they had only to wait one year to find out that this was not to be.

The Oscarcast on April 2, 1974, was so star-glutted that buses were sent to Los Angeles International Airport to collect the herds winging in from England and France. There was Twiggy and François Truffaut, Liza Minnelli and Linda Blair, Susan Hayward and Alfred Hitchcock. And, as an added Roman candle, Katharine Hepburn, appearing at the ceremony for the first time. Onstage to present the Thalberg Award, she won over the audience with her candor: "I'm so glad," she said, "that I didn't hear anyone call out, 'It's about time.'"

While Hollywood was bowing low to Kate, an offstage drama began unfolding in the half-world behind the curtains. Before it was finished, reporters were running to the phones and the staid Academy officers were gulping Valium like Life-Savers.

The man who caused all the trouble, Robert Opel, had no trouble

ner—a buffo move so cagy that, although TV viewers at home only saw him from the waist up, all six of the onstage cameras captured him head to toe. "I looked up and saw him times six," said the show's director, Marty Pasetta. "And I can tell you a couple of things about him: the 'shortcomings' mentioned by David Niven were anything but . . . and he wasn't Jewish."

★ P.R. man Robert Levinson, who once worked for the Academy, suggested in 1980 that the entire gambit "might have been an internal, secret network job to juggle the ratings."

Whatever the truth may be, the streaker himself will never tell his story. On July 9, 1979, he was shot to death in the San Francisco sex paraphernalia shop he owned. Two men armed with sawed-off shotguns burst through the door of the shop (called Fey Way) and blew Opel away for five dollars, a used camera, and a new backpack.

Police records in both Los Angeles and San Francisco have shown that Opel's professional streaking time lasted from 1973 until late 1974, when he streaked one time too many—in front of the Los Angeles city council. He was convicted for public lewdness and put on four-year probation.

Opel then disappeared into the murkiness of San Francisco's sexual underbelly, only to surface in a blaze of national publicity surrounding his murder.

In 1975, Howard W. Koch was back as producer, and the backstage area exploded into a battlefield for superstars.

Bert Schneider, who won the Oscar for Best Documentary (feature) for *Hearts and Minds*, a controversial anti-Vietnam War film, thanked Hollywood for the award and then took out a telegram sent that day from Hanoi. Thanks, America, said the wire. Thanks for liberating South Vietnam. As Schneider read the words haltingly, the celebrity audience was a bit slow on the uptake. Many people thought the producer was delivering his own sentiments.

While the audience may have been slow, celebrities backstage were not. Bob Hope's face turned ruddy, Frank Sinatra's chin jutted out in hostility, and both men headed for Howard Koch. "This is too serious to let slide," Sinatra said. And Koch later remembered that Hope was furious.

Hope began scrawling a message on a program with Sinatra adding a phrase here and there. With Academy president Walter Mirisch out in the audience, he could not be consulted. So Hope and Sinatra showed Koch what they had written. The producer nodded.

"If you don't want to do it, I *will*," said Hope. Sinatra just shook his head. "I'll do it," he said.

Shirley MacLaine, also backstage, took immediate offense. She spat out a few words to Sinatra, a longtime buddy.

But the singer walked onstage and read the simple statement: "We are not responsible for any political references made on the program. And we are sorry they had to take place this evening."

Shirley collared Sinatra the minute he came offstage. "Why did you do that?" she asked. "You said you were speaking on behalf of the Academy. Well, *I* am a member of the Academy."

"Well, did you agree with that telegram?" asked Sinatra.

"It seemed like a very positive, friendly telegram to me," she answered.

Sinatra, one of the most popular winners in the history of the awards, realized, as perhaps nobody else did that night, that a blatantly political statement like Schneider's would only lead the Oscar show into deeper and deeper political waters. (Network stations reported that the thousands of calls which came in were running at least three-to-one against Schneider's action.)

"The attempts to keep the world of rain and thunder out of the Academy work better some years than others," wrote Charles Champlin in the *Los Angeles Times*. "This year the fact that Hollywood is sharply divided politically, as it always has been, slipped through the smooth, self-congratulatory surfaces."

There was a permanent hole, however, in Oscar's public relations dike. On April 3, 1978, Oscar's fiftieth birthday celebration, the hole became a crashing waterfall. Those putting together the birthday show had their first bout of nerves when they realized that Vanessa Redgrave was the odds-on favorite to win the supporting award for *Julia*. Worse than that, Vanessa was flying into town to collect the award in person. Nerves were certainly in order.

Redgrave, then a four-time nominee for *Morgan!; Isadora; Mary, Queen of Scots;* and *Julia*, is one of the world's finest actresses. But she has never made for smooth sailing on Oscar waters. To the Academy, she was Vanessa of the Hanoi headband, Vanessa the socialist candidate for Parliament, and Vanessa the free spirit. She brought down the house in the sixties when she showed up in a billowing sari with lantana blossoms intertwined with her flying red tresses. In 1978 she was better known for her recent film *The Palestinian*, a movie considered inflammatory and anti-Zionist. (Ironically, Miss Redgrave's nomination and eventual win was a triumph of mature thinking among the Academy's heavily Jewish voters.)

"It wasn't too hard to tell," said Gregg Kilday, a film writer for the *Los Angeles Times*, "that it was going to be a bumpy evening." Indeed, Nazi storm troopers and growling members of the Jewish Defense

Fred Zinneman directing Vanessa Redgrave in Julia *(1977).*

League were hardly grouped outside to root for singer Debby Boone, whose appearance onstage would also become an international issue before the evening was over.

Finally, Redgrave arrived. She was in black, with her red hair catching the rays of a California sunset. She was neither unnerved nor upset by the chanting and hostility outside. In fact, the minute she realized what was going on, she began rewriting her acceptance speech in her head.

Then there were sirens! Forty policemen from ten divisions were rushed to the streets near the Los Angeles Music Center, which, as the Oscar curtain went up, was turned into a battlefield for the JDL and the neo-Nazis. Suddenly, in the dusk, two men rushed up to the steps of the theater, hoisted an elaborate effigy with red hair flying, and then set it afire. The sign dangling from the doll's feet read: VANESSA IS A MURDERER.

Into this maelstrom marched still a third little band—the Arabs, members of the Palestine Liberation Organization. And their signs read, ZIONISM IS RACISM. The Los Angeles police SWAT troopers linked arms and began steering the four hundred away from the theater and into isolated groups. But the disappearance of the press proved to be the final wet blanket, and the militants on all sides, seeing their chances of fame disappearing, hightailed it for home.

If only it had ended there.

But the problem would not disappear. Redgrave won. After her thanks, she added: "You should be very proud that in the last few weeks you stood firm and you refused to be intimidated by the threats of a small bunch of Zionist hoodlums whose behavior is an insult to the stature of Jews all over the world and to their great and heroic . . ." And on, and on, and on.

Even if it had ended there, the Academy would still have had much to be thankful for. No such luck. Presenting an award, playwright Paddy Chayefsky couldn't resist mounting the soapbox to say, "I'm sick and tired of people using the occasion of the Academy Awards for the propagation of their own political propaganda. . . . I'd like to suggest to Miss Redgrave that her winning an Academy Award is not a pivotal moment in history. A simple thank you would have been sufficient."

Chayefsky was so overcome with the sound of his own words that he completely forgot to read the names of the nominees for the Oscar he was presenting, until the uproar in the audience forced him to do so.

That same night there was Debby Boone in virgin white, singing the nominated "You Light Up My Life," as cloyingly sweet a song as the Oscarcast had heard in many a year. Daddy Pat Boone and his wife, Shirley, sat out in the audience, holding hands, saying "wow," and fighting the tears. To make it even more touching, Debby was surrounded, like Dorothy by the Munchkins, with darling ten-year-old girls who interpreted the song in sign language. And within minutes there wasn't a dry eye in the house.

Bob Hope stepped out and announced in an awesome whisper that the girls were from the John Tracy Clinic, named for the deaf son of Oscar winner Spencer Tracy. Who could top that? Right?

The Academy quickly found out as the first calls began jamming the network switchboards. The sign language, as it turned out, was basically inept. And the deaf members in the TV audience had picked up on it. Oscar officers had to shamefacedly admit that the girls were not deaf and that they had come from the Sam Levy public school in nearby

Torrance. "After all," said a P.R. spokesman for the Academy, "nobody actually *said* the children were really deaf. And a doctor at the Tracy Clinic *did* recruit them."

"But we're offended," said the president of the newly founded Alliance for Deaf Artists. "Because we have many, many deaf children who could have done the same thing if only they'd been given the opportunity. What happened on the Oscar show was really the last straw in that it represented the industry's traditional misrepresentation of the deaf."

The Academy blushed and began looking hopefully ahead to the 1979 show.

But 1978 was the year the movies finally came to grips with the Vietnam War; it was a case of better late than never. The fact that Jane Fonda had to fight for six years to scrape together the cash to film *Coming Home* speaks for itself. Hollywood was afraid of Vietnam films and more afraid of the ultraconservative audiences who might boycott them. But *Coming Home* with Fonda and Jon Voight, and Michael Cimino's *The Deer Hunter* with Meryl Streep and Robert De Niro, broke the Vietnam embargo. They were fine movies, and the public lined up to see them. Both had fat parcels of nominations, and *The Deer Hunter* was the two-to-one favorite to win the big one—Best Picture of 1978.

These odds were well earned. Academy voters were wined, dined, and otherwise wooed by Universal in the most cold-blooded and calculated campaign since the one for *Gone With The Wind*. The fact that

A touching moment in Oscar history: Debby Boone singing the Oscar-winning song of 1977—"You Light up My Life"—with a staircaseful of girls signing the lyrics for the international television audience. But the performance turned into a scandal when deaf activist organizations learned that the girls were far from deaf.

neither film needed help was of no consequence to fearful Hollywood executives. They had learned to their distress and heartburn that a good campaign for a lousy picture could easily get it a nomination over a really great film. Columbia Pictures, for instance, had achieved an Oscar nomination for the dreadful *Oliver!* at the expense of one of the finest films ever made, Stanley Kubrick's *2001: A Space Odyssey*. Even worse was the fact that *Oliver!* was named Best Picture of the Year.

But the campaign for *The Deer Hunter*, costing more than $250,000, blazed new trails of hype in a town gorged on public relations. From the day the film was finished until the night it won the Oscar, the studio made no move that was not geared toward the Academy's estimated 3,500 voters. Universal even turned to Tinseltown's king of hype, Allan Carr, producer of that celluloid bit of bubble gum, *Grease*. Carr's orders were to sell the movie, and to sell it by first winning the Oscar. First, Carr had to see the movie. He said he came away from his private screening "crying like a baby. Why, I was crying so hard I had to go to the men's room and put cold water on my face. I was having dinner with Governor Brown that night, and I was so emotionally undone I had to apologize personally to Jerry Brown." Carr told the gov, "I've been affected so deeply I just can't speak tonight."

Carr left a trail of salt water all the way to the offices of those entertainment bibles *Daily Variety* and the *Hollywood Reporter*. But he was certainly dry-eyed when he designed lavish supplements to those papers, loaded with color stills from the film and heavily burdened with positive reviews. Special editions of the ads were immediately mailed to the homes of the Academy members.

Billboards soaring above Hollywood's Sunset Boulevard blazed in the winter sun, with a minimal message. "I sensed right away that this is an 'event' movie. It's not *Grease,* where it's ninety minutes in and out and turn over the box-office grosses," Carr told a Los Angeles columnist. So Carr waited until the hype in New York and Hollywood neared hysteria and then opened the film for eight showings in L.A.'s university suburb, Westwood, and in Manhattan. "I knew it would be the Christmas-cocktail-party subject in New York," said Carr. "Everybody would be asking if you were one of the five hundred people who saw one of the eight shows. They said to me, 'You can't give a film to New York and then just take it right away.' I answered, 'That's how you treat New York.'"

The opening of *The Deer Hunter* in Westwood is now legend. People mobbed the box office and everybody who was *anybody* bombarded Universal with requests for "house tickets." Lauren Bacall asked, so did Charlton Heston and Rudolf Nureyev. "Imagine everybody's reaction when we told them, 'There aren't any. We're saving this film for the Academy.'"

It worked! The members of the Academy of Motion Picture Arts and Sciences took the bait like underfed trout in the Colorado River. Universal royally used all of its Oscar screening time to virtually guarantee that the film would be shown at times that would fit the schedule of the busiest Oscar voter. The studio even put a full-time staff member at the door who carefully counted the number of voters showing their Academy cards to get in. The final tally was an unheard of 2,400 of the 3,500 eligible voters; most studios estimate that only 25 to 40 percent of the Oscar voters see any eligible film.

Carr has expressed his belief that the campaign was helped greatly by opening the film out of town. "L.A. is jaded and spoiled by the movies. At previews in Westwood they cheer for Telly Savalas chasing an airplane."

Then Carr scheduled a golden-circle showing with an audience of two—directors Steven Spielberg and Vincente Minnelli. The young lion (Spielberg) and the old master (Minnelli) represented opposite poles of the powerful Directors Guild of America. When Carr bundled his select audience into the screening room, the DGA Awards were only a week or two away. And Carr was obviously relying on that audience to be impressed and to spread the word: for most of the past twenty years the director winning the DGA Award has also directed the film ultimately winning the Oscar.

Right on target! *The Deer Hunter*'s Cimino was quickly named director of the year—an honor he would have undoubtedly won in any case.

Analyzing the strategy, the *Los Angeles Times* noted, "The making of the campaign for *The Deer Hunter* is a case study of what happens when a major studio incorporates a run for the Oscar into its overall marketing strategy for a commercially shaky film. And eight months ago *The Deer Hunter* (the *Times* story appeared two months after the Oscars) was both a box-office long shot and an Oscar dark horse.

"Carr's campaign seemed to have pinpointed timing and strategies of exposure. He was backed by the highest levels at Universal, who obviously counted on the Oscar to help them with a very tough marketing job."

But Carr hastened to add: "Of course, none of this would have worked if we hadn't had a brilliant film." (Many Oscar watchers worry that the strategy will spread to films that aren't quite so worthy, creating an entirely new way to buy the Oscar.)

With their Oscars in hand, Best Actor Jon Voight, Best Actress Jane Fonda, and Best Director Michael Cimino, greet four hundred of the world's reporters. This photograph notwithstanding, it was not all cookies and milk backstage. Neither the Coming Home *alumni nor* The Deer Hunter *veterans could contain their animosity, and Cimino, at one point, pulled away from Fonda. Still later, Best Supporting Actor Christopher Walken of* The Deer Hunter *said, "I'm glad I beat him," referring to Bruce Dern of* Coming Home, *his major competition. Oscar had come light years since the Best Picture of 1946. The* Best Years of Our Lives *was cheered by a unanimous audience—many of them, like Clark Gable, still in World War II uniforms.*
(© A.M.P.A.S.)

So that's how *The Deer Hunter* came into the Oscar arena as a two-to-one shot. The film's only real competition, Jane Fonda's *Coming Home*, a soap opera about one woman's odyssey into the soul of a handicapped veteran of the war in Vietnam, was an odds-on favorite to take the two best acting awards, with Bruce Dern a dark horse for Best Supporting Actor.

Unfortunately, on the night of the awards, Vietnam also dominated the streets and sidewalks outside the Music Center as members of Vietnam Veterans Against the War, the Association of Vietnamese Patriots, and the We Won't Go Away Committee came to cheer Fonda and boo Cimino. *The Deer Hunter*, they claimed, was pro-war and anti-vet. Their placards—NO OSCAR FOR RACISM, *THE DEER HUNTER* IS A DIRTY LIE, and PROFIT IS THEIR HOLY WORD—were waved above the limos as Robin Williams, Christopher Reeve, and Donna Summer alighted and headed through Hollywood's golden arches. The protests were echoed inside in a chilly feud between the *Coming Home* Oscar winners and *The Deer Hunter* champs.

Film writer Lee Grant, of the *Los Angeles Times*, was backstage from the first shout to the last yawn, which allowed for a rare view from behind Oscar's curtain of hype: "Like everybody else, working or not, you root silently [and some reporters even openly] for the pictures you want to win. I was happy for *The Deer Hunter*, but I thought Robert De Niro gave the performance of a lifetime in the same film. But Jon Voight won."

The sparks of bad feeling between the *Coming Home* gang and Cimino's guys first erupted when *The Deer Hunter*'s Christopher Walken walked off with the Oscar for Best Supporting Actor. Of Bruce Dern, his competitor, Walken said, "I'm glad I beat him."

Grant said that Fonda was a popular winner among the press "because she's always good for a quote. However, professionally, most reporters felt the best performance of the year was Geraldine Page's in Woody Allen's *Interiors*, followed by Jill Clayburgh's in *An Unmarried Woman*.

CHAPTER NINE

Backstage

Nice speech, Eve, but I wouldn't worry too much about your heart. You can always put that award where your heart ought to be.

—BETTE DAVIS (AS MARGO) TO ANNE BAXTER (AS EVE) IN *ALL ABOUT EVE*, 1950

Although the warm California sun beamed brightly that February day in 1963, 3,000 miles away in New York, the frown on Joan Crawford's face matched the dark, wintry sky above as she sat stiff-backed at her writing table in the elegantly appointed apartment she had shared with her late husband, Pepsi president Alfred Steele.

Over black coffee, Joan was reading the *New York Times* story on the 1962 Oscar nominations. For Best Actress: Anne Bancroft for *The Miracle Worker,* Geraldine Page for *Sweet Bird of Youth,* Katharine Hepburn for *Long Day's Journey into Night,* Lee Remick for *Days of Wine and Roses,* and (gasp!) Bette Davis for *Whatever Happened to Baby Jane?*

The other nominations didn't matter. Joan flung the newspaper across the room and grabbed for her pale blue stationery all in one angry motion. Dashing off handwritten congratulatory notes to Bancroft, Page, Hepburn, and Remick, she closed by declaring she would be "delighted" to accept their Oscars should they be unable to attend the ceremonies six weeks later.

Bancroft, appearing on the New York stage at the time, had already asked *Miracle Worker* co-star Patty Duke to accept should she be lucky enough to win, a request that had been turned down by the Academy, since Patty herself was also nominated for an Oscar.

Joan followed up her notes with six weeks of rigorous campaigning among the Academy's New York contingent to get the Oscar for Bancroft, an actress she didn't know and probably had never met. In truth, it was as much a campaign *against* Davis as it was *for* Bancroft.

When it came time for Oscar night, Joan and Bette were both on hand. Davis was there to present the writing awards (and would certainly be available to receive her *own* Oscar). Crawford had also been asked to present an award, to the year's Best Director. And Bancroft, undoubtedly moved by Joan's appreciation of her performance as Annie Sullivan, had agreed to have her Oscar picked up by Crawford.

158

It should have begun and ended with that. However, Joan seized the opportunity to repay the affronts, real or imagined, she had suffered at the hands of Bette prior to, during, and following the shooting of *Baby Jane*. (Davis had completely upstaged Crawford at the press conference arranged by Jack Warner the day filming began on the picture by wearing a simple frock of basic black to Crawford's out-of-place, completely outrageous couture original. And because she had waived a salary of $75,000 in favor of a lucrative percentage arrangement, Davis cooperated fully with nationwide personal appearances, assuring the huge grosses the film later garnered.)

It was now time for Crawford to exact sweet revenge. She turned her star dressing room backstage at the Santa Monica Civic Auditorium into a huge party, with Pepsis all around and tables fairly groaning with the choicest morsels. It began with the first Oscar presentation and did not let up until the last award was given. Everyone was invited: winners, losers, presenters.

At last time came for the Best Actress award. The nominees were announced one by one. Davis was waiting in the wings hoping to hear her own name read as the winner. It was not to be. "And the winner is . . . Anne Bancroft for *The Miracle Worker*." At first, there was a silence. And then applause. Davis started as she felt an icy hand on her shoulder and turned to see Joan Crawford. Staring straight at the podium, Joan intoned, with venom dripping from every word, "Pardon me, but I have an Oscar to accept."

Old hurts apparently die hard. Fully twenty-three years after the events of that Oscar night (and nearly a decade after Joan Crawford had gone to her reward), Davis was still unwilling or unable to forgive and forget.

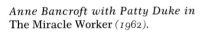

Anne Bancroft with Patty Duke in The Miracle Worker *(1962).*

On May 21, 1986, the seventy-eight-year-old Davis was the sole guest on Johnny Carson's "Tonight" show. Still the movie queen, resplendent in a scarlet silk organza, she felt obliged to correct the record, and while it may not yet be the final word on Joan Crawford, this is what she said:

Responding to Carson's question "Is there any film you think you should have won the Oscar for and didn't?"

"Not one—*three!*" bellowed Bette, between great clouds of cigarette smoke. "There was *Dark Victory* in 1939. But that was the year of *Gone With The Wind*, and I was gone with the wind. Then I always felt I should have won for Margo [in *All About Eve*]. But I was not under contract to Fox. Miss Baxter was. The studio got the word out that it was throwing its weight behind their contract player. That's the way they did it in those days. But the one I was *really* robbed of was *Jane*. Miss Crawford went to New York and announced to anyone who would listen that she would gladly accept the Oscar for any of the nominees who could not attend the presentations. Sure enough, Miss Bancroft won and could not attend as she was appearing in *Mother Courage* on Broadway. But the Widow Steele was there to receive the prize. She carried the Oscar around for a year selling Pepsi-Cola. She bathed it in the waters of the world. A year later—*one year later*—she threw a party onstage at the theater where *Mother Courage* was still playing and finally presented Miss Bancroft with her Oscar."

Thus it was that two of the cinema's greatest and most dignified actresses reduced themselves to bitchy gutter cats—clawing each other, stabbing each other's friends in the back, and mauling the industry which made them rich and famous. And all over a hunk of tin, brass, and a teensy-weensy bit of gold.

Those two black-widow queens of the thirties, Bette Davis and Joan Crawford, beam at each other ever so sweetly at the start of the filming of a comeback movie for both, What Ever Happened to Baby Jane? (1962). But the smiles faded as the atmosphere on the set became increasingly stormy. When Bette was nominated and Joan passed over, an Oscar vendetta erupted—the likes of which hadn't been seen before and hasn't been seen since.

The top lineup for the Oscar-winning All About Eve *(1950). Left to right: Anne Baxter, Bette Davis, Marilyn Monroe, and George Sanders (who took home the Best Supporting Actor award). Since Baxter and Davis were pitted against each other for Best Actress, Bette blamed studio politics for her defeat by Judy Holliday in* Born Yesterday. *Since Fox threw its support to Anne, Bette had to fend for herself. "Hell yes, I should have won," she recently snapped to Johnny Carson.*

One of Oscar's most touching moments: Best Actress Louise Fletcher signing along with her acceptance speech. The daughter of deaf parents, Fletcher said she wanted to tell them of her "special gratitude." Jill Ireland, presenter of the award for One Flew over the Cuckoo's Nest, *stands at left.* (© A.M.P.A.S.)

An Oscar ceremony is like the world's largest Kiwanis Club luncheon gone stark-raving mad with greed, covetousness, envy, and hate.

Those almost unbearably ugly little statuettes are like Kewpie doll trolls which spring to life in the dark and lash out at those who possess them—those who fight to gain them with all the ferocity of pit bulls.

Friend turns against friend, sister against sister, agent against client, director against star in the maniacal rush to take home this golden bitch toy.

And to what purpose?

Will an Oscar buy good roles? The finest to be had? Ask Warner Baxter, Faye Dunaway, Louise Fletcher, Luise Rainer, or Mercedes McCambridge.

Will it bring you peace of mind? Ask the troubled Richard Dreyfuss, who descended into a private hell with an Oscar held tightly in one fist. Or Mary Pickford, who retreated—with her statuette—into a dark bedroom to become a real-life Norma Desmond, hiding in perpetual night.

Will it buy immortality? Ask Emil Jannings, who died alone and unremembered in a Swiss chalet. Or Anne Revere, who although innocent, was hounded out of town during the shameful period of the blacklist and even with an Oscar alongside her, could never revive a brilliant career.

The fierceness of competition and the divisiveness of the ceremony itself has turned Oscar's backstage into a jungle where fear and hysteria prevail, often wreaking havoc on the lives of those who come in contact with this tempting, glittering and seductive rite.

It would be foolish to believe that the parameters of the ceremony's "backstage" begin and end behind the curtains at the Music Center. Far from it: once Oscar season starts in January, the entire town becomes the stage for a sun-drenched passion play in which actors, producers, and studio executives start rushing for the gold—tawdry and tainted though it may be.

Oscar-winning sisters Olivia de Havilland and Joan Fontaine, however, have acted out the shabbiest, though by far the most classic, case of Oscar envy in a feud which has spread over four decades and across three continents, and which has left a dozen Oscar ceremonies scarred by emotional rocket blasts.

It started in a simple, touching way.

The year was 1939, and Olivia's performance as Melanie Hamilton in *Gone With The Wind* was considered by some to have been the best in the film—finer-toned than Vivien Leigh's and less obtrusive than Clark Gable's. De Havilland called up Errol Flynn late one night to mull over her chances for a Best Actress Oscar. "Don't count on it," said Flynn. "You're a Warner Bros. star, and David O. Selznick has a lot of

A classic triumvirate from Gone With the Wind *(1939). Left to right: Olivia de Havilland, Leslie Howard, and Vivien Leigh. Olivia's loss that night to Hattie McDaniel as Best Supporting Actress apparently created in her a mighty thirst for Oscar glory, which was not to be satisfied for nearly a decade. To make it worse, her baby sister, Joan Fontaine, got an Oscar first.*

money riding on Vivien Leigh. As for MGM [distributors of the film], they won't care about you at all."

Then Selznick informed de Havilland that he was entering her in the Best Supporting Actress category. He told her flatly: "I don't want you hurting Vivien's chances to win as Best Actress."

This put her up against Hattie McDaniel, the beloved black actress who played Mammy in the same film. Still, Olivia hoped against hope that her powerful presence would win out.

She was in for a disappointment. The actress was seated at a table with David O. Selznick when McDaniel's name was announced. As McDaniel delivered a succinct and elegant speech, de Havilland dissolved in tears and sobs, which she tried to stifle with an embroidered handkerchief.

Finally, in embarrassment, Irene Selznick (David's wife and the daughter of Louis B. Mayer) dragged Olivia—silk dress bustling—into the kitchen at the Coconut Grove. "She took my shoulders and shook me again and again," said de Havilland, "telling me there would be plenty of Oscars in the future, and then hugged me while I cried into an immense bowl of consommé destined for the post-awards banquet. 'Compose yourself,' Irene ordered. 'And then go right out there and congratulate Hattie.' "

Like the good little contract player she was, Olivia sailed back out into the spotlight and played the gracious, all-forgiving Melanie Hamilton, as she was to do again and again in her long career.

But the seeds of envy were planted.

Then her lissome blond sister sallied forth as a budding actress—an abnormally pretty thing who burst on the film scene almost on a dare by her older sister that she "couldn't make it." And, indeed, for four years Fontaine was a blonde awash in an entire industry of blondes, languishing in such films as *No More Ladies*. Then Fred Astaire, tired of an increasingly difficult Ginger Rogers, hired her to co-star with him in *Damsel in Distress,* with music by George Gershwin. Fontaine was on her way to full stardom.

De Havilland's own career had been stalled in the stalwart mud of Errol Flynn pictures—as Maid Marian in *The Adventures of Robin Hood,* and as the downstairs lover in *The Private Lives of Elizabeth and Essex*. Miss Olivia was soon tripped up in her own crinolines and heaving bosom. But she stayed at Errol's side. "It's true, I fell in love with him," she said in 1986. "He was the most wonderful, most exciting man I had ever been around. It was thoroughly unrequited, but I loved him all the same."

As her sister dallied in Flynn's arms, Fontaine scurried under her skirt and stole the part of a lifetime—that of the terrified heroine in Alfred Hitchcock's *Rebecca*. De Havilland, Hitchcock's first choice, seethed. Jack Warner refused to loan her out. "I'm sorry I loaned you out for *Gone With The Wind,*" he yelled at her. "I've learned my lesson . . . you stay at Warner Brothers"—which meant at Flynn's side, playing out a dozen attacks of the vapors.

Joan snatched up the part and negotiated the very first of Hollywood's independent pacts—picture-by-picture deals which let her pick and choose like a prize grocer at Hollywood's Farmers' Market.

Oscar voters gave the younger sister a rush of approval and nominated her as Best Actress in 1941 for *Rebecca*. She lost to the ubiquitous Ginger Rogers for *Kitty Foyle,* but by the barest of whiskers.

Polling all the voters, Hedda Hopper declared that Rogers had beaten Fontaine by only three votes.

The older sister just squeezed into another crinoline and hiked off into the Errol Flynn sunset to make *Santa Fe Trail*.

The subject of Academy Awards became taboo at the teas their mother held each Sunday in a vain hope that crumpets and cucumber sandwiches would serve to hold together her collapsing family.

Olivia had fought for a key part in *Hold Back the Dawn* and was rewarded with a second Oscar nomination in 1942. "You got it in the hat, kid," Louella Parsons assured her this time.

Nobody counted on the Academy atoning for its guilt. Perhaps the members had taken a good, hard look at Ginger Rogers's ridiculous performance and melted into the cement at Grauman's Chinese Theater. In any case, with another Oscar-nominated, Hitchcock-directed performance (in *Suspicion*), it looked like Joan would easily triumph over sister Olivia.

The day before the ceremonies, Fontaine decided it would be difficult for her to attend, still being somewhat new to the Hollywood Oscar experience. De Havilland felt that her sister's absence would damage her own stature in the film community.

Fontaine was working at RKO when she received a call from de Havilland, who said: "You must attend the dinner. Your absence would look odd; the contestants in all categories are expected to be there and moreover I'm an Academy member. You must be there."

Finally Fontaine said, "I haven't anything to wear."

Joan Fontaine recoils from Cary Grant in Suspicion, *which brought her the Oscar—years ahead of her older sister. She claimed she never flaunted it. But Louella Parsons disagreed, saying, "Joan wouldn't let Livvy forget who had the statuette."*

An hour later de Havilland arrived at RKO in a limousine with the saleslady who attended both sisters at I. Magnin in Beverly Hills. They deposited in Fontaine's dressing room seven tan-and-white-striped boxes containing all the size-six dresses that the store possessed.

Between takes, Fontaine tried on one dress after another. Finally she decided on one.

Just before the ceremony, a limousine arrived (ordered by de Havilland), picked up Fontaine from her home and delivered her to the Biltmore Hotel, where the dinner was held that year.

The big picture of the year was *How Green Was My Valley*, but the Best Actress award was considered a toss-up. The nominees were Bette Davis for *The Little Foxes*, Greer Garson for *Blossoms in the Dust*, Barbara Stanwyck for *Ball of Fire*, de Havilland for *Hold Back the Dawn*, and Fontaine for *Suspicion*.

After several anxious moments Fontaine's name was announced. She sat as if transfixed. De Havilland, two seats away, finally leaned over and jabbed her with an elbow. "Joan," she said, "get up there and accept that award!"

There's no reason to disbelieve de Havilland's graciousness that night—perhaps there was still more than a soupçon of Melanie Hamilton in her. So she pulled in her fingernails and posed ever so cutely with her baby sister and her Oscar. This was to be a first and a last; it was total war from then on.

Hoisting her Oscar as a banner, Fontaine sailed from one triumph to another—working in Britain, Hollywood, and France during the same era and at a yearly salary in the millions.

Alas, Olivia became the unfortunate step-sister—sent back to Warner Bros. Oscarless and at the mercy of Jack Warner—never the best of Hollywood bosses and quite often the worst. He told her she would be bound to her contract.

After coming so close to two Oscars, the tea at the Warner Bros. commissary was bitter as she was relegated to playing maidens with heaving bosoms—who were usually in thrall to Errol Flynn.

"I liked Errol Flynn, don't get me wrong," de Havilland said recently. "But my parts consisted of wearing fancy gowns and smiling quite a bit." Her films seemed to deteriorate with each year—from *The Adventures of Robin Hood*, to *Hard to Get* and *Wings of the Navy*. By 1943, Jack Warner had shoved her into a clutch of B films such as *Princess O'Rourke* and *Government Girl*.

So she walked out the gates and refused to return for nearly three years. In the meantime, she turned to the courts.

She did give Warner a chance to make amends. One fine spring day she walked into his office with an ultimatum: she was to be treated "as good as Bette Davis. I get good parts or I walk."

Warner's pudgy hand indicated the door.

De Havilland was off the screen for thirty months—an absence that would have completely collapsed most careers.

She spent her entire savings and even took out a loan to pay a battery of attorneys. De Havilland and her legal eagles zeroed in on an unenforced California law which limited to seven years the period any employer could enforce a contract against an employee. Jack Warner scoffed at this effort. De Havilland had options in her pact which would have, Warner felt, allowed him to keep her under his thumb for at least twelve years.

How sweet it is. Joan Fontaine stops by sister Olivia de Havilland's table the night Joan won the Best Actress Award for Suspicion *(1941), a victory which ignited a forty-five year feud between the famous siblings.*

It was a black and bitter day for the studio moguls when the California courts ruled in de Havilland's favor—a ruling reaffirmed by the state's supreme court. It gave freedom to dozens of Hollywood actors and artists, and the majority opinion is known to this day as the "De Havilland Decision."

The actress returned to work with a vengeance, starting with two important films, *The Dark Mirror* and *To Each His Own,* a 1946 film which won her the Best Actress Oscar.

This should have ended the petty rivalry and Oscar vengeance which swirled about the sisters, the rest of their family and even friends, who, engulfed, were forced to take sides as the feud grew and grew, becoming the gossip item that swallowed Hollywood.

At the height of the Oscar season, 1946, Joan and her husband William Dozier went to Pebble Beach for a riding weekend only to meet Olivia and her new husband, Marcus Goodrich. "I don't know who Olivia talked to," exclaimed Joan. "But I have already seen it printed that 'Olivia can't even go on a vacation without her sister trailing her.' "

This only fanned an already raging newsprint fire.

Louella Parsons, noting the teensy little feud at Pebble Beach, ran this item: "I have never, never scolded Joan Fontaine in print because I like her, but I think she should not discuss this quarrel with her sister. When Olivia read what Joan had to say, they had to call a doctor in to administer a sedative."

Goodrich then telephoned Hedda Hopper to say, "Can't you shut Joan up? Olivia is in hysterics."

Hedda instantly called Joan.

"This is horrible, simply horrible," said Fontaine. All of this over the Academy Awards."

As she accepted the award, de Havilland gushed, "At last, at last."

Olivia, Oscar firmly in hand, was sailing back to her seat when Fontaine grabbed her hand. "I'm so happy for you," Joan tried to say as Olivia brushed by in a cloud of Chanel No. 5.

Gossip columnists swarmed both tables.

"Why did she do that, when she knows just how I feel?" lamented Olivia that same night.

Joan countered, "Do you know what she said as I tried to congratulate her? Do you know what my own sister said? She said, 'Ugh.' "

The next morning Louella Parsons, *the* columnist in town, was awakened by a sobbing Joan: "After I stuck my hand out that night at the Academy Awards and said, 'Good girl,' Olivia issued a thing to the press that was printed all over the world saying, 'Oh, Joan just did that to get publicity for herself.' "

The feud, though, died down over the years as both actresses drifted further and further from the Oscar-caliber roles.

But you can imagine the consternation when an Academy Awards director peeked through the ceremonial curtain to see Miss Melanie Hamilton (Olivia)—with crinolines at full sail—heading directly for an empty seat next to Jane Eyre (Joan), who was hovering in sedate velvet. An enterprising young page had noticed that the sisters were seated apart and made a very difficult switch so they could be together.

"My God almighty," said the director. "Get out there and put her in another seat—*any* other seat—but not next to her sister."

Oscar often brings out the worst in people, so important is it to the economic and social realities of Hollywood. To be seen on the arms of an Oscar nominee is often the entree to Tinseltown society. Seats to the ceremonies are coveted to such an extent that the Academy is stormed each year by its members, strangers, families of the nominees, and hangers-on—all of them wanting to don evening clothes and bathe in the sweet glow of Oscar fame.

One bitter fight over an Oscar appearance led indirectly to a tragedy: the killing of Johnny Stompanato in Lana Turner's bedroom. According to Turner, Stompanato, the handsome Hollywood hanger-on, who had been her beau for almost a year, assumed he would escort her to the 1958 ceremony. The actress, who at that time was trying to break off with him, later said, "I certainly wasn't going to appear before the leading lights of the industry with John on my arm." Her refusal to take him inflamed Stompanato, who yelled, "Well, you're not going to the ball afterward. You're coming home to me!"

Turner, nominated for Best Actress for *Peyton Place*, made a spectacular entrance, minus her escort. She went to a private party after the ceremony and returned home to find Stompanato in a rage.

"He told me I was never to cut him out of anything again," Turner said. "And he roughed me up for the first time in front of my daughter Cheryl." A week later, on the night of April 4, 1958, their fighting intensified, causing Cheryl to rush to the bedroom to protect her mother. When Stompanato pulled the door open abruptly, Cheryl careened into him, accidentally stabbing him in the abdomen with the knife she was carrying. After the tragedy, it took Lana Turner five years to muster up enough courage to appear again at the Oscars.

Some stars are willing to mask heartbreak for the annual rite. In April 1966, Kim Novak and her husband of one year, British actor Richard Johnson, made a dazzling entrance: she in a golden knit by Jean

John Garfield and Lana Turner, two fine performers who were destined never to win Oscars, in a bleakly lighted scene from The Postman Always Rings Twice *(1945). Tay Garnett, the film's director, knew there was only one actor who could duplicate the range required to play the James M. Cain character. Several years later Garfield, one of the biggest names to be blacklisted, died of a heart attack the night before he was to testify before HUAC.*

Louis and he in dinner clothes fashioned by one of Prince Philip's tailors. The orchestra struck up "Love Walked In" as they stepped on-stage. That morning the couple had agreed to file for divorce. "We were a phony couple that night," Kim later told her longtime friend Mac Krim. "Even though I could barely fight back the tears, I put my arm through Richard's and looked up at him lovingly, as he looked at me with the same expression. I had to go through with it, and that was rough, but I went through it for the sake of the industry. Millions of people would have been disappointed."

Some special appearances, however, proved to be triumphs. For Oscar-show producer Howard W. Koch, the all-time high point of the Academy Awards was the presentation in 1972 to movie great Charlie Chaplin, who years earlier had fled Hollywood after being blacklisted for alleged Communist sympathies. At first, Koch wondered if Chaplin would still be bitter about his years of exile—there was even some question as to whether or not he'd show up.

One night shortly before the awards, Koch saw a newsreel of Chaplin literally being carried out of a limousine in New York City. "I wondered, my God, was he going to make it? What's going to happen when he gets up in front of eighty million people? A heart attack? A stroke? What if he dies right there on camera? I know it was terrible to think that, but it was going through my head. So to be safe, I called the Academy and suggested we put him on at the end.

Kim Novak and fiancé Mac Krim at an Oscar banquet in the fifties.

"I got an okay from the board. We brought Chaplin out in his wheelchair and put him behind a special screen on which we ran a twelve-minute clip of his life [a stunning montage put together by Peter Bogdanovich]. I watched carefully to see if he was okay. He didn't seem to be moving. I got very nervous. Time was flying. Was he sleeping or was he . . . ? Then, without rehearsal, about a minute before he was to make his appearance on stage, he got his cue. They moved him into full view of the audience. The lights shone on him, and all of a sudden the adrenaline flowed. He stood up, and the blood rushed through him, and he was *alive*—lucid, touching, and wonderful. The most incredible moment I've ever known."

"When John Wayne finally made the decision that he would appear on the 1979 Oscars," said the show's producer, Jack Haley, Jr., "it was on the condition that nobody know that Wayne was dying of cancer. So besides the Duke, his son Pat, and myself, nobody knew."

John Wayne's appearance went smoothly, offstage and on. And the shouting was just about over in Wayne's dressing room when two guys showed up from the audience just to pay their respects. "Now, Wayne had said he was ready to go home," said Haley. "But I told him he might want to talk to these guys because they, too, had been waiting around for a long time."

Wayne agreed and the two old guys came through the door and offered their hands. "The Duke's face lit up like a western sunset," said a longtime Academy publicist, "because those two guys were, of course, Cary Grant and Larry Olivier."

171

Many of the juiciest backstage stories take place *far* from the Dorothy Chandler Pavilion, in the snug confines of Beverly Hills and Bel Air.

Rock Hudson learned about Oscar rigors in the filmy pink bedroom of Mae West's towering Hollywood penthouse. They had been tagged to sing "Baby, It's Cold Outside" at the 1958 Oscarcast, but Mae refused to rehearse anywhere but home—kitsch though it was.

Rock was told to arrive at 2:00 P.M. precisely on the Saturday before the show. He showed up in Levi's and a white T-shirt only to find Mae in a shocking-pink negligée through which you could see all the way to . . .

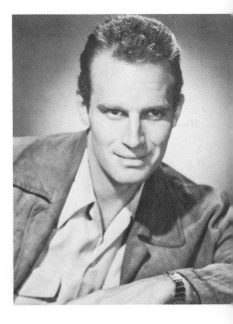

The tip of one tiny Westian toe poked through the silken gauze and traced an imaginary line across a glittering pink carpet. "We'll do our little dance right here, Rock," she said before putting on the phonograph a record of the song originally done by Esther Williams and Ricardo Montalban in *Neptune's Daughter*.

As Hudson tried bravely to sing the special, racier words, West folded herself into his arms and shoved her hands in the back pockets of his jeans.

He stopped dead. "This isn't, uh, the way we're going to do it," he protested.

"Well, sure," said West. "Only you're gonna be wearing a tux."

"I don't think so," said the blushing Hudson. "You're gonna be on the couch, and I'll be singing in front of you."

"We'll see. We'll see," cooed West as her hands continued to explore.

When Rock tried on his tuxedo for a run-through Sunday afternoon, he discovered that Miss West had ordered it altered, making the pants so tight that Rock couldn't sit down. "I immediately knew why," he said. "That way I couldn't get nearer by kneeling down and she could steal the show."

Hudson dashed home to change with his tux in hand. The garment was dropped off at a tailor's for restoration, which wasn't completed until eighteen minutes before curtain time.

Hudson drove by the tailor's, grabbed the tux, and speeded to the Pantages Theater still wearing jeans and a T-shirt. "I discovered they forgot to give me a parking place, and the cop refused to let me go in."

The actor yelled, "I'm Rock Hudson, can't you see that?"

"I don't care who you are, buddy," snarled the cop. "You aren't getting into that parking lot." Rock's face reddened and he floored the gas pedal, causing his convertible to roar up over the curb and into a fire lane. He pulled into a priority space outside the stage door. "I jumped out, bounded up the steps, and shrugged on my tux as a makeup man worked on my face and a barber tousled my hair.

The music had already started when I raced out onstage to stand in front of Mae. I noticed that she had turned the couch in such a way that she was in front of the audience. I would have been completely upstaged."

Hudson edged Mae off the couch, turned it around, and flopped down on it himself just as the stage turned toward the audience. "I upstaged *her*."

One infamous backstage story occurred entirely in the mind. In 1969 the outrageous psychic Kenny Kingston staged a massive séance to reach Clifton Webb and Fannie Brice so that he could poll them about the Oscar races. Kingston was particularly interested in Fannie's reply because Barbra Streisand was up for an Oscar in *Funny Girl*, playing Miss Brice.

"You know what Fannie told me," Kingston said to a waiting press. "She said *Funny Girl* will not win Best Picture, but another musical will. And she said Barbra Streisand will not win as Best Actress—but that she will not lose either."

For some reason, this news was flashed around the world, with amusing results. Ray Stark, producer of *Funny Girl* and Miss Brice's son-in-law, called up Kingston to roar, "Damn you; you've just cost me the spiritual vote."

But Kingston was right. Barbra tied with Katharine Hepburn on Oscar night and another musical, *Oliver!*, won the Oscar.

Mrs. Ray Stark, the former Fran Brice, chastised the psychic for still another reason. Kingston had reported that, in his dream-séance, he had accompanied Fannie and Clifton Webb to a restaurant in the San Fernando Valley. "That just couldn't be true," sniffed Mrs. Stark. "Mother wouldn't have been caught dead in the San Fernando Valley."

Psychic powers aside, Oscar ceremonies can cause jitters in the breasts of the most stouthearted.

In 1974, Katharine Hepburn was set to present the Irving Thalberg Award to her friend Lawrence Weingarten. But according to Marty Pasetta, the show's director, she declined to attend rehearsal unless the stage was cleared for her. Pasetta called an early lunch, motioned for Hepburn to enter, and watched her take an ancient typewriter downstage to write her speech. She delivered it perfectly—from memory—in a single run-through.

The next night, Pasetta said, Hepburn remained outside the pavilion watching a TV monitor in her limo while awaiting her cue. She then hurried inside, presented the award, returned to her car, and left.

According to Pasetta, another star of Hepburn's magnitude was afraid to appear as a Best Actor nominee lest he be seen showing dis-

Charlton Heston, one of the most popular Oscar winners in history, has given a touching, indelible portrait of what it feels like to win. Writing in his diary at 5:00 A.M. the day after he won as Best Actor for Ben-Hur (1959), *Heston noted: "Just before Susan Hayward read it off, something popped into my head. 'I'm going to get it.' And I did. I kissed my wife and walked to the stage dripping wet, except for a pepper-dry mouth: classic stage fright. I'll never forget that moment, or the night. Backstage, posing with William Wyler, I said, 'I guess this is old hat to you.' 'Chuck,' he said, 'it never gets old hat.'" Wyler was also a winner as Best Director for* Ben-Hur.

In her only appearance at the Academy Awards, Katharine Hepburn gave the Thalberg Award to producer-executive Lawrence Weingarten in 1974. The four-time Oscar winner proved to be so shy of attention that she insisted on appearing alone (with director Marty Pasetta) during the run-through. At the ceremony itself, she had her limo parked just a few feet from a back door so that she could rush in, present the Oscar, and then dash away. The entire mobilization took only twelve minutes.

appointment in the face of defeat. So the producers barred any reaction shots when the winner was named, and Dustin Hoffman collected the gold for *Kramer vs. Kramer.*

If fear of being shown in defeat made Hoffman camera shy, this was not the case with another Hollywood figure of equal magnitude. In fact, when it seemed that a seven-month pregnant Amy Irving would be denied a presenter's spot on the Oscar cast, her lover, Steven Spielberg, protested: "No Amy; no Spielberg." Both appeared, of course, and New York columnist Liz Smith wrote of the incident, "Just imagine anybody in Hollywood these days taking a high moral attitude over an unwed mother! These people are denizens of a business that gives us things like *Porky's Revenge.*"

Once the final Oscar ballots are in, a form of madness settles onto the film community. Nervous agents stay later in their offices; nominees try on dozens and dozens of dresses, hoping to find that "right look" in which to win the Oscar; and a fight for seats at the Oscarcast and for places on the elite list of Oscar presenters gets under way in earnest.

Obtaining seats is no small feat, because the Dorothy Chandler Pavilion in the Los Angeles County Music Center holds only 2,900 people. Nominees, their families, and sometimes their agents gobble up as many as five hundred places. The remaining tickets, at forty dollars, sixty dollars, and a hundred dollars each are sent out to the first 2,400 Academy members who mail in their checks.

A byzantine hierarchy rules the seating plans. The nominees and superstar presenters are seated in a "golden horseshoe" pattern so the famous faces are within view of the eleven television cameras.

Bitter Hollywood rivalries have created awkward seating problems through the years. Four times the Academy had to seat Bette Davis and Joan Crawford on opposite sides of the theater to prevent a visible outburst of their longtime enmity.

Though most Oscar nominees wouldn't miss the ceremony for the world, circumstances have prevented some stars from attending. In 1967, Elizabeth Taylor and husband Richard Burton, both nominees for *Who's Afraid of Virginia Woolf?*, were in the south of France, filming *The Comedians.* Having completed her scenes, Taylor, knowing that she was almost certain to win an award, ordered a gown from Givenchy, booked a bungalow at the Beverly Hills Hotel, and made plane reservations to L.A. At the last minute Burton, perhaps sensing that he would lose the Best Actor Oscar to Paul Scofield in *A Man For All Seasons*, ordered his wife to stay at his side. She pleaded. He stood firm. So, two days before the Oscars, she tearfully canceled, telling her press agent, "The only thing that means more to me than the Academy Awards is my husband."

Oscar day itself dawns with a dash for as many as three hundred limousines, booked up to a year in advance by the Academy for the royal progressions to the theater. Included are about twenty chauffeured Rolls-Royces for such cinematic royalty as Sophia Loren and Sir Laurence Olivier. Even unpretentious stars like Meryl Streep and Robert De Niro opt for the official Academy limos.

For stars trying to make a spectacular entrance, *the* time to arrive is between 5:40 and 5:57 P.M.—just before the overture focuses all attention inside the theater. The most prized limo drivers are those who can keep a holding pattern until just the right time to pull up to Oscar's red carpet. In three of their last four appearances, both Cher and Raquel Welch have managed to arrive during the primest of television time.

Shirley MacLaine's car has always been equally punctual, with the exception of 1984, when she was thrown an emotional curve. Heading toward the Los Angeles County Music Center from her home in Malibu, the limousine made an unscheduled detour to the office of MacLaine's agent. A messenger opened the door and handed the actress a small package. She opened the box to find a gift from her brother, Warren Beatty. Although she has refused to identify the gift, the actress says it expressed five affectionate memories she shares with him. As the limousine rolled on, she dissolved in tears, which necessitated a repair job that almost made her late for the show.

As with arrivals, there is definitely an "in" time to depart—about half an hour before the Oscar show is over. In years when they aren't nominated or booked to appear in the big finale, such luminaries as Jack Lemmon, Walter Matthau, James Stewart, Lauren Bacall, and Lily Tomlin are already at the exclusive, post-Oscar parties that round out the evening.

For those unfortunate stars caught in the crush, the exit from downtown Los Angeles is not unlike an earthquake evacuation, as the rich and famous climb all over each other in their race to the action in Beverly Hills, about ten miles away. Some of the smartest have their chauffeurs meet them on darkened side streets that can be reached by an alley behind the Music Center. Thus, fans who have waited outside in front of the Center for glimpses of Bette Midler, Meryl Streep, Warren

William Wyler with the Irving Thalberg Award in his hand and Shirley MacLaine on his shoulder. MacLaine, a perennial at the Oscars, has been a notorious devil's advocate backstage, once almost decking Frank Sinatra in a nasty political dispute during the protest era. Later, she annoyed brother Warren Beatty by mixing with his current lover and several ex-lovers just offstage.

Beatty, and Robert Redford have kept vigil in vain, the stars having escaped in the darkness.

Some celebrities, however, insist on braving the crush for the ego-stroking summons of the official cars. A special majordomo stands near the edge of the red carpet to bellow, "Mr. Heston's car" and "Miss Loren's car" and so on. Sometimes this backfires. One year Lana Turner waited an embarrassing thirty minutes as the man periodically bellowed for her limo. The driver had fallen asleep at the wheel.

The post-Oscar parties have always been an integral part of the rite. Of the half-dozen bashes, the one party that's most definitely "out" is the official ball of the Academy's board of governors. The chic place to be is the informal affair hosted by super-agent Irving "Swifty" Lazar. In 1986 the gathering was at Spago, the current hot spot.

Chatter at the parties focuses on who wore what, who looked dazzling, and who looked dreadful. Quipped Zsa Zsa Gabor, "I'll tell you one thing we *don't* talk about, darling—those deadly dull awards."

CHAPTER TEN

Oscar Curse

The Oscar can be a jinx, bringing with it envy, hatred, and ill wishes—uneasy is the winner. —JOAN FONTAINE, BEST ACTRESS OF 1941

A human storm broke over Rod Steiger's shoulders. Mikes were jammed into his exhausted face. Flashbulbs blinded him. A pack of rapacious journalists yelled at him, bullied him with questions, dared him not to answer. Hands yanked at his satin lapels. Cords from a dozen TV cameras wound around his legs.

Suddenly he was a prisoner of fame—caught in a hornet's nest of unreality. It was, he would remember, exactly like the crowd scene from *Day of the Locust.* But at the time, in April 1968, he felt only a slightly bitter hangover after the hefty taste of sweet victory. Within three months, Steiger had won the top acting prizes from the National Society of Film Critics, the New York Film Critics, the Hollywood Foreign Press Association, and the British Film Academy.

And now the Oscar! It had been five minutes since he had bounded toward the stage, and they had gone by in slow motion. First, Audrey Hepburn languidly read the nominees: "Warren Beatty for *Bonnie and Clyde,* Dustin Hoffman for *The Graduate,* Paul Newman for *Cool Hand Luke,* Spencer Tracy for *Guess Who's Coming to Dinner?*" Then the words, "Rod Steiger, *In the Heat of the Night.*"

Then the roar. Wave after wave of shouts—because Steiger was an "inside winner, an actor's actor." Probably no winner since Paul Muni and Laurence Olivier had as much respect from his peers.

Steiger tightened his longshoreman's fist around the Oscar and rubbed it across his wrist in a gesture which seemed to ask, "It's real, isn't it?"

He'd almost had it in his hand two years before for *The Pawnbroker.* That year, even the oddsmakers in Vegas said he'd win. But Lee Marvin, another guy who came up the hard way, took home the prize for the lightweight *Cat Ballou.* Even as an "also ran" Steiger was boosted into the golden circle whose names are above the title on the movie marquee. With *In the Heat of the Night* he broke the bank.

So Steiger shrugged off the clamoring mob, hoisted his Oscar over his head, and smiled across the room at the gossip columnist who had just asked him a question. "Oscar curse—what's that? Not for me." He sailed out to his limo, hanging ten on a wave of glory.

The gossip columnist just smiled, twisting one ruby red lip into a sneer. "Just wait, mister, just wait."

During the next decade Rod Steiger had little time and no inclination to look back. His salary soared to $750,000 a picture, and his tough-guy mug became one of the ten best-known in the world.

He traded his Oscar chit for chances to play the greatest roles in history: Mussolini, Lucky Luciano, and that Waterloo of parts, Napoleon. But the Oscar propulsion ran out—as it so often does. Steiger faced his 51st birthday a physical wreck (he needed open heart surgery), an artistic casualty (critics were blasting his performance in *W.C. Fields and Me*), and an emotional fatality (his third marriage had just crumbled in a bitter court confrontation).

"I was scared to death, and couldn't work," he said. "To get out of bed and brush my teeth was a big accomplishment. 'The bed is death,' I used to say to myself. 'Go ahead, lie here and talk to yourself, but the goddamned bed is going to kill you.' "

It was there, in his solitude, that Steiger looked back over the decade to Oscar night, 1968, when the columnist had asked him about "the Oscar curse" and then folded her arms to wait.

"From the minute you get off the stage, it seems they're looking for you to fall," said George Kennedy, who won his best supporting Oscar the same year, for *Cool Hand Luke*. "There was a guy waiting for me behind the curtain. 'Hey, George,' he said. 'Do ya think it'll be a jinx for you?' He didn't so much as say congratulations or good going. Then I heard that question over and over and over again during the next few weeks. What a bunch of bunk."

Kennedy's beef is on target.

The so-called "Oscar curse" was invented during the Academy's early days by that mama of all columnists, Louella Parsons. For Louella, whose view of Hollywood allowed for all superstition, the jinx was born on a Tinseltown Ouija board. "Beware, beware," Louella cautioned many a dewy-eyed winner, "the Oscar will get you if you don't watch out."

This was just so much emotional claptrap, of course. But the Oscar curse became real, and it was born in that era. It was born of greedy agents who priced their Oscar-winning clients out of existence. It was born of studio bosses who shoved their Oscared stars into quickie films designed merely to cash in on the Academy's largesse. And, in some cases, it was born of the stars themselves as they turned piggish and "high hat."

"I don't know if it should even be called a jinx," said Rita Moreno, an Oscar winner who has tasted of the curse. "But the award can quickly be turned into a downer by people who try to cash in on it as a promissory note. That is the curse."

Moreno's own victory over the burden an Oscar places on a career is telling because it took her almost twenty years to climb out of the shadow cast on her by the statue.

Her flirtation with the Academy Awards began on April 9, 1962. It was a banner year for the Oscars: a hundred million fans would watch the ceremony through new TV hookups, and the largest contingent of superstars since the forties was jammed into the Santa Monica Civic Auditorium.

Like many other stars, Rita Moreno learned painfully that Oscar holds a two-edged sword. Her Best Supporting Actress for West Side Story *(1961) brought her acclaim and with it a deluge of offers to play the demeaning stereotype of a Latin spitfire—tawdry duplicates of her "Anita" role. George Chakiris, named Best Supporting Actor for the same film, suffered a similar problem. His agents hustled him into a string of quickies, all flops, thus negating the power of the Oscar. Young performers in particular are easy prey in a typecasting industry.*

While Greer Garson and Natalie Wood were having their hair done in Beverly Hills, Moreno, then a moderately successful ingenue, flew into Los Angeles from Manila—tourist class. She blew her savings on a Paris gown, picked up her mom, and joined the crush of cars heading toward the searchlights.

The next two hours slipped by in a daze as Moreno sat in a row awash with mink, Dior, and custom-cut tuxedos.

Then the envelope—*that* envelope. "And the winner is, for *West Side Story*, Rita Moreno."

She gave her mother a hug, ran the fifty yards to the stage, took her Oscar, shook it a little, and started to cry.

Then she rushed back to the airport, boarded a midnight flight for Manila, and disappeared from Hollywood sound stages for seven years. Her Oscar turned back into a pumpkin, and her career was back at the starting point.

Louella could hardly wait to list her as the latest victim of the curse.

In reality, Rita Moreno's problems proved to be more scientific and more intriguing than those invented by the columnists. She rolled the dice—took a gamble on a hunch. She should not, she decided, doom herself to play and replay the Puerto Rican spitfire character until she became a Hollywood stereotype (like Judy Holliday's dumb blonde or Yul Brynner's bald and macho Oriental—career types that grew directly out of Oscar victories).

"It wasn't easy," said Moreno. "I was terrified at first. I knew I had to get out of town because there was too much temptation here. I could have taken any of those spitfire roles and made a bundle. Luckily I was so demeaned—I mean, it's really demeaning after you've won the Oscar to be offered the same role over and over again. They only wanted me to drag out my accent-and-dance show over and over again. And boy was I offered them all: gypsy fortune tellers, Mexican spitfires, Spanish spitfires, Puerto Ricans—all those 'Yankee peeg, you steel me people's money' parts.

"The only thing I could do was turn my back on it."

Moreno was luckier than most Oscar winners—she'd been dancing and singing on Broadway since she was thirteen. So, when she finished her Manila quickie, she bought a ticket for New York.

Rita stayed off the screen for eight crucial years between the time she won the Oscar until she found "the right film" (*The Night of the Following Day*) in 1969.

Meanwhile, she put together a club act (which is now earning her more than $1 million a year in Las Vegas and Atlantic City), immersed herself in lucrative television roles, and finally made it to Broadway where she has worked, occasionally, for two decades.

After a spectacular cameo role in Mike Nichols's *Carnal Knowledge*, Rita took a recurring role on James Garner's television show *The Rockford Files*. It was this role that not only earned her a bouquet of Emmy nominations, but made her one of TV's highest priced character actresses. (She earned $50,000 and higher for several segments.)

Oscar's history certainly boasts of more success stories—rescued careers and quick fortunes—than it boasts of reversals. But evidence of Oscar backlash goes as far back into the Academy's past as the era when Luise Rainer won two Best Actress awards in a row (for 1936 and 1937) and then virtually never made another decent film. Her career quickly became a curiosity—a Hollywood footnote.

Some veteran stars like Oscar winner Joan Fontaine continue to speak of an Oscar jinx. "The Oscar was a marvelous concept of some very responsible people," said Fontaine. "It was supposed to be an event to make our business more dignified. But it quickly became just another monetary spectacle."

Fontaine has always felt that the source of the Oscar hangover is the massive publicity that comes with the territory. "In the forties, and still today, winners of the Oscar seemed like members of royalty suddenly elevated to the throne. You suddenly have international recognition, preferential treatment. Naturally, there is many an ill-wisher, many a doubter.

"They are gunning for you after you win. If you fail for any reason to see the press on the set, you've suddenly gone 'high hat.' And the critics are so hard on you that they seem to be in a hurry to tear you down from that supposed high place that the Oscar won for you.

"Everybody is jealous—especially the producers and directors, because the Oscar winner is suddenly the one they want to see. And producers are used to being top dog."

Indeed, in Fontaine's case David O. Selznick, who had called Joan the "hardest woman in Hollywood to get a performance out of," quickly took public credit for building her to her Oscar peak. "She could have become a top star no place else but at Selznick," he wrote in a letter. "I nurtured her."

"Then I got typed," Fontaine stated. "One critic for the *Saturday Review* said I could probably only play simps. But my simping became suddenly more expensive—Selznick charged a lot more for my services . . . then I had a publicity glut—my picture was everywhere at once."

Joan was photographed in fifty different suits for Easter promos in 1943, was decked in twenty fur coats for Sunday supplements, and modeled hair styles especially for blondes. The Selznick flaks made certain that entertainment editors were sick and tired of Fontaine within three years. "An Oscar can damage irreparably one's relations with family, friends, co-workers, and the press—certainly the press."

Meanwhile Selznick loaned her out, using her as a made-to-order simp in movies like *Jane Eyre.*

In recent Academy history, nobody has taken more Oscar aftershocks than Rod Steiger—and from all sides.

For five years after his Best Actor award, he rode the Oscar high with all the trimmings—the media blitz, the six-figure salary, and, he has said, the chance to try his greatest acting challenges.

"It's like any other contest. You're number one for a while. Then you slip to number two. Then number three. Then it's every man for himself."

Eighteen months after his win, Steiger's face was still seen in slick double-page spreads of a dozen magazines. LET US NOW PRAISE THE FAMOUS ME, read a headline in *Esquire* magazine. And a London tabloid, in a case of the sillies, proclaimed Steiger and Claire Bloom, his wife at the time, "The King and Queen of Hollywood," even painting British crowns over their Technicolor faces.

Steiger traded his Oscar for chances to make a wide range of films—from the bizarre *Illustrated Man* to *The Sergeant,* a frank and daring exploration of macho homosexuality. In this, Steiger veered sharply from the course usually followed by Oscar winners. Normally, winners happily kiss their statuette and then sign multi-million-dollar pacts to make routine box-office films. Then they ride their Rolls-Royces into the sunset of Beverly's top hills.

A prime example of this cash-in is Lee Marvin, from Steiger's own generation of winners. Marvin, after giving tour de force performances in *Ship of Fools* and *Cat Ballou* in the same year, consigned himself to forgettable movies. For consolation he has taken home massive paychecks. " 'Just tow the mark and say the lines.' That's Bogart's line, and, in the long run, he's right," Marvin said recently. He pulls a million a movie, and, he says, "I'm satisfied."

But Steiger forsook the millions and plowed into highly experimental waters. Some critics feel he will reap rewards in cinema history books for his troubles. One of his movies, *No Way to Treat a Lady*, has come to be regarded as one of the medium's "flawed classics" and another, *Happy Birthday, Wanda June,* is on its way.

"Suddenly it began to dawn on me that I felt like a ballplayer who had hit a home run in an empty ball park."

He'd also come to the end of his third marriage, through the expensive failures *Waterloo* and *W.C. Fields and Me,* and through open-heart surgery. He was face-to-face with both physical and artistic mortality. "Confronting death is a big shock to the ego," Steiger said. "It scares the shit out of you."

When the critics turned on him, he was hit in a somewhat more private part of his anatomy. "I felt like I was under siege on the set of *F.I.S.T.;* I was in the midst of terror. I didn't think I could even remember my lines."

But the actor knew his Oscar honeymoon was over long before that. "It was over the minute I did a film that didn't do well." During his year of researching Napoleon's final days for *Waterloo,* he began to feel that Oscar glory (and Hollywood fame, for that matter) could well be compared with the fickleness of Parisians that dogged the French emperor.

Steiger, in spite of it all, views the Academy Awards with a schizophrenic mixture of disdain and awe. "It becomes a fad every April. I respect their decisions. But then, I don't even like to lose a tennis game. When I was up for *The Pawnbroker* and lost, that ceremony goes by in a haze. And did I have to lose to *Cat Ballou?*"

Maybe some of the actor's awe harks back to his experience with a British film, *The Pawnbroker.* "Winning that nomination was an enormous help in getting directors to listen to me when I feel a scene isn't going right," he later told an interviewer. "The year I was nominated happened to be Hollywood's year. When *The Sound of Music* wins an Academy Award, you know it's Hollywood's year. The year before, England walked off with the honors, so Hollywood had to say, 'Wait a minute. This has got to be Hollywood's year.'

"If you've given a performance that you believe is good, there's nothing the matter with taking pride in the recognition an Academy Award symbolizes. I didn't kiss anybody's ass to get it. And its main value is that it protects an actor's position and power. It helps him in the tactical maneuvers that you have to have—if you want to keep your self-respect."

In 1980 the Oscar curse began lifting for Steiger, with five of his pictures going into release within a seven-month period, ranging from *The Chosen* with fellow Oscar winner Maximilian Schell (Best Actor

for the 1961 film *Judgment at Nuremberg*) to a Nazi occupation film, *The Lucky Star*, with Louise Fletcher (also a former winner in 1976 for *One Flew Over the Cuckoo's Nest*).

Oscar's prestige, in any case, has never been in question, and its economic worth to an actor is, with rare exception, a big plus.

A London tabloid fixed the value of Julie Christie's Oscar for *Darling* (1965) at $10 million. "That's what she'll get during the next ten years," said a columnist, writing under the headline OCAR FOR JULIE. Estelle Parsons found that her fee had been multiplied by ten the day after she won the Best Supporting Actress award for *Bonnie and Clyde* (1967). And George Kennedy has freely admitted that his supporting Oscar for *Cool Hand Luke* (1967) made him Hollywood's richest character actor.

The "cash value" of an acting Oscar was a subject taboo during the Academy's first three decades. But an Oscar has almost always brought treasure with it.

In 1941 Joan Fontaine's official loan-out fee jumped from $25,000 to $100,000 after she was nominated for *Rebecca*. A year later, after her Oscar-winning performance in *Suspicion*, Selznick International Pictures, which held her contract, began charging as much as $200,000 per picture. "I never saw a cent of those increased fees," said Fontaine, who continued to receive $12,500 a week (her pre-Oscar paycheck). The inflation chased off producers who otherwise might have used the actress.

She described the futility and frustration of the post-Oscar blues in her caustic book about Hollywood, *No Bed of Roses:* "I sat idle for six months after *Suspicion*. He [David Selznick] was trying to get the highest bid for my services . . . but that was only common practice then." Selznick also used his Oscar inflation scale when he loaned out Ingrid Bergman, Jennifer Jones, and others in his stable of stars.

In the thirties and forties stars were often "rented" from their home studios by rival producers, and it was no secret that an Oscar moved a star into a higher rent district. Fontaine felt that these salary hikes, along with publicity hype, contributed greatly to the post-Oscar syndrome: "It gave people a chance to say—or at least to think—is she worth it? If the picture was a success, fine. If not, this was the first step back down."

Stars who won Oscars in the fifties began talking about salary gains as early as the morning after—and the stakes grew higher every year. Civil-court records give plenty of examples.

Marlon Brando got $75,000 for *A Streetcar Named Desire* and, after winning the Oscar for *On the Waterfront*, took a whopping jump to $1.2 million for the Technicolor turkey *Mutiny on the Bounty* in 1962. His fee was scaled downward in the late sixties but was up again to about $1.5 million for *The Missouri Breaks* after his second Academy Award in 1973 for *The Godfather*. That price doubled for *Apocalypse Now* and increased by another $1.5 million for his "cameo" in *Superman*.

William Holden was in the moderate price range for *Sunset Boulevard*, *Born Yesterday*, and *Stalag 17*, but joined the ranks of the multimillionaires after his Oscar for the last-named film.

Such inflation filtered down in descending value, depending on the award. Dorothy Malone, for instance, was taking home about $90,000 a year from her contract with Universal in 1955. She had been in Hol-

Dorothy Malone was able to weather the Oscar curse mainly because she was rescued by the juiciest role in the television series Peyton Place. *Starring with Ryan O'Neal, Mia Farrow, and Barbara Parkins in a top-rated show gave Malone the exposure she had failed to get from the second-string productions her agent signed her for.*

lywood for twelve years, having been spotted by a talent scout in an amateur play at Southern Methodist University. First she tried RKO, where the bosses felt she was their answer to such girls-next-door as MGM's Donna Reed and Fox's Jeanne Crain. Films like *The Falcon and the Co-Eds* and *Too Young to Know* quickly put her to sleep.

Then she tried Warners. There her hair was lightened to "blondine" and she was draped on the arms of a succession of screen cavalry lieutenants who fought off the Indians and romanced Dorothy in their tight Helen Rose uniforms. Then she landed a steamy role in *Battle Cry*, where she tempted Tab Hunter while changing clothes in a butterfly chair.

Universal, her new studio, relegated her back to junk. "By 1955, I was spending more time in Dallas, my hometown, than I was in Hollywood. It was more challenging for me to do public relations for an insurance company and a Texas airline than to play the roles they gave me."

She decided to give it one more try. In late 1955 she hired a press agent and bleached her hair platinum for sexy "other woman" parts. The change was breathtaking, and she was penciled in as Robert Stack's sister in *Written on the Wind*.

The 1956 Best Supporting Actress Oscar for her performance in that film resulted in instant salary inflation. From her pre-award $90,000, Malone's salary jumped to $125,000 in 1956, to about $160,000 in 1958, to $164,000 in 1959. By then the Oscar honeymoon had waned and her salary headed down: to $98,170 in 1960, $58,013 in 1961, and $32,456 in 1962.

It's an old Academy Award story in Hollywood, with greedy agents and studio bosses pushing their winning stars to higher salaries and shoving them into quickie movies or TV shows. The star is rarely at fault, but the results usually mirror the eventual salary drop that hit Dorothy Malone.

When an Oscar winner fails, it's usually a big failure—a million-dollar failure. The Hollywood executives, who seem to see the Oscar as a golden four-leaf clover, soon feel that a winner can sprinkle Oscar dust on even the dreariest of films. "Executives suddenly lose their perspective with a big Oscar winner," said Bosley Crowther of the *New York Times*. "The safeguards they normally have fail to operate. Disasters easily follow."

The Oscar often creates an artistic and economic Peter Principle for these stars—they rise to their level of least effectiveness. Then they fall.

This is what happened to Julie Andrews, who won the Oscar in 1965 for her cloyingly sweet performance in *Mary Poppins*. Neither she nor the big studio movies she represented have been the same since. Twentieth Century–Fox rushed her into *The Sound of Music* and then watched in amazement as that movie, a Broadway vehicle tailored for Mary Martin, became the most successful film in Hollywood's history; overtaking *Gone With The Wind* after only a month in release. It seemed that Julie could do no wrong, and the Fox brass offered her the moon to make the splashiest musical ever made. It was such a sure thing that they decided to call it simply *Star!* No explanation needed. Right? I mean, after all, this was Julie Andrews—folks in Calcutta, for Chrissakes, were going to see her four and five times.

But in 1968 *Star!* waltzed into the box-office records as a musical *Cleopatra*. And Andrews plummeted from Oscar superstardom to the stages of Vegas, where they gave her $250,000 a week to sing, sweetly, the songs from *Mary Poppins*.

In early 1980 Julie reported to a Hollywood sound stage to make a film intriguingly titled *S.O.B.,* which was written and directed by husband Blake Edwards and was about, he said, an actress who won an Oscar for *Peter Pan*, but had to bare her bosom to make a comeback.

Julie Andrews's Oscar story is hauntingly familiar. It echoes through all the other Oscar cash-ins of Hollywood's history. Again, the industry's normal artistic and economic safeguards were ignored in deference to Oscar, allowing Andrews's career and Fox's product to plunge past the fail-safe mark.

It all started back in September 1964, when *Mary Poppins* opened in New York City. One of the drooling reviews in the *Hollywood Reporter* summed up the hysteria: "This is the kind of film and the kind of performance that creates not fans but evangelists." Which is precisely what happened. Out in Foggy Bottom, Alabama, and Shenandoah, Iowa, women's clubbers told their friends, who told their friends, that here, finally, was "a gal you can take the family to see—*all* the family."

Miss Andrews had already finished *The Sound of Music,* which opened only a month before the 1965 Oscar ceremony. Here is how the *Hollywood Reporter* welcomed her: "This lady is not just a great star. She is not just an ordinary film personality. She is a whole, whirling galaxy. Once there was Mary Pickford, then there was Garbo, now there is Julie."

This would seem silly were it not for the fact that Hollywood reads the *Hollywood Reporter* as gospel. It's the first thing Peter Bogdanovich reads as he heads off the racquetball court. Cher carries it to her fanny-tightening class, and Ryan O'Neal scans it while he's pumping iron. So what does this mean? Julie Andrews had just become a box-office saint.

Miss Andrews, then twenty-nine, with only three films behind her, was rushed into *Torn Curtain* and then *Hawaii* at a salary of $700,000 and her pick of co-stars. When she jetted to the islands, she couldn't have known that James Michener's book about the tropics would become her last truly successful film of the seventies.

In quick succession, *Star!*, *Darling Lili*, and *The Tamarind Seed* bombed at the only place it counts—the box office.

"I think *Star!* failed because the public wasn't very happy with seeing me in drunken scenes," she told writer Charles Higham. "It was hard for me to play drunk scenes. I had to force myself to do it, but I think it worked. Then the public refused to accept me as a spy, and that disappointed me awfully," she said about *Darling Lili*, which is fast becoming a critical success in cult cinema circles. "I was a victim of typecasting. I can't knock *The Sound of Music* and *Mary Poppins*, because they gave such an awful lot of pleasure to a lot of people. But that kind of exposure puts you into the greatest danger. I won an Oscar

The success of Julie Andrews in The Sound of Music *came back to haunt her by typing her almost forever in the saccharine image of the Rodgers and Hammerstein heroine. The image has dogged her steps, greatly limiting an actress of incredible range, much as the gift of sweetness and light typed Doris Day a decade earlier.*

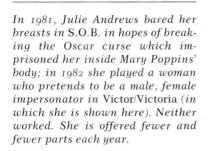

In 1981, Julie Andrews bared her breasts in S.O.B. *in hopes of breaking the Oscar curse which imprisoned her inside Mary Poppins' body; in 1982 she played a woman who pretends to be a male, female impersonator in* Victor/Victoria *(in which she is shown here). Neither worked. She is offered fewer and fewer parts each year.*

for *Mary Poppins* and then went into the most successful musical up to that time. Now I can see that I was too quickly bracketed in one category. And I couldn't escape."

She was also a victim of the Oscar hangover. Because she won the award and was so quickly nominated again for *The Sound of Music*, film executives felt they could hardly just put her into a little, well-made movie. They had to show her rising full-blown in CinemaScope conch shells like Venus rising from the sea. So she quickly sank.

It looks like she's going to have the last laugh. In the film *S.O.B.* Andrews gave it right back—in the gut. Which is where she had to take it. Even after having—literally—bared her bosom in *S.O.B.*, it remained for her to play a "female impersonator" in the critically and financially successful *Victor/Victoria* (1982) in order to finally shake loose from her sugary image.

Scores of Oscar-winning actors have played the money game and won permanently fat paychecks—Holden, Sinatra, Ernest Borgnine, and Gene Hackman to name only a few. Hackman's win for 1971's *The French Connection* led directly to the $1.3 million super-agent Sue Mengers got him when he replaced George Segal in the disastrous *Lucky Lady* (1975).

Among those who took Oscar and ran with it up monetary Himalayas, George Kennedy is somewhat of a legend. "Here's an actor who won thirteen years ago," said a major agent in 1981. "He hasn't made an economic stumble since."

"My salary was multiplied by ten the minute I won," said Kennedy, who went to the Oscar ceremony the year he was nominated for Best Supporting Actor thinking he would lose to Michael J. Pollard in *Bonnie and Clyde*. "We weren't supposed to win. I wasn't thinking about it, even. My performance in *Cool Hand Luke* had already changed things for me. People were saying, 'Hey, this guy can do something besides kill people.'

"Everything changed for me after the Oscar. I got a certain figure for *Cool Hand Luke* and a new [higher] figure for everything that followed. But the happiest part was that I didn't have to play only villains anymore. In that film [*Cool Hand Luke*] I was able to show the compassionate side of the character. The Oscar flooded this with attention. I began to get roles that were sympathetic. Now, three out of four roles offered to me are likable characters."

Like many other Oscar winners, Kennedy began feeling the winds of change even before the nominations were announced: "I was working on *Bandolero!* with Jimmy Stewart, Raquel Welch, and Dean Martin. Stewart went to the producers and told them the word was getting around about *Cool Hand Luke*. Then he asked that my name be put above the title. In some ways that means as much to me as the Oscar."

Kennedy shares the belief of many when he says, "You would be hard pressed to find one example to prove that the Oscar, by itself, can hurt you."

But he has admitted that new salary demands that begin with Oscar can cause trouble. "When a star's salary jumps to superstar level—the next big, big step above my level—the salary jump can backfire.

"It has nothing to do with whether a star like Rod Steiger is a good actor. The real question is, 'Does he or she have enough charisma and luck—that's a lot of it—to justify a million dollars?' "

Kennedy, who had piloted the Concorde in *Airport '79 Concorde*, ridden the steamer in *Death on the Nile*, polished off the *Brass Target*, and been shaken apart in *Earthquake*, has seen a "lot of winners price themselves right out of existence. But that has nothing to do with the quality of an actor's performance."

The cash registers have been ringing since the first Oscar ceremony in 1929, when inexpensive ingenue Janet Gaynor's salary tripled. Some other examples from Oscar's early years: James Cagney, $140,000 a year before his 1942 Oscar for *Yankee Doodle Dandy*, $362,000 after; Wallace Beery (1931–32, *The Champ*), $75,000 before, $200,000 a year after; Claudette Colbert (1934, *It Happened One Night*), $100,000 before, $350,000 after; Katharine Hepburn (1932–33, *Morning Glory*), $120,000 before, $206,000 after; Victor McLaglen (1935, *The Informer*), $50,000 before, $165,000 after.

There is another form of Oscar cash-in—a more subtle and perhaps more damaging misuse of an Academy Award.

Since the thirties, Hollywood's money men have never been able to resist herding the winners through projects that are designed to cash in, quickly and hugely, on the prestige of an Oscar.

"Almost the morning after I won for *Charly*, a film I had to hand-guide through production, I was descended upon by the same myopic

Monday-morning quarterbacks who hadn't wanted to make the movie in the first place," said Cliff Robertson, who won the Best Actor award in 1969. "In all cases, their creative credentials had not improved over the weekend. They came up with a lot of money and a lot of junk."

This post-Oscar stampede toward the box office has resulted in some notable career casualties. Susan Hayward, for instance, never made a critically successful film after winning for *I Want to Live!*

But the career disasters inflicted on Luise Rainer and on Dorothy Malone, although two decades apart, are perhaps the most typical. Both emerged from the semishadows to national prominence and both were pushed out of the business by greedy producers and agents.

It was Rainer's post-Oscar problems that caused Louella Parsons to coin the term "Oscar jinx" in the first place. Louella was trying to endow the Oscar with an emotional power and superstition, while Rainer's problems were really a case of striking too quickly while the Oscar was hot.

The "Luise Rainer Affair" reeks of *Sunset Boulevard* and has become one of the prime skeletons in Oscar's closet. Rainer (the "Viennese Teardrop"), an actress who was brought to MGM from Vienna as a "threat" to Garbo, hit it so big and disappeared so completely that an erroneous folk tale has grown up around her name.

The story goes that Rainer, who some said was more beautiful than Garbo, refused to sit on Louis B. Mayer's lap when she asked him to renegotiate her contract after her first Oscar. So, say the snipes, Luise was quietly set out in the MGM sun to wither and die.

According to another legend, Rainer, a Thalberg creation, was systematically destroyed by the Mayer regime after Thalberg died.

The real story of Luise Rainer, the first woman to win two Oscars in a row, has remained buried in a slag heap of gossip—perhaps because it reveals a highly unflattering portrait of the Academy Awards during their golden era.

Stripping away the decades shows that Luise Rainer, and her two Oscars, were a political accident, an accident that was a powerful symptom of Oscar's ills in the mid-thirties, even though she did win the New York Film Critics Award for *The Great Ziegfeld.*

The term "Oscar curse" was invented for Luise Rainer, here with William Powell and appearing as Anna Held in The Great Ziegfeld, *(1936) which brought her the first of two Oscars in a row. (The second was for playing a creaky Chinese peasant in* The Good Earth.*) MGM publicists liked to say that Miss Rainer's sixty-second scene on the phone was studied, dissected, and shown to acting classes around the world. And this may have been true: it seems more likely, however, that the scene was used to show effectively* how not *to handle a short bit. The writer Dalton Trumbo used to tell his colleagues, "Don't take the Oscars so seriously. . . . After all, they gave two of them to Luise Rainer."*

The week Rainer was nominated for *The Great Ziegfeld* in February of 1937, the Academy was at its weakest point, with hundreds of actors, writers, and directors having resigned, enraged over the organization's domination by the Hollywood establishment and its interference in the formation of labor unions.

Only a handful of people were involved in selecting candidates for the 1936 awards. That year, the Best Actress Award pitted Rainer against Irene Dunne in *Theodora Goes Wild*, Gladys George in *Valiant Is the Word for Carrie*, Carole Lombard in *My Man Godfrey*, and, much closer to home, Norma Shearer in MGM's *Romeo and Juliet*. Rainer's part was so small in *The Great Ziegfeld* that she would be classed as a supporting player today. And Shearer's vehicle had been handpicked for her by husband Irving Thalberg. If ever a part was designed to win the Oscar, it was Shearer's. Voters would have easily taken the bait, too, except for Oscar's weakened condition.

Rainer's first Oscar led to the second through still another set of political circumstances. Since Academy president Frank Capra and the organization's officers, trying frantically to bring the Oscar race back into perspective, had opened the vote to about fourteen thousand extra players, writers and others in Hollywood, it was this huge group that chose Rainer's performance in *The Good Earth* over Garbo's in *Camille*. Rainer, a self-effacing newcomer, was far better liked, generally, than Garbo and other Best Actress nominees that year: Irene Dunne, Janet Gaynor, and Barbara Stanwyck. And she had the publicity from the previous year on her side.

Insiders at MGM say that *this* was the real story behind Luise Rainer's sudden fame and sudden fall. "They never planned for her to win

When Cliff Robertson picked up his Oscar for Charly *he also picked up the Oscar curse. He had played* Charly *on television in 1961 (on the "U.S. Steel Hour") and became obsessed with taking the property to the big screen. It was a delicate, bittersweet portrait of a young mentally retarded man who undergoes an experimental operation which gives him superior intellect for a brief, heart-breaking period. Robertson carted the project from producer to producer before scraping up the financing. But, like Barbra Streisand with* Yentl, *he worked outside the system. A crippled career followed.*

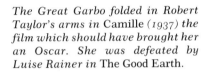

The Great Garbo folded in Robert Taylor's arms in Camille (1937) *the film which should have brought her an Oscar. She was defeated by Luise Rainer in* The Good Earth.

in the first place," said a former MGM publicist. "You must remember that 'they' wanted to decide what to do with whom. So they didn't treat her as a winner."

In Rainer's own words: "For my second and third pictures I won Academy Awards. Nothing worse could have happened to me."

James Robert Parish, in his encyclopedic work *The MGM Stock Company*, wrote, "She won unprecedented audience sympathy. Almost by default, she was considered a dramatically versatile actress. Today, her acting technique in those films seems more mannered monotony than versatility. Compared to other actresses of more enduring qualities, such as Ingrid Bergman, Luise seems simply not of flesh and blood."

Two years later Rainer was a has-been, having finished five hasty pictures so dreary that they don't even show up on "Movies 'Til Dawn": *The Emperor's Candlesticks, The Big City, The Great Waltz, Dramatic School,* and *The Toy Wife.* "I was just a piece of machinery with no rights," said Rainer. "They completely abused me. I was catapulted into the position of being a box-office attraction. Nothing could have been worse."

Enough of that callous, commercial attitude toward the Oscar remained twenty years later to relegate Dorothy Malone to the same fate. But there was one difference between the two: Malone's performance on the set of *Written on the Wind* was so sensational that gossip was already giving her the Oscar even before the nominations were made.

Her agents got the word also. She was bound, body and soul, to the huge MCA organization. And MCA had nepotistic ties to Malone's contract company, Universal. "The word got out so quickly on my work in the film that I was grossly overworked when I went to get the Oscar. Both the studio and my agents rushed to cash in. They put me into every dog made that year."

Incredibly, she made fifteen films in eighteen months—all of them quite forgettable: *Quantez, Tip on a Dead Jockey, Warlock, The Last Voyage,* and *The Fast and the Furious* being some of the "better" ones. "If somebody had just been honest with me and said, 'Let's wait and get some really good parts' or if they'd just stopped to think about it. But I had very bad advice and am quite bitter about it. I was in the top fifteen box-office stars the three years before the Oscar. It was pretty much downhill afterwards," she said in 1960.

It took a TV series, "Peyton Place," at another studio (Fox) to put Malone back in the mainstream of Hollywood. But the momentum was gone. The actress eventually moved back to Dallas, where she became a TV free-lancer and a star of regional theater. In 1985, *Peyton Place: The Next Generation* brought together Malone and eight of the original series performers in a successful television "Movie of the Week."

Even when the award isn't waved before the faces of producers as a bargaining tool, it can cause career aftershocks for many winners by forever identifying them with the role or type of role for which they won the Oscar. History is full of examples: Gloria Grahame, who became typed as the bad girl with the heart of gold; Charles Coburn, who was forever locked into his dotty-old-man character; and Hattie McDaniel, who was forced to repeat her Southern mammy time and again just to keep working.

Gale Sondergaard became welded to her performance as the archetypal villainess; Audrey Hepburn was linked to the wide-eyed gamine; Shelley Winters is still making money off her portrayals of blowsy women far beyond their prime.

"When Red Buttons won the Oscar for *Sayonara,* his career was at a standstill," said his agent, Martin Baum. "That Oscar and the way the industry reacted to it gave him a whole new career—now he's done twenty films and goes back to Vegas as a highly paid headliner."

Baum has learned the hard way about the other side of Oscar typing: when client Sidney Poitier became the first black performer to win the Best Actor Oscar (for *Lilies of the Field* in 1963) the industry seemed to view the win as a "one time thing—unlikely to be repeated," said Baum. And Poitier's Oscar came as a real surprise to the big movietown bosses. The "in money" was on Paul Newman for *Hud* or maybe Albert Finney for *Tom Jones.*

Hollywood's myopic bosses felt the city had done enough by tossing him the nomination as a bone. "We tried for months, unsuccessfully, to get financing for Poitier's next picture, *To Sir, With Love,* but nobody

Sidney Poitier became the first black to win a Best Actor award for Lilies of the Field *(1963).*

was interested," said Baum. "Finally, James Clavell agreed to write the script for nothing and to direct for only a percentage of the film. Sidney had to work at no salary just to prove himself all over again— and that was all after the Oscar."

"The only real change in my career was in the attitude of newsmen," said Poitier. "And they started to query me on civil rights and the Negro question incessantly. Ever since I won the Oscar, that's what they've been interested in—period." (Hollywood apparently decided that one Oscar was enough. Poitier has never been nominated again, even for *In the Heat of the Night*, which brought an Oscar to co-star Rod Steiger, or for *Guess Who's Coming to Dinner*, although practically everyone else who acted in that film was nominated—Spencer Tracy, Katharine Hepburn, Cecil Kellaway, and Beah Richards.)

A year after his Oscar, Poitier turned over the final print of *To Sir, With Love* to Columbia Pictures. The brass there looked at the print, were frightened by its inter-racial theme, and put it on the shelf for more than a year. Poitier threatened to go public, however, and Columbia sneaked the film in two locations: an art theater in Manhattan and a theater in Westwood near the University of California at Los Angeles. The sneak in Los Angeles was given no ballyhoo and no advertising. The opening titles simply rolled onto the screen after the first show of the evening. At first, there was restless stirring among the packed student audience. But the English rock star Lulu's rendition of the title song became hypnotic. When Poitier appeared on the screen, the student audience cheered. There was a near riot of approval when Poitier made his first breakthrough as a black teacher trying to win over a classroom of London toughs.

But there was only one representative from Columbia Pictures at the showing, and nobody passed out rating cards. The studio released the film anyway, and it went on to earn $50 million worldwide. It was so popular that Columbia hired the Gallup Poll to find out why. The answer turned out to be Sidney Poitier. That only served to rankle Columbia's brass. When Oscar time rolled around again, *To Sir, With Love*—one of the major hits of 1967—was not nominated, not even for the title song.

Another of Baum's clients, the British actress Maggie Smith (named Best Actress of 1969 for *The Prime of Miss Jean Brodie*), hasn't had a major film offer from Hollywood since she won her second Oscar, a Best Supporting Actress award, for *California Suite* in 1979.

"Maggie's Oscars have, I think, typed her as a quote—actress—unquote," Baum said. "Those awards clearly typed her as a great actress—but not necessarily as a leading lady. They'll probably call when they have a part for a quote—great actress—unquote."

This type of industry reaction to the Oscar stretches far back to the early decades of the award and was firmly entrenched when a newcomer named Anne Baxter won the Best Supporting Actress award in 1947 for *The Razor's Edge*.

Maggie Smith, whose excellent performance as the viper-tongued schoolteacher in The Prime of Miss Jean Brodie *earned her the Best Actress Oscar for 1969. She found the dark side of Oscar's rainbow after winning a second award, for Best Supporting Actress, in* California Suite *(1978). She didn't receive a single film offer for three years and has had only twelve major movie roles in the decade since she earned the first award.*

Anne Baxter, as Eve Harrington in All About Eve, a 1950 backstage classic with George Sanders.

She was a dark horse if there ever was one. Hollywood's smart money wasn't riding on Baxter as the ballots went out. For one thing, she was still a starlet—a girl who would be gilded and groomed at the whim of Twentieth Century–Fox, following a pattern that had been set for Alice Faye and Betty Grable. For another, Baxter, only 23, was up against four heavyweights: Ethel Barrymore in *The Spiral Staircase,* Lillian Gish in *Duel in the Sun,* Flora Robson in *Saratoga Trunk,* and Gale Sondergaard (winner of the first Best Supporting Actress award ten years earlier) in *Anna and the King of Siam.*

"So when Fox found I had won the Oscar for *Razor's Edge,* they put me in a very special position. You see, the part I played, Sophie, was an alcoholic and on drugs—every bit a character part. I was twenty-two and labeled a 'character actress.' Fox had been used to calling for a 'Betty Grable script' or an 'Alice Faye script.' They really didn't know what to do with me."

While the studio was trying to read Oscar tea leaves, it loaned Baxter out to MGM to play the role of Clark Gable's long-suffering wife in *Homecoming.* Then somebody got sick and she took over a leading role in *The Walls of Jericho.* "Secretly, I was delighted," Baxter said. "To me, every part was a character part. Ironically, my Oscar kept me from being typed. Those were the days of ironclad stables of stars. If you played wives—you played wives forever. I managed, through a series of crazy flukes, to keep from falling into the Hollywood mold." Consequently, her forty-year career included such diverse experiences as *All About Eve, The Ten Commandments,* and scores of star performances on television, culminating in her role on the hit series "Hotel." "Along the way, I've been directed by Lewis Milestone, Billy Wilder, Otto Preminger, Fritz Lang, Mervyn LeRoy and Cecil B. De Mille. Some of that I owe directly to Oscar," recalled the actress shortly before her death in 1986.

Many others failed to make that leap over the artificial barriers in the minds of casting agents. Dean Jagger, Edmond O'Brien, Celeste Holm, Teresa Wright, Wendy Hiller, George Sanders, and Ed Begley all stayed in the supporting mold.

Oscar typecasting is a trap that can be avoided only by deft maneuvering. No one knows this better than Estelle Parsons, who, after a long Broadway career of great depth, won the 1967 Best Supporting Actress award for *Bonnie and Clyde*. Parsons, Broadway's woman of a thousand faces, played the hysterical and silly Blanche—the dramatic antagonist to Warren Beatty's Clyde and Faye Dunaway's Bonnie.

"I must have been offered dozens of Blanche parts in the years right after the Oscar," said Parsons. "For that matter, I still get those offers. My salary went up immediately; there was a lot more interest in me by the press and my name went up over the title."

Parsons routinely turned down carbon copies of the hysterical Blanche. "There were suddenly a lot of people who wanted me to trade on the award—some of them people who should have known better. I could have cashed in on it big. But who wants to do the same part over and over again? I made a pact with myself early on never to play the same role again—and I haven't." After a second tour de force in 1968's *Rachel, Rachel* (for which she got a second nomination), the actress had to turn from movies to TV and to Broadway for *And Miss Reardon Drinks a Little* and *Miss Margarida's Way* and to regional theater, where she played Lady Macbeth.

Parsons has said she has few hopes that the chances in films will change for her and for many others who give performances of Oscar caliber: "The kind of work I do is found much more often in TV than in films. Films have become very stereotypical lately. They're not as interesting as TV, which has far more 'good actress' parts—and besides what I'd really like to do is a stand-up routine in Vegas. To hold my own there would be a *real* challenge."

Though today's best supporting awards are no guarantees of future challenging work, the situation may have been far worse in the years of the big studios. Thelma Ritter, for instance, was nominated six times for playing basically the same character. And she never got a really good film role.

In 1942 Mary Astor, who had just won the Best Supporting Actress award for *The Great Lie*, found her illusion about the Oscar's mystique dashed the minute she reported for her new Metro contract. "I was offered a long-term contract at MGM with its secure income plus a forty-week year—great security for an aging actress," she said. Suddenly coming off a career high that included not only an Oscar but the female lead in *The Maltese Falcon*, Astor found that she was "a piece of property and typed for mother roles. Even the people at the studio started calling me 'Mom.' "

Astor got her lifetime studio pass and her key to the dressing room on a Friday morning; Friday afternoon she got a phone call. The caller told her to be in makeup at 8:00 A.M. Monday. "You'll play Susan Peters' mother." No script, no instructions. "Oh, yeah," said the voice on the phone. "The script isn't out of mimeo yet—don't worry, you'll get one."

"And that's what happened to the power and the glory of the Oscar?" Astor asked herself. "And how long will it be before another *Maltese Falcon* comes along? Or a play on Broadway? Oh, shut up, Mary, and be happy; you've got that check coming in every week."

Of all the morning-after stories about the Oscar, few are more poignant than the one told by Beverly Hills realtor Elaine Young, former wife of Oscar winner Gig Young, who, in an apparent murder-suicide, shot himself to death after killing his wife of three weeks in 1978.

"For Gig the Oscar was literally the kiss of death, the end of the line. It was a case of the old saying, 'Be careful what you wish for—you may get it,'" said Young. "You know what Gig truly, really wished for? He wanted, at least once, to be given a chance to star in a good movie; his own movie. He wanted to be more than just supporting in somebody else's film.

"He started out as a strong dramatic actor. . . . Then he turned to comedy. After that, he couldn't get out of his own way. He supported Doris Day; he supported James Cagney; he supported Clark Gable. And finally he supported Jane Fonda in *They Shoot Horses, Don't They?*

"What he was aching for, as he walked up to get the Oscar for *They Shoot Horses, Don't They?*, was a role in his own movie—one they could call, finally, a 'Gig Young movie.'"

She called him an "actor's actor." And the record bears this out: when his name was announced as the winner in 1970, the audience of his peers gave him a roar that hadn't been heard since the fifties—the kind of roar that greeted Ingrid Bergman or Susan Hayward.

Gig Young's victory in the Oscar race was the best thing that ever happened to him . . . and the worst. For years Young had been fighting to gain recognition as an actor and star in his own right rather than as just a second fiddle to Doris Day, Clark Gable, James Cagney, and others. They Shoot Horses, Don't They? *(1969) seemed to be just that chance. But it was not to be. The Oscar only welded Young forever to his own personal purgatory as a supporting player . . . a great one, but a second fiddle nonetheless.*

But he made only four pictures in the eight years between his Oscar win and his death, all in supporting roles. He never got his wish for "a Gig Young picture."

"Look over Oscar's record for the futile exercises in shallow honor," said Elaine Young. "There you'll find Oscar's ultimate sadness."

The most recent victim of the Oscar curse was the crown prince of mirth, Richard Dreyfuss, who won an Academy Award in 1978 for *The Goodbye Girl* and then promptly turned into a Peck's Bad Boy. Already burdened by a major case of the cutes, Dreyfuss ran amok in Hollywood almost from the time he won the Oscar he was so certain he would get. (Those in the know claim that he already had his speech written and typed by a secretary before he limoed off to the Dorothy Chandler Pavilion to gobble up the gold.)

Then he took the Oscar with its little pointed head and used it to commit emotional and artistic hara-kiri. His weight ballooned up to 180 pounds, he ceased taking showers regularly, and he ultimately drifted into a *Götterdämmerung* of drugs and booze, all but destroying a major acting career.

Not since the days of the silents has one young actor gone so far on the emotional tightrope that can be fashioned from a monumental ego.

His antics—none of them truly harmless—could fill half a book. But here are a couple which speak volumes about the actor's misuse of sudden superstardom.

One afternoon, after lunch in a swank Beverly Hills restaurant, Dreyfuss paid his check, scornfully surveyed the room through reflector sunglasses, and then drifted over to a table full of major studio executives.

He stood arrogantly before their table, sunk to his designer-jeaned knees, and snorted an imaginary line of cocaine off the tabletop.

The men reddened and looked away as Dreyfuss straightened up and turned his back on them to coyly stroll out of the eatery for the rich and famous.

The actor carried this childishness one step further at a meeting packed with the top brass of Columbia Pictures, where the actor had a million-dollar deal in the works.

The day before, Dreyfuss had scoured the thrift shops of West Los Angeles seeking a costume for the self-destructive passion play he had in mind. He found a crumpled white sailor hat, a small blue dickey, and sailor pants inches too tight for his increasingly bloated figure. To complete this "look" he didn't shave for two days before the meeting and found an old 1960s shirt to make him look even more bedraggled. The result was horrendous: he looked like a cross between Baby LeRoy and Charles Manson on a very good day. Dreyfuss looked in the mirror and was perfectly satisfied. Then, stinking like a monkey in a small-town zoo, he strode into the meeting with a half-assed smile on his face which dared any of his pinstriped audience to make the slightest comment.

"I looked not only like a fool but I looked thirteen years old," Dreyfuss recalled. "I walked into this meeting with all these people and their calculators. They were standing around in corners talking, then coming back to the table with new offers for me. I'm standing there looking thirteen years old because I didn't want them to think I was smart. I wanted to be a clown."

He later tried to explain his descent into the black hole of the Oscar curse: "I had enormous, enormous guilt about how easily things had always gone for me. I drank, did drugs, ate too much, and, finally, even denigrated my talent.

"It really took me by surprise, this success," he said. "Here I was, this guy who knew he wanted to be a star his whole life, who knew he wanted to win the Academy Award: and suddenly I found myself acting like a small child. I just didn't anticipate the guilt and the fear of success. I didn't anticipate the down side of success at all."

As soon as he carted the Oscar home for *The Goodbye Girl*, Dreyfuss began his descent into the witch's cauldron stirred by Oscar, the almighty. "Soon I stopped making thirty thousand, forty thousand, sixty thousand a year and they were talking two or three million. What it did was to make me the only one of my friends who had money. They were suddenly uncomfortable around me. A producer at Fox bribed my answering service to get my private number. People were coming at me but at the same time stepping back away from me. I needed cool heads around me, and all I got were sycophants."

The actor became inaccessible, hiding behind the none too ample torso of Oscar. Shortly after he took home the big award, *US* magazine, in a profile, wrote, "Richard Dreyfuss has been called brash, vain, vulgar, and an arrogant s.o.b., BUT ONLY BY THOSE WHO KNOW HIM WELL."

Insecurity, that worm in Hollywood's golden apple, assaulted Dreyfuss in a hailstorm of fury. For days after his victory, the good fortune was almost too much for him to accept. He sat home in the dark before his videotape machine and replayed the ceremony half a dozen times—as if to assure himself that he really had been there and had won the Oscar. "That whole night is a fog," he said much later. "What I remember most was going back to New York with the statue on my lap and turning it with my hands in disbelief."

Richard Dreyfuss with Marsha Mason in The Goodbye Girl, *which brought Dreyfuss an Oscar and a series of major problems, including cocaine abuse and egomania.*

Richard admitted that he made two fatal mistakes after his victory: "The very night I won the Oscar I decided rather than act—not to act. I had a fun time for seven or eight months, but I became yesterday's news real fast. The other error I made was that I chose to be picky."

Meyer Mishkin, the agent who discovered Dreyfuss in a high-school play in Beverly Hills, said that the actor felt the Oscar mantle weighing heavily on his shoulders. "You're afraid that your next role won't quite be up to snuff and you become alarmed over making the right choice."

Howard Koch depicted the "Richard Dreyfuss Syndrome" as a classic example of Oscar panic, which in turn becomes an Oscar jinx. "Actors say, 'God, I've won the Oscar. Now I must be very, very picky about what I do.' On the other hand, agents and producers get just as jittery about hiring a recent Oscar winner: will he be difficult? will he charge too much? will he overvalue the Academy Award? All this contributes to the so-called Oscar jinx," Koch concluded.

It didn't help that Dreyfuss used the prestige of his statuette to make a series of post-Oscar clinkers unequaled since the days of Luise Rainer. *The Big Fix* came first—an amateurish private-detective epic in which he tried to glamorize himself into a cross between Alan Ladd and Ricky Schroeder. Then came *The Competition*, a soap opera set around the competition for a classical piano prize. Then *The Buddy System* . . .

Ironically, the increasingly difficult Dreyfuss had a chance at a classic mood piece—*All That Jazz*—the singing, dancing, thinly disguised autobiography of choreographer turned film director Bob Fosse.

Whatever happened on that set (a story we will probably never know), Dreyfuss and Fosse began sniping at each other on the first day. Everybody called the trouble "a classic case of creative differences." Fosse has always remained mute on the subject, playing the gentleman in a very tough situation, but the ugly rumors from the set indicated that Dreyfuss was using his Oscar to ride herd on the entire production in order to make it "The Richard Dreyfuss Story."

Just days before the film was to have started shooting, Dreyfuss walked out, leaving the movie which had been designed for him to flounder about like a beached codfish. (His departure reportedly cost the producers more than $350,000; some say the figure was much nearer $600,000. Supposedly, Dreyfuss somehow paid back this money or atoned for it in some other way, but the details of that agreement remain secret.)

"Richard's behavior not only caused severe mental anguish to all involved," said an assistant director on the set of the film, "but it left a tidal wave of hostility which threatened to pockmark the entire film."

The film went on to win a bouquet of Oscar nominations in 1980—for Best Picture, for Roy Scheider (who took over the Dreyfuss part) as Best Actor, for Bob Fosse as Best Director, for writing, and cinematography —and won the gold for art direction, for original song score, editing, and costume design.

After Dreyfuss's walk-out, a reporter for the *Washington Post* asked a studio head: "Have the post-Oscar jitters made Richard absolutely unhirable?"

"No," answered the exec. "But it's made him very hard to place."

By that time, however, Dreyfuss had problems far worse than juggling movie roles. His self-admitted cocaine habit careened him into a personal and professional slump from which he didn't emerge until 1984.

In true "Oscar Curse" style, these problems reached their apex when his sports car flipped over on a Beverly Hills street, pinning the actor beneath the twisted wreckage and almost killing him.

Tests by the Beverly Hills Police Department revealed moderate levels of cocaine in his bloodstream, enough to bring him into municipal court on drug charges. He eventually got probation with the provision that he do community-service work and make a film about cocaine abuse.

"When an actor is successful enough to win an Oscar, all Hollywood and the rest of the country cheers loudly," said Mishkin. "But they take even greater delight when an actor stumbles as Richard did. Hollywood fans are like sports fans—they'll kick you when you're down."

By 1986, a cocaine-free Dreyfuss seemed to have cleaned up his post-Oscar act and regained control of his multi-million-dollar career. With the big Disney hit *Down and Out in Beverly Hills*, he was on the comeback trail.

CHAPTER ELEVEN

Oscar: The Perfect Gift

Hearst, with his whim of iron, became obsessed with winning an Oscar for Marion Davies—no matter the cost. . . . The quest loomed like a holy grail.

—F. SCOTT FITZGERALD IN *ESQUIRE*, 1940

Marion Davies was already one of Hollywood's ghosts by 1942—a film star of fast-fading beauty and evaporating fame.

On Oscar night, 1942, she was far out of the Hollywood swim, whiling away the war in a dank hunting lodge with her megamillionaire lover William Randolph Hearst at her side. Her dressing bungalow of sixteen rooms was now only so many cartons in a Los Angeles warehouse, and untouched prints of her films were sealed in an air-conditioned bin.

The career of Marion Davies lasted from 1917 to 1937 (a long career by Hollywood standards), and is remembered mainly as a bizarre footnote to Hollywood's history. But on February 26, 1942, Marion's shadow fell over the Academy Awards ceremony like a cultural fog bank, and her silent voice drowned out the silly sentences of the presenters. Category by category, Orson Welles's masterpiece, *Citizen Kane*, lost to far inferior nominees:

Gary Cooper's "yup" and "nope" portrayal of Sergeant York beat out Welles's incendiary Kane; Gregg Toland's masterful photography lost to Arthur Miller's so-so work on *How Green Was My Valley*; Robert Wise's editing was bested by William Holmes's for *Sergeant York*; Welles lost again, as Best Director, to John Ford for *How Green Was My Valley*; and the film was shut out in the categories of interior decoration, scoring, and sound recording. *Citizen Kane*'s only Oscars went to Welles and Herman J. Mankiewicz for Best Original Screenplay.

It was an Oscar slight with the Tinseltown establishment throwing its weight behind *How Green Was My Valley* and, said Hedda Hopper, "almost any other film EXCEPT *Citizen Kane*." So *How Green Was My Valley* was named Best Picture with no surprised gasps from Hollywood. "The REAL surprise," hissed Hedda, "was that this 'little' picture got any nominations at all." Then she threw one arm around Coop, the other around Joan Fontaine (who had taken the Best Actress award for *Suspicion*), and posed with the happy winners.

Today that faded picture serves as a blatant reminder of one of Oscar's lowest artistic points. Staunch Academy defenders would repeat through the years that *Citizen Kane* would not be thought of as the greatest film in American movie history until a number of years had passed. Back in 1942, they would plead, there was only a mild twitter of acclaim for Welles's study of power and egomania.

That is, of course, apologetic hogwash. The reviews at the time the picture opened were as strong as they would ever be. And even in Hollywood, at the cozy little parties given by Basil Rathbone and producer Walter Wanger, some iconoclasts whispered the word *genius* when talking about Welles. For the first time since the heydey of D. W. Griffith, Hollywood's moviemakers felt bested. To quote Dorothy Parker, "The town was upended, and Welles could have whatever he wanted— except an Oscar and a job."

Nobody has ever denied that Welles's Oscar K.O. was a political defeat, not an artistic one, and that the knockout was sealed the minute Hollywood realized that the doomed, alcoholic mistress in *Citizen Kane* was meant to be Marion Davies. (Dorothy Comingore's performance was eerily correct, right down to Davies's walk and hand mannerisms.)

And nobody has denied that Welles's withering depiction of Davies would never have occurred if Hearst had not become morbidly obsessed with having the actress crowned as the dramatic queen of Hollywood, with her Oscar becoming the scepter royal.

Marion Davies busy emoting in a thirties film. "The Oscars were designed to create incentive, but they became a cruel joke. It was only natural that they create jealousy," said Davies. "You would go to the show and think you were going to win and somebody else did." If Marion was pessimistic about her chances for an Oscar, Hearst only became angrier as each year passed: he pushed her into lavish musicals, bought the services of Clark Gable, Bing Crosby, and Gary Cooper to star with her, and, finally, when nothing worked, pulled her off the MGM lot and switched her to Warner Bros.

"To him, it would have meant the seal of approval for his whole relationship with Marion Davies," said Hollywood correspondent Zelda Cini. 'The Oscar, he felt, would make up for the marriage Hearst could not give her. And Lord knows it wasn't the first or the last time that somebody would try and buy an Oscar."

Hearst's quest for Davies's Oscar followed by *Citizen Kane*'s defeats resembled nothing so much as one of Hollywood's own gothic scripts. Underneath their Adrian gowns and silk tux coats, the Academy voters who gathered at the Biltmore all had a warm spot in their hearts for Marion Davies—the hostess of Hearst's massive castle at San Simeon, a lady who knew most of them by nicknames and who had sent their children christening gifts. By anybody's standards Davies had been the official hostess for the movie capital from 1925 to 1939.

It must have been soul-wrenching for Oscar voters to decide whether to vote for a film they knew to be a monumental work of art or honor social debts to an old friend, a Hollywood damsel in distress.

"It was easy for everyone to assume, since Hollywood is a community conditioned to think the worst of anyone rather than the best, that they were at last getting the truth about Marion's erratic career," said Fred Laurence Guiles, in his 1972 book, *Marion Davies*. "Word of this reached Marion quickly. Bad news always travels the fastest. But Marion pretended that it didn't bother her, and she could not guess how far the film would go in obliterating her name as a film queen."

Guiles, in his exhaustive study of Hearst and Davies during the *Citizen Kane* period, does not buy Welles's later apologies that Susan Alexander in *Kane* was never meant to be Davies. "There was no doubt in anyone's mind, once the film was released, that it *was* Hearst. And before many months passed, people in Hollywood would be referring to Susan Alexander as 'the Marion Davies part.' "

The day Hedda saw the film, she borrowed a phone in the lobby and called Hearst directly at San Simeon. Louis B. Mayer of MGM, the studio that made the best of Davies's movies, wept as he came out of a private screening. The next day Mayer tried to buy the negative from RKO for $800,000. "*Kane* is an important film, and we're proud of it," answered George J. Schaeffer of RKO. "No sellout."

There was good reason for the tears. *Citizen Kane*'s scriptwriter Herman Mankiewicz, who had been the guest of Davies dozens of times, had virtually created Susan Alexander in the actress's image. The film star's sad and growing affair with alcohol, her loneliness among the crowds at the Hearst mansions, and her gnawing wish to become Mrs. Hearst were all paraded before Welles's cameras. But Mankiewicz used these "details only a friend would know" to create a portrait of a failure, a lady totally unredeemed by talent.

"In this they went too far, and Mankiewicz, of all people, knew better; he'd seen all Marion's triumphs, and he *knew*," said one of Hearst's managing editors. "But the millions who have seen the movie accept it as the gospel truth—so goes history."

The movie myth so completely engulfed the truth that if Marion Davies is remembered at all, it's as the inspiration for Susan Alexander.

But six decades ago—about the time Hearst began creating her in the image of the Virgin Mary—Marion Davies was a big star, on her own and with no help from any of her sugar daddies. Ziegfeld had seen her in the second chorus line of a minor Broadway musical and signed her on for his *Follies*. There, while coming down a stage staircase as a

March daffodil, she was spotted by Hearst. She was eighteen; he was fifty-four, and restive from his marriage with an earlier chorine, Millicent Hearst.

"I don't know if he decided then and there to make her the second Mary Pickford," said screenwriter Frances Marion. "But he had definitely decided on that course by the time he, and she, came out to Hollywood." Hearst summoned the writer to his office after finding out that she was the one who wrote Mary Pickford's cutesy filmplays.

"He looked at me, and I could tell he was going to ask me to write Marion's movies," she said. "My heart sank. I liked this warm-hearted Irish girl who was prettier than peonies in a horticulture catalogue. But her pictures were weighted down with such elaborate sets and bejeweled costumes that they dwarfed the actors."

The writer hedged her way through a second cocktail and finally blurted out: "Mr. Hearst, I really don't want to work on Marion's pictures."

Hearst's eyelids dropped a little: "Why not? Don't you like her?"

"I like her very much," said the writer. "And that's exactly why I don't want to do anything that would hurt her career."

She waited for Hearst, who finally said: "I don't understand what you're saying. I'm willing to spend a million dollars on each picture."

The publishing magnate had given Frances Marion the opening she was looking for: "Lavishness doesn't guarantee a good picture, Mr. Hearst. Marion is a natural-born comedienne, and you are smothering her with pretentious stories and such exaggerated backgrounds that you can't see the diamond for the setting." Frances Marion then took in a relieved gasp of air. She'd gotten it out, told Hearst what all Hollywood had been wanting to tell him.

And Hearst, the writer said, gave her a "look that curled me up on the edges."

She had hit it on the head. Hearst, who had decided he could as easily be a Svengali of the film world as he had been czar of a publishing empire, remained on his pigheaded course, virtually smothering Marion Davies's fragile gifts under an avalanche of hokum. She was never able to crawl out.

When the Academy was established ten years later, Hearst was the first to see its little statue as a vial of holy oil just meant to anoint his lover's saintly gifts. So he pulled her out of the simple comedies (for which she might have legitimately won an Oscar) and shoved her into a dismal parade of bad musicals (*Going Hollywood*), weary soap operas (*Peg o' My Heart*), and sorry backstage epics (*The Floradora Girl*).

Hearst had contracted all the symptoms of a Tinseltown blight that *Time* magazine later called "Oscarmania—an irrational search for awards at the expense of all reason."

In this, the newspaper mogul was an original. He blazed a course of silly lavishness that would be repeated in later decades by other idealistic swains trying to pick off an Oscar for their ladies as if it were a Kewpie doll with pink feathers on its head.

In the forties, movie genius David O. Selznick lost all reason grappling for a second Oscar for his wife, Jennifer Jones. Several decades later Peter Bogdanovich would apparently suffer cultural amnesia as he created the dubious *Daisy Miller* for his blond nymphet Cybill Shepherd. For entirely other reasons, Samuel Goldwyn would spend $10 million on a forgettable star, Anna Sten. And Joseph Kennedy helped

Hearst at San Simeon with his beloved dachshund, Helen. The publishing magnate used the considerable magnificence of San Simeon to lobby for Marion Davies during Oscar season. But no amount of champagne and imported food could persuade the film community to take Davies seriously. When San Simeon failed him, Hearst threatened Louis B. Mayer with the wrath of his newspaper empire, telling L.B. to deliver the MGM votes for Marion or else. But MGM's second-in-command, Irving Thalberg, always delivered the studio's votes to his wife, Norma Shearer.

Gloria Swanson spend most of her fortune on an Oscar-aimed movie, *Queen Kelly.*

These Oscar campaigns, in all fairness, have always been discouraged by the Academy. However, since Academy voters quite often honor even dreadful films which cost too much (*Cleopatra*, *The Alamo*, *Doctor Dolittle*, *Hello, Dolly!*, and *Gandhi*), spending in any form often takes precedence over common sense and good taste.

This form of greed reared its head a second time in 1934—quite early in Oscar's history—in an artistic cold war between Marion Davies and Norma Shearer, and therefore between Hearst and MGM's boy genius Irving Thalberg, Shearer's husband and the man who had guided her to her first Oscar (in 1929–30 as Best Actress for *The Divorcée*).

Thalberg, who siphoned off all the best MGM properties for Shearer, seemed to view her first Oscar as basically "an early sound launching pad" for Norma. And who should have known better than he that the Academy Awards race was held in the hands of a few studio bosses in 1930? So Shearer really needed a second Oscar to bring her career to its harvest point.

Thalberg, then only thirty-five and two years away from his death, drew up an acting plan for Norma Shearer that was as cold-blooded as a fighter plane and as ambitious an undertaking as the construction of the Maginot Line. First, Shearer would get out her lace handkerchiefs to play Elizabeth Barrett Browning in *The Barretts of Wimpole Street*. Then, at thirty-six, she would take on Shakespeare's love tragedy *Romeo and Juliet* as the sixteen-year-old Juliet. Finally, in 1938 Norma would shrug off her youthful demeanor to play Marie Antoinette from minuet to guillotine. So ambitious was Thalberg's plan that scouts were sent to France to buy the French queen's own furniture and wigs; meanwhile, MGM artistic wizard Cedric Gibbons began building Verona on the back lot.

This was like waving a red flag in front of Hearst. And he responded like a raging bull. After all, hadn't Hearst draped $80,000 worth of pink roses around the screen when Marion's *Cecilia of the Pink Roses* opened (sending hundreds of moviegoers rushing home with hay fever)? And hadn't he hired Victor Herbert, at almost $100,000, to compose the "Marion Davies March" for the opening of *When Knighthood Was in Flower* (at a premiere so lavish that Dorothy Parker said, "Well, at least we now know what the Second Coming will be like")?

The newspaper publisher pushed his way into Louis B. Mayer's office without an appointment and began pounding on the sacred desk. "I brought my film company to you with an agreement that Marion would get a choice of properties. We had our hearts set on *The Barretts of Wimpole Street* and *Marie Antoinette*."

But Mayer was having trouble keeping Thalberg happy. And, since the studio's prestige and much of its success depended on the whiz kid, Mayer let Shearer keep her gilded bouquet of roles.

Hearst trumpeted like a wounded elephant. He called up Jack Warner and said, "We're bringing our business to Burbank." Warner, of course, was delighted. And why shouldn't he have been? Marion Davies meant Hearst; Hearst meant the combined power of the old man's newspapers; and the papers meant Louella Parsons, a lady who could make or break an Oscar nomination with a remark over her morning croissant. That night a construction crew on double time pulled down Marion's two-story bungalow (with its Renoirs on the wall) and drove it out the MGM gate. Louella said that L.B. cried as he watched it drift out of

Culver City. (But if Mayer had cried as many times as Louella recorded, there would have been a salinity problem in Culver City.)

The Barretts of Wimpole Street came out in 1934. Norma got her nomination, but Claudette Colbert won for *It Happened One Night*. Thalberg was unconcerned: *The Barretts* was only a curtain raiser for *Romeo and Juliet*, which George Cukor was hired to direct.

"Juliet will win Norma an Academy Award in her maturity as an actress just as *The Divorcée* did for her in her young womanhood," Thalberg told his friends. "It's true that Norma is past thirty and Juliet a teen-ager, but her artistry will easily overcome the discrepancy." To balance the scale, he hired an artist even older than Norma, forty-two-year-old Leslie Howard, to play Romeo.

Because of the movie's endless budget, the balcony scene used up all of MGM's huge sound stage 15. Director Cukor needed thirty arc lamps to light the set and took seven days to film the scene.

While it was being shot, Cukor noticed a man standing in the shadows and sent an assistant director to investigate. "It's Mr. Thalberg, sir," said the kid.

"Tell him to come on over," said Cukor.

"But he said to ignore him."

And for hours Irving Thalberg watched his wife toil through the most famous love scene in history.

A year later Thalberg was dead, and *Romeo and Juliet* was well on its way to losing more than a million dollars. Neither it nor Norma won an Oscar. (*Marie Antoinette*, filmed after Thalberg died, would fare no better, with Shearer receiving a sympathy nomination for her twittering, inept portrayal of the French queen.)

Across the hills at Warners, Davies's sugar daddy bought her the services of Dick Powell (for *Hearts Divided*), Clark Gable (for *Cain and Mabel*), and Robert Montgomery (for *Ever Since Eve*). By the time *Cain and Mabel* opened in 1936, the Oscar election was at its most vulnerable, with the race decided by only a handful. And while the film did manage a nomination for dance direction, Hearst couldn't wangle one for Davies.

It was this legacy that brought Hollywood to the Oscar table in 1942 when Marion Davies and Orson Welles would both become victims.

Whenever Welles's name was mentioned (as it was for his personal nominations as Best Actor, Best Director, producer of the Best Picture, and co-author of the Best Original Screenplay) there were loud hisses and boos. Everybody looked the other way when the words *Citizen Kane* were spoken. "People fiddled with their furs, adjusted a hat pin—anything to get past the shame," said an actress who was there. "This was a freeze-out that was decided long before the voting."

Critic Pauline Kael, in writing her brilliant *New Yorker* series "Raising Kane," spent months researching the background for this public crucifixion of the film. And she has expressed her belief that the Hollywood establishment denied the film distribution access not because of any overt threats from Hearst, but because it feared what he "might" do. "Had it not been for the delays and the nervous atmosphere that made the picture 'seem' so unpopular and so become unpopular, it might have swept the Academy Awards. But the picture had an aroma of box-office failure about it when the Awards were given—an aroma that frightens off awards in Hollywood."

But more than aroma clobbered *Citizen Kane*. Hollywood was hit with the full brunt of a Hearst power machine that had been a-building for a half-century. The first sign came when the premiere, set for February 14 at the Radio City Music Hall, was suddenly canceled. George Schaeffer, RKO's top production chief, called the Rockefeller offices in New York City (they owned the Music Hall) and asked, "What gives?" The first answers were vague. Finally, after Schaeffer went all the way to Nelson Rockefeller, he was told: "Louella warned me off it. She asked me, 'How would you like the *American Weekly* magazine section to run a double-page spread on John D. Rockefeller?'"

It took the pressure of a lawsuit to finally get Warners Theaters, which had agreed to distribute, to offer booking dates for *Citizen Kane*. Then Schaeffer had trouble getting papers to take ads for the movie. Some theaters paid for the film but then sat on it, according to Kael's research. And a campaign by Mayer in Los Angeles not only got Welles evicted from his offices at RKO but cost Schaeffer his job as well. RKO employees who had cooperated with Welles were given assignments on B pictures.

Only magazine and newspaper critics (working for non-Hearst magazines and papers, of course) showed any courage.

To quote Kael, "Contrary to rumor [the film] got smashing reviews."

Like this one in *Time*, March 17, 1941: "To most of the several hundred people who have seen the film at private showings, *Citizen Kane* is the most sensational product of the U.S. movie industry. It is a work of art created by grown people for grown people."

And this one by John O'Hara in *Newsweek*, also on March 17, 1941: "[I] have just seen a picture that must be the best picture I've ever seen. And I've just seen the best actor in the history of acting. Name of picture: *Citizen Kane*. Name of actor: Orson Welles."

And this one by Gilbert Seldes for *Esquire*: "Welles has shown Hollywood how to make movies. . . . He has made the movies young again, by filling them with life." And this one by Archer Winsten in the *New York Post*: "It goes without saying this is the picture that wins the majority of 1941's prizes in a walk. For it is inconceivable that another will come along to challenge it."

And this, by Cecilia Ager in *PM*: "It's as if the motion picture was a sleeping monster; a mighty force stupidly awaiting a fierce young man to come and kick it to life: to rouse it; shake it and awaken it to its potentialities. Seeing it, it's as if you never really saw a motion picture before."

This chorus of praise was the final ingredient needed to convert the Oscar ceremony of 1942 into a full-blown tragedy of classic proportions.

"The members of the Academy destroyed Orson Welles that night," wrote Kael in *The Citizen Kane Book*. "*Kane* was Welles's finest moment. Their failure to back him was the turning point. He had made *Citizen Kane* at twenty-five, and he seemed to have the world before him. The Academy members had made their token gesture to *Citizen Kane* with the screenplay award. They failed in what they believed; they gave in to the scandal and to the business pressures. They couldn't know how much guilt they should feel: guilt that by their failure to support *Kane* they started the downward spiral of Orson Welles, who was to become perhaps the greatest loser in Hollywood history."

Nineteen forty-two is one of those years that puts a permanent chink in Oscar's fragile armor of objectivity. If only the Oscar weren't held up by the mass media as a high watermark of quality. But it is. If only a

Orson Wells as the older Citizen Kane, in a still that is a token reminder of Welles' lost Oscars for that masterpiece. He was to suffer from that defeat until the day he died.

single nomination couldn't make the difference between a big career and a moderately successful one. But it can.

Unlike Hearst's pursuit of an Oscar for Davies, the normally tasteful Samuel Goldwyn's quest, on behalf of Anna Sten, caused several bits of high farce in Hollywood's rather humorless history.

The "Anna Sten Affair" began in 1932. Oscar was still young, and Goldwyn was prickly with jealousy over the nominations being chalked up by Dietrich and Garbo.

With two foreigners packing the theaters of America, a third, newer one could only do better, to Goldwyn's way of thinking.

Goldwyn saw the Russian-born actress emoting in a German-made production when he was on a tour of Europe in 1932. The film was *The Murderer Dmitri Karamazov* and the producer was entranced. "Listen to her," he told an adjutant. "She sounds like Garbo—only better."

"But Mr. Goldwyn, Garbo's Swedish, not German."

Goldwyn would hear none of it. He met Anna Sten, toasted her with champagne, and then, with the producer bobbing his head and speaking English and Sten bobbing her head and speaking German, the star was signed up at $3,000 a week plus expenses. Sten stuffed the fat Goldwyn marks into her almost empty wallet, headed for Paris shops, and left her new boss to overcome the fallout from his own largesse.

A month later, American movie magazine editors found their mail suddenly cluttered with a barrage of German cheesecake. Sten! Sten as an Arabian temptress; as a coy milkmaid with Clara Bow lips; as an

*You can be forgiven if the screen credits of Anna Sten have escaped your memory; her major films—*Nana, Resurrection, *and* The Wedding Night*—hardly set the thirties on fire. Sten, shown here during her "Garbo period," was imported from Europe by Samuel Goldwyn. By the time she docked in New York and was being driven into Manhattan, Goldwyn already had billboards plastering the city. When* Nana *was released, her face, in this kerchief pose, stood seventy-five feet above Times Square. Goldwyn said quite frankly that she "is better than Garbo, sexier than Dietrich, and a finer actress than Norma Shearer." But the Oscar voters were unimpressed.*

apple-cheeked hussar popping out of her vest. "Sexier than Dietrich; more mysterious than Garbo," said the releases from the purple pen of Goldwyn publicist Lynn Farnol.

Sten was in Hollywood by then, fatter and speaking much less English than Goldwyn remembered. No English, in fact. The producer told Gary Cooper that she seemed able to do only two things—nod her head and gain weight.

Goldwyn made her sign up at the Beverly Hills Tennis Club to cure the latter and sent her to a passel of language instructors to cure the former. As for Goldwyn, he took an Alka-Seltzer and screamed for his story editors. "She has to start at the top," he told writer Willard Mack. "In a classic by *another* foreigner. You know, Zola or something. Yeah, Zola'll do fine."

And Zola it was. *Nana,* to be specific—the story of a whore adrift in nineteenth-century Paris. The scripters started sweating while Goldwyn's bills piled up.

"Teach her to sing," he ordered a studio vocal coach.

"But Sam," the coach cried, "this is a woman with a small but disagreeable voice."

"Change it, then," answered Sam.

"Teach her to dance," he ordered a veteran ballet master.

"But she has no coordination," said the master.

"I'll come see myself," said Goldwyn.

Which he did. According to Goldwyn's biographer Arthur Marx, the producer, after about five minutes of watching the lessons, "jumped off his chair and hopped around the rehearsal hall on his left foot to show that anyone, even a middle-aged man, could learn to do the can-can."

The evidence was dismal, but Goldwyn set a starting date for *Nana* anyway. "This is the girl that's going to win the next Academy Award," he said. "Just you watch." And this was the girl Hollywood would soon be calling "Goldwyn's Last Sten" as Oscar voters chuckled over their ballots.

George Fitzmaurice took the helm, slowly coaching Sten line by line through a script that was waterlogged by attempts to make it fit Goldwyn's standards of "Academy seriousness." The producer tried to ignore the rumors coming from the set, but finally ordered a rough cut to gauge the progress of "Project Sten."

"When he saw a picture that was definitely without the Goldwyn touch, Sam ordered the whole thing scrapped and announced that he was starting over from page one with a new director," wrote Marx in *Goldwyn.*

"I don't care how much money it costs," he yelled at his distraught accountants. "It is my money I'm spending. We will shoot until I'm happy."

Sam brought in the town's only woman director, Dorothy Arzner, and tried to tell Anna things would be better from that point on. Sten thought he was talking about her dress and asked, "What's wrong with it?"

Arzner pulled Sten through the picture with a maximum of artistry and a minimum of confusion. But even Arzner could not correct what the Goldwyn scriptwriters had done to Zola. They had changed Nana from a prostitute into a nice girl in trouble and jettisoned her gruesome death from smallpox; in the Goldwyn version Nana commits suicide, freeing two brothers who love her to fight for France.

And the producer had an alternate plan in case the critics caught on. A week before *Nana* opened in New York, 25 percent of the city's downtown billboards were plastered with Sten—billboards a full story high carrying the subtle hint that here was next year's Academy Award winner.

"By the time *Nana* opened at the Music Hall on February 2, 1934, Anna Sten was better known to some Americans than Charles Lindbergh and the Burma Shave sign," said Marx.

It was futile: *Nana* lost money—only Goldwyn knew how much. To dampen the rumors of "failure," he quickly put Sten with Gary Cooper in a sure winner, *Barbary Coast*, with William Wyler directing. Nobody ever talked about what happened on that set, but Anna came tumbling out of the role after only four days, succeeded, successfully, by Miriam Hopkins.

"Well," said Goldwyn, unruffled, "we'll try Tolstoy." Then he hauled out and dusted off the Russian's difficult novel *Resurrection*. The critics liked it; the public didn't. No Oscar.

Sam again drafted Cooper and scrapped together a little pastiche called *The Wedding Night*, with King Vidor at the controls. "He can direct anybody," Lillian Gish had said, not counting on Sten.

Halfway through filming, Goldwyn showed up on the set to watch a love scene. "I tell you that if this scene isn't the greatest love scene ever put on film, the whole goddamned picture will go right down the sewer." Which is exactly what it did.

The fourth time was a knockout. Goldwyn threw in the towel and said good-bye to Sten, who reemerged in minor roles during the forties.

Years later Rosalind Russell, after losing the Oscar for her almost certain win in *Mourning Becomes Electra*, said: "It seems to be a case of the gods saying to those self-conscious 'Oscar pictures'—Well, just you watch, you aren't going to win."

David O. Selznick knew all this when he began tilting Academy Award windmills in the name of his love (later his wife), Jennifer Jones. She'd already won an Oscar for her second feature film, *The Song of Bernadette* (1943). That only put more pressure on Selznick: not only did he have to top himself (after the Oscar-rich *Gone with the Wind*), he had to find the role of roles, the film of films, for Jennifer.

The producer shuffled through a couple of minor projects before settling on *Duel in the Sun*, which in Selznick's hands became an overblown western that critics would call "Lust in the Dust." The five-million-dollar film, with King Vidor as director and Gregory Peck, Lionel Barrymore, and Lillian Gish as co-stars, also had, as a special consultant to Jones, Dietrich's former mentor, Josef von Sternberg.

"From an artistic little western, *Duel in the Sun* grew to epic size," wrote Bob Thomas in *Selznick*. "David was especially meticulous in matters concerning Jennifer. Her costumes were redesigned again and again. Her makeup and hairstyles were tested again and again."

Then came the "Affair of Orgasm Music." Dimitri Tiomkin found out about that only after Selznick hired him, sending him a Western Union telegram, declaring that the film's score must have eleven separate themes: Spanish theme, ranch theme, love theme . . . Desire, too. And, oh yes, the orgasm theme. Tiomkin told Thomas it might have been funny if Selznick hadn't been so serious. "Love themes I can write. Desire, too. But orgasm? How do you score an orgasm?"

"Well, you'll just have to try," said Selznick. The composer came up with a heavy air that he thought might fit his employer's idea of orgasm

Jennifer Jones in Love Is a Many-Splendored Thing (1955).

music. Selznick seemed to like it. At a sneak preview, however, the producer began stirring in his theater seat. He rushed back to Tiomkin: "Whistle the orgasm theme for me!"

The composer wet his lips and whistled a weak approximation of the score. "No, that isn't it," said Selznick. "That's just not an orgasm." Back to the music sheets. Weeks later, Tiomkin unveiled the new theme, combining cellos, trombones, and the pulsating of a handsaw.

Selznick still wasn't happy, but the score stood as it was after Tiomkin blew up, yelling, "Meestair Selznick, you . . . your way, I . . . mine. To me, *that* is . . . music. Case closed."

The low point of Selznick's movie meddling came as King Vidor was finally filming the death scene. Jennifer Jones and Gregory Peck were sprawled in the hot sun, expiring for the camera. Vidor loomed over them in intense concentration.

Suddenly, new splashes of blood slopped onto the actors. Then a hand appeared dabbing more Indian makeup on Jones's contorted face.

It was Selznick. Vidor closed his script, rose from his chair, and looked Selznick in the eye. "David," he said, "you can take this picture and shove it."

Many another producer would have been shaken from his obsession by this incident, and the embarrassing publicity which followed. Not Selznick. And when the Oscar nominations were announced, they confirmed the success of his carefully mounted ad campaign: Jones was nominated for Best Actress of 1946. (This kind of P.R. strategy is what makes Oscarmania so venal: even in the case of lapses of taste, this strategy works; it ropes in the voters long enough to get a nomination.)

In his biography of Selznick, Bob Thomas wrote: "David became obsessed with Jennifer and with her career. She was unlike any woman he had known before—enigmatic, enchanting, quintessentially feminine. He saw in her the limitless potential of a consummate actress. There was nothing she was incapable of; no role she could not play. And David took charge of every aspect of her career."

So Selznick began writing the "Jennifer memos," a series of insanely long instructions to directors, makeup artists, lighting technicians, and producers, advising them *ad infinitum* on the intricacies of handling Miss Jones (by then Mrs. Selznick). One memo to the cameraman on *A Farewell to Arms* ran for twenty single-spaced pages. Selznick, point by point, told the cinematographer how to photograph Jones properly.

A Farewell to Arms (1957) was Selznick's last grab for the gold ring on the Academy's Oscar merry-go-round. He hired John Huston to direct, Rock Hudson to co-star, and every extra in Italy for support. Huston, on location in Italy, was soon buried under paper.

"I am very much on my guard, and unless I hold you to the line on this as a love story, with the war as the background, the military emphasis is going to throw the picture way off balance," Selznick wired.

Huston was still dizzy from this one when he received a second cable, costing seven hundred dollars to send.

If this picture is going to fail, it must fail on my mistakes, not yours, Selznick said in the telegram. He also hinted strongly that Huston should resign, which he did.

In came Charles Vidor (no relation to King). Vidor had a week's grace before the memos started. In one of his most comical, Selznick pointed out to Vidor that Jennifer knew what she was doing when she asked Selznick for a "business appointment" to discuss her deep disturbance concerning changes that had been made in her first scene with Henry [Rock Hudson] in the Milan hospital. He said that they had, with the rewrite, lost entirely the desperate hunger of these two people for each other—in what Hemingway has called his *Romeo and Juliet*. As I think you will discover, he suggested, Jennifer is a very creative artist, who brings to every scene the benefits of intense study. Incidentally, he added, I think you would be well-advised to always let her play the scene for you first, of course, then feel free to redirect her as you see fit.

The memo exposes for public scrutiny some of the hysteria Selznick felt during this last attempt to bag an Oscar for his wife. Rock Hudson told Thomas that he quietly watched as Selznick, lost in concentration, walked into a wall. Another time, when Hudson was in a deep embrace with Jones, he looked up at the camera to see Selznick whispering in Vidor's ear.

"David," said the actor.

"Oh, sorry," said Selznick.

Several days later Selznick told an associate producer, "This picture has got to have love, love, love. And there isn't enough of it yet."

Finally Selznick and Jones headed home with their picture.

An advisor to Selznick took one look at the film, then suggested that his boss release it gradually in California to get audience reaction. But the bigwigs at Fox wanted it out quick, whispering sycophantic nothings into David's ear.

It was painful, contemporaries said, to see how much David O. Selznick wanted to create an Oscar-winning role for his future wife, Jennifer Jones. Under the pressure of competition from his early success with Gone with the Wind *and her Oscar-winning first feature film,* Song of Bernadette, *Selznick's artistic judgment faltered. He smothered her talent in overblown productions that bombed with the critics, (exceptions were* Portrait of Jennie, Since You Went Away, *and* Madame Bovary). *Some of the most powerful men in Hollywood have mounted similarly massive and doomed efforts to win statuettes for their favorite starlets—Samuel Goldwyn for Anna Sten, William Randolph Hearst for Marion Davies, and Irving Thalberg for Norma Shearer.*

That was just what he wanted to hear. Being anxious to have *A Farewell to Arms* qualify for both the Oscars and the New York Film Critics Awards, the producer was seduced by the yes-men at Fox. And he let the film go out without viewing the final cut, sailing to Jamaica with his wife.

The reviews were crushing, with critics calling the picture old-fashioned, overproduced, poorly acted, and ineffective. Even Hemingway, who had been offered a share of the profits, cabled Selznick to say he thought little of the profits from a film in which "the forty-one-year-old Mrs. Selznick portrayed the twenty-four-year-old Catherine Barkley."

Bob Thomas wrote, "Selznick was devastated by the failure of *A Farewell to Arms*, and what hurt him most was the feeling that he had failed Jennifer. He had intended the picture to be the crowning achievement of her career. David, his confidence shattered, never made another film."

A Farewell to Arms received only a single nomination, a Best Supporting Actor nod to Vittorio De Sica, a man with whom Selznick had feuded during this and an earlier movie, *Indiscretion of an American Wife*.

And the Oscar Svengali tradition didn't die there.

What else, after all, was megaproducer Robert Evans when it came to Ali MacGraw, the frozen-faced girl who got an Oscar nomination for "never saying I'm sorry" to Ryan O'Neal in *Love Story*?

Evans, an incredibly handsome man who made a million in the women's sportswear business and then worked his way up the Hollywood production ladder, showed almost unerring judgment as a Paramount helmsman (with *The Godfather*, *Rosemary's Baby*, and *Love Story* to his credit). When it came to the human sleepwalker Ali MacGraw, however, Evans finally lost all sense of taste in 1979. That year he tried to create a tennis version of *Rocky* with MacGraw and the equally vapid Dean-Paul Martin (son of big Dean) in *Players*.

While *Rocky* had won the Oscar, Ali MacGraw, as a female cross between Sylvester Stallone and Burgess Meredith, drew only laughter. At a foreign-press preview the audience snickered; they chuckled in Westwood; and they laughed out loud in Atlanta. The frightful dramatic climax of the film featured the masklike MacGraw pushing Martin of the bleached hair through a tennis training workout.

You have pigeon toes," said Ali, squinting over her Gucci scarf.

Dino rolled his eyes (buried in blue contacts) and mumbled: "Segura was pigeon-toed; Laver was pigeon-toed; Gonzales was pigeon-toed. And me—now me."

Then they called it game, set, and match.

"How can two people who look so good, act so bad?" groaned Gene Shalit on "Today."

According to Marie Brenner's stylish 1978 book, *Going Hollywood*, Evans's grand dramatic design for MacGraw was formed long before *Players*. "Ali had plans for *The Great Gatsby*," wrote Brenner. "Gatsby's Daisy was her literary self-image. She nagged Paramount for two years, convinced Evans it had to be *Gatsby*."

But first came *The Getaway*. And Steve McQueen. And then a romance the whole world would know about. According to Brenner, MacGraw forgot Evans but remembered *Gatsby*. "Evans had an ultimatum for her. If she stayed with him, she'd be in the movie. If not, . . ." So Mia Farrow played Daisy to Robert Redford's Gatsby, saving MacGraw from one of cinema's five biggest flops.

There are echoes of both Selznick and Hearst in Evans's "Ali fixation." And while Evans is not the kind to admit right out that he's been

Ali McGraw with Steve McQueen in The Getaway *(1972).*

tilting for an Oscar, his campaigns for *Love Story* and *The Godfather* long ago unmasked his Academy Award fever.

Peter Bogdanovich's celluloid Tinker Toys for Cybill Shepherd fit more easily into the classic mold set by Hearst. Shepherd, an also-ran for Miss Teenage America, might have made it farther on her own than with Bogdanovich's heavy directorial hand. After she blazed to glory in Bogdanovich's 1971 film *The Last Picture Show,* her mentor proceeded with plans for a film that would be far more "important": a hand-tailored version of Henry James's *Daisy Miller.* He then surrounded his protégée with the immense talents of Cloris Leachman and Eileen Brennan. Cybill came off like a living Barbie doll in a Hollywood wax museum.

Ho-hum, one down. Then Bogdanovich bought much of Cole Porter's song catalogue and cast Shepherd in a dinosaur of a musical called *At Long Last Love.* A singing Burt Reynolds, literally crammed into a tight thirties tux, reported as Miss Shepherd's co-star, along with Eileen Brennan and Madeline Kahn—all of whom wheezed and whined their way through the score. "It's a good thing Cole wasn't alive to see this," Ethel Merman said through clenched teeth after seeing the film.

As if this weren't enough, Bogdanovich pulled Cybill into one of America's best recording studios to make an album of naughty Porter songs, such as "In the Morning, No." While trying to play one of the songs, a New York disc jockey laughed so hard the needle jumped through an entire band.

The picture temporarily ruined not only Bogdanovich's career but Shepherd's as well. Is it any wonder that Cybill retired to Memphis—with no Oscar on her bookcase?

"To some," said Hedda Hopper, "the Oscar is like a one-armed bandit. They just have to pull that lever—no matter the cost."

After all these years—years in which his tryst with Cybill died a slow, agonizing death, years in which his career nosedived spectacularly—Bogdanovich smarts from "L'Affaire Cybill."

He recalled: "I came into the town like gangbusters and had three hit pictures in a row. I was never particularly humble, and these hits gave me a power I didn't even realize I had. Besides, a lot of people in town didn't know me. All they saw was the plot: this guy leaves his wife for a beautiful model—a model he makes into a movie star and then flaunts.

"After this string of hits, everyone says, 'Well, let's see what he can do next.' But then I had *Daisy Miller*, a flop starring my girl friend. Well, then, the knives were ready."

The Oscar campaign for *Daisy Miller* was based on a string of rave reviews. "Interestingly enough," Peter continued, "*Daisy Miller* got infinitely better reviews than *Paper Moon*. The *New York Times* and *Newsweek* both gave *Daisy Miller* raves and panned *Paper Moon*."

The charismatic director admitted that he was soon viewed as "a fool for love." "They were trying to make me replay the Marlene Dietrich–Josef von Sternberg saga. After Hollywood broke them up they didn't let Joe work very much. They sort of killed Joe for his arrogance; they thought he was hiding behind Marlene. I think a lot of people believed that Cybill and I were going to play that scene. Then Cybill went into a sort of a decline, I didn't make any pictures for 'endless years,' and we broke up. By that time Cybill and I were being kicked around by the whole country because we made *At Long Last Love,* and it was treated

*Cybill Shepherd in Peter Bogda-
novich's* The Last Picture Show
*(1971), the film which ignited Bog-
danovich's infatuation with the ingenue.*

as if we had committed one of the most heinous crimes ever, including child-murdering and rape." A *New York Times* writer observed, "It's hard to recall a time when so many people derived so much pleasure from one director's decline and fall."

Several years later Bogdanovich, still much the Svengali, stumbled into a love affair and subsequent tragedy so intense that it eventually launched two doomed Oscar campaigns of lavish proportions.

It all began with one heartbreaking tragedy: the murder of starlet Dorothy Stratten (who would be called the "Cybill Shepherd Substitute") at the hands of her former husband, Paul Snider.

This lurid death in a high-tech Hollywood apartment sent emotional and artistic vibrations through a shocked town and industry.

But Bogdanovich was the first victim—bereft director chased by a shroud of guilt over the loss of a girl he was grooming into an Oscar-caliber comedic actress.

He had just finished filming a showcase (*They All Laughed*) for Dorothy, a *Playboy* playmate, and was all but entombed in the editing room polishing the film he felt would propel him back into the top ranks of Hollywood auteurs.

On August 14, 1980, an emergency call from Hugh Hefner was put through to the telephone at his elbow. Hefner, in a quaking and halting voice, told Peter that the director's lover—his fiancée—had been sodomized and then slain by her Hollywood hustler husband, who then took his own life.

The director felt the floor give way as his mind tried to cope with the impossible: the death of not only his star but his lover. More than anything else, he wanted to rush out to find her—to prove she was still alive, still vibrant.

As tragedy built upon tragedy, as the bright California sun turned dark for him, as the lurid details were published of Dorothy's rise from the ranks of a *Playboy* centerfold to a starlet and finally into Peter's bed, Bogdanovich began to cling to *They All Laughed* as if it were a life preserver.

Dorothy Stratten's story was the *classic* case of the Hollywood dream gone mad. She was a two-dollar-an-hour soda-fountain clerk in Canada when Paul Snider took her under his romantic wing (and into his bed).

It was Snider, looking for a shortcut to Hollywood fame and power, who engineered and promoted Dorothy's centerfold—which, in turn, made her Playmate of the Year in 1980. Armed with her achingly poignant "small-town girl" beauty, Dorothy made such an impact at the Playboy mansion that it catapulted Snider out of her life and Peter Bogdanovich into it.

"Peter B. is doing the town with a new young girl whose resemblance to Cybill Shepherd is uncanny," wrote one gossip columnist. "It's love; it's love between Bogdanovich and Dorothy," predicted another.

Dorothy drifted into love with Bogdanovich. All at once, the man who had produced four celluloid disasters in a row was bounding with energy.

He showcased his new love with an astounding cast for *They All Laughed*: Audrey Hepburn, in yet another return to the screen, John Ritter, Ben Gazzara, and the newly discovered character actress Colleen Camp.

Bogdanovich designed the movie to be filmed entirely in New York. That decision took on monumental importance because it marked the true life separation of Snider and Stratten. In fact, she had to tell her estranged husband that "due to Miss Hepburn's wishes, the set will remain closed to *everyone*."

But Snider continued to feed his impossible and dark plans for the girl he had so valiantly rescued from small-town life. "I'm going to make her into the biggest star Hollywood has ever seen," he bragged to friends at Chippendale's, the male strip emporium he had begun to frequent. "Peter Bogdanovich won't even be able to afford her before I'm through."

Snider turned increasingly to alcohol and cocaine as he tried to cope with Dorothy's sudden success and his equally sudden collapse. Bogdanovich no longer accepted his calls; Hugh Hefner had him barred from the L.A. Playboy Club; and debts piled up in the mailbox of the apartment which he had turned into a showcase for Dorothy's photographs.

The idyll Bogdanovich shared with Stratten during the seven weeks of filming in New York was suddenly over as they flew home to face their divergent destinies during one of the hottest summers in the history of Los Angeles.

The chain of events leading to the murder began several weeks later, when Dorothy officially moved into Bogdanovich's movie-star mansion tucked in the rarefied Holmby Hills above Bel Air. Snider pleaded with her to see him, cried, and threatened until his rages became more than Stratten could stand.

So, on that afternoon in August, she left Bogdanovich's house and drove to her death.

It was then Hugh Hefner who placed the call to Peter with the news, his hand shaking violently as he dialed the private number in Bogdanovich's den.

"There was no conversation after I broke the news—just silence," Hefner recalled. "I was afraid Peter had gone into shock or something.

When he wouldn't respond to my questions, I called the house under another number. A male friend was there to make sure he was all right. But I could tell Peter was overcome by grief."

It was Peter who arranged for cremation five days later—with the urn buried in a casket only 500 yards from Marilyn Monroe's mausoleum.

Four days later, the director issued this statement:

Dorothy Stratten was as gifted and intelligent an actress as she was beautiful. And she was very beautiful indeed—in every way imaginable —most particularly in her heart. She and I fell in love during the filming of our picture (They All Laughed) *and planned to be married as soon as her divorce was final. The loss to her mother and father, her sister and brother, to my children, to her friends, and to me is larger than we can calculate. But there is no life Dorothy's has touched that has not been changed for the better through knowing her—however briefly. Dorothy looked at the world with love, and believed that all people were good down deep. She was mistaken, but it is among the most generous and noble errors we can make.*

—*Peter Bogdanovich*

Dorothy Stratten in a portrait made to publicize Peter Bogdanovich's film They All Laughed, *which the director later fashioned into a memorial to the slain actress.*

After the funeral, Peter took increasing solace from the film as it flickered before him in the darkened editing rooms. It would be, he decided, a memorial to Dorothy—perhaps even an Oscar-nominated memorial.

They All Laughed became the exorcist for his guilt and sorrow.

Fate struck again. Just weeks before the film was to open with great splashes in Los Angeles and New York, Time-Life Films (the producer of the project) collapsed and announced, among other things, that *They All Laughed* would be shelved permanently. Several companies made tentative offers only to be rebuffed.

Bogdanovich instantly decided to sacrifice his fortune, part of his future, and his bankability. He took his five-million-dollar fortune, liquidated it, and bought the film back from Time-Life.

He spent still more money releasing the film and paying for a marketing campaign which splashed Dorothy's image (predominantly) across the pages of America's newspapers and the screens of fifty million television sets.

Though ticket sales earned back only $900,000 of Bogdanovich's fortune, the director was encouraged enough to spend $100,000 for an Oscar campaign to tout the film generally and Colleen Camp particularly. *They All Laughed* received not a single nomination.

The still-distraught director sorrowfully pulled the film back in to start work on a reedited version still in the works in 1986.

Oscar wasn't through with Dorothy Stratten—yet. Bob Fosse became intensely interested in her story, from beginning to end, after reading an essay on the murder in the *Village Voice*. And from the beginning, he was as interested in Snider's story as he was in Stratten's. "It was this guy's story which interested me," Fosse said. "His milieu—sleazy nightclubs—I could deal with that portion of the story and it's also about Hollywood. I suppose there is still quite a bit of anger in me about Hollywood."

Fosse tested twenty actresses, most of them unknown, before turning to Mariel Hemingway—but only on the condition that she find some way to duplicate Dorothy Stratten's greatest asset: her breasts. Mariel responded by having plastic implants.

Fosse insisted publicly that the "breast issue" was incidental. "I cast Mariel because she has a certain innocence—an innocence so like Dorothy Stratten's own."

Hemingway also quickly denied she was trying to *Playboy*-ize her look. "I didn't do it for the role," she told *People* magazine. "It was for me, truly . . . I decided I didn't want to go through life being looked on as just an athletic tomboy."

The sometimes brilliant Eric Roberts played the contemptible Snider to both raves and pans by the nation's film critics. "He seems certain to be a front-runner in the Oscar race," said columnist Marilyn Beck.

The Ladd Company quickly found that the ungainly title of the film, *Star 80*, and the downbeat tempo kept ticket buyers away in droves. Even when Hemingway appeared mostly undraped in *Playboy* to show off her charms, the film continued to die on the box-office vine. It also received no Oscar nominations.

"The real movie on Dorothy is yet to be made," Peter Bogdanovich promised, as a final word on the subject.

Unlike the attempts of Hearst, Selznick, Bogdanovich, and the others, there was one Oscar quest—that by a daughter for her father—that succeeded admirably.

Jane took that Oscar of her Dad's and held it in her hands; she held it with a pride and joy she lavished on neither of her own Academy Awards.
—Rona Barrett, 1981

On Golden Pond director Mark Rydell was in a Hollywood lab preparing to make the final sound dubbing on the film when he received a late-night call from one of the film's producers, Jane Fonda.

"Mark, you've got to show this picture to my father," she said in a somewhat injured voice.

"I'm still finishing work on adding the score," he said. "It will be completely finished in a couple of weeks."

"No, Mark, you have to show *On Golden Pond* to my father now—he may not live to see it."

"God, Jane," Rydell replied. "I didn't know it was that serious. Of course, I'll set up a screening for tomorrow night." The director then worked around the clock to prepare as finished a product as he could to show his celebrated star.

"I was very anxious about it. I wanted very, very much for Henry Fonda to like it. I was, I'll confess it, afraid of his wrath."

As Rydell sat in that deserted screening room, his mind drifted back to the genesis of the project almost a year earlier.

By then, Jane's production company, IPC Films (now Fonda Films), had bought Ernest Thompson's play to crown her father's long career with one last masterpiece. And from the start, the movie was designed to win the Academy Award Henry Fonda had so richly deserved for any one of a score of performances since his film debut in the mid-thirties.

With the exception, perhaps, of Greta Garbo, Henry Fonda was, by 1980, the most prestigious actor who had never won an Oscar.

When her dad had been given one of those tedious "special" Academy Awards several years earlier, Jane was pleased. "But she told close associates she had a work in mind which would bring Henry the Best Actor prize at long last.

And Ernest Thompson's mellow play about a strong New England couple who look death squarely in the eye seemed ideal. The play's setting was as golden as the play itself—a shimmering summer retreat in the New Hampshire mountains.

"The major move, of course, was Jane's purchase of that play—in the sense that it was an objective of hers to give her father this final golden moment," Rydell remembered. "I don't recall any conscious knowledge that an Oscar was the ultimate achievement. The award merely followed naturally."

The Oscar-winning deal was put together by William Morris's Stan Kamen, the much beloved super-agent, who represented Rydell as well.

Henry told Kamen that he particularly admired Rydell's *The Reivers*, *The Cowboys* and *Cinderella Liberty*. So the deal was struck and an Oscar odyssey was begun.

What Rydell couldn't have known as he waited in that theater for the one-man screening was the story of Henry's own bitterness over being passed by with just a single nomination (in 1940 for *The Grapes of Wrath*), despite a rich body of work which included: *Young Mr. Lincoln*, *Jesse James*, *The Lady Eve*, *The Ox-Bow Incident*, *My Darling Clementine*, *The Fugitive*, *Twelve Angry Men*, *Mister Roberts*, *Advise and Consent*, and *Once Upon a Time in the West*.

The New Hampshire sunset frames Katharine Hepburn, Henry Fonda, and his daughter Jane just before they start shooting On Golden Pond *(1981). Moments earlier, Kate walked up shyly to Henry and handed him a crumpled-up hat. "This was Spencer's," she said. "He wore it on each film. I want to pass it on to you." Even the crew broke down.*

Once the financial deal for *On Golden Pond* had been worked out, Jane, playwright Thompson, and Mark Rydell sat down and drew up a battle plan to strengthen the work for the screen by making an ominous, foreboding sense of approaching death creep into the golden autumn setting.

"Once Katharine Hepburn was cast (what dream casting!), we had the opportunity to confront very, very profound issues," the director declared. "And we operated on one basic premise: that the film was basically about Fonda's character—a man confronting his own final moments while making peace with his daughter at the same time. It was tailored to the Fondas—purely and simply. But before we were through, we would find that art was merely shadowing real life."

From the beginning, Rydell admired Jane's gutsiness. "She was not the least bit reluctant. She made a conscious choice to rectify her life with her father through this extraordinary situation in which she was *playing* an alienated daughter who wanted to resolve her relationship with an infirm and dying father."

The crucial scene for both Henry and Jane came when the fictional daughter had to face the professor father to settle their own emotional relationship before it was too late.

Though she had enormous doubts about her ability to bring her full powers to the scene, she didn't confide them to Rydell. But she turned to Hepburn with a mind full of doubts. "Nonsense! You can do it. You can do it!" Hepburn told her. And, as Rydell moved his cameras in a circle about the elder and younger Fonda, Hepburn stayed behind Henry with her fists in knots and her mouth forming a silent: "Come on, Jane. Come on!"

"I watched Jane in complete awe," recalled Rydell. "Remember she still had this enormous job of acting to do—hitting the marks, speaking the text which was written for fictional characters. But as Jane fumbled with her words, and looked deeply into her own father's eyes, she drew deeply and richly from her personal life and bared her own fears and vulnerability."

Before that one scene was finished, Henry Fonda was so touched that he was weeping uncontrollably. "We had to remove that footage because it just wasn't right for the fictional character."

"She literally bared her soul in that scene," Rydell said analytically. "But never once did she let me—or any of the rest of the company—know how hard it must have been for her . . . she just looked up and headed straight through it."

Katharine Hepburn, too, "headed straight through," regardless of difficulties. Just six weeks before location shooting started, the actress had suffered a shoulder separation which necessitated painful surgery. "We started rehearsing in the hospital," Rydell said. "The doctors told her there was no way she could make this film, and she just laughed at them."

By the time filming began, Hepburn had loosened up her shoulder just enough to allow her to swim in the icy New Hampshire lake every morning and evening.

"She even insisted on carrying a heavy canoe through the woods herself—just because the script called for it. She had that Yankee determination. She was, by damned, going to carry that heavy canoe. And when friends told her that I had been forced to cut that small scene, she became furious—they tell me. I'm not sure she has even seen the film yet."

When Jane arrived with husband Tom Hayden and their children, the entire *On Golden Pond* process became a "family affair," with the basic unspoken goal of making a film so good, so intimate, so openly vulnerable that not even the Academy could afford to ignore Henry Fonda this time.

"Once the full cast and their families were assembled, a great burst of camaraderie blossomed," Rydell remembered. "It became a genuinely familial experience. Most of the people came to the set even when they were not needed. Tom and Jane lived in an enlarged outbuilding right on the grounds, and the others lived in the main house."

Jane and Hayden hosted regular political and philosophical sessions every Sunday afternoon where guests were invited to plunge into the stances Fonda began perfecting during her militant days in the sixties.

By far the gutsiest scene came when the script called for Henry and a young fishing companion, played by Doug McKeon, to plunge into the lake waters—where they cling to rocks until they are rescued by Hepburn and a postman she recruits.

"We were all deeply concerned about this—and Hank's stamina," Rydell confessed. "We did it at the very end of the shooting schedule. And by then fall was upon us and the lake was winter cold. It was also stormy, so even the crew was chilly beneath the warmest of clothes."

Rydell maneuvered the cameras in place and delayed, as long as

An obviously touched Henry Fonda finally got his Oscar—however honorary—from a gracious Robert Redford. Fonda had received only one nomination in his five-decade career. His hands shook visibly as he took the statue. The roar of the crowd was thunderous.
(© A.M.P.A.S.)

possible, Fonda's descent into the lake. "Finally, he had to jump in. We were fully aware of how fragile he was after doing the scene in the woods where he became temporarily disoriented and had to run around through the sun, seeking a familiar tree or clearing. Even then, early in the filming, he was only able to run about ten paces at a time, and he would be literally exhausted from his heart condition."

Rydell was forced to put Henry in and out of the water a number of times as he painstakingly filmed the vignette where the old professor and the boy are rescued.

"We thought of alternatives, but Hank wanted to and *insisted* on doing it himself. But when he was in the water, I couldn't believe it. This old man plunged into that scene and played it straight through until he must have been as exhausted as possible before physically caving in."

As a capper, when the boat carrying Hepburn came within camera range, the actress herself—bandaged shoulder and all—dived into the water (in a departure from the script). "We had been shooting in that water for many days," said Rydell, "but when she dived in, my jaw dropped at the audacity and courage of this actress!"

During a long, emotional interview with the authors of this book, Rydell returned again and again to Jane's courage, which allowed her own real emotional character to be revealed for the sake of this one film.

"She had very, very little to hide behind," he said. "Before those terrible, strenuous scenes, she would sink into that role and take it on as her own. I never once saw the slightest hint of stardom there. Her feet were always on the ground. But she was always close to real and genuine anxiety when she had to come to grips with her father. There was a real sense of disturbance before those scenes."

Ordeal though it was, it was over too soon for Mark Rydell. "It was a lifetime experience. I'll probably never make another movie with that much heart."

So this experience replayed in Rydell's mind as he waited for Henry Fonda to arrive at that dark theater. And the director was stunned when Fonda, using two canes, emerged from the limo with the help of a chauffeur.

"He had aged so much since the filming ended. I saw him to his seat and then left him to watch the film alone. . . . I could not sit with him when he watched it—that's how much I cared about his opinion."

While Henry watched the almost finished film, Rydell paced about the studio, wrenching his hands and continually watching the clock. Eventually, he knew the final credits were running, so he walked back into the theater to find Fonda stumbling toward him.

"He was struggling toward me down the side of the row, so I moved quickly forward. Then he stumbled and fell, so that I had to catch him in my arms. I was suddenly aware of how fragile he had become. He began to shudder, so that I thought he might be dying in my arms. But he regained his strength and whispered to me: 'Thank you for the most important film of my life. Thank you!' "

Rydell had to turn away as he talked. "That moment became the most important in my life. I needed no award—no Oscar—after that. I had my award."

CHAPTER TWELVE

Little Red Oscar

Who the hell is Robert Rich and why are we giving him an Oscar?
—HEDDA HOPPER, MAY 16, 1957

Deborah Kerr had an ungodly time with the envelope. She flicked at the edge of it again and again until an uncomfortable silence settled on the audience—an omen perhaps of the bitter irony to follow.

She tore at the envelope one last time, tugged out the card and announced expectantly: "And the winner for Best Motion-Picture Story is Robert Rich for *The Brave One.*"

All through the ermined, minked, and tuxedoed crowd in the vast Pantages Theater, America's most famous heads craned to catch their first glimpse of Hollywood's hottest new writer—Maureen O'Hara, Carroll Baker, Rock Hudson, Elizabeth Taylor—they all looked on with some awe. After all, this suddenly Oscared wunderkind might easily write their next film.

But there was no motion among the writers' contingent, an anonymous mass of penguin suits.

Animation was suspended for the usual number of seconds. But, finally, a handsome young man dashed toward the stage and into the spotlight of instant fame.

As fate would have it, it was the *wrong* young man, and it was the closest he would ever get to an Oscar.

"That's Jesse Lasky, Jr.," said Hedda Hopper suspiciously. "What's going on?"

Lasky tugged at his black tie and smoothed the lines of a seven-hundred-dollar custom tux. The words of a hastily prepared speech grew muddled in his mind as he silently asked the same qustion: Who is Robert Rich?

The thought had been on his mind for twenty-four hours—ever since the Screen Writers Guild had told him to accept the almost certain Oscar for a fellow writer. The Hollywood gossip underground, as accurate as the CIA, had already decreed that the mysterious Robert Rich would walk off with an award for his dazzling authorship of *The Brave One,* an RKO film up for two other Oscars.

But gossip began and ended with that terse bit of information. Lasky dashed about Hollywood all afternoon trying to harvest the slightest description of Rich—or at least enough facts to determine why the screenwriter couldn't claim his own Oscar. The president of RKO said tersely, "No, I've not met him. Know nothing about him—except he can write."

The King Brothers, producers of the low-budget film, were also no help. "We dealt through an agent," they said, with no small degree of anxiety. Talking through a public relations man they declared that "the film came to us through the mail."

Lasky despaired of finding anything to say before the Hollywood crowned heads assembled for the 1956 Academy Awards. He planned to mumble "Thanks. Mr. Rich can't be here tonight but sends his gratitude." Then, while Lasky was already donning his tux, the Writers Guild received a frantic telephone call from a man claiming to be Robert Rich. "My wife is at this minute in labor at the hospital," the man explained with careful emotion. "I have to be with her . . . doctors say she's going to have a difficult delivery."

"I'm sorry," said a relieved secretary at the Guild—relieved because the Guild *finally* had something to explain Robert Rich's elusive absence.

This was all a great comfort to Jesse Lasky, scion of one of the oldest Hollywood dynasties. In a town which thrives on histrionics, an Oscar-winning writer at his wife's bedside presented just the right touch. So Jesse bounded up, embraced Deborah Kerr, and took the Oscar in his well-tanned hand. He proudly announced Rich's dramatic predicament, adding that his "good friend was attending the result of another creative effort. . . ." There was a collective "aah" from the audience. And the ordeal was over—or so Lasky thought, as he tucked the Oscar into the trunk of his sports car for delivery to the Writers Guild the next day.

But the saga of Robert Rich was only beginning. The Oscar for *The Brave One* left Lasky, the Writers Guild, and the Academy with a particularly nasty hangover. Lasky found that out for the first time at 7:00 A.M. the next day.

"I'm sorry to wake you, Mr. Lasky," said an officer of the Guild. "But we've checked all the lists here for an address—or even a phone number. But Robert Rich isn't even a member."

"Better call the Academy," Lasky cautioned, with a sense of foreboding which would become a painful déjà vu.

For the next four hours Lasky's telephone rang like a repeater rifle. Everyone called: the Associated Press, UPI, the *Los Angeles Times*.

"Who is Robert Rich?" became the entertainment news of the hour.

Across Beverly Hills from Lasky's home, Louella Parsons tried in vain to find Rich and told her assistant, Dorothy Manners, "I have a funny feeling about this one. I don't think there *is* a Robert Rich." Within hours, the afternoon editions of American newspapers were referring to his win as an infamous Oscar scam. "Jesse Lasky, Jr., Accepts Award for Non-Existent Writer," trumpeted the *New York Post*. "Who is Robert Rich and Why Did He Win an Oscar?" questioned the *Chicago Tribune*.

By 5:00 P.M. even the Academy had to officially conclude: "We have no records on him other than the fact that his fellow writers nominated him and the Academy as a whole voted him the Oscar."

The acidly wicked gossip columnist Hedda Hopper didn't bother telephoning the Writers Guild. The morning after, she was whisked by limo over to RKO and began the real Rich hunt. Executives told the old war horse that they hadn't actually met Robert Rich either. "He's been kind of a phantom," said Robert Shriver. "[The script] came through the William Morris Agency; RKO bought it, sent a sizable check to a bank account—and we made the picture," he told a dubious Hopper.

That afternoon she barged into the office of Rich's agent—a man whose phone had been tolling all day. "Bug off," he told her tersely. "This is a very, *very* private man. Case closed."

"A certifiable kook—this man Robert Rich," Hedda told her assistant, Jake Rosenstein.

Thus it was that Rich's Oscar was sent back to the Academy, Robert Rich was erased from the record books as if he never existed, and the mystery quickly faded into Hollywood's past . . . but not before it brought a touch of sweet revenge to a screenwriter whose fame had turned to ashes in the fire ignited by the Communist witch-hunt which had hit movieland in 1950 and was holding sway in a still-frightened town.

His name was Dalton Trumbo, the brilliant writer of *Kitty Foyle*, *Thirty Seconds Over Tokyo* (a divinely all-American film), and *Our Vines Have Tender Grapes*. His career in film had been sacrificed on the altar of sanctimony which Hollywood had erected to save itself from massive anti-Communist rages tearing through the United States during the early 1950s thanks to Sen. Joseph McCarthy and his loathsome Senate Investigations Subcommittee.

In the late 1940s, Trumbo had been called to Washington by J. Parnell Thomas's House Un-American Activities Committee to explain his so-called "pinko" leanings and then dragged off to jail when he refused to turn in his Hollywood friends and colleagues suspected of harboring vaguely Socialist ideas. This made him one of the "Hollywood Ten," all of them jailed for refusing to "name names."

Twenty years after Dalton Trumbo won an Oscar for scripting The Brave One *(1956), he finally received the award from Academy president Walter Mirisch—shown here offering the golden idol at the writer's deathbed. This was one of the few injustices of the blacklist era that was finally corrected. The Academy knew then that Trumbo had also earned a second Oscar for his original story used by Paramount for* Roman Holiday. *The man under whose name Trumbo wrote the story, Ian McLellan Hunter, admitted long ago that he had only passed the story to Paramount, in exchange for $40,000—money that kept a roof over Trumbo's head during the blacklist years.*

Back in Hollywood, Trumbo became an artistic leper, shunned by studio heads, avoided by his own agents, and feared by former friends and colleagues. (On his birthday one year, a friend telephoned to say, "Happy birthday, Trumbo. I hope you understand that I don't dare be seen entering your house.")

To feed his family and pay the rent, Robert Rich was born—a man with surprising talent and absolutely no past.

As Hollywood searched for the elusive Rich, Trumbo toyed with the press. Shortly before his death in 1976 he told the authors of this book that he took "some small pleasure in the histrionics following the 1956 Oscars. They checked the obstetrics wards with no luck," he said. "And it wasn't long before rumors began to fly—from reporter to reporter, from news service to news service.

"Pretty soon many began to believe that Robert Rich was only a pseudonym for Dalton Trumbo. I denied nothing, and it was the Robert Rich thing that gave me the key to unlock at least part of the blacklist. All the reporters came to me, and I dealt with them in such a way that they knew bloody well I had written *The Brave One*. I would suggest that it was Mike Wilson. They would call Mike and he would deny it. This bounced them back to me, and I would suggest that they try somebody else—another blacklisted writer.

"I suddenly realized that eleven of the journalists were sympathetic to my cause. There had been a sudden change in the atmosphere. The terror was breaking up."

But panic still reigned in the august offices of the Academy. And on February 6, 1957 (when the witch-hunt was dying out elsewhere and McCarthy had already been censured and stripped of his committee assignments by his fellow senators), the Academy of Motion Picture Arts and Sciences board, alarmed by the number of past nominees and winners implicated in the hunt, enacted a dastardly "loyalty oath" and ushered in the Academy's most shameful hour.

Their new rule stated: "Any person who, before any duly constituted Federal legislative committee or body, shall have admitted that he is a member of the Communist Party (and has not since publicly renounced the party) or who shall have refused to answer whether or not he is, or was, a member of the Communist Party or shall have refused to respond to a subpoena to appear before such a committee or body, shall be ineligible for any Academy Award so long as he persists in such a refusal."

In plainer words: *Turn in your friends or forget about an Oscar.*

"Of course we never meant it to be taken literally," said someone who was an Academy leader during the fifties, talking off the record and laughing nervously. "We were only protecting our rear. How could we openly give Oscars to people all the studios were blacklisting? How could we? Anyone else in our shoes would have done the same."

Nevertheless, the "Robert Rich Affair" quickly became the *cause célèbre* of the entire decade, a rallying point for supporters of the blacklist and, eventually, salvation for those persecuted in the anti-Communist conflagration. This happened for several reasons:

First, Trumbo/Rich was a solid member of the "Hollywood Ten," courageous writers and directors who may or may not have been Communists but refused to say, refused to name others, and thus went to prison. Second, Trumbo quickly became the most successful (and richest) of the scores of writers who used ghost names to continue their

Oscar nominee Adolphe Menjou, who bought his own ticket and a new London suit to voluntarily testify about his former friends before HUAC. Menjou's list included more than twenty-five fellow Oscar nominees and several winners.

careers. And finally, Trumbo became such a successful screen writer (for such successful films as *Roman Holiday, Spartacus, Exodus, The Sandpiper,* and *Papillon*) that his renown and the humor of the "Robert Rich Affair" poked the first enormous holes in the dike built up by the town's ultraconservatives.

It hadn't seemed so funny, however, when Oscar formed his own blacklist. "The name of the game was Un-Americanism, and the referee was blowing the whistle on everyone," wrote Jesse Lasky, Jr., in his book, *Whatever Happened to Hollywood?* "With a so-called prevalence of witches, the only problem was: Which witch to hunt? That not-too-bright producer who had risen too quickly? That story editor who hired only guess-what-kind of writers? The actor who got the part you were up for?"

Screenwriter Philip Dunne, an Oscar nominee for *How Green Was My Valley* and *David and Bathsheba,* saw the Academy's blacklist rule as a simple outgrowth of the general Red Scare in Tinseltown, begun by Thomas's HUAC in the forties and revived by McCarthy in the fifties. "The list expanded from the 'Hollywood Ten' to the several hundred, from suspected Communists to their suspected sympathizers, and eventually involved the several thousand who tried to defend them. The fear spread and spread until there was even a 'gray list,' consisting of those people who could be hired, but, just to be on the safe side—you better not."

While the Academy's own list of "pinkos" was never written down, it was based on the industry-wide record of "suspected artists" and on a list which, all denials to the contrary, *was* written down.

The real blacklist still sits moldering in libraries and in the executive suites of studios. And it was in the Academy's own library that the authors of this book found a copy.

A librarian reached far into the recesses of a locked case and pulled it out—a rare and tattered copy of *Red Channels*, the very Bible of the blacklist.

It looked so harmless and insignificant with its hand-lettered cover and crooked, almost amateur, printing. Some of its pages had been printed on a crude mimeograph machine and apparently shoved in at the last minute.

"Nobody asks for it now," said the librarian. "Sometimes years go by before anyone asks for it."

Thus the true blacklist—the blacklist from which the careers of so many artists turned to ashes, the blacklist used by the Academy to make certain Oscar wasn't tainted by Communist hands—seems a quaint anachronism now. It is treated like an evil footnote to the texts of Hollywood history.

In the early fifties, however, *Red Channels* was the hottest periodical in the bookstores on Madison Avenue and at the newsstands clustered at Hollywood and Vine, the spiritual center of the film community. Originally the list was issued in parts—bulletins later bound with a red cover. This made it a pulp manual of suspects which was updated by weekly, and sometimes daily, supplements as new names were revealed by the dreaded HUAC.

Oscar Peterson worked at Universal Newsstand in downtown Hollywood, and he remembers that the all-powerful studio moguls used to dispatch runners to furtively grab the latest lists. "They would look over the bulletins with darting eyes and then drive off in their black cars," Peterson recalled. "And I knew somebody else's head would be on the chopping block before morning."

The publishers of *Red Channels* were former FBI agents and conservative businessmen loosely organized into a group known as Aware. And it was they who wrote down, permanently as it turns out, the Hollywood blacklist—a long roll call of artists (most of them innocent) who were stigmatized during the McCarthy era.

Leonard Bernstein is there. And Melvyn Douglas, Dalton Trumbo, and Gale Sondergaard, along with three hundred others, including writers, costume designers, story editors, character players, set decorators, and renowned directors. So there *was* a written blacklist—still is.

It was upon this hit list that the Academy built its case for a loyalty oath. Suddenly, Oscar winners had to be certifiable flag wavers to even qualify for a nomination.

Dalton Trumbo in Robert Rich's clothing wasn't the first blacklisted writer to win an Oscar. That honor went to veteran scripter Michael Wilson, who won for the blockbuster *A Place in the Sun* the very year his name later appeared in *Red Channels* for the first time. (He made all seven editions of the book.) Two weeks later and partly as a reaction to Wilson's Oscar, the Hollywood Film Producers Association ruled that no blacklisted writer was to receive *any* screen credit—even for work already done. And for a time, Michael Wilson's name was erased from release prints of the film.

In the end, however, it was Wilson's work on a second film, *Friendly Persuasion* (1956), which led to the Academy's fervor over its own loyalty oath. Although Wilson had written the first draft of this film about pacifism long before the blacklist existed in any form, his name was excised from the writing credits. Then when Wilson won the Writers Guild Award, the board of the Academy ruled that "under no circumstances can a blacklisted writer be nominated for an Oscar."

But negotiations between the producers of *Friendly Persuasion* and the Academy paved the way for an official screenplay nomination "if Michael Wilson's name is omitted from the ballot." All parties (except Wilson) agreed and the nomination followed. The Academy's official records still read "Screenplay—*Friendly Persuasion*—writer Michael Wilson ineligible under Academy bylaws." Wilson's script lost to *Around the World in Eighty Days,* in the same year that Robert Rich's phantom presence clouded the writing awards.

A ghostwriter wasn't a candidate for nomination again until late 1958, when the gossip mill predicted that Nathan E. Douglas (actually a pseudonym) was almost certain not only to be nominated but also to collect the statuette for co-scripting *The Defiant Ones,* a racial epic starring Tony Curtis and Sidney Poitier. An anonymous caller alerted several Academy board members that Nathan E. Douglas was none other than Ned Young, a writer who, for personal reasons, had taken the Fifth Amendment before HUAC.

The late director Otto Preminger gathered a circle of Academy members around him and warned, "Ned Young is going to put all of us to shame. He's gonna win. And he's gonna tell the world." And Preminger was not alone: the Academy was warned by veteran columnist Sidney Skolsky, Gary Cooper, Kirk Douglas, and finally even by Louella Parsons.

Finally, to stave off massive embarrassment, Academy officers took steps to rescind the rule—but only after high-level meetings between *The Defiant Ones* writers Harold Jacob Smith (a real name) and Nathan E. Douglas/Ned Young. Over cheesecake and coffee at the old Brown Derby, the Henry Kissingers of the Academy told Nathan/Ned that he could take home the Oscar if he won. In return Young had to promise that he wouldn't embarrass the Academy on national television.

At that brief lunch Oscar shucked his loyalty oath.

But one thing that diplomatic luncheon failed to achieve was public disclosure of Ned Young's right to have the Oscar he took home. In the record books he is still listed as Nathan E. Douglas. The Academy maintains that Young, or someone acting in his behalf, must present an affidavit from the producers of *The Defiant Ones* stating that Douglas is indeed Young—a fact the Academy is fully aware of.

If this misconception is mildly confusing to film researchers, the mystery surrounding *The Bridge on the River Kwai,* one of the landmark films of all time, is more befuddling and, arguably, far more serious. The film walked off with seven Oscars in 1957, including Best Picture, Best Actor (Alec Guinness), Best Director (David Lean), Best Cinematography (Jack Hildyard), Best Film Editing (Peter Taylor), Best Score (Malcolm Arnold), and Best Screenplay for Pierre Boulle, the author whose novel had inspired the film.

There's no doubt that Alec Guinness is Alec Guinness, that Lean is Lean. But no one who has ever seriously followed the making of the film believes that Pierre Boulle wrote the screenplay. Super-writers Carl Foreman and the ubiquitous Michael Wilson, both blacklisted, fashioned the sprawling script in a Herculean partnership which lasted more than a year. "Well, *all* Hollywood knows that," sniffed Hedda Hopper to a BBC interviewer in 1964. "All Hollywood!"

"I owned the rights to *The Bridge on the River Kwai* all along," said the late Carl Foreman. "I had signed a deal to write *and* produce the film through an agreement with Sir Alexander Korda [the famed British film magnate]. But the British market was suddenly glutted with World War II prisoner-of-war stories, and the financing fell through." Foreman trekked back to America with the exclusive rights to Boulle's novel and worked out a deal with the dreaded head of Columbia Pictures, Harry Cohn. Sam Spiegel agreed to produce through an unwritten agreement which forced Foreman and Wilson to remain anonymous. "We were forced into it," Foreman recalled bitterly. "And too much of *The Bridge on the River Kwai* was in our hearts for us to turn it down. It was a film that cried out to be made.

"At the time I never thought for a minute that Pierre Boulle would retain the screenplay credit for eternity. The film became legendary, as you know. And everyone in Hollywood knew that I wrote it in concert with Wilson. Eventually that slowly spreading knowledge broke the blacklist for me and a number of others."

Foreman, who came back big as a producer-writer-director of such films as *The Guns of Navarone, The Victors, Born Free*, and *MacKenna's Gold*, expressed only mild annoyance at the web of deception forced on him—and his films—by the witch-hunt. Others were far angrier for him. Henry Rogers, founder of the world's largest public relations firm, Rogers and Cowan (which handled Foreman), was still angry two decades later. "It was a shaft and it cheated film history," Rogers fumed. "Pierre Boulle had nothing to do with the screenplay. He could barely speak English—much less write it! Mild pressure put on the Academy to change the record has still had no effect. And the producer, Sam Spiegel, doesn't want to admit that he succumbed to such subterfuge—at least, that's the way it seems to me."

The Academy still maintains that "rules are rules. Unless we get affidavits giving Foreman and Michael Wilson official credit, there's nothing we can do about it." It's much the same at the Writers Guild: "We can only go by the film's official screen credits," said Alan Rivkin, a longtime official of the Guild. "I may know that it was written by Foreman and Wilson; you may know it was written by Foreman and Wilson; the whole Academy may know that. But we're helpless until the film's credits are officially changed."

Sam Spiegel has always refused to discuss the matter.

An even wilder mystery has grown into legendary proportions, involving a brilliantly crafted comedy, *Roman Holiday*, for which a writer named Ian McLellan Hunter earned and publicly accepted an Oscar for Best Motion-Picture Story of 1953. To this day, William Wyler, who produced and directed the film, says there's no question about the film's authorship. "Hunter wrote the story—it's as simple as that," Wyler angrily told a reporter two years ago.

Yet all artistic evidence points directly to Dalton Trumbo, who must have earned a second uncredited Oscar. The handwriting shown on the original story matches Trumbo's to a T, and the author had been telling his friends about a suspiciously similar script to the finished *Roman Holiday* tale he planned to make into a full screenplay.

But there was never a shred of proof until an intrepid UCLA film professor, Dr. Howard Suber, watched director Otto Preminger make a slip in introducing Trumbo as the author of *Exodus*. "Here's a man with two Oscars to his credit already," Preminger boasted. "And he'll get a third for *Exodus*."

Suber picked up on it instantly. Ah, Trumbo wrote *Roman Holiday* as well, he said to himself. But how do I get him to admit it?

The professor bombarded Trumbo with letters asking for a confession or at least a halfhearted admission. Trumbo remained silent.

"The more I learned, the more certain I became," said Suber. "I was convinced that Trumbo had produced the story for Wyler through an agreement that allowed the fainthearted director to avoid a conflict with the blacklist."

Then Trumbo and Suber were invited to address a radio seminar concerned with the blacklist, and the professor saw it as the one chance to drag the truth from the reclusive writer. First Suber buttered him up with safe small talk. "I already knew that Trumbo had written the film and was not a little obsessed with proving it," Suber said. The professor waited until the right moment and said softly, "Trumbo, did William Wyler actually know that you had written *Roman Holiday*?"

Trumbo answered with silence, and an uncomfortable five minutes followed.

Finally, Trumbo turned toward Suber: "You bastard! Who the hell told you?"

It was all the proof Suber needed.

Unfortunately for film historians yet to be born, the official list of Oscar winners still credits Ian McLellan Hunter with writing the story for *Roman Holiday*. But Hunter gladly admitted that the Oscar "really belongs to Dalton."

According to Hunter it happened this way: "Trumbo was just out of jail for his refusal to answer HUAC and he was broke. He had written this perfectly charming story, but he knew he couldn't sell it. I agreed to front, and it was quickly bought by Paramount for forty thousand dollars."

Hunter forwarded the cash to Trumbo and then started to write the shooting script, first for Frank Capra and then for William Wyler (who, as producer, replaced the director with himself).

"It became a nightmare for me," Hunter remembered. "Nobody likes to get public credit for something he didn't do. I just took the Oscar home and tossed it in a box up in the attic of my New York town house. Looking back, I don't know what else I could do. The blacklist was still very much in effect when *Roman Holiday* was made: at least Dalton got his money. Ironically, I was forced to use fronts myself as the black-list grew and grew."

The era also exacted a painful toll on the careers of dozens of Oscar winners and nominees in acting categories—most notably from Larry Parks, whose career had skyrocketed when he portrayed Al Jolson in the 1946 film *The Jolson Story*. He won an Oscar nomination and earned a new, six-year contract with Columbia Pictures which would have jumped to $90,000 a picture by the mid-fifties. After his years of struggle in B pictures, this single, stunning performance promised to make him one of Hollywood's superstars within a matter of years.

"I'm going to make this kid the greatest actor in modern films," bragged his boss, Harry Cohn, the tough ruler of the Columbia lot. Cohn quickly optioned a series of properties for his up-and-comer, including *Down to Earth* (a musical teaming Parks with queen of the studio Rita Hayworth), *A Force of Arms* (eventually filmed with William Holden), *Phffft!* (which would star Jack Lemmon, not Parks), *Three for the Show* (also made with Lemmon), and *The George Jessel Story* (which was never made).

Most of these magnificent plans crumbled during the very first months of the Hollywood witch-hunt when the House Un-American Activities Committee learned that Parks and a circle of friends had been involved in the Communist Party.

Parks was the first of the big-name actors to be hog-tied and dragged before the hearings being held by J. Parnell Thomas and his coven of right-wingers. It was so early in the game that Parks served as a human guinea pig for both the commission and the Hollywood lawyers hired by Harry Cohn—a bitter foe of the HUAC and the blacklist—to defend him. The studio lawyers told him that he "must hand over the names of the actors associated with him or go to prison for as long as ten years."

Larry asked for time to think it over.

Two days later he appeared in Harry Cohn's office to plead with the boss. "If I give those names, I won't have a friend left in Hollywood. I'll be a Judas."

Cohn snapped back: "And if you don't give those names, you will have neither a career nor a paycheck. I can kick you off this lot and out of your contract legally."

Larry Parks as Al Jolson. When he returned to Hollywood after agonizing through his appearance on the House Un-American Activities Committee stand, derogatory headlines greeted him. JOLSON SINGS AGAIN, *read the* Hollywood Citizen. A STOOL PIGEON SINGS TOO LATE, *read a line over Hedda Hopper's scathing column. Parks was finished from that moment—unjustly tarred and feathered by zealots. Only in the seventies were the records set straight—too late for Parks.*

Then Cohn dismissed him with a sharp rap on the desk.

Watching his deflated star retreat, Cohn confided to his executive assistant, Max Arnow, "I hate this business. That kid is damned if he does and damned if he doesn't."

Three days later Parks; his wife, Betty Garrett; and two attorneys entrained for Washington and the dreaded HUAC hearings. TAINTED OSCAR WINNER SPILLS TO HUAC TODAY, screamed a headline in the *New York Daily News*. In Hollywood, Hedda Hopper offered the beleaguered actor some stern advice: PLAY IT SMART, LARRY, read her headline. And the story that followed urged Parks to give name, chapter, and verse to the HUAC folks. "Prove to us all that you're an American."

Ironically, those who did name names—the "stoolies"—often fared the worst. Parks pleaded with the committee: "Don't make me do it. . . . Don't make me crawl in the mud. . . ." Then his voice trailed off and his eyes grew moist.

The committee counsel became more threatening: "Who were the members of the Communist party cell to which you were assigned?" There was a pause—a silence that filled the chamber. Then, in a hoarse voice, Parks began his list: "Lee J. Cobb, Dorothy Tree, Gale Sondergaard, Anne Revere . . ."

Two days later, Columbia tore up Parks' seventy-five-thousand-dollar contract for a picture he had already started. A week after that, Harry Cohn bought out his contract. "We picked that kid up off the street," said Cohn. "We got a traitor."

When Parks arrived by train in Los Angeles, an afternoon newspaper headline read: JOLSON SINGS AGAIN. Parks's loss was to be complete. He would play only one more Hollywood film role, a cameo for his old friend John Huston. The film was *Freud*. The year was 1962, eleven years after his 1951 appearance before HUAC. In another thirteen years he would be dead.

The post-Oscar experiences of two actresses—Lee Grant and Gale Sondergaard, winners of the Best Supporting Actress Oscar—best symbolize the ravages of the blacklist.

Lee Grant, who didn't net the Best Supporting Actress award until 1976 for *Shampoo*, felt a great, welling feeling of triumph when she finally took the Oscar in her hand.

"As I stood there with the Academy Award in one hand and the other fist clenched, I heard wave upon wave of applause wash over me. And it was applause within applause. I understood then. They *knew*. They knew what I had been through; what I had suffered; what I had borne so silently. It was a wonderful sign of approval and a sort of sweet revenge on those who had persecuted all of us."

By then, the long ordeal of Lee Grant had been over for some time. But in 1952, the year after her triumphant screen debut in *Detective Story* (for which she earned the first of four Best Supporting Actress nominations), she found herself barred from films, TV, and even from radio, which was a major source of income for her.

And it all had nothing to do with her personal politics. She was, however, married to a suspected Communist, writer Arnold Manoff. Worse, she was a close friend and student of another self-admitted Communist, well-known character actor J. Edward Bromberg.

While still under investigation and banned from all stage and screen work, Bromberg died of a heart attack (probably brought on by the stress of the investigation). Lee Grant organized a funeral, held a memorial service, and delivered a fiery eulogy. She found herself black-listed two days later.

"She was just a seventeen-year-old kid with a tremendous career before her," said TV actor John Henry Faulk, who wrote a classic work on the blacklist, *Fear on Trial*. "But she was a fighter. She just decided it wasn't going to get her down, by damn. She was aiming to whip them —and she did!"

The actress showed her colors at a meeting of the American Federation of Television and Radio Artists, who had convened to discuss the blacklist and its effect on its members.

An angry buzz filled the room as one of the AFTRA officers, with considerable nerve, calmly explained that there were no HUAC traitors in the room, no snitches.

Lee Grant leaped to her feet and began pointing one by one to the actors and actresses who had voluntarily gone to Washington to turn in their fellow artists as traitors. "You turned on us," she shouted at one woman. "So did you," she said to another. "And you. And you. And you."

Without exception Grant singled out AFTRA members whose testimony was later proven to be false.

"I was still a teen-ager all fired up with idealism," Lee recalled. "And it was fun for a few months to be Joan of Arc. I didn't fully realize what I was doing to my own future career. And I didn't care."

So Lee Grant, an Oscar nominee at seventeen, didn't get a single decent film job for seventeen years. ("I was tossed a part here and there," she said, "but nothing that would revive my career.")

The most iron-willed dramatic actress in town, Lee Grant, in a key scene from In the Heat of the Night *(1967). She is virtually the only one of the three dozen blacklisted actresses to make a major comeback. But after her first nomination, in 1951, it was seventeen years before she could get a decent job either in films or on television (the haven for so many blacklisted actors). Her great error was holding a memorial service for her blacklisted mentor, J. Edward Bromberg.*

Then, finally, after an attorney worked for five years to prove her personal innocence, her name was taken off the list. HUAC leaders still in Congress sent her a reluctant, written apology.

Then came *Terror in the City, In the Heat of the Night, Valley of the Dolls, Buona Sera, Mrs. Campbell, Plaza Suite,* and eventually *Shampoo* and the Oscar.

"I rushed into films as if I'd never had an acting job in my life," said Grant. "I was high on acting. Since the blacklist got so little publicity —at least not mass publicity—nobody really knew where I had been or, in some cases, even *that* I'd been gone. This all gave me a head-wind. . . . I had limitless energy and staying power."

Now, in the eighties, Lee Grant has come all the way back—and gone further, including direction of her own film, *Tell Me a Riddle*, starring Lila Kedrova and Melvyn Douglas. Her agent turns down an average of twenty scripts a month for her.

"But that's not to say that there haven't been permanent legacies. No matter how successful I am, I remain paranoid—afraid that it all might crumble again as it did after *Detective Story* in 1951.

"One afternoon in the early fifties, I suddenly couldn't remember anyone's name, and that came directly from the months when I deliberately tried *not* to remember names. I wanted to forget the names of friends and associates so that I wouldn't even *be able* to give them names—if they asked me."

She leaned out onto the veranda of her lush, rambling house in Malibu on a sunny afternoon in 1982, and her eyes misted: "It's not easy to feel the fear well up inside your chest over something that happened twenty-five years ago."

The day Grant finally walked back onto a Hollywood sound stage after almost two decades, she found her past waiting to confront her. "One of the men I faced down years before—a turncoat—was featured in the film in which I had the leading role. Our eyes locked for a minute. Then he looked down toward the floor. Finally, he came slowly over and introduced himself.

"I took his hand and looked directly into his eyes.

"He knew and I knew—and that's the way this whole thing ended for most of us . . . with a slow, drawn-out whimper."

The afternoon sun added a shading to Lee Grant's still-angry eyes and highlighted her blond hair. She was silent for several minutes before saying sadly: "You know, the way the blacklist worked was not through sinister design, but by innuendo and omission. For instance, a producer would say, 'Let's get him or her,' and somebody else would say, 'Wasn't she *involved* in something back then? But I don't remember the exact circumstances. Better not hire them—just in case.'

"It's fear that runs this town and fear which allows the blacklist to continue," the actress said. "For some people the blacklist continues. For some people it will never be over."

Of those who labored under that shadow, the late Gale Sondergaard, the legendary actress who won the first Best Supporting Actress Oscar (for *Anthony Adverse,* 1936) was perhaps the most notable casualty— what happened to her was a shameful waste of Oscar-caliber talent.

Sondergaard, who made three abortive comebacks in Hollywood since the blacklist, remained under such a dark shadow that not even the greedy money men of television were able to hew a career out of the ashes of the blacklist.

She almost made it back the first time, in 1969—ironically on the old Warner Bros. lot, where she achieved her legendary position among the screen's character actors. "I was out here at the Mark Taper in *Uncle Vanya,* when Robert Wagner came backstage one night. He talked to me about guesting on his new series, 'It Takes a Thief.' Since I would be following an appearance by Bette Davis, it seemed appropriate."

When she drove onto the lot five days later it was as if *Sunset Boulevard* had come to life and a latter-day Norma Desmond were emerging from fossildom into the light of a new era. As her car came up to the gate, Murray, a Warner Bros. guard from the old days, leaned down to the side window and said, "It's great to have you back, Miss Sondergaard." It was the same in the wardrobe department. The women dropped their work to gather around the actress who had made *The Life of Emile Zola* and others during the golden decade from 1935 through 1945.

She recalled in an interview at her Echo Park home: "When I got on the Wagner set, they had managed to wind up shooting early and asked me to come back the next day for an 'early call.' "

Gale Sondergaard as photographed by MGM's George Hurrell in her costume-makeup tests for The Wizard of Oz *(her dress by Irene). Sondergaard was the original choice to play the wicked witch. Then the decision was made to use an ugly witch, and Gale was out. This photo captures her at the height of her glory—one facet of which was her adeptness as a character actress. By 1936 she was among a handful of performers for whom the Academy created best supporting categories. Gale won the first Best Supporting Actress award for* Anthony Adverse. *She also created a new type, the svelte, sexy, and gorgeous villainess. But from the minute her husband, director Herbert Biberman, was named as a possible Communist party member, Sondergaard's career was virtually over. Only in 1970, when Robert Wagner talked her into a guest shot on "It Takes A Thief," did she return to a Hollywood soundstage.*

But she lingered on the big empty stage where *The Jazz Singer* began talking pictures. She walked across a ramp and down a staircase where a key scene in *Emile Zola* was filmed. Robert Wagner caught her eye, and she started to talk: "You know, this is the first time I've been on a Hollywood sound stage in twenty years."

"They were aghast," the actress remembered. "I had to sit down and explain it all again. When I was through, a great relief spread through me. It was a sort of exorcism for all the pain and sorrow I had been holding inside for decades. To look up at Robert Wagner's sympathetic face and see his own distress went a long way toward ridding me of my own burden."

Her appearance on "It Takes a Thief" drew critical raves but achieved little for Gale Sondergaard's career.

"They—that great unknown gray mass that runs the studio system—they were still afraid of me, hiring me, of being linked to me."

Gale reached over to a bookcase and grabbed her Oscar. "And this, this did me no good. My Oscar was tainted."

So the comeback didn't take: the wife of director Herbert Biberman, a blacklisted artist who went to prison for taking the Fifth, still suffered a hangover from the time of agony.

It was six years before she got the next call from Hollywood, from the producers of *The Return of a Man Called Horse*, in which she portrayed a role originated by Dame Judith Anderson two years earlier in *A Man Called Horse*.

History repeated itself: Sondergaard was lionized, welcomed back, and critically acclaimed once again as one of Hollywood's great ones.

Again, it was a useless exercise; she was not more employable then than she had been in the worst years of the blacklist. Some took the easy way out, describing her as "too old; too hard to place; too strong for today's smaller, less pretentious dramas." "Gale Sondergaard is just too old now," proclaimed an executive at CBS when she was mentioned for a major series.

"Producers and casting directors were very condescending to me," she recalled shortly before her death. "They trotted me out like an old horse, a prize exhibit as one of the blacklisted matriarchs. I was like an exhibit at a carnival. There was a lot of shouting about still another comeback, then I was forgotten again."

To prove them wrong, the actress climbed up onto the comeback trail a third time in 1980. She took the central role in a new Broadway play, *Goodbye Fidel*. It ran only a few weeks, but long enough for the *New York Times* to call her "a bright, vibrant oasis in a year of dismal performances on the New York stage." When the last curtain fell, Sondergaard packed her things and returned, jobless, to Hollywood.

In 1978 she had been put back into harness as the major centerpiece for the "Fiftieth Birthday of Oscar," joining such former MGM musical mainstays as Jane Powell, who sang the fluttery "Slipper and the Rose Waltz" off-key, and Cyd Charisse, who displayed her gorgeous legs in period costumes from *The Band Wagon*.

The crowd of old-timers roared. Fan mail poured in to Sondergaard's agent. By then joblessness had forced her to sell the fantastic Hollywood mansion she built with her husband in the lush years of the thirties, and she had scaled down her lifestyle in a modest compound in fading Echo Park. She greeted interviewers in a darkened house—with her Oscar spotlighted in the entryway. Portraits showing her in glam-

Gale Sondergaard returns to the big screen after twenty-five years on the blacklist to co-star with Richard Harris in The Return of a Man Called Horse *(1976).*

orous poses from *Anthony Adverse* were scattered about the rambling flat as if the Oscar and its trappings were the centerpiece of her life.

She reached over and gently took the Oscar out of its nook, holding it up to catch the afternoon light from a stained-glass window. "This typifies the best and the worst Hollywood brought me," she reflected ruefully. "It was euphoric to win the Academy Award, but the award itself represents the confusion inherent in the industry. There is constant pressure to win at all costs. And the blacklist and its casualties were forms of losing—of losing faith and dollars at the box office.

"I was condemned by the money-makers and by the establishment."

(In one confrontation with Jack Warner, the mogul actually hinted to Sondergaard that she should give back the award.)

"An Oscar is window dressing only," she said with a sad smile. "You want to know what was really fulfilling? I'll show you," she said, pointing to a picture of the early Sondergaard in a red velvet dress and monkey-fur coat walking on her husband's arm at the world premiere of *The Life of Emile Zola*. "*That* was exciting!"

Then she reflected: "I have no real bitterness about what *they* did. I didn't even know who *they* were. *They* was actually a system—a force which was there, a force which grabbed out at the innocent and pulled them down."

Gale Sondergaard and Larry Parks were the era's most tragic casualties in that they never really came back, at least not successfully. But the most bizarre victim of Oscar's flirtation with the blacklist was the movie *High Noon*—the ultimate western masterpiece and the creation of director Fred Zinnemann and blacklistee Carl Foreman.

In Academy history only the loss of *Citizen Kane* to *How Green Was My Valley* created as much uproar. And the screams started the minute Cecil B. De Mille's potboiler, *The Greatest Show on Earth*, won 1952's Best Picture honors over the now classic western.

No other story in Oscar's history reveals as well the basic and pervasive fear of the Academy's block voters and the occasional courage of those creative forces who choose to fly against a withering headwind of disapproval.

This time, the hero of the shoot-out was the same on and off the screen—Gary Cooper.

Even the setting was unlikely: sleepy Sonora, California, a city far enough into northern California for the town folks to be wary of those city slickers, the moving-picture people. Gary Cooper reported to the set in the fall of 1951 as the second choice for the lead. (Producer Stanley Kramer had asked for Gregory Peck but was turned down flat.) From his first cup of coffee with the crew, Cooper knew he had landed amid a covey of cinema's young turks: Kramer, who was becoming known for producing "message pictures"; Foreman, who'd written the scripts for *Home of the Brave* and *Cyrano de Bergerac;* and Zinnemann, whose major works had pitted man against his conscience.

It was a congenial crew—it almost had to be in isolated Sonora. But bits and pieces of gossip about the anti-Communist developments back in Hollywood began seeping in.

Suddenly the situation hit home with a thud when Foreman's name was added to the growing list of suspects being assembled by the House Un-American Activities Committee in Washington (a list that was leaked to the press before some committee members got a copy).

Foreman received the dreaded summons, went to Washington, took the Fifth. He would be blacklisted as soon as he finished *High Noon*.

Foreman arrived back on the set frightened but inspired. He put his script back into the typewriter. Slowly, on those dusty days on the set, Foreman began crafting *High Noon* to fit the McCarthy era like a Saville Row suit fits the newest member of the House of Lords.

"So much of the script became comparable to what was happening," said Foreman decades later. "There are many scenes taken from life. One is a distillation of meetings I had with partners, associates, and lawyers. And there's the scene with the man who offers to help and comes back with his gun. 'Where are the others?' he asks. 'There are no others,' says Cooper."

Cooper, Kramer, and Zinnemann all knew about the subtle shifts in the script and agreed to them—even to the point of leaking their strategy to Columbia's boss, Harry Cohn.

One day, near the end of shooting, Cooper wandered over to Foreman and said, "Thanks. This is a good one." He shook the writer's hand and headed back to his dressing room.

Cooper seemed anxious to give Foreman even further support, but the gesture was wordless, an unspoken promise.

The writer was puzzled but forgot about it back in Hollywood, where all hell broke loose when Hedda Hopper and John Wayne demanded publicly that Foreman be fired and that, as Hedda wrote, "he never be hired here again."

The next day, Kramer, in a frantic attempt to salvage the Kramer Company, publicly announced he was disassociating himself from the beleaguered writer. Foreman was never to forgive Kramer even though

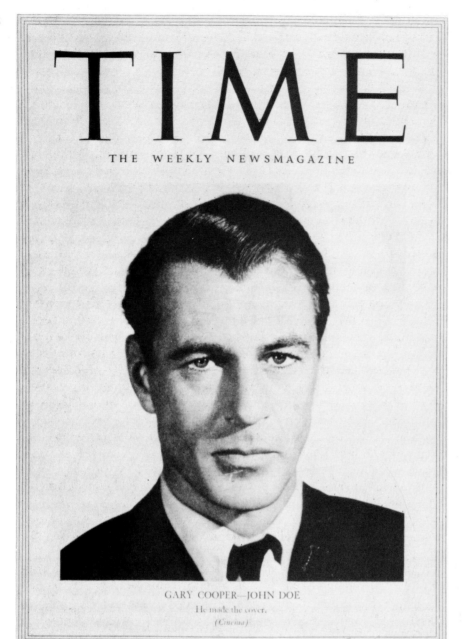

TIME

THE WEEKLY NEWSMAGAZINE

GARY COOPER—JOHN DOE
He made the cover.
(Cinema)

Gary Cooper, shown here on the cover of Time *after starring in* Mr. Deeds Goes to Town *(1936), was not only one of the finest actors in the business, but was one of the few Hollywood heroes during the black-listing of the fifties, when he openly gave his support to black-listed* High Noon *scriptwriter Carl Foreman. Cooper won his first Oscar, oddly enough, for his rather one-dimensional performance in* Sergeant York, *and his second for his spectacular performance in* High Noon *(1952). He received a special award in 1960; James Stewart broke down while accepting the award for his friend and revealed that Cooper was dying.*

the producer revealed it was either cut bait or lose the entire company, including Foreman's own investment. The bitterness continued into the eighties.

The day Kramer sliced free his close friend, Foreman got a call at home, late in the evening. "How's it going?" It was Gary Cooper. The writer explained that, since he owned some properties himself (including *The Bridge on the River Kwai*), he was going to form his own company. "Count me in—now. Use my name," said Cooper. "I mean it."

Foreman waited a couple of minutes and then called another Hollywood pal, publicist Henry Rogers. "What should I do?" he asked. Rogers, fast emerging as the most important public relations man in town, told him to set a press conference and come out in the open with it.

The announcement made page one of *Daily Variety* and the *Hollywood Reporter*. Cooper, several others, and Rogers himself were named as members of the board. But somebody had tipped off Hedda before press time. Rogers's switch phones at home were jammed before the P.R. whiz got home. First on the line was the acid voice of Hedda, who had long ago boycotted Rogers: "Now I know why I got mad at you years ago," she said. "You're just no good. You've got yourself mixed up with that Commie bastard Carl Foreman. That washes you up in this town. I'm going to see to it that you're driven out of business."

The next couple of calls came from John Wayne, Ginger Rogers, and Ward Bond—all members, with Hedda, of the right-wing Motion Picture Alliance for the Preservation of American Ideals, an organization of more than a thousand actors, writers, and directors.

So many calls came through in the next six hours that Rogers began to realize they had been staged. "It was," he said later, "a calculated plan of terror."

At this point, *High Noon* was still in post-production, but Cooper gave his support openly to Foreman, which had made the Hollywood establishment a mite skittish about the movie.

Cooper had given his word to Foreman, confirmed it, and then taken off into the wilds of Montana, fishing. On his first morning there, Cooper and pal, Ernest Hemingway, were casting for trout when a Western Union man showed up at the stream with a fistful of telegrams. One was from Warner Bros.—they wanted to break Cooper's contract, using an outdated "morals clause." And there were threats from Louis B. Mayer and producer Walter Wanger warning Cooper he might never get a decent role if he didn't back off.

The hero of *Sergeant York* and *Meet John Doe* hiked back to the lodge and got the long-distance operator.

"Carl—"

But Foreman stopped him. "I know. Nobody can hold up against this . . . not even you."

Cooper admitted defeat. Not even his broad shoulders were strong enough to fight the political current. "But he was the only big one who tried," said Foreman. "The only one."

Henry Rogers, in his own hot box, got a call from the biggest agent in town. "He said he'd have to pull his clients if this kept up. He told me

Columnist Hedda Hopper, right, shown here with Joan Crawford, was one of Hollywood's fiercest anti-Communist crusaders during the fifties.

Gary Cooper and Grace Kelly in High Noon.

to back down. But I didn't . . . refused. But I was scared." So Rogers held on, giving up only after Foreman himself made him do it. "Nobody can hold out against all this . . ." Foreman told Rogers. "I'm giving up."

A couple of weeks later Foreman packed up his typewriter and his family and moved to England, where he stayed until *The Bridge on the River Kwai* restored his career and then some.

Meanwhile, *High Noon* made money so quickly and won over critics so completely that it squeezed out seven nominations, including Best Picture. Over at the Academy, the rafters of that twenty-five-year-old institution were shaking from the news that a sizable list of past winners was banished from Tinseltown. Back-fence gossip made the membership painfully aware of the subtle propaganda written into *High Noon.* "A great film but mighty political."

The nervousness increased when the New York Film Critics named *High Noon* Best Picture of 1951.

Luckily for everybody, a circus soap opera, *The Greatest Show on Earth*, became the biggest box-office hit in twenty years, taking in $12 million in only a year. A good excuse, right? The voters had often (too often, some said) named economically successful movies over artistic triumphs. It was to be so again. Cecil B. De Mille walked off with the Best Picture Oscar on the back of an elephant and a train wreck, the movie's only touch of excitement. The one choice everybody agreed on was Gary Cooper as Best Actor.

It is important thirty years later to see that the Academy was not an actual participant in these sorry episodes. Actress Lee Grant prefers to call the Academy just another victim. "At first, it looked like this was going to be permanent. The fear became *the* reality."

Dalton Trumbo seems to have written the last word: "When you who are in your forties look back with curiosity at that dark time, as I think occasionally you should, it will do you no good to search for villains. There were none. There were only victims."

CHAPTER THIRTEEN

Oscar Follies

Who Is the Academy?

JOINERS

The Academy of Motion Picture Arts and Sciences has grown from less than a dozen members in 1927 to 4,747 in 1986. But because the Academy has gone in and out of fashion over the decades, it's been a bumpy ride. For instance, by 1932 about 1,200 had signed up. Then came the attempt by the studios to use the organization as a company union. Actors, writers, and musicians resigned by the hundreds. Frank Capra said the Academy was down to forty people in 1936. The long climb back finally hit its stride in 1970 when the membership went above 3,000. One becomes a member only after being first nominated by two current members, then voted in by the Board of Directors. Rumor has it that *many* are rejected.

THE BRANCHES

Actors 1,201 members, ranging from Monica Lewis and Henny Backus to Patti Andrews and Peggy Lee, from Bert Convy and Severn Darden to Abe Vigoda and Bill Zuckert. There was some hesitation to join during the late sixties, when the anti-Academy movement became chic; but many of the "new Hollywood" belong, including such second-generation thespians as Peter and Jane Fonda, Keith Carradine, Tatum O'Neal, Beau and Jeff Bridges, Patrick Wayne, Andrew Stevens, and Michael Douglas. And while hundreds of yesterday's leading lights—Luana Anders, June Allyson, Anna Maria Alberghetti, May Britt, Corinne Calvet, Peggy Cass, Marge Champion, Sally Forrest, Mona Freeman, Kathryn Grayson, David Hartman (yes, *that* David Hartman), *ad infinitum*—still cling to their Academy membership cards, Hollywood's hard-at-work "Brat Pack" actors—Emilio Estevez, Rob Lowe, Matt Dillon, Tom Cruise, Molly Ringwald, Ally Sheedy, Sean and Christopher Penn, Judd Nelson, Anthony Michael Hall, Kevin Bacon, and Charlie Sheen—are sadly missing from the Academy's membership rolls.

Directors 230 members, ranging from Joshua Logan and Roy Rowland to Hal Ashby and Karel Reisz; from Steven Spielberg and Robert Rafelson to Martin Scorsese and Herbert Ross.

Executives 304 members, including Donald and Marvin Mirisch, Alan Ladd, Jr., Frank Capra, Jr., Sherry Lansing, and Motown's Berry Gordy.

Musicians 242 members, ranging from Burt Bacharach and Marvin Hamlisch to Al Kasha and Stevie Wonder. Others include Irving Berlin, Paul Jabara, David Rose, Carmine Coppola, and John Green.

Also Art directors, 245 members; cinematographers, 108 members; film editors, 172 members; producers, 326 members; writers, 367 members; short subject filmmakers, 197 members; public relations directors, 255 members; sound technicians, 282 members; members-at-large, 299.

Finally, the Academy now carries 519 on its nonvoting associates list —a highly significant number, since that list, decided upon by the Academy board, is purgatory for Academy members who have been out of the swim too long. The longer that list grows, the closer the Academy comes to true representation of Hollywood today. Regrettably, the Academy has found it impossible to retire any of its "name" actors—no matter how retired they actually are—so the actors' branch remains top-heavy with dead wood.

SURPRISING MEMBERS

Peter Bogdanovich A director-writer who went Hollywood quickly, Bogdanovich is a deputized critic of the Academy Awards. His incisive essays in *New York* and *Esquire,* on the occasion of Oscar's golden anniversary, were some of the only credible commentaries written at that time. He was nominated for writing and directing *The Last Picture Show*, but his virtuoso work on *Paper Moon, What's Up Doc?*, and *Mask* went unrewarded. His mild jabs at St. Oscar may have contributed to these lockouts.

Marlon Brando A member from 1950 through 1982, he refused to take his 1972 Oscar for *The Godfather*, sending an Indian maiden, Sacheen Littlefeather, to turn it down. He had sent a three-and-a-half-page speech along with her. She never got to read it, but stated simply and movingly that Brando was shunning the Oscar because of the country's treatment of Native Americans. The Academy fully expected a cancellation of his membership forthwith. Instead, Brando simply let his membership expire and has refused invitations to rejoin. After retrieving Brando's Oscar from the new 007, Roger Moore, who had taken the statuette along on a Mexican holiday, the Academy placed it in its vaults, where it rests today.

Dustin Hoffman Now forty-nine, Hoffman is considerably wiser about the commercial ways and means of Hollywood. But back in his early thirties, when he was passed over for *Little Big Man, Papillon,* and

Straw Dogs, Hoffman was Oscar's bitterest and most public enemy. He called it a cruel charade—pointless and patently unfair. Hoffman was nominated for *Lenny, Midnight Cowboy,* and *The Graduate.* The actor had a brief lull in the late seventies with the minor flops *Agatha* and *Straight Time.* And sometime during that period, he decided he'd play the Academy's game—winning the big one for *Kramer vs. Kramer* in 1980. He came back strong three years later with the brilliant, but unrewarded, *Tootsie,* a role that showed virtually all of Hoffman's dramatic and comedic skills.

Oscar Brass

The Academy of Motion Picture Arts and Sciences, buffeted by the political currents in Hollywood, has eaten up its presidents, making many of them victims of Oscar's general ill will. Below is an incomplete annotated list of the Academy's leaders.

Douglas Fairbanks, Sr. (1927–29) Fairbanks lent his position as Hollywood social leader to the Academy's first stumbling years. His main accomplishment was, appropriately, an Oscar for his wife, Mary Pickford—one of the first victories for politics rather than acting ability.

William C. De Mille (1929–31) The selection of Cecil's brother kept the helm of the Academy firmly in the hands of the studio executives. A popular choice, De Mille was a screen behind which Louis B. Mayer and others turned the Academy into a company labor union.

M. C. Levee (1931–32) A man who left no discernible mark one way or the other.

Conrad Nagel (1932–33) Nagel, a popular actor and Hollywood social figure, was bounced by the Mayer clique as it tried to block the actors, writers, and directors out of legitimate labor unions.

J. Theodore Reed ((1933–34) A president who went down in history as the unfortunate helmsman the year the Academy's producers tried to shove wage and agent controls through the new National Recovery Administration. More than 1,500 members resigned during this period.

Frank Lloyd (1934–35) The Academy fell apart during Lloyd's regime, dropping from more than a thousand members to less than a hundred.

Frank Capra (1935–39) Capra, the director of *American Madness,* was elected only once and then declared Oscar emperor until 1939. There were forty members when he took over, Capra has written. And those forty weren't all gung-ho. Capra forced the Academy to drop out of the labor union business and went about the task of saving the organization. "I had to beg the [artists and crafts] guilds to let me send them ballots," said Capra. "It was touch and go for awhile."

Walter Wanger (1939–45) Wanger guided the Academy through the war years and has maintained that the organization had "less than fifty active members" during most of that time. (Bette Davis was elected president in 1941 but quickly resigned when she found she was only "a figurehead for the producers.")

Jean Hersholt (1945–49)   Hersholt moved the Oscar voting into higher artistic waters—and that meant recognition and votes for the increasingly fine British product. By the time *Hamlet* was named Best Picture of 1948, the producers had already pulled all of their cash out of the Oscar ceremony and were ready to gut the Academy. It was touch and go again.

Charles Brackett (1949–55)   Brackett was the man who turned to TV in order to pay for the Oscars, and thereby created the publicity-glutted monster we know and love today. The first TV rights were bought for $100,000 a year. Now the price is near $2 million.

George Seaton, George Stevens, B. B. Kahane, Valentine Davies, Wendell Corey, and Arthur Freed (1955–67)   These were uneventful but lucrative years as Oscar grew increasingly bloated on television cash.

Gregory Peck (1967–70)   Along with Charles Champlin, Los Angeles columnist and staunch Academy critic, Peck is the man who's done the most to bring Oscar voting into the space age. He worked steadily to update bylaws and weed out aged voting members while increasing the number of those who actually voted, which many believe was down to 40 percent of Academy membership in the early sixties.

Daniel Taradash, Walter Mirisch, and Howard W. Koch, (1970–77)   All have slowly but surely upgraded the Academy's image and voting practices. And it all shows in the Oscar nominees and winners.

Fay Kanin, Gene Allen, and Robert Wise (1978–present)

The Winner's Circle

BEST FILM

Award first given 1927–28 *Wings, The Broadway Melody* (1928–29), *All Quiet on the Western Front* (1929–30), *Cimarron* (1930–31), *Grand Hotel* (1931–32), *Cavalcade* (1932–33), *It Happened One Night* (1934), *Mutiny on the Bounty* (1935), *The Great Zeigfeld* (1936), *The Life of Emile Zola* (1937), *You Can't Take It with You* (1938), *Gone With The Wind* (1939), *Rebecca* (1940), *How Green Was My Valley* (1941), *Mrs. Miniver* (1942), *Casablanca* (1943), *Going My Way* (1944), *The Lost Weekend* (1945), *The Best Years of Our Lives* (1946), *Gentlemen's Agreement* (1947), *Hamlet* (1948), *All the King's Men* (1949), *All About Eve* (1950), *An American in Paris* (1951), *The Greatest Show on Earth* (1952), *From Here to Eternity* (1953), *On the Waterfront* (1954), *Marty* (1955), *Around the World in Eighty Days* (1956), *The Bridge on the River Kwai* (1957), *Gigi* (1958), *Ben-Hur* (1959), *The Apartment* (1960), *West Side Story* (1961), *Lawrence of Arabia* (1962), *Tom Jones* (1963), *My Fair Lady* (1964), *The Sound of Music* (1965), *A Man for All Seasons* (1966), *In the Heat of the Night* (1967), *Oliver!* (1968), *Midnight Cowboy* (1969), *Patton* (1970), *The French*

Frank Capra coaches Clark Gable and Claudette Colbert on the set of It Happened One Night *(1934), the film that brought the director an Oscar, which was his personal "Holy Grail," as he called it. "I was Oscar crazy," Capra said. "Did everything in the world to get one." But he learned quickly that "making good films was not good enough." Capra had to join the Academy and work his way up to the board of directors before he won the big one. A familiar story.*

Connection (1971), *The Godfather* (1972), *The Sting* (1973), *The Godfather Part II* (1974), *One Flew over the Cuckoo's Nest* (1975), *Rocky* (1976), *Annie Hall* (1977), *The Deer Hunter* (1978), *Kramer vs. Kramer* (1979), *Ordinary People* (1980), *Chariots of Fire* (1981), *Gandhi* (1982), *Terms of Endearment* (1983), *Amadeus* (1984), *Out of Africa* (1985).

Even in Out of Africa *(1985), which took home seven Oscars, Redford walked off without so much as a nomination. Is he too pretty? Is he too independent? Or did the Academy assume that it had already given him a bone—his Best Director Oscar for* Ordinary People *(1980)?*

Award first given 1927–28 Emil Jannings, Warner Baxter (1928–29), George Arliss (1929–30), Lionel Barrymore (1930–31), Wallace Beery and Fredric March (a tie) (1931–32), Charles Laughton (1932–33), Clark Gable (1934), Victor McLaglen (1935), Paul Muni (1936), Spencer Tracy (1937), Spencer Tracy (1938), Robert Donat (1939), James Stewart (1940), Gary Cooper (1941), James Cagney (1942), Paul Lukas (1943), Bing Crosby (1944), Ray Milland (1945), Fredric March (1946), Ronald Colman (1947), Laurence Olivier (1948), Broderick Crawford (1949), José Ferrer (1950), Humphrey Bogart (1951), Gary Cooper (1952), William Holden (1953), Marlon Brando (1954), Ernest Borgnine (1955), Yul Brynner (1956), Alec Guinness (1957), David Niven (1958), Charlton Heston (1959), Burt Lancaster (1960), Maximilian Schell (1961), Gregory Peck (1962), Sidney Poitier (1963), Rex Harrison (1964), Lee Marvin (1965), Paul Scofield (1966), Rod Steiger (1967), Cliff Robertson (1968), John Wayne (1969), George C. Scott (1970), Gene Hackman (1971), Marlon Brando (1972), Jack Lemmon (1973), Art Carney (1974), Jack Nicholson (1975), Peter Finch (1976), Richard Dreyfuss (1977), Jon Voight (1978), Dustin Hoffman (1979), Robert De Niro (1980), Henry Fonda (1981), Ben Kingsley (1982), Robert Duvall (1983), F. Murray Abraham (1984), William Hurt (1985).

A triumphant Jack Nicholson holding aloft his Oscar for Terms of Endearment—*one of the most popular wins since Frank Sinatra's for* From Here to Eternity. (© A.M.P.A.S.)

Gene Hackman, Best Actor for The French Connection *(1971).*

Best Actor William Hurt. It was a shock to critics when Hurt captured the 1985 award for Kiss of the Spider Woman, *in which he played a distraught yet heroic homosexual. All of the seers had feared that Jack Nicholson's hammish turn in* Prizzi's Honor *would doom Hurt's chances.*

BEST ACTRESS

Award first given 1927–28 Janet Gaynor, Mary Pickford (1928–29), Norma Shearer (1929–30), Marie Dressler (1930–31), Helen Hayes (1931–32), Katharine Hepburn (1932–33), Claudette Colbert (1934), Bette Davis (1935), Luise Rainer (1936), Luise Rainer (1937), Bette Davis (1938), Vivien Leigh (1939), Ginger Rogers (1940), Joan Fontaine (1941), Greer Garson (1942), Jennifer Jones (1943), Ingrid Bergman (1944), Joan Crawford (1945), Olivia de Havilland (1946), Loretta Young (1947), Jane Wyman (1948), Olivia de Havilland (1949), Judy Holliday (1950), Vivien Leigh (1951), Shirley Booth (1952), Audrey Hepburn (1953), Grace Kelly (1954), Anna Magnani (1955), Ingrid Bergman (1956), Joanne Woodward (1957), Susan Hayward (1958), Simone Signoret (1959), Elizabeth Taylor (1960), Sophia Loren (1961), Anne Bancroft (1962), Patricia Neal (1963), Julie Andrews (1964), Julie Christie (1965), Elizabeth Taylor (1966), Katharine Hepburn (1967), Katharine Hepburn and Barbra Streisand (a tie) (1968), Maggie Smith (1969), Glenda Jackson (1970), Jane Fonda (1971), Liza Minnelli (1972), Glenda Jackson (1973), Ellen Burstyn (1974), Louise Fletcher (1975), Faye Dunaway (1976), Diane Keaton (1977), Jane Fonda (1978), Sally Field (1979), Sissy Spacek (1980), Katharine Hepburn (1981), Meryl Streep (1982), Shirley MacLaine (1983), Sally Field (1984), Geraldine Page (1985).

Award first given 1927–28 Frank Borzage, Lewis Milestone, Frank Lloyd (1928–29), Lewis Milestone (1929–30), Norman Taurog (1930–31), Frank Borzage (1931–32), Frank Lloyd (1932–33), Frank Capra (1934), John Ford (1935), Frank Capra (1936), Leo McCarey (1937), Frank Capra (1938), Victor Fleming (1939), John Ford (1940), John Ford (1941), William Wyler (1942), Michael Curtiz (1943), Leo McCarey (1944), Billy Wilder (1945), William Wyler (1946), Elia Kazan (1947), John Huston (1948), Joseph L. Mankiewicz (1949), Joseph L. Mankiewicz (1950), George Stevens (1951), John Ford (1952), Fred Zinnemann (1953), Elia Kazan (1954), Delbert Mann (1955), George Stevens (1956), David Lean (1957), Vincente Minnelli (1958), William Wyler (1959), Billy Wilder (1960), Jerome Robbins and Robert Wise (co-directors) (1961), David Lean (1962), Tony Richardson (1963), George Cukor (1964), Robert Wise (1965), Fred Zinnemann (1966), Mike Nichols (1967), Carol Reed (1968), John Schlesinger (1969), Franklin J. Schaffner (1970), William Friedkin (1971), Bob Fosse (1972), George Roy Hill (1973), Francis Ford Coppola (1974), Milos Forman (1975), John G. Avildsen (1976), Woody Allen (1977), Michael Cimino (1978), Robert Benton (1979), Robert Redford (1980), Warren Beatty (1981), Richard Attenborough (1982), James L. Brooks (1983), Milos Forman (1984), Sydney Pollack (1985).

The most honored actress of the eighties, Meryl Streep. She is the archetypal Oscar winner of today —actress first, then star. Besides her Best Supporting Actress Oscar for Kramer vs. Kramer, *and her Best Actress win for* Sophie's Choice, *Streep has garnered nominations for* The Deer Hunter, The French Lieutenant's Woman, Silkwood, *and* Out of Africa, *topping any other actress of her generation.*

Warren Beatty in Reds *(1981). Oscar voters can accept him as a director; as an actor—not yet.*

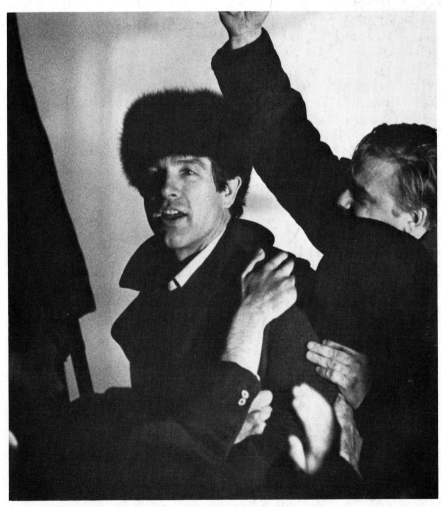

Award first given 1936   Walter Brennan, Joseph Schildkraut (1937), Walter Brennan (1938), Thomas Mitchell (1939), Walter Brennan (1940), Donald Crisp (1941), Van Heflin (1942), Charles Coburn (1943), Barry Fitzgerald (1944), James Dunn (1945), Harold Russell (1946), Edmund Gwenn (1947), Walter Huston (1948), Dean Jagger (1949), George Sanders (1950), Karl Malden (1951), Anthony Quinn (1952), Frank Sinatra (1953), Edmond O'Brien (1954), Jack Lemmon (1955), Anthony Quinn (1956), Red Buttons (1957), Burl Ives (1958), Hugh Griffith (1959), Peter Ustinov (1960), George Chakiris (1961), Ed Begley (1962), Melvyn Douglas (1963), Peter Ustinov (1964), Martin Balsam (1965), Walter Matthau (1966), George Kennedy (1967), Jack Albertson (1968), Gig Young (1969), John Mills (1970), Ben Johnson (1971), Joel Grey (1972), John Houseman (1973), Robert De Niro (1974), George Burns (1975), Jason Robards (1976), Jason Robards (1977), Christopher Walken (1978), Melvyn Douglas (1979), Timothy Hutton (1980), John Gielgud (1981), Louis Gossett, Jr. (1982), Jack Nicholson (1983), Haing S. Ngor (1984), Don Ameche (1985).

BEST SUPPORTING ACTRESS

Award first given 1936   Gale Sondergaard, Alice Brady (1937), Fay Bainter (1938), Hattie McDaniel (1939), Jane Darwell (1940), Mary Astor (1941), Teresa Wright (1942), Katina Paxinou (1943), Ethel Barrymore (1944), Anne Revere (1945), Anne Baxter (1946), Celeste Holm (1947), Claire Trevor (1948), Mercedes McCambridge (1949), Josephine Hull (1950), Kim Hunter (1951), Gloria Grahame (1952), Donna Reed (1953), Eva Marie Saint (1954), Jo Van Fleet (1955), Dorothy Malone (1956), Miyoshi Umeki (1957), Wendy Hiller (1958), Shelley Winters (1959), Shirley Jones (1960), Rita Moreno (1961), Patty Duke (1962), Margaret Rutherford (1963), Lila Kedrova (1964), Shelley Winters (1965), Sandy Dennis (1966), Estelle Parsons (1967), Ruth Gordon (1968), Goldie Hawn (1969), Helen Hayes (1970), Cloris Leachman (1971), Eileen Heckart (1972), Tatum O'Neal (1973), Ingrid Bergman (1974), Lee Grant (1975), Beatrice Straight (1976), Vanessa Redgrave (1977), Maggie Smith (1978), Meryl Streep (1979), Mary Steenburgen (1980), Maureen Stapleton (1981), Jessica Lange (1982), Linda Hunt (1983), Peggy Ashcroft (1984), Angelica Huston (1985).

BEST SONG

Award first given 1934   "The Continental" by Con Conrad and Herb Magidson; "Lullaby of Broadway" by Harry Warren and Al Dubin (1935); "The Way You Look Tonight" by Jerome Kern and Dorothy Fields (1936); "Sweet Leilani" by Harry Owens (1937); "Thanks for the Memory" by Ralph Rainger and Leo Robin (1938); "Over the Rainbow" by Harold Arlen and E. Y. Harburg (1939); "When You Wish upon a Star" by Leigh Harline and Ned Washington (1940); "The Last Time I Saw Paris" by Jerome Kern and Oscar Hammerstein II (1941); "White Christmas" by Irving Berlin (1942); "You'll Never Know" by Harry Warren and Mack Gordon (1943); "Swinging on a Star" by James van

Heusen and Johnny Burke (1944); "It Might As Well Be Spring" by Richard Rodgers and Oscar Hammerstein II (1945); "On the Atchison, Topeka and Santa Fe" by Harry Warren and Johnny Mercer (1946); "Zip-A-Dee-Doo-Dah" by Allie Wrubel and Ray Gilbert (1947); "Buttons and Bows" by Jay Livingston and Ray Evans (1948); "Baby, It's Cold Outside" by Frank Loesser (1949); "Mona Lisa" by Ray Evans and Jay Livingston (1950); "In the Cool, Cool, Cool of the Evening" by Hoagy Carmichael and Johnny Mercer (1951); "High Noon (Do Not Forsake Me, Oh My Darlin')" by Dimitri Tiomkin and Ned Washington (1952); "Secret Love" by Sammy Fain and Paul Francis Webster (1953); "Three Coins in the Fountain" by Jule Styne and Sammy Cahn (1954); "Love Is a Many-Splendored Thing" by Sammy Fain and Paul Francis Webster (1955); "Whatever Will Be, Will Be (Que Sera, Sera)" by Jay Livingston and Ray Evans (1956); "All the Way" by James van Heusen and Sammy Cahn (1957); "Gigi" by Frederick Loewe and Alan Jay Lerner (1958); "High Hopes" by James van Heusen and Sammy Cahn (1959); "Never on Sunday" by Manos Hadjidakis (1960); "Moon River" by Henry Mancini and Johnny Mercer (1961); "Days of Wine and Roses" by Henry Mancini and Johnny Mercer (1962); "Call Me Irresponsible" by James van Heusen and Sammy Cahn (1963); "Chim Chim Cher-ee" by Richard M. Sherman and Robert B. Sherman (1964); "The Shadow of Your Smile" by Johnny Mandel and Paul Francis Webster (1965); "Born Free" by John Barry and Don Black (1966); "Talk to the Animals" by Leslie Bricusse (1967); "The Windmills of Your Mind" by Michel Legrand and Alan and Marilyn Bergman (1968); "Raindrops Keep Fallin' on My Head" by Burt Bacharach and Hal David (1969); "For All We Know" by Fred Karlin, Robb Royer, and James Griffin a.k.a. Robb Wilson and Arthur James (1970); "Theme from *Shaft*" by Isaac Hayes (1971); "The Morning After" by Al Kasha and Joel Hirschhorn (1972); "The Way We Were" by Marvin Hamlisch and Alan and Marilyn Bergman (1973); "We May Never Love Like This Again" by Al Kasha and Joel Hirschhorn (1974); "I'm Easy" by Keith Carradine (1975); "Evergreen (Love Theme from *A Star Is Born*)" by Barbra Streisand and Paul Williams (1976); "You Light Up My Life" by Joseph Brooks (1977); "Last Dance" by Paul Jabara (1978); "It Goes Like It Goes" by David Shire and Norman Gimbel (1979); "Fame" by Michael Gore and Dean Pitchford (1980); "Arthur's Theme (Best That You Can Do)" by Burt Bacharach, Carole Bayer Sager, Christopher Cross, and Peter Allen (1981); "Up Where We Belong" by Jack Nitzsche, Buffy Sainte-Marie, and Will Jennings (1982); "Flashdance . . . What a Feeling" by Giorgio Moroder, Keith Forsey, and Irene Cara (1983); "I Just Called to Say I Love You" by Stevie Wonder (1984); "Say You, Say Me" by Lionel Ritchie (1985).

Give Me Your Tired Plots, Your Clichés

Only certain types of films and performances win Oscars—the same few favored by Hollywood's money men for nearly sixty years. Musicals, obvious comedies, tepid war movies, an occasional message movie—Oscar has been a dull creature of habit. And to the great detriment of the Academy's image, some genres are routinely shut out (for instance, science fiction, *Close Encounters of the Third Kind;* and youth, *Sixteen Candles* and *The Breakfast Club*). Here is a scoreboard of prominent Oscar-winning genres:

FILM GENRES

Adventure   *Around the World in Eighty Days, Ben-Hur, Lawrence of Arabia,* and (yawn) *Gandhi.*

Comedy   *It Happened One Night, You Can't Take It with You, The Apartment, Tom Jones, The Sting,* and *Annie Hall.*

Crime   *The French Connection, The Godfather,* and *The Godfather Part II.*

Melodrama   *Cavalcade, Grand Hotel, Mrs. Miniver* (a war soap opera), *Casablanca* (likewise), *The Greatest Show on Earth* (a circus soap opera), *All About Eve* (a Broadway soap opera), *Gone With The Wind* (a Civil War soap opera), *Rocky* (a boxing soap opera), *Ordinary People* and *Terms of Endearment* (both pure soap operas), *Chariots of Fire* (an Olympic Games soap opera), and *Amadeus* (a "period" soap opera, with classical music).

Message (or Crusading) Films   *The Lost Weekend, Gentlemen's Agreement, In the Heat of the Night, One Flew over the Cuckoo's Nest,* and *Kramer vs. Kramer.*

Musicals   *Broadway Melody, The Great Ziegfeld, An American in Paris, Gigi, West Side Story, My Fair Lady, The Sound of Music,* and *Oliver!*

War   *Wings, All Quiet on the Western Front, Mrs. Miniver, The Best Years of Our Lives, From Here to Eternity, Bridge on the River Kwai, Patton,* and *The Deer Hunter.*

PERFORMANCE GENRES

Adulterers   Norma Shearer, *The Divorcee;* Simone Signoret, *Room at the Top;* Helen Hayes, *The Sin of Madelon Claudet;* Gloria Grahame, *The Bad and the Beautiful;* and Julie Christie, *Darling.*

Biographies   George Arliss, Disraeli; Charles Laughton, Henry VIII; Paul Muni, Louis Pasteur; Spencer Tracy, Father Flanagan; Gary Cooper, Sergeant York; James Cagney, George M. Cohan; Luise Rainer, Anna Held; Patty Duke, Helen Keller; Anne Bancroft, Annie Sullivan; Alice Brady, Mrs. O'Leary of Chicago fire fame; Anthony Quinn, Paul Gauguin; Paul Scofield, Sir Thomas More; Katharine Hepburn, Eleanor of Aquitaine; Barbra Streisand, Fanny Brice; Robert De Niro, Jake La Motta; Sissy Spacek, Loretta Lynn; Maureen Stapleton, Emma Goldman; Ben Kingsley, Mahatma Gandhi; F. Murray Abraham, Antonio Salieri.

Joan Crawford giving Patty Duke an Oscar for The Miracle Worker *(1962).* (© A.M.P.A.S.)

Mental Disturbance Fredric March, *Dr. Jekyll and Mr. Hyde;* Joanne Woodward, *The Three Faces of Eve;* Ronald Colman, *A Double Life;* Emil Jannings, *The Last Command;* and Jack Nicholson, although feigned, in *One Flew over the Cuckoo's Nest.*

Prostitutes with Hearts of Gold Shirley Jones, *Elmer Gantry;* Janet Gaynor, *Seventh Heaven;* Judy Holliday, *Born Yesterday;* Elizabeth Taylor, *Butterfield 8;* Susan Hayward, *I Want to Live!;* Donna Reed, *From Here to Eternity;* Jo Van Fleet, *East of Eden;* and Lila Kedrova, *Zorba, the Greek.*

DYING CAN BE GOOD FOR YOU

José Ferrer, Best Actor for Cyrano de Bergerac *(1950).*

And regardless of genre, it helps greatly to die before the end of the picture: Emil Jannings, *The Last Command;* Fredric March, *Dr. Jekyll and Mr. Hyde;* Wallace Beery, *The Champ;* Victor McLaglen, *The Informer;* Spencer Tracy, *Captains Courageous;* Robert Donat, *Goodbye, Mr. Chips;* Donald Crisp, *How Green Was My Valley;* Teresa Wright, *Mrs. Miniver;* Jennifer Jones, *Song of Bernadette;* Ethel Barrymore, *None but the Lonely Heart;* Ann Baxter, *The Razor's Edge;* Ronald Colman, *A Double Life;* Laurence Olivier, *Hamlet;* Broderick Crawford, *All the King's Men;* José Ferrer, *Cyrano de Bergerac;* Gloria Grahame, *The Bad and the Beautiful;* Frank Sinatra, *From Here to Eternity;* Yul Brynner, *The King and I;* Alec Guinness, *Bridge on the River Kwai;* Red Buttons and Miyoshi Umeki, *Sayonara;* Burl Ives, *The Big Country;* Susan Hayward, *I Want to Live!;* Simone Signoret, *Room at the Top;* Shelley Winters, *The Diary of Anne Frank;* Elizabeth Taylor, *Butterfield 8;* George Chakiris, *West Side Story;* Melvyn Douglas, *Hud* and *Being There;* Paul Scofield, *A Man for All Seasons;* Ben Johnson, *The Last Picture Show;* Marlon Brando, *The Godfather;* Jack Nicholson, *One Flew over the Cuckoo's Nest;* Peter Finch, *Network;* Vanessa Redgrave, *Julia;* Christopher Walken, *The Deer Hunter;* John Gielgud, *Arthur;* Meryl Streep, *Sophie's Choice;* Ben Kingsley, *Gandhi;* Linda Hunt, *The Year of Living Dangerously;* William Hurt, *Kiss of the Spider Woman.*

Liza Minnelli and Joel Grey in Cabaret *(1972).*

Big Winners

These movies won record numbers of Academy Awards.

FILM	OSCARS
Ben-Hur (1959)	11
Gone With the Wind (1939)	10
West Side Story (1961)	10
Gigi (1958)	9
Gandhi (1982)	9
From Here to Eternity (1953)	8
On the Waterfront (1954)	8
Cabaret (1972)	8
Bridge on the River Kwai (1957)	7
Lawrence of Arabia (1962)	7
My Fair Lady (1964)	7
Patton (1970)	7
The Sting (1973)	7

Big Losers

These films were heavily honored in the nominations but were slighted or left out in the cold by the final voters.

FILM	NOMINATIONS	OSCARS
Johnny Belinda (1948)	12	1
Becket (1964)	12	1
Mr. Smith Goes to Washington (1939)	11	1
Chinatown (1974)	11	1
The Turning Point (1977)	11	0
The Color Purple (1985)	11	0
Giant (1956)	10	1
Airport (1970)	10	1
Citizen Kane (1941)	9	1
For Whom the Bell Tolls (1943)	9	1
Since You Went Away (1944)	9	1
Quo Vadis (1951)	8	0
The Sand Pebbles (1966)	8	0
Mutiny on the Bounty (1962)	7	0

What follows is a selected comparison between the New York Film Critics Awards (a relatively unbiased body) and the Academy Awards.

BEST FILM

YEAR	NEW YORK FILM CRITICS	THE ACADEMY
1968	*The Lion in Winter*	*Oliver!*
1969	*Z*	*Midnight Cowboy*
1970	*Five Easy Pieces*	*Patton*
1971	*A Clockwork Orange*	*The French Connection*
1972	*Cries and Whispers*	*The Godfather*
1973	*Day for Night*	*The Sting*
1974	*Amarcord*	*The Godfather Part II*
1975	*Nashville*	*One Flew over the Cuckoo's Nest*
1976	*All the President's Men*	*Rocky*
1977	*Annie Hall*	*Annie Hall*
1978	*The Deer Hunter*	*The Deer Hunter*
1979	*Kramer vs. Kramer*	*Kramer vs. Kramer*
1980	*Ordinary People*	*Ordinary People*
1981	*Reds*	*Chariots of Fire*
1982	*Gandhi*	*Gandhi*
1983	*Terms of Endearment*	*Terms of Endearment*
1984	*A Passage to India*	*Amadeus*
1985	*Prizzi's Honor*	*Out of Africa*

One of the toughest contests of the eighties erupted when Shirley MacLaine took on the equally strong Debra Winger in the Best Actress race for Terms of Endearment *(1983). MacLaine, who had gone Oscarless since her first nomination twenty-eight years earlier (for* Some Came Running*), finally grasped the little golden man and sighed: "I've wondered what this would feel like for twenty-eight years. Thank you for ending the suspense."*

YEAR	NEW YORK FILM CRITICS	THE ACADEMY
1968	Alan Arkin, *The Heart Is a Lonely Hunter*	Cliff Robertson, *Charly*
1969	Jon Voight, *Midnight Cowboy*	John Wayne, *True Grit*
1972	Laurence Olivier, *Sleuth*	Marlon Brando, *The Godfather*
1973	Marlon Brando, *Last Tango in Paris*	Jack Lemmon, *Save the Tiger*
1974	Jack Nicholson, *Chinatown*	Art Carney, *Harry and Tonto*
1976	Robert De Niro, *Taxi Driver*	Peter Finch, *Network*
1977	John Gielgud, *Providence*	Richard Dreyfuss, *The Goodbye Girl*
1978	Jon Voight, *Coming Home*	Jon Voight, *Coming Home*
1979	Dustin Hoffman, *Kramer vs. Kramer*	Dustin Hoffman, *Kramer vs. Kramer*
1980	Robert De Niro, *Raging Bull*	Robert De Niro, *Raging Bull*
1981	Burt Lancaster, *Atlantic City*	Henry Fonda, *On Golden Pond*
1982	Ben Kingsley, *Gandhi*	Ben Kingsley, *Gandhi*
1983	Robert Duvall, *Tender Mercies*	Robert Duvall, *Tender Mercies*
1984	Steve Martin, *All of Me*	F. Murray Abraham, *Amadeus*
1985	Jack Nicholson, *Prizzi's Honor*	William Hurt, *Kiss of the Spider Woman*

Robert De Niro's portrayal of Jake LaMotta in Raging Bull *(1980) finally earned him the Best Actor Oscar, and the New York Film Critics Award to boot.*

YEAR	NEW YORK FILM CRITICS	THE ACADEMY
1977	Diane Keaton, *Annie Hall*	Diane Keaton, *Annie Hall*
1978	Ingrid Bergman, *Autumn Sonata*	Jane Fonda, *Coming Home*
1979	Sally Field, *Norma Rae*	Sally Field, *Norma Rae*
1980	Sissy Spacek, *Coal Miner's Daughter*	Sissy Spacek, *Coal Miner's Daughter*
1981	Glenda Jackson, *Stevie*	Katharine Hepburn, *On Golden Pond*
1982	Meryl Streep, *Sophie's Choice*	Meryl Streep, *Sophie's Choice*
1983	Shirley MacLaine, *Terms of Endearment*	Shirley MacLaine, *Terms of Endearment*
1984	Peggy Ashcroft, *A Passage to India*	Sally Field, *Places in the Heart*
1985	Norma Aleandro, *The Official Story*	Geraldine Page, *The Trip to Bountiful*

Ten Films that Shouldn't Have Won . . . What Were They Thinking?

Mrs. Miniver (1942)   William Wyler's propaganda film was greatly sweetened by the talents of Greer Garson and Walter Pidgeon. But many find it unwatchable today, bathed as it is in the school of the crying towel. That's not the point, of course. *Mrs. Miniver* defeated such fine films as *The Magnificent Ambersons*, *The Pride of the Yankees*, and *Kings Row*.

Going My Way (1944)   Whatever it was that persuaded the Academy to overlook the powerful, hard-edged *Double Indemnity* and the suspenseful, psychological melodrama *Gaslight* in favor of Leo McCarey's sappy, sentimental series of sketches involving an aging Catholic priest and his younger replacement will forever remain a mystery. Not even nominated for Best Picture were *Lifeboat*, *Laura*, and *Meet Me in St. Louis*, all classics of their genres. No doubt the Academy membership, like the rest of America, simply felt safer with sentiment, since the war was still being waged at full tilt. And don't forget that the film introduced that Hit Parade chart topper "Swinging on a Star," the Best Song Oscar winner, sung by Bing, of course.

An American in Paris (1951)   In another year it might have been an obvious champ. But in 1951 Vincente Minnelli's musical triumphed over such milestone works as *A Streetcar Named Desire*, *A Place in the Sun*, and *Quo Vadis*. *The African Queen* and Hitchcock's *Strangers on a Train* were not even nominated.

The Greatest Show on Earth (1952)   When Cecil B. De Mille's tawdry soap opera about the circus plays on TV, even children turn it off. It beat *High Noon*, *The Quiet Man*, and *Moulin Rouge*. *Come Back, Little*

Gene Kelly and Leslie Caron in the Oscar-winning film An American in Paris (*1951*).

Sheba, The Bad and the Beautiful, and *Viva Zapata!* weren't even on the Academy's list of five. The vote was taken at the height of the McCarthy era, and the obvious winner, *High Noon,* was caught up in the House Un-American Activities furor because of its scriptwriter, Carl Foreman. Hedda Hopper personally campaigned against it.

My Fair Lady (1964)   Nobody, not even her staunchest fans, believed for a moment that the elegant Audrey Hepburn was a Cockney guttersnipe in what was essentially a stylish, lovely film version of a hit Broadway play and little else. Also, Hepburn's vocals, by the overworked, little recognized Marni Nixon, were crucial to the success of this filmusical. And yet it won seven Oscars out of a total of twelve nominations. Shut out was Stanley Kubrick's brilliant black comedy *Dr. Strangelove: Or How I Learned to Stop Worrying and Love the Bomb,* one of the most shattering motion pictures extant. The message of this landmark film is as potent today as it was when it was made nearly a quarter of a century ago, while George Cukor's creaky, but colorful, *My Fair Lady* seems merely another Hollywood conceit.

Sylvester Stallone in Rocky (*1976*).

Oliver! (1968)   Carol Reed's overblown musical valentine to Dickens and Victorian England was pleasant entertainment, but little else. The acting was turgid, cartoonish. The script could have been written in 1920. But the film beat out *Romeo and Juliet, Funny Girl, The Lion in Winter,* and *Rachel, Rachel,* any one of them better than the winner. Finer films, such as *2001: A Space Odyssey, Faces* and *The Heart Is a Lonely Hunter,* weren't even nominated.

Rocky (1976)   Just when critics said "box-office voting" was over, the Academy gave John Avildsen's entertaining bit of hokum its highest award. *Rocky,* a fairy tale about a losing boxer who is turned into a winner, was quite inferior to all of its fellow nominees: *All the President's Men, Network, Bound for Glory,* and *Taxi Driver.*

Meryl Streep on the set of Kramer vs. Kramer *(1979).*

Ben Kingsley as Gandhi, in one of the rare films to win the Best Picture Award from both the Academy and the New York Film Critics.

Kramer vs. Kramer (1979)   As entertainment reporter Lee Grant pointed out, Robert Benton's *Kramer vs. Kramer* "was not a particularly popular winner. . . ." And Rona Barrett called it "a soap opera and antifeminist in nature." The strongest entry that year was unquestionably *Apocalypse Now*, Francis Coppola's definitive epic about war, containing some of the most remarkable footage ever captured on film, particularly the helicopter attack on a Vietcong village. In the Hollywood wars, timing is apparently everything and it was *Apocalypse Now*'s misfortune to have been released the year after *The Deer Hunter*, another Vietnamese War epic, and a Best Picture Oscar winner in 1978.

Chariots of Fire (1981)   Losers were *Atlantic City, On Golden Pond, Raiders of the Lost Ark*, and *Reds*—any one of which would have been preferable to Hugh Hudson's heavy-handed, predictable, preachy soap opera set against the 1924 Olympic Games. Or for that matter, the unnominated *The French Lieutenant's Woman* and *Ragtime* would have been better choices. Academy voters, mistaking catchy theme music for compelling moviemaking, gave this British entry four Oscars, prompting *Chariots*' producer David Puttnam to gush, "You are the most extraordinary, generous people on God's earth, not just the Academy, to whom we are thankful, but as a country—to have taken what is an absolutely Cinderella picture and awarded it this . . ." It seemed as incredible to Puttnam as it does to us.

Gandhi (1982)   Simply because it took Sir Richard Attenborough twenty years to get this dismal, boring spectacle to the screen, the Academy membership passed over the Steven Spielberg masterpiece, *E.T.—The Extra-Terrestrial*, in what must rank as the most blatant, inexcusable oversight in Oscar history. Slobbering after Sir Dickie's artless indulgence, the Academy voted an incredible eight additional Oscars (including statuettes for Best Director and Best Actor) to *Gandhi*, a film that seemed as long as India's struggle for independence. The utterly charming, ultimate fantasy film *E.T.* had to be content with getting millions of delighted moviegoers back into theaters.

Today wives can still be heard luring their husbands to the suburban movie theater with the soothing call, "Well, it must be good—it *was* nominated for an Oscar." By its very presence within Oscar's golden circle, the most mundane film acquires the trappings of legend, cinema to be savored to the last inch of celluloid. How often we have seen this phrase tagged on to the ad for an unlikely-looking movie on TV: "Nominated for an Oscar"? Alas, the Best Picture nomination is hardly a guarantee of quality. At least 10 percent of the films in Oscar's golden circle are turkeys. Here are some of the most flea-bitten dogs from Oscar's golden lists.

Bad Girl (1931–32) A bit of sentimental slop starring Sally Eilers and James Dunn, this film probably owes its place on the Best Picture list to the social and financial position of its director, Frank Borzage, who had won the first Best Director Oscar for *Seventh Heaven.* Bizarrely, with this bit of claptrap Borzage beat out King Vidor for *The Champ* and, more tragically, Josef von Sternberg for *Shanghai Express.* The plot of *Bad Girl* revolves entirely around the difficulties a young couple has in finding the right doctor for their soon-to-be-born child. The husband finally takes to the boxing ring to find the cash for that special pediatrician. The key line in the film comes when the boxer shows up at the doc's office to plunk down the cash. The dad looks around, mugs at the camera a bit, and says, "Gee, Doc, you got a swell dump here." With luck , you'll never be called on to see this one. It's so obscure that *Movies on TV, Halliwell's Film Guide,* and *The New Encyclopedia of Film* don't list it at all. One of the few places it appears is on Oscar's proud master list.

Here Comes the Navy (1934) This nominee features a young James Cagney changing from a cocky ne'er-do-well into a cocky navy hero, with ho-hum support from Pat O'Brien and Gloria Stuart. Lloyd Bacon provided what direction there was, and studio boss Jack Warner let the Oscar people know that this was *his* personal selection for the finest film of the year. In order to nominate such drivel, the Academy had to slight such giants as King Vidor's *Our Daily Bread, Of Human Bondage* with Bette Davis and Leslie Howard, *Twentieth Century* with Carole Lombard and John Barrymore, *Death Takes a Holiday, The Count of Monte Cristo,* and *The Scarlet Empress* with Marlene Dietrich.

Three Smart Girls (1936) This is the film that made a star out of shrill-voiced Deanna Durbin, who played one of three teen-age girls who bring their parents back together—a feat they supposedly accomplish by merely singing. "A movie idiotically tuned in on happiness," wrote *The New Yorker*'s film critic, while Graham Greene described it as "laundered and lavendered." Nobody—least of all the film's producer, Joe Pasternak—pretended it was a good film. But it sure made money: $2 million in the first six months, thereby ensuring itself a nomination. While rushing out to nominate this frippery, the Academy bypassed *Show Boat, The Petrified Forest* with Bogart and Davis, *Charge of the Light Brigade* with Errol Flynn, Lillian Hellman's *The Children's Hour* (filmed as *These Three*), *The General Died at Dawn,* Charlie Chaplin's *Modern Times,* and Fritz Lang's *Fury.*

Test Pilot (1938)   This jerky little melodrama starred Gable and Tracy as, you guessed it, test pilots and Myrna Loy as their soft-hearted stay-at-home. With most of the action taking place in airfield coffee shops and most of the dialogue centering on "how dangerous it is up there," the film is quite a yawner. And it beat out Hitchcock's *The Lady Vanishes, Angels with Dirty Faces, The Dawn Patrol,* and Selznick's *The Adventures of Tom Sawyer.*

Anchors Aweigh (1945)   Though it's a pleasant MGM musical, with Kathryn Grayson, Gene Kelly, and Frank Sinatra, the film had no business on the Oscar list in a year when movies were entering an era of postwar realism. But Louis B. Mayer decided it would make the list—and make the list it did, although MGM had to sacrifice its own far superior products *The Picture of Dorian Gray, National Velvet,* and *Our Vines Have Tender Grapes.* Consider other fine films sacrificed to gain this soprano-eaten epic a place on the top five: *The Story of G.I. Joe, Love Letters, Keys of the Kingdom, Leave Her to Heaven, The Clock,* and *A Song to Remember.*

Kill 'Em with Silence

The films that follow, listed in the American Film Institute's Top Twenty, were not even nominated for Best Picture by the Academy of Motion Picture Arts and Sciences. The AFI polled thirty-five thousand of its members to determine the list.

The General (1927)   Buster Keaton finished this classic comedy in time to qualify it for the first Academy Awards. But by then he was at MGM, which controlled the newly formed Academy. Louis B. Mayer saw no reason to nominate a film made for another company. And that was that. The comedy plays for laughs against a bittersweet panorama of the Civil War.

The Crowd (1928)   King Vidor's silent masterpiece about the futility and fear of life in the faceless big city. It was the first film to deal with the loss of identity in the urban canyons, and was ahead of its time in treating the monetary crisis of the lower middle class. Louis B. Mayer, Vidor's boss and the man who founded the Academy, let it be known that a nomination for "Best Director is sufficient." So *The Crowd* was overlooked (except for a nomination for Best Artistic Quality of Production) in the name of splashiness and melodrama: *Wings, Seventh Heaven,* etc. Five people did the final voting, and Vidor said he lost because Mayer maintained that the film was not financially successful enough to win. So the director's prize went to a lion of Hollywood society, Frank Borzage, for *Seventh Heaven.*

City Lights (1931)   Silent clown Charlie Chaplin was at his height in this film, which capped twenty years of comedy work. But the film was just that—silent. Once sound came in, the Academy immediately became its slave. There was little chance of a nomination. The Academy was happy with the sappy *Skippy* and the forgettable *East Lynne.*

King Kong (1933)   It's hard to imagine today, but the Academy blindly nominated ten films and still managed to exclude this fantasy-horror classic. Merian C. Cooper, a dashing pilot in World War I who became the genius of adventure films, produced *King Kong* for RKO. That was the rub. RKO knew it had a breakthrough film on its hands, but still could not manage to repeat its earlier triumph with *Cimarron*, Best Picture of 1930–31. Had the film been made at MGM, it probably would have not only been nominated, but would have won.

Modern Times (1936)   Charlie Chaplin's mostly silent masterpiece of the thirties stood head and shoulders above the other Best Picture nominations—it even made money, about $2.5 million worldwide. But it failed to pull a single nomination—not even for cinematography or art direction. There was certainly room for it on the 1936 Oscar list for Best Picture, which included such junk as Jean Harlow's *Libeled Lady* and Deanna Durbin's teen-age soprano opus, *Three Smart Girls*.

Singin' in the Rain (1952)   A film that spoke in music's international language and became an instant hit in America, France, England, Germany, and Japan, it was cut adrift to face the Oscars when MGM decided that *Ivanhoe* had to be nominated or it would not make back its cost. So *Ivanhoe* it was. MGM also had other pictures in the fire for Best Art Direction (*The Merry Widow*) and Best Cinematography (*Million Dollar Mermaid*)—both categories in which *Singin' in the Rain* might have won. The film was also a major box-office hit—which worked against it in the bastardized Oscar politics of the fifties. Then the studios felt hits did not need Oscar's help but flops like *Ivanhoe* did.

Psycho (1960)   *The* horror classic of all time. Hollywood was aware of the film's stature from the minute it was released, instantly achieving both box-office success and critical acclaim. In 1960, however, Hollywood was firmly locked into the habit of lavish, even shameful, Oscar campaigning. Alfred Hitchcock considered such ads demeaning and pointless. So *Psycho* lost its place in the nominations to John Wayne's trivial film, *The Alamo*, on which at least $100,000 was spent in advertising.

No Room on the List

Great films that were not nominated for Best Picture, listed chronologically: *City Lights, The Crowd, King Kong, Modern Times, The Jazz Singer, Hallelujah!, Anna Christie, Little Caesar, Morocco, Of Human Bondage, Camille, Snow White and the Seven Dwarfs, The Sea Hawk, Laura, Lifeboat, Meet Me in St. Louis, Body and Soul, The Third Man, Death of a Salesman, Strangers on a Train, Singin' in the Rain, Rear Window, To Catch a Thief, Some Like It Hot, North by Northwest, Inherit the Wind, Psycho, Long Day's Journey into Night, The Manchurian Candidate, The Miracle Worker, Hud, Cool Hand Luke, In Cold Blood, 2001: A Space Odyssey, Faces, Easy Rider, They Shoot Horses, Don't They?, Women in Love, Ryan's Daughter, Carnal Knowledge, McCabe and Mrs. Miller, Sunday, Bloody Sunday, Alice Doesn't Live Here Anymore, A Woman Under the Influence, Close Encounters of the Third Kind, Interiors, Manhattan, The China Syn-*

drome, Prince of the City, S.O.B., Body Heat, Victor/Victoria, Diner, An Officer and a Gentleman, Yentl, Zelig, Risky Business, The Natural, Greystoke: The Legend of Tarzan, Lord of the Apes, Cotton Club, Broadway Danny Rose, The Breakfast Club, St. Elmo's Fire, Sweet Dreams.

Lead, Kindly Light

Hollywood is full of cases wherein less than leading lights were perfectly paired with the "role of a lifetime." While many of these performers have in fact put the "act" in "char*act*er," others, after their moments of cinematic glory, often faded from view and were rarely given a second chance to shine so brightly. While the following list is highly subjective, the authors stand by it, categorically speaking—character actors who won Oscars for leading roles:

Emil Jannings, *The Last Command* and *The Way of All Flesh*, 1927–28; George Arliss, *Disraeli*, 1929–30; Marie Dressler, *Min and Bill*, 1930–31; Lionel Barrymore, *A Free Soul*, 1930–31; Wallace Beery, *The Champ*, 1931–32; Charles Laughton, *The Private Life of Henry VIII*, 1932–33; Victor McLaglen, *The Informer*, 1935; Paul Muni, *The Story of Louis Pasteur*, 1936; Paul Lukas, *Watch on the Rhine*, 1943; Broderick Crawford, *All the King's Men*, 1949; José Ferrer, *Cyrano de Bergerac*, 1950; Shirley Booth, *Come Back, Little Sheba*, 1952; Ernest Borgnine, *Marty*, 1955; Alec Guinness, *The Bridge on the River Kwai*, 1957; Lee Marvin, *Cat Ballou*, 1965; Paul Scofield, *A Man for All Seasons*, 1966; Rod Steiger, *In the Heat of the Night*, 1967; George C. Scott, *Patton*, 1970; Gene Hackman, *The French Connection*, 1971; Art Carney, *Harry and Tonto*, 1974; Richard Dreyfuss, *The Goodbye Girl*, 1977; Dustin Hoffman, *Kramer vs. Kramer*, 1979; Ben Kingsley, *Gandhi*, 1982; Robert Duvall, *Tender Mercies*, 1983; F. Murray Abraham, *Amadeus*, 1984; Geraldine Page, *The Trip to Bountiful*, 1985.

An Oscar by Any Other Name . . .

The Academy is notorious for giving best acting awards to those who in no way gave the best performance of the year. Oscar is a gentleman of tradition and sentiment—qualities more highly prized by the voters than dramatic ability. But every once in a while even Oscar has gone too far. A few examples:

Ingrid Bergman (Best Supporting Actress: *Murder on the Orient Express,* 1974) Ingrid Bergman walked out to the end of the stage after getting her Oscar and directed the Academy's attention to Valentina Cortese, the actress who actually deserved the Oscar, for *Day for Night.* Charles Champlin called the gesture a high point of the Oscar decade. Bergman's Oscar, her third, is typical of the sins committed in the name of best supporting performances; the voters, having to choose between established names and dazzling newcomers, almost always pick the old favorites. Other examples are Helen Hayes, who won for the 1970 film *Airport* over Karen Black in *Five Easy Pieces;* George Burns in

The Sunshine Boys (1975) over Chris Sarandon in *Dog Day Afternoon* and Brad Dourif in *One Flew over the Cuckoo's Nest;* and Jason Robards for *Julia* (1977) over Peter Firth in *Equus* and Mikhail Baryshnikov in *The Turning Point.*

Bette Davis (Best Actress: *Dangerous,* 1935) A guilty-conscience Oscar. In 1934 Bette Davis *had* given the best performance of the year, in *Of Human Bondage,* in which she created an entirely new type of screen heroine—the bitch without redemption. Davis had made that for RKO and not her home studio, Warner Bros. Therefore, neither RKO nor Warner put her on its list. So she wasn't even nominated. The Oscar voters raised a ruckus, gaining the right to vote for Davis as a write-in. Even then, the Warner brass sent out a memo hinting to voters that a vote for Bette was not a vote for Warner Bros. Claudette Colbert got the Oscar for *It Happened One Night.* The Davis fever was raging so furiously in 1935 that the Academy would probably have given her an Oscar for reading the phone book. Other nominees: Elizabeth Bergner, *Escape Me Never;* Katharine Hepburn, *Alice Adams;* Miriam Hopkins, *Becky Sharp;* Merle Oberon, *The Dark Angel;* and Claudette Colbert, *Private Worlds.* All of them had bigger challenges than Bette. Bergner, Oberon, and Hopkins were never to get an Oscar.

Katharine Hepburn (Best Actress: *Guess Who's Coming to Dinner,* 1967) The only actress with four best acting awards, Hepburn probably won in 1967 because of the maudlin nature of this integration soap opera— with extra brownie points because she had nursed her friend Spencer Tracy through his last film. Any one of her four competitors could have qualified as Best Actress of 1967; Hepburn could not. The other nominees: Anne Bancroft, *The Graduate;* Faye Dunaway, *Bonnie and Clyde;* Audrey Hepburn, *Wait Until Dark;* and Dame Edith Evans, *The Whisperers.* This was one of the years which make you wonder about the taste of the average Oscar voter.

Lee Marvin (Best Actor: *Cat Ballou,* 1965) By 1965 Marvin had turned in performances in more than fifty films, almost single-handedly carrying such movies as *Pete Kelly's Blues, The Comancheros,* and *The Killers* of 1964. The Oscar voters were just itching to give him an Academy Award. *Cat Ballou* was a change of pace for Marvin, and he was capable in his portrayal of the satirical cowboy. But this was *not* the best performance of the year. Rod Steiger was the odds-on critical favorite for *The Pawnbroker.* (In fact, voters committed another miscarriage two years later when they gave Steiger the Oscar he should have gotten for *The Pawnbroker* and thereby denied it to Warren Beatty for *Bonnie and Clyde.*) Runner-up to Steiger was Richard Burton in *The Spy Who Came In from the Cold.*

James Stewart (Best Actor: *The Philadelphia Story,* 1940) This is one of the Academy's classic cases of a "better late than never" Oscar. Stewart had certainly earned the Academy Award the year before for *Mr. Smith Goes to Washington.* But the competition that year—including Clark Gable for *Gone With The Wind*—was stiff, and the winner, Robert Donat for *Goodbye, Mr. Chips,* was Stewart's equal. The voters picked 1940 to set the record straight. It must have been difficult to pick a winner that year, a year of classic performances: Charles Chaplin, *The Great Dictator;* Henry Fonda, *The Grapes of Wrath;* Raymond Massey, *Abe Lincoln in Illinois;* and Laurence Olivier, *Rebecca.* Not nominated were William Holden, *Our Town;* Herbert Marshall, *The Letter;* Charles Boyer, *All This, and Heaven Too;* and Errol Flynn, *The Sea Hawk.*

Elizabeth Taylor (Best Actress: *Butterfield 8,* 1960)   The headlines on Los Angeles's tabloid newspapers screamed LIZ DYING the day Oscar voting started. It threw the voters into a panic. This might be, they thought, the last chance to give Liz her Oscar—which, arguably, she deserved for *Cat on a Hot Tin Roof* (1958) or for *Suddenly, Last Summer* (1959). She barely survived, flew into town, and walked up to get her Oscar leaning heavily on husband Eddie Fisher's arm. Again, Liz was the sole nominee who obviously did not deserve the Oscar. Her competitors: Melina Mercouri, *Never on Sunday;* Shirley MacLaine, *The Apartment;* Greer Garson, *Sunrise at Campobello;* and Deborah Kerr, *The Sundowners.* Not even nominated were Jean Simmons for Elmer Gantry and Wendy Hiller for *Sons and Lovers.* Even Taylor has said, "I won it because I almost died."

Oscarless

Some artists have been Oscar bridesmaids so often that they've become a *cause célèbre* for Academy critics. Many say the circle of Oscar losers is more illustrious than the winners' list.

Richard Burton (seven nominations)   In Hollywood films since 1952 (*My Cousin Rachel,* for which he was nominated Best Supporting Actor),

The Oscarless Richard Burton in Becket (1964).

Burton has been the victim of Oscar trends or voter sentimentality almost every time he lost. His performance in 1965's *The Spy Who Came In from the Cold* should have easily defeated Lee Marvin's broad charade in *Cat Ballou*. His portrait of the man without hope in *Who's Afraid of Virginia Woolf?* (1966) is one of the great acting feats of the decade but lost to Paul Scofield's *A Man for All Seasons*. Even Burton's role in 1969's *Anne of the Thousand Days*, not one of his best, was still a head higher than John Wayne's in *True Grit*. Ex-wife Liz Taylor has expressed her belief that "they had to go out of their way to deny him the Oscar for *Who's Afraid of Virginia Woolf?*"

Other nominations: *The Robe*, 1953; *Becket*, 1964; and *Equus*, 1977.

Peter O'Toole (seven nominations) Beginning with *Lawrence of Arabia* in 1962 and lasting through two decades of Oscar-nominated acting stints, O'Toole's career has covered an astonishing array of roles in wide-ranging genres: historical pageants (*Becket*, 1964, and *The Lion in Winter*, 1968), soap opera (*Goodbye, Mr. Chips*, 1969), farce (*The Ruling Class*, 1972), screwball comedy (*My Favorite Year*, 1982), and melodrama (*The Stunt Man*, 1980). Although he has appeared in a number of films whose artistic merit is highly suspect (*What's New Pussycat?*, *Great Catherine*, *Rosebud*, and *Zulu Dawn*, among others), he nonetheless has amassed an impressive body of work that should soon qualify him for, like Paul Newman, a Lifetime Achievement Oscar.

Peter O'Toole in The Bible (*1966*).

Deborah Kerr

Deborah Kerr (six nominations)   *From Here to Eternity* (1953) should have won her an Oscar, but Paramount launched a dazzling and expensive campaign for Audrey Hepburn, who took the award home for the frothy *Roman Holiday*. In 1956, it was a toss-up between Kerr as Anna in *The King and I* and Ingrid Bergman, who won for *Anastasia*. In 1960's *The Sundowners* she was certainly better than Liz Taylor, the winner for *Butterfield 8*. The British actress was too good an actress and too weak a box-office star. That tells the story in an era when the Oscar was tossed to stars who made money, not to actresses who made fine films.

Other nominations: *Edward, My Son*, 1949; *Heaven Knows, Mr. Allison*, 1957; and *Separate Tables*, 1958.

Paul Newman (six nominations)   Starting his film career shakily in 1955 with the unfortunate biblical epic *The Silver Chalice*, he recovered remarkably the following year as Rocky Graziano in *Somebody Up There Likes Me*, a role that was ignored in the Oscar-nominating process. His performance in 1958 in *The Long Hot Summer* met a similar fate, although that slight was somewhat softened by the Prix International he received at Cannes. While Oscar-nominated that year for his limning of Brick in Tennessee Williams's *Cat on a Hot Tin Roof*, he came up short on awards night, losing to David Niven's wimpish, waspish turn in *Separate Tables*. Nominations for *The Hustler* (1961)

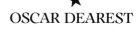

Paul Newman, who hasn't yet received a Best Actor Oscar. In 1985 —as if to atone for its transgressions—the Academy voters gave Newman a special Oscar. "What is he to assume from that?" asked columnist Robert Osborne acidly. "That his career is over?"

and *Hud* (1963) followed. His unnominated performance in 1962's *Sweet Bird of Youth,* in the role he created on Broadway, was considered by many to be at least their equal. Another nomination was his in 1967 for *Cool Hand Luke,* and another shutout. Two brilliant, back-to-back, Oscar-nominated performances, his fifth and sixth, resulted in shutouts numbers five and six—for *Absence of Malice* (1981) and *The Verdict* (1982). His 1982 loss was to newcomer Ben Kingsley, a character actor from the British stage, in the overblown, overrated, overlong Sir Richard Attenborough yawner, *Gandhi.* 1986 - The Color of money - win

Agnes Moorehead (five nominations) Arguably the finest all-round actress in Hollywood's history, she began her film career playing Kane's mother in *Citizen Kane* in 1941 and exited in a gothic film, *Dear Dead Delilah* in 1975. She was an actress so skilled that she disappeared deep within her celluloid characters. Without doubt, she deserved to win several of the Best Supporting Actress awards for which she was nominated. In 1942 her work in Orson Welles's *The Magnificent Ambersons* was easily better than Teresa Wright's work in the soapy *Mrs. Miniver.* She was also better in *Mrs. Parkington* (1944) than the showy Ethel Barrymore in *None but the Lonely Heart.* Ironically, she reaped more honors for her work as Endora, Elizabeth Montgomery's mother, on TV's "Bewitched." And she could have done that one on the phone.

Other nominations: *Johnny Belinda,* 1948; *Hush . . . Hush, Sweet Charlotte,* 1964.

The forever Oscarless Agnes Moorehead.

Al Pacino

Al Pacino (five nominations)   These included *The Godfather* (Best Supporting Actor, 1972) and *Dog Day Afternoon* (1975). During the 1980 Oscar ceremony, a kaleidoscope of Pacino's career flashed across the screen as Jane Fonda announced him as a nominee for . . . *And Justice for All* (not one of his best roles). "*Jee*sus," said a reporter for the *Los Angeles Times*, "what a range." Pacino, along with De Niro, has shown a range unequaled in modern cinema. His most deserved nomination came for his performance in 1974's *The Godfather Part II*, which was neck and neck with Jack Nicholson's for *Chinatown*. But the Academy being the Academy, voters bypassed them both to choose Art Carney for *Harry and Tonto*.

Other nominations: *Serpico*, 1973.

Montgomery Clift (four nominations) The classic Hollywood outsider, Clift gave Oscar-class performances at least ten times in films that ranged from 1948's *The Search* (his debut film and one of his nominated roles) to *Freud*, a fine but flawed portrait of the father of psychoanalysis. Clift was oriented to New York and to Broadway—a fact that counted him out in the opinion of many Oscar voters. In 1951, Bogart's performance in *The African Queen* outpolled Clift's dazzling work in *A Place in the Sun*. (The maudlin tribute to Bogie also aced out Brando's performance in *A Streetcar Named Desire*.) And there is little doubt that he should have won for *From Here to Eternity* in 1953, but the film's studio, Columbia, threw its votes to Burt Lancaster in the same

Montgomery Clift, never an Oscar winner, in The Heiress *(1948).*

film. Both Clift and Lancaster were defeated by the wooden William Holden in *Stalag 17*. (But Holden was really winning for *Sunset Boulevard*—for which he was passed by several years earlier.) "What do I have to do to prove I can act?" Clift asked a New York critic.

Other nominations: *Judgment at Nuremberg* (Best Supporting Actor).

Greta Garbo (four nominations) The classic victim of studio politics, Garbo was nominated for *Anna Christie* and *Romance* in 1930, for *Camille* in 1938, and for *Ninotchka* in 1940. In 1930 and 1938 she would have won easily if MGM had not rigged the races against her. In 1930 MGM production chief Irving Thalberg delivered the studio votes on a platter to his wife, Norma Shearer, the winner for *The Divorcée*. It was the same in 1938, when the studio commanded its members to vote for the winner, Luise Rainer, for *The Good Earth*. MGM prexy Louis B. Mayer virtually ruled the Academy from 1927 until 1935, so he must have been somewhat responsible when Oscar failed to even nominate Garbo for *Queen Christina*, *Anna Karenina*, and *Mata Hari*.

Greta Garbo in her earliest MGM glamor shot.

Barbara Stanwyck (four nominations) She was nominated for *Stella Dallas* (1937), *Ball of Fire* (1941), *Double Indemnity* (1944), and *Sorry, Wrong Number* (1948). Her career, arguably the longest and certainly one of the most distinguished in film, began on the Broadway stage in 1926 and spans six decades, including her role as Constance Colby on the TV soap opera "The Colbys." Her four Oscar nominations could have easily expanded to twice that number, including those in *The Bitter Tea of General Yen, Union Pacific, The Lady Eve,* and *Meet John Doe.* The acting careers of many of Hollywood's brightest stars were given impetus by having appeared in support of her—namely Bette Davis *(So Big),* Clark Gable *(Night Nurse),* Anthony Quinn *(Union Pacific),* Marilyn Monroe *(Clash by Night),* Kirk Douglas *(The Strange Love of Martha Ivers),* and Burt Lancaster *(Sorry, Wrong Number).* Undeniably one of the most woeful injustices ever inflicted by the Academy was its failure to honor this enormously talented and beloved lady with a Best Actress Oscar, a slight it limply tried to rectify with a career achievement Oscar in 1982—the same award that was given to Paul Newman for his contribution over the years.

Barbara Stanwyck in The File on Thelma Jordan *(1950).*

Kirk Douglas (three nominations) Douglas was so fine in *Champion* (1949) that he seemed destined to rank with the legendary Oscar actors. His portrait of a driven fighter was a hard act to follow. But he did it—first as a sharkish studio head in *The Bad and the Beautiful* (1952) and then as Vincent van Gogh in *Lust for Life* (1956). Both brought him Best Actor nominations. Also of Oscar class, but unnominated, were his performances in *Young Man with a Horn, Detective Story, The Devil's Disciple, Spartacus,* and *Two Weeks in Another Town.* While other actors of his generation got Oscars (Lancaster, Peck, and Borgnine), Douglas was beaten by Broderick Crawford for *All the King's Men* (1949); Gary Cooper beat him for *High Noon* (1952); and Yul Brynner, for *The King and I* (1956), got the award that truly belonged to Douglas.

Kirk Douglas as Vincent van Gogh in Lust for Life *(1956).*

Cary Grant (two nominations)   The debonair Grant has made even life look easy, so why not acting? In this respect he has been his own worst enemy—Oscarwise. "I play myself beautifully," he has said again and again. The town came to believe it. But Grant remained the champ of America's comic actors, with more range than Richard Dreyfuss and more subtlety than Jack Lemmon. He never cared about the Oscar particularly and maintained that the institution was fine "back in the days when it was still just a party—a chance for some fun." His two nominations were for *Penny Serenade* (1941) and *None but the Lonely Heart* (1944). But he could as easily have been picked for *The Awful Truth*, *His Girl Friday*, *Indiscreet*, *Topper*, *Bringing Up Baby*, *The Philadelphia Story*, *Arsenic and Old Lace*, *To Catch a Thief*, *Notorious*, and *North by Northwest*.

Cary Grant, never an Oscar winner.

Eddie Albert, Jane Alexander, Dame Judith Anderson, Ann-Margret, Fred Astaire, Lauren Bacall, Carroll Baker, Tallulah Bankhead, John Barrymore, Alan Bates, Warren Beatty, Barbara Bel Geddes, William Bendix, Charles Bickford, Jacqueline Bisset, Claire Bloom, Dirk Bogarde, Timothy Bottoms, Charles Boyer, Jeff Bridges, Genevieve Bujold, Billie Burke, Michael Caine, Dyan Cannon, John Carradine, John Cassavetes, Lon Chaney, Charles Chaplin (except for special award), Lee J. Cobb, Gladys Cooper, Joseph Cotten, Tony Curtis, James Dean, Marlene Dietrich, Jeanne Eagels, Clint Eastwood, Peter Falk, W. C. Fields, Albert Finney, Geraldine Fitzgerald, Errol Flynn, Nina Foch, Lynn Fontanne, Glenn Ford, Ava Gardner, John Garfield, Judy Garland, Jackie Gleason, Sydney Greenstreet, Ann Harding, Sir Cedric Hardwicke, Jean Harlow, Barbara Harris, Julie Harris, Bob Hope, Miriam Hopkins, Leslie Howard, Trevor Howard, John Ireland, Boris Karloff, Danny Kaye, Sally Kellerman, Gene Kelly, Kay Kendall, Shirley Knight, Alan Ladd, Elsa Lanchester, Angela Lansbury, Piper Laurie, Gertrude Lawrence, Carole Lombard, Myrna Loy, Alfred Lunt, Herbert Marshall, James Mason, Marsha Mason, Raymond Massey, Joel McCrea, Steve McQueen, Adolphe Menjou, Sal Mineo, Robert Mitchum, Marilyn Monroe, Robert Montgomery, Don Murray, Mildred Natwick, Merle Oberon, Pat O'Brien, Jack Palance, Anthony Perkins, Walter Pidgeon, Dick Powell, William Powell, Tyrone Power, Claude Rains, Robert Redford, Sir Michael Redgrave, Sir Ralph Richardson, Paul Robeson, Edward G. Robinson, Flora Robson, Mickey Rooney, Gena Rowlands, Rosalind Russell, Peter Sellers, Robert Shaw, Martin Sheen, Sylvia Sidney, Jean Simmons, Kim Stanley, Margaret Sullavan, Gloria Swanson, Franchot Tone, Lana Turner, Liv Ullmann, Robert Vaughn, Eli Wallach, Clifton Webb, Tuesday Weld, Orson Welles, Richard Widmark, and Natalie Wood.

Marlene Dietrich—never a winner.

Oscarless John Barrymore.

Two of the biggest reasons why the list of Oscar losers often seems more illustrious than the winner's circle—Cary Grant and Irene Dunne, in The Awful Truth (1937). *It's hard to believe that Dunne and Grant—on almost everybody's list of Hollywood's finest performers— never won the big one. Irene Dunne was nominated for* Cimarron, Theodora Goes Wild, The Awful Truth, *and* I Remember Mama. *Her work in* Anna and the King of Siam *and* The Mudlark *was ignored by Oscar voters. Cary Grant was nominated only twice—for* Penny Serenade *and* None but the Lonely Heart *—and his ignored triumphs are too numerous to mention. In 1970 the Academy finally honored him with an honorary statue for "unique mastery of the art of screen acting."*

James Dean—never a winner.

Martin Sheen had a heart attack (then open-heart surgery) after his grueling and brilliant work in Apocalypse Now, *but was not nominated for that film. He never has been nominated, despite a spate of fabulous performances.*

Nary an Oscar Nomination

In the course of this book, much has been made of the Academy's lock-out of what should have been obvious choices for the golden idol. Such names as Cary Grant, Greta Garbo, and Thelma Ritter come to mind immediately. But *they*, at least, were nominated. Consider those performers that have never received an Academy nomination:

Alan Alda, Dana Andrews, Edward Arnold, Lauren Bacall, Lucille Ball, Tallulah Bankhead, John Barrymore, Constance Bennett, Claire Bloom, Carol Burnett, John Carradine, Lon Chaney, Ina Claire, Sean Connery, Dolores Costello, Joseph Cotten, Noël Coward, Dolores del Rio, Catherine Deneuve, Colleen Dewhurst, Michael Douglas, Douglas Fairbanks (Sr. *and* Jr.), Mia Farrow, Mel Ferrer, W. C. Fields, Errol Flynn, Glenn Ford, John Gilbert, Betty Grable, Harry Guardino, Sir Cedric Hardwicke, Jean Harlowe, Rita Hayworth, John Hodiak, Bob Hope, Betty Hutton, Al Jolson, Louis Jourdan, Boris Karloff, Danny Kaye, Kay Kendall, Alan Ladd, Veronica Lake, Gertrude Lawrence, Peter Lorre, Myrna Loy, Ida Lupino, Joel McCrea, Roddy McDowall, Fred MacMurray, Herbert Marshall, Gary Merrill, Marilyn Monroe, Zero Mostel, Pat O'Brien, Maureen O'Hara, Lilli Palmer, Christopher

Plummer, Dick Powell, Tyrone Power, George Raft, Ronald Reagan, Burt Reynolds, Paul Robeson, Will Rogers, Zachary Scott, Martin Sheen, Ann Sheridan, Donald Sutherland, Robert Taylor, Max von Sydow, Eli Wallach, and Mae West.

By the same token, through the years, some oddly out-of-place names have managed to crop up among the Oscar nominees. It is not for their lack of talent that they appear here. Rather, it is because their peerless peers saw something in their work that we have failed to see.

Miliza Korjus, Marjorie Main, Dan Dailey, Ellen Corby, Jeff Chandler, Arthur Hunnicutt, Terry Moore, Maggie McNamara, Dan O'Herlihy, Joe Mantell, Betsy Blair, Robert Stack, Peggy Cass, Martha Hyer, Cara Williams, Chill Wills, Nick Adams, Bobby Darin, Lilia Skala, Debbie Reynolds, Grayson Hall, Lila Kedrova, Elizabeth Hartman, Ian Bannen, Michael Dunn, Ida Kaminska, Mako, Michael J. Pollard, Carol Channing, Seymour Cassel, Daniel Massey, Jack Wild, Lynn Carlin, Sondra Locke, Rupert Crosse, Catherine Burns, Sylvia Miles, Ali MacGraw, Carrie Snodgrass, Richard Castellano, John Marley, Chief Dan George, Karen Black, Richard Jaeckel, Stuart Whitman, Topol, Janet Suzman, Leonard Frey, Ryan O'Neal, Jeannie Berlin, Susan Tyrell, Vincent Gardenia, Candy Clark, Doris Day, Carol Kane, Jocelyn Lagarde, Vivien Merchant, Isabelle Adjani, and Ann-Margret (in *Tommy* only).

Errol Flynn was never nominated, was never even suggested by his home studio, Warner Bros. "I guess swashbucklers don't act," he said.

Thank You, Very Much . . .
Musings on Winning the Oscar Literate

Every now and again (but not often enough) an Oscar winner will be short, clever, and amusing when accepting an award:

Loretta Young (Best Actress: *The Farmer's Daughter,* 1947):   "At last!"

Jane Wyman (Best Actress, playing a deaf mute: *Johnny Belinda,* 1948):   "I accept this very gratefully for keeping my mouth shut; I think I'll do it again."

Mercedes McCambridge (Best Supporting Actress: *All the King's Men,* 1949):   "I just want to say to all beginning actresses: Never get discouraged. Hold on! Just look what can happen."

Edith Head (Best Costume Design: *Roman Holiday,* 1953):   "I'm going to take it home and design a dress for it."

Dimitri Tiomkin (Best Scoring of a Dramatic or Comedy Picture: *The High and the Mighty,* 1954):   "To all those who helped me get where I am: Brahms, Bach, Beethoven, Richard Strauss, Johann Strauss . . ."

Lee Marvin (Best Actor: *Cat Ballou,* 1965):   "I think half of this belongs to a horse somewhere out in the Valley."

Barbra Streisand (Best Actress: *Funny Girl,* 1968):   "Hello, gorgeous."

John Wayne (Best Actor, playing a one-eyed sheriff: *True Grit,* 1969):   "I should have put on that eye patch years ago."

Meryl Streep (Best Supporting Actress: *Kramer vs. Kramer,* 1979):   "Holy mackerel!"

Maureen Stapleton (Best Supporting Actress: *Reds,* 1981):   "I'm thrilled, happy, delighted . . . sober!"

Pardon Our Oscar

Oscar history is loaded with oversights, embarrassing winners and nominees, and lapses of taste. But occasionally, the Academy Award voters outdo even themselves. Here are a few examples:

The *Scenes from a Marriage* Affair   The critical elite on both coasts were bowled over by a three-hour Ingmar Bergman film, *Scenes from a Marriage.* It appeared to be an Oscar shoo-in for Best Director, Best Picture, Best Actress, and Best Film Editing for 1974. But the preliminary ballots (containing approximately 350 names of eligible pictures) went into the mail without the Swedish film on the list. A furor erupted. Directors including Frank Capra and George Cukor ran ads in the trade papers begging the Academy to put the film onto the list. Gregory Peck, then Academy's president, ruefully explained that a highly technical point excluded *Scenes from a Marriage*. The saga had been first shown as a television movie in Sweden in 1973. It was the date of the film that excluded it rather than its origin as a television show. The controversy became a rage as the final Oscar voting neared. The Academy's board of directors, however, would not back down. Finally Charles Champlin wrote: "As it stands, the luster of the top awards in many categories will be tarnished because Bergman's brilliantly observed and superbly executed drama was not on the ballot. It is crazy and unfair to the winners and losers alike and a seemingly needless blow to the credibility and prestige of the Academy Awards."

A Penny for Your Expensive Turkeys   Or, how Twentieth Century–Fox bought nominations for three disasters (*Doctor Dolittle*, *Hello, Dolly!*, and *Star!*) by trading on studio politics, waging shameless ad campaigns, and wooing Oscar voters with expensive food and very private screenings. It all started in 1967, when the brass at Fox released *Doctor Dolittle* to widespread derision and apathy. This overproduced children's film wasn't one of the top twenty films of the year, much less a member of the top five. John Gregory Dunne has shown in his book *The Studio* how Fox waged the *Doctor Dolittle* campaign voter by voter as if it were fighting street by street in a besieged city. Each of the Academy branches had a series of private showings, preceded by a buffet dinner and followed by a midnight champagne supper. Further, Fox mailed out copies of the film's soundtrack, ran a massive ad campaign, and even held a telephone campaign. Worse for history, the studio used its clout in the Academy's branches to see that its own *Two for the Road* was dropped from the preliminary cinematography and editing lists. Never mind that the editing and photography on *Two for the Road* were excellent, while *Doctor Dolittle* was only mediocre in those areas. *Doctor Dolittle* needed the Oscar nominations to help it at the box office, and Fox saw that the film got them. The studio P.R. department did the same thing in 1969, gaining the musical dud *Hello, Dolly!* nominations for Best Picture, Best Cinematography, Best Art Direction, Best Sound, Best Film Editing, Best Score of a Musical Picture and Best Costume Design.

Music? That's Just Noise: The Oscar Case Against *Saturday Night Fever*   In 1977, *Saturday Night Fever* gave the movies a new type of hero—the daytime loser who becomes a prince by night—and a new star: John Travolta. It made so much money so fast that even the Academy couldn't ignore it. (The Academy can overlook *anything* but a hit.) The Hollywood voters tossed the film a prize bone—a Best Actor nomination for John Travolta. But the Academy's music branch excluded it from competition in any of its categories. The score, in fact, was counted out before the quarterfinals. "They could have played any music during those scenes," said a spokesman for the music branch. "We have to consider the appropriateness of the music to the plot."

The Gibb brothers, better known as the BeeGees, had created an entirely new score for the disco movie, a score that fit the action in a subtle manner. Nobody who saw John Travolta walking through the opening song, "Stayin' Alive," doubted the power of the song or the score as a whole. But did the music voters even see *Saturday Night Fever*? Probably not. To exclude the BeeGees from the category of Best Original Score, the music branch had to nominate *Mohammad—Mes-*

senger of God. The nominees for Best Song were laughable: "The Slipper and the Rose Waltz," "Someone's Waiting for You," "Candle on the Water," "Nobody Does It Better," and "You Light Up My Life," the winner. "Stayin' Alive" became the theme for a new generation, while "You Light Up My Life," an international hit, came from a stupid film of the same name that was purposely written to justify the song.

The Godfather
and the Academy

Paramount's saga of the underworld establishment was planned as one sprawling chronicle (and that was the way it came to network television). Although it was released as two films, *The Godfather* in 1972 and *The Godfather Part II* in 1974, many film critics view the two as a whole. Following that line of thinking, *The Godfather* has received more nominations—twenty-one—and has launched more Oscar-class stars than any project in film history.

THE ALUMNI

Actors Marlon Brando, Best Actor, 1972; Robert De Niro, Best Supporting Actor, 1974. Al Pacino, Best Actor nominee, 1974; Lee Strasberg and Michael V. Gazzo, Best Supporting Actor nominees, 1974; James Caan, Robert Duvall, and Al Pacino, Best Supporting Actor nominees, 1972; Talia Shire, Best Supporting Actress nominee, 1974.

Direction Francis Ford Coppola, Best Director nominee, 1972; Best Director, 1974.

Production Best Picture, 1972; Best Picture, 1974 (Albert S. Ruddy, producer).

Writing Mario Puzo and Francis Ford Coppola, Best Screenplay, 1972; Best Screenplay, 1974.

Technicians Anna Hill Johnstone, Best Costume Design nominee, 1972; Bud Grenzbach, Richard Portman, and Christopher Newman, Best Sound nominees, 1972; William Reynolds and Peter Zinnen, Best Film Editing nominees, 1972; Dean Tavoularis, Angelo Graham, and George R. Nelson, Best Art Direction, 1974; Theodora Van Runkle, Best Costume Design nominee, 1974; Nino Rota and Carmine Coppola, Best Original Dramatic Score, 1974.

. . . But Fans Still Love Him

Oscar or no Oscar, one thing Steven Spielberg has going for him, both as producer and/or director, is audience support.

He is acknowledged as the world's most financially successful filmmaker, and his nine most popular films have been seen by 546 million people in the United States alone and have sold $1.6 billion worth of tickets throughout the country. His worldwide audience is estimated at over a billion people, accounting for more than $3 billion in ticket sales.

FILM	TICKET SALES (in millions)	AUDIENCE (in millions)
E.T.—The Extra-Terrestrial	$400	133
Jaws	$228	76
Raiders of the Lost Ark	$203	68
Indiana Jones and the Temple of Doom	$191	64
Back to the Future	$165	55
Close Encounters of the Third Kind	$146	48
Gremlins	$138	46
The Color Purple	$100	34
Poltergeist	$65	22
Total	$1,636	546

Little Red Oscar

The Oscar races became so intertwined with the anti-Communist movement in Hollywood that the Academy drafted a loyalty oath required of all nominees. But many of those blacklisted officially had been nominees or even winners. Here is a partial list of blacklisted nominees and winners, followed by writers in the same category.

BLACKLISTED WRITERS

John Bright, one nomination; Sidney Buchman, three nominations, one Oscar; John Howard Lawson, one nomination; Dalton Trumbo, one nomination, one Oscar under the pseudonym "Robert Rich" and another under the "front" of Ian McLellan Hunter; Donald Ogden Stewart, one nomination; Howard Koch, one nomination, one Oscar; Lillian Hellman, two nominations; Dashiell Hammett, one nomination; Alvah Bessie, one nomination; Albert Maltz, one nomination; Abraham Polonsky, one nomination; Carl Foreman, five nominations, one Oscar incorrectly attributed to novelist Pierre Boulle; Michael Wilson, one nomination, one nomination disqualified due to the loyalty oath, one Oscar; Waldo Salt, one nomination, two Oscars; Ned Young, one nomination, one Oscar—both under the pseudonym "Nathan E. Douglas" and still listed incorrectly in the Academy records.

BLACKLISTED PERFORMERS

John Garfield, twice nominated, died of a heart attack the night before he was to appear before the House Un-American Activities Committee.

Lee Grant, four times nominated and the winner of the Best Supporting Actress award for *Shampoo,* was blacklisted, resulting in her being kept out of the industry for eighteen years.

Kim Hunter, Oscar winner as Best Supporting Actress in *A Streetcar Named Desire,* was unjustly implicated and, except for four minor films from 1956 to 1958, kept off the screen for a dozen years.

Anne Revere, a Best Supporting Actress winner and a nominee two other times, was never able to revive her movie career because of the HUAC stigma.

Gale Sondergaard, winner of the first Best Supporting Actress award, and a later nominee, was blacklisted and could not get a job in Hollywood from 1950 until 1970.

Kim Hunter, here with Vivien Leigh in A Streetcar Named Desire *(1951), made perhaps the most sensational ingenue splash in the history of the industry as Tennessee Williams's troubled young heroine. Everybody wanted to sign her, and she walked off with the Best Supporting Actress Oscar in a hands-down contest. Six months later her name was engraved in granite on the blacklist. She was never to make an adequate comeback.*

The Ultimate Oscar Quiz

(THE ANSWERS TO THIS QUIZ MAY BE FOUND ON PAGE 298.)

1. What Oscar-winning actor co-wrote the screenplay for *Jane Eyre*? This film also marked an early screen appearance for what two-time Oscar-winning actress?

2. The dubious distinction of having given the longest Academy Award acceptance speech belongs to whom?

3. *A Letter to Three Wives* was the first of Joseph L. Mankiewicz's back-to-back Oscar wins for direction and screenplay. Name the Oscar-winning actress whose voice was used as the writer of the letter in that film.

4. Only two performers have won all four major entertainment awards—the Oscar, the Emmy, the Tony, and the Grammy. Name them.

5. Besides its Oscar-winning music score by Max Steiner, *Now Voyager* is also remembered as the film in which Paul Henreid lighted the famous twin cigarettes for Bette Davis and himself. Despite Henreid's claim of having "invented" this bit of business, proof exists that George Brent actually did this several years earlier. Name the film in which Mr. Brent offered the cigarette to his co-star. Name his co-star.

6. *All About Eve*, with fourteen Oscar nominations, has yet to be equaled. The film boasts an early appearance of Marilyn Monroe in the role of Miss Caswell, a "graduate of the Copacabana School of Dramatic Art." According to Addison DeWitt, played by that film's Best Supporting Actor winner, George Sanders, what is Miss Caswell's first name?

7. On two occasions, Oscar winner Ruth Gordon was cast early in her career as the wife of Oscar nominee Raymond Massey. Name the films.

8. This Oscar-winning actress appeared in the 1920s in a silent version of *Brewster's Millions*. Name her.

9. There have been some sixteen reincarnations of the character Zorro. But the first time he appeared was in a silent film directed by what director-turned-Oscar-winning actor?

10. What film received the industry's first Best Special Effects Oscar?

11. What do Rex Harrison and Yul Brynner have in common? (Two things, please.)

12. Two films share the record for being the non–Oscar winner with the greatest number of nominations. Name them.

13. This Oscar-winning director also directed a 1932 film that served as the inspiration for the three versions of *A Star Is Born*. Name the director and the 1932 production.

14. What do Shirley Booth and Barbra Streisand have in common? (Two things, please.)

15. This Oscar-winning actress began her career on Broadway in 1923 in a play called *The Barker*. She made her film debut in 1928 and her final film (so far) in 1960. Who is she? For what film did she receive her Oscar?

16. This Oscar-winning actor was often glimpsed as a chorus boy in such film-musicals as *Gentlemen Prefer Blondes*, *White Christmas*, and *Brigadoon* in the 1950s and, during the 1960s appeared in support of such Oscar winners as Charlton Heston, Yul Brynner, and Simone Signoret. Name this actor and the film for which he was awarded an Oscar.

17. The first of this actor's four Oscar nominations came in 1948 for the leading role in his film debut. Name the actor and the film.

18. Symphony conductor Leopold Stokowski's infrequent movie appearances began in 1937 in a film that was awarded an Oscar for Best Musical Score. Name the film.

19. Composer-conductor André Previn has earned four Oscars for Best Musical Score. Only one, *Irma La Douce*, was for a nonmusical film. Name the three musicals for which Previn won Oscars.

20. Name three films in which double Oscar winner Jane Fonda was paired with multiple Oscar nominee (and Oscar winner as Best Director) Robert Redford.

21. What Oscar-winning actress made her film debut in 1933 in *Life in the Raw*?

22. What 1938 Oscar-nominated actor wrote the popular classic song "The World Is Waiting for the Sunrise?"

23. Name two actors who were nominated for reprising roles for which they were also nominated in the originals of those films.

24. The 1950 Best Supporting Actor winner, George Sanders, had four wives, two of whom were sisters. Name the sisters.

25. A Best Supporting Actor nominee in 1947 was a 1940 Golden Gloves amateur boxing champion. Name him.

26. Another actor—an Oscar winner—was once a professional prizefighter who even fought Jack Johnson. Name him.

27. Robert Mitchum and Shelley Winters co-starred in 1955's brilliant *Night of the Hunter*. It was the only film directed by an Oscar-winning actor. Name him.

28. What Oscar-winning actress returned to the screen—after a fifteen-year absence—to play Troy Donahue's mother in *Parrish*?

29. What two-time Oscar-nominated actor won a Tony Award for *The Changing Room*?

30. Match the Oscar-winning songs with the films in which they were introduced:

1) "The Last Time I Saw Paris"	(a) *Lovers and Other Strangers*
2) "The Continental"	(b) *Lady Be Good*
3) "Thanks for the Memory"	(c) *Holiday Inn*
4) "The Way You Look Tonight"	(d) *State Fair*
5) "I Just Called to Say I Love You"	(e) *The Big Broadcast of 1938*
	(f) *The Woman in Red*
6) "White Christmas"	(g) *Gold Diggers of 1935*
7) "You'll Never Know"	(h) *The Gay Divorcée*
8) "All the Way"	(i) *Breakfast at Tiffany's*
9) "It Might As Well Be Spring"	(j) *An Officer and a Gentleman*
10) "Lullaby of Broadway"	(k) *Calamity Jane*
11) "For All We Know"	(l) *The Harvey Girls*
12) "Secret Love"	(m) *Hello, Frisco, Hello*
13) "Moon River"	(n) *The Joker Is Wild*
14) "On the Atchison, Topeka and the Santa Fe"	(o) *Swing Time*
15) "Up Where We Belong"	

31. What singing actor has introduced the most Oscar-winning songs? Name the songs.

32. What Best Song was introduced by an insect?

33. What is the only nominated song to serve as the musical signature of a cartoon bird?

34. What Oscar-nominated song was sung by a stuffed frog?

35. What Oscar-winning actor made an early film appearance as a postal-service employee in *Miracle on 34th Street*?

36. What Oscar-winning actor once taught classes in acting at Missouri's Stephens College?

37. A twice-nominated actress narrated the 1962 film *To Kill a Mockingbird*. Name her.

38. Three best supporting Oscar winners have also won lasting fame as playwrights. Name them.

39. A multinominated, but nonwinning actor reportedly turned down leads in the following films: *Sunset Boulevard*, *East of Eden*, *Somebody Up There Likes Me*, and *On the Waterfront*. Name him.

40. What two sets of actors were approached for *Casablanca* before Humphrey Bogart and Ingrid Bergman were signed?

41. Name the only star to have won Best Actor Oscars back to back.

42. Name the two Best Pictures in which the stars also received Oscars for Best Actor and Best Actress.

43. What do Woody Allen, Robert Redford, and Warren Beatty have in common?

44. What two things do Laurence Olivier, Anne Bancroft, and Barbra Streisand have in common?

45. What Oscar nominee once wrote an advice column in the 1960s for *16* magazine?

46. What two Oscar-winning actors appeared in the 1930 Paul Whiteman musical *King of Jazz*?

47. What three musicals were directed by Oscar winner Francis Ford Coppola?

48. This Oscar-winning actress made an early film appearance in support of Alec Guinness in *The Lavender Hill Mob.* Name her.

49. Name two films whose entire casts were nominated for an Oscar.

50. Under her real name of Phyllis Isley, this Oscar-winning actress appeared in the Republic serial *Dick Tracy's G-Men.* Name her.

51. What do Fay Bainter, Teresa Wright, and Jessica Lange have in common?

52. Who was Joseph Farnam?

53. Name Oscar's first posthumous nominee for acting.

54. What do James Dean, Spencer Tracy, and Peter Finch have in common?

55. What do *Mutiny on the Bounty* (1935), *On the Waterfront, Tom Jones, The Godfather,* and *The Godfather Part II* all have in common?

56. Why was the 1981 Oscarcast delayed by one day?

57. What was unusual about Robert De Niro's and Sissy Spacek's Oscar wins in 1981?

58. Who won the Thalberg Award for 1981 and why is his name so familiar?

59. What was unusual about the Oscar-winning Best Original Dramatic Score for 1972?

60. Name the films for which the following stars received their only Oscar nominations: Dan Dailey, Doris Day, Lana Turner, Ava Gardner, and Bette Midler.

61. Name the film for which the Beatles won the Oscar for Best Original Song Score.

62. What Oscar-winning actor sang on Broadway in *The Sound of Music?*

63. Only one director (so far) has received the Best Director Oscar four times. Name him. Give yourself a bonus if you can name the films.

64. Name the three films for which Frank Capra received Best Director Oscars.

65. On January 11, 1933, a Frank Capra–directed film starring Barbara Stanwyck opened the landmark movie palace Radio City Music Hall in New York. Name the film.

66. Name the Oscar-nominated film that was on the marquee of Radio City Music Hall in *The Godfather*.

67. What do Meryl Streep, Ingrid Bergman, Helen Hayes, Maggie Smith, Jack Lemmon, Jack Nicholson, and Robert De Niro have in common?

68. Warren Beatty has received a total of twelve Oscar nominations—for acting, directing, writing, and producing. How many has he won?

69. Barbara Stanwyck, four times Oscar-nominated, starred in a 1937 Paramount film that spawned the popular MGM series, *Dr. Kildare*. Name the film. Who played Dr. Kildare?

70. What do David Niven and Charlton Heston have in common?

71. Leo McCarey wrote and directed both *Going My Way* and its sequel, *The Bells of St. Mary's*, both nominated as Best Picture, in 1944 and 1945, respectively. Each was also the year's top box-office attraction. Name the studio(s) which produced these blockbusters.

72. Name the "prequel" to Samuel Goldwyn's Oscar-nominated film *The Little Foxes*.

73. Name the Oscar-winning actresses top-billed in the turkey *A Matter of Time*. Who was the Oscar-winning director of this bomb?

74. This grandfatherly Oscar-winning actor played a heartless murderer in Alfred Hitchcock's *Foreign Correspondent*. Name him.

75. In 1939, the consummate charactor actor Thomas Mitchell appeared in four classic films: *Stagecoach*, *Gone With The Wind*, *Only Angels Have Wings*, and *Mr. Smith Goes to Washington*. For which of these did he win an Oscar?

76. Name five actors who received Oscars for Best Song.

77. Name the only back-to-back Oscar winners for Best Song.

78. Name the only Oscar winner to present an Oscar to himself.

79. Name the films for which the following stars received their only Oscar nominations: Debbie Reynolds, John Travolta, Sylvester Stallone, Tony Curtis, Cornel Wilde, and Lee Remick.

80. Oscar-winning performers Charles Laughton and Bette Davis each portrayed a royal father and his daughter on two occasions, but in different films. Name the king and queen essayed and the four films in question.

AN ANNOTATED

Bibliography

The story of the avarice and heartbreak surrounding the Academy Awards comes out in bits and pieces which are scattered through the history of Hollywood. More than 150 books, 500 magazine articles, and hundreds of daily newspaper stories were used in the compilation of this book. The most useful are included in this bibliography. When they were available, we have listed paperback editions.

But three works stand out from the rest:

OSBORNE, ROBERT. *Fifty Golden Years of Oscar: The Official History of the Academy of Motion Picture Arts and Sciences.* ESE California Books; La Habra, California; 1979. The full history of the Academy is told by Osborne in a massive work of scholarly nature. Osborne, a film writer for the *Hollywood Reporter*, the respected trade paper, has also offered a decent actor-by-actor index.

SHALE, RICHARD. *Academy Awards: An Ungar Reference Index.* Frederick Ungar Publishing Company, New York, 1978. Organized so thoroughly that all of the body of Oscar data is available in a few minutes, the book has bridged the gap for writers and scholars.

WILEY, MASON AND BONA, DAMIEN. *Inside Oscar: The Unofficial History of the Academy Awards:* Ballantine Books, New York, 1986. A welcome addition to the reference books of Robert Osborne and Richard Shale, this meticulously researched volume proved invaluable, especially with the details of the ceremonies themselves.

BOOKS

BAKER, FRED AND FIRESTONE, ROSS. *Movie People.* Lancer Books, New York, 1973. Good interview with Rod Steiger.

BEHLMER, RUDY, editor. *MEMO from David O. Selznick.* Viking Press, New York, 1972. Selznick's paranoia about Jennifer Jones' career and the Oscar makes for riveting reading.

BOSWORTH, PATRICIA. *Montgomery Clift.* Bantam Books, New York, 1978.

CAPRA, FRANK. *The Name above the Title.* The Macmillan Company, New York, 1971. Invaluable account of the Oscar intrigue during the Academy's most turbulent decade is spiced throughout the book. And Capra even reveals his own morbid obsession with winning the Oscar.

CAREY, GARY. *Brando.* Pocket Books, New York, 1973.

CARPOZI, GEORGE. *The John Wayne Story.* Dell Books, New York, 1972. Hidden well in these pages is the shameless story of Wayne's attempt to buy an Oscar for his film, *The Alamo.*

294

CRAWFORD, CHRISTINA. *Mommie Dearest*. William Morrow and Company, New York, 1979. Joan Crawford with her Oscar showing—only part of a unique and agonizing book.

CROWTHER, BOSLEY. *Hollywood Raja*. Holt, Rinehart and Winston, New York, 1960. Crowther unmasks the greed behind Louis B. Mayer's founding of the Academy of Motion Picture Arts and Sciences.

DAVIS, BETTE. *The Lonely Life*. Lancer Books, New York, 1962.

DUNNE, JOHN GREGORY. *The Studio*. Bantam Books, New York, 1969. This stylish study of Hollywood studio politics is now a classic—must reading at most film schools. In fact, almost everybody learned from it *except* the studio politicians themselves. It holds up because nothing has changed.

EELS, GEORGE. *Hedda and Louella*. Warner Books, New York, 1973. To understand the world of Hedda and Louella is to understand the gamesmanship that created the Oscar. This portrait is essential.

FOWLER, GENE. *Good Night, Sweet Prince*. Ballantine Books, New York, 1950. How could Hollywood exclude John Barrymore from the Oscar? This book tells part of the story.

GRAHAM, SHEILA. *Confessions of a Hollywood Columnist*. Bantam Books, New York, 1968. Inside stuff on Monroe, etc.

GUILES, FRED LAWRENCE. *Marion Davies*. McGraw-Hill, New York, 1972. This out-of-print book restores Marion to her original place among Hollywood's best comediennes. It also sheds light on the Oscar politics that defeated Orson Welles and his *Citizen Kane*.

GUSSOW, MEL. *Don't Say Yes Until I Finish Talking*. Doubleday Books, New York, 1971. So-so work on Darryl Zanuck.

HARBISON, W. A. *George C. Scott*. Pinnacle Books, New York, 1977. To study Scott's picture career is to follow the Oscar through its trends.

HOPPER, HEDDA. *The Whole Truth and Nothing But*. Pyramid Books, New York, 1963.
From Under My Hat. MacFadden Books, New York, 1960. A lot of old rumors and some biting remarks about the Oscar.

HIGHAM, CHARLES. *Celebrity Circus*. Dell Books, New York, 1980.
The Celluloid Muse. Signet Books, New York, 1969.

HYAMS, JOE. *Bogie*. Signet Books, New York, 1966.

KAEL, PAULINE. *The Citizen Kane Book*. Bantam Books, New York, 1974. Kael follows *Citizen Kane* from its release through its hallowed status as perhaps the best film ever made. On the way she discovers the rotten cesspool of the Oscar voters. This and Guiles' *Marion Davies* nail the Oscars to their deserved infamy for this episode.

KOBLER, JOHN. *Damned in Paradise: The Life of John Barrymore*. Atheneum Books, New York, 1977. Perhaps *too much* gossip.

LA GUARDIA, ROBERT. *Monty*. Avon Books, New York, 1977.

LAMBERT, GAVIN. *On Cukor*. Capricorn Books, New York, 1972.

LIKENESS, GEORGE. *The Oscar People*. Wayside Press; Mendota, Illinois; 1965. This out-of-print and hard-to-find book is an interesting look at the varied fates of Oscar winners. It was written in 1964 when the Oscar was adapting to a "new Hollywood."

LINET, BEVERLY. *Alan Ladd: A Hollywood Tragedy*. Berkley Books, New York, 1979. Why wasn't Alan Ladd nominated for *Shane*? Linet gives a partial answer.

MARCHAK, ALICE. *The Super Secs*. Bantam Books, New York, 1976. Alice Marchak, Marlon Brando's secretary, writes with humor and insight about life with the great one. And she gives a satirical picture of her boss and his *Godfather* Oscar.

MARION, FRANCES. *Off with Their Heads*. The Macmillan Company, New York, 1972. The Oscar's first decade, critically viewed by a winner and her friends. Not entirely a happy picture.

PARISH, JAMES ROBERT. *The MGM Stock Company.* Bonanza Books, New York, 1977. This trail-blazing reference book portrays every MGM contract star and helps explain the careers of such people as Luise Rainer.
Lisa. Pocket Books, New York, 1975.

PERRY, LOUIS B. AND PERRY, RICHARD S. *A History of the Los Angeles Labor Movement.* University of California Press, Berkeley, 1963. The pitiful attempt by the studio bosses to make a slave of the Academy they created emerges in great detail in these pages. There's no doubt—the Academy was created in Louis B. Mayer's image.

PHILLIPS, GENE. *Stanley Kubrick: A Film Odyssey.* Popular Library, New York, 1977.

ROSENBERG, BERNARD AND SILVERSTEIN, HARRY. *The Real Tinsel.* The Macmillan Company, 1975.

RUSSELL, ROSALIND. *Life Is a Banquet.* Grossett and Dunlap, New York, 1977. "In her own words."

SANDS, PIERRE NORMAN. *A Historical Study of the Academy.* Arno Press, New York, 1966. Sands studied the Academy's first three decades for his doctoral thesis at the University of Southern California. He defends the Oscar races, but his statistics unlock the key to the Academy's dark decade —the thirties.

SARRIS, ANDREW. *Interviews with Film Directors.* Avon Books, New York, 1967.

SHEPPARD, DICK. *Elizabeth.* Warner Books, New York, 1974. If there ever was any doubt that Liz Taylor got her first Oscar because she nearly died, this book erases it.

STEELE, JOSEPH HENRY. *Ingrid Bergman.* Popular Library, New York, 1959.

STEINBERG, COBBETT. *Reel Facts: The Movie Book of Records.* Vintage Books, New York, 1978. The best raw reference book ever published on the movies. It gives the results of all top film contests plus salary and profit data.

SWANBERG, W. A. *Citizen Hearst.* Bantam Books, New York, 1961. Valuable inside look at the *Citizen Kane* Affair.

THOMAS, BOB. *Selznick.* Doubleday Books, New York, 1970.
Joan Crawford. Bantam Books, New York, 1978.
Thalberg, Life and Legend. Doubleday Books, New York, 1969.
King Cohn. Bantam Books, New York, 1967.
Walt Disney, An American Original. Pocket Books, New York, 1976.
The One and Only Bing. Grosset and Dunlap, New York, 1977.
Bob Thomas, Hollywood reporter for three decades, tells thoroughly the story of the Oscar in his many biographies.

WATERBURY, RUTH. *Elizabeth Taylor: Her Life, Her Loves.* Popular Library, New York, 1964.

ZOLOTOW, MAURICE. *Shooting Star: A Biography of John Wayne.* Simon and Schuster, New York, 1975. Wayne, the good and the bad. But still not an unbiased account of Wayne and the *Alamo* Affair.

ARTICLES

BERKOWITZ, STAN AND LEES, DAVID. "A Race for Fame and Money." *Los Angeles Times.* April 8, 1979. A capsulized look at the greed involved in a representative Oscar race. A view you don't get from columnists.

BOGDANOVICH, PETER. "The Oscar at Fifty." *Esquire.* April, 1978. An insider stands back to look at the Academy Award monster: entertaining, with good views from Cary Grant and James Stewart.

CANBY, VINCENT. "Hooray, Another Awful Oscar Evening." *New York Times*. April 4, 1974. Criticism from a voice of experience.
"In the Afterglow of the Oscars." *New York Times*. April 16, 1978. Ditto.

CHAMPLIN, CHARLES (Entertainment Editor, the *Los Angeles Times*). "Oscar, the Tail That Wags the Academy." *Los Angeles Times*. February 23, 1980.
"A-Z Rating for Oscar." *Los Angeles Times*. January 3, 1975.
"Oscar Ceremony, Reflection of a Tense Era in Film History." *Los Angeles Times*. April 18, 1971.
"Oscar, Forty Years Old and Still an Adolescent." *Los Angeles Times*. March 2, 1969.
"The Awards, a Rundown of Possible Winners." *Los Angeles Times*. April 7, 1968.
"Craft Over Content, an Oscar Tradition." *Los Angeles Times*. April 2, 1978.
"Brando, and the Offer He Refused." *Los Angeles Times*. March 30, 1973.
"Hollywood's Multi-Million Dollar Question: How Right?" *Los Angeles Times*. January 28, 1971.
"The Oscar Nominations, an Assessment." *Los Angeles Times*. February 28, 1971.
"Signs of Change for the Better in Oscar Nominations." *Los Angeles Times*. February 27, 1972.
"Oscar, '78, It's Business As Usual." *Los Angeles Times*. February 22, 1978. Taken as a whole, Charles Champlin's year-by-year chronicling of the Academy Awards mirrors the Oscar as a troubled institution. His is the closest the Academy has to a voice of conscience, being the only major critic who takes a middle ground between those who crucify the Academy and those who glorify it. Some of his complaints have helped to produce major changes in the process, lessening greed and manipulation.

GRANT, LEE. (film writer, the *Los Angeles Times*). "Redgrave Remarks Arouse Jewish Group." *Los Angeles Times*. April 5, 1978.
"War and Peace at the Awards." *Los Angeles Times*. April 11, 1979. Virtually the only unbiased reporting of Oscar's backstage. Most others play the glamorous Oscar game.

HARMETZ, ALJEAN. "How to Win an Oscar Nomination." *New York Times*. April 3, 1970. She gets inside a year's worth of Oscar hype and the view is devastating.

HOBERMAN, J. "Hearst's Lady of Hollywood." *Village Voice*. April 2, 1979. A rare look at Hearst's obsessive quest for the Oscar—which he wanted to present to Marion Davies.

KNIGHT, ARTHUR. "Assessing the Oscar." *Hollywood Reporter*. March 7, 1980.

LINDSEY, ROBERT. "Oscars Stir Redgrave Dispute." *New York Times*. February 1, 1978.

MANN, KLAUS. "Emil Jannings and Life after Hitler." *Los Angeles Times*. June 8, 1945.

NEWSWEEK. "Perils of an Oscar." April 2, 1958.
"Electioneering for Oscars." March 5, 1973.

NEW YORK TIMES. "German Leaders Grew Wealthy on Favoritism." August 5, 1945. The article depicts Emil Jannings and his connection with Nazi propaganda films which made him wealthy. He won the first Oscar for *The Way of All Flesh*.

POWERS, CHARLES. "Jack Lemmon: The Long Wait Before Oscar." *Los Angeles Times*. April 7, 1974. An interesting look at the general hysteria surrounding the Oscar.

ROYKO, MIKE. "So Mary Pickford Has Grown Old. So What?" *Los Angeles Times*. April 2, 1976. Exposes the Oscar and its annual trading off the tears and pathos of its aging stars.

SAN FRANCISCO CHRONICLE. "Sacheen Littlefeather, a Profile." March 30, 1973. A revealing portrait of the maiden who refused Brando's Oscar for *The Godfather.*

SARRIS, ANDREW. "The Oscars: Why 'Chinatown' Lost." *Village Voice.* April 21, 1975. Sarris has the voters pegged in this piece which not only focuses on one Oscar year, but flashes back to the skeletons in the Academy Award closet.

SCHULBERG, BUDD. "How My Daddy Won the Oscar." *Los Angeles Times.* April 13, 1969. A clever look at Oscar greed.

SKOLSKY, SIDNEY. "Film Flam," *The Hollywood Citizen,* February 11, 1935.

STUMBO, BELLA. "Oscar Show Arouses Protest by Deaf." *Los Angeles Times.* April 8, 1978.

TUSHER, WILL. "Oscar Aftermath Torn by Viet Passions," *Hollywood Reporter.* April 10, 1975.

WARGA, WAYNE. "A Half Century of Movie Arts and Survival." *Los Angeles Times.* May 8, 1977.
"Academy Spadework, a Long Row." *Los Angeles Times.* February 28, 1971.
Two of the many articles by Wayne Warga, associate arts editor of the *Times,* and an observer of the Oscars for a decade. He's gone to the source with Mary Pickford and King Vidor to separate fact from Oscar hokum.

YEAMAN, ELIZABETH. "The Awards Puzzle." *Hollywood Citizen.* February 1, 1936.
"Hollywood's Film Prize under Scrutiny." *Hollywood Citizen.* March 2, 1935.

VIDEO SOURCES

BARRETT, RONA. *Good Morning, America.* "Rona Comments on Oscar Winners." ABC Television. March 29, 1977.
Good Morning America. "Rona Looks at Oscar Winners." ABC Television. April 4, 1978.
These lively spot commentaries catch the flavor of the modern Oscars.

CHAMPLIN, CHARLES. "On the Film Scene with Jane Fonda." Interview on Theta Cable Television. March, 1980.
"On the Film Scene with I. A. L. Diamond." Interview on Theta Cable. Winter, 1979.
"On the Film Scene with Walter Mirisch." Interview on Theta Cable. Summer, 1980.
These shows managed to catch, in capsulized fashion, the feelings of Fonda, Diamond, and former Academy President Mirisch on the current film scene.

Answers to the Ultimate Oscar Quiz

1 John Houseman. Elizabeth Taylor.

2 Greer Garson.

3 Celeste Holm.

4 Rita Moreno and Helen Hayes.

5 *The Stamboul Quest.* Myrna Loy.

6 Claudia.

7 *Abe Lincoln In Illinois* (1940) and *Action in the North Atlantic* (1943).

8 Jane Darwell.

9 Donald Crisp.

10 *The Rains Came* (1939).

11 Both actors won Oscars for screen versions of roles they originated on the Broadway stage—Harrison for *My Fair Lady* (1964) and Brynner for *The King and I* (1956). Of course, both actors have essayed the role of the King of Siam.

12 *The Turning Point* (1977) and *The Color Purple* (1985), both with 11 nominations and no wins.

13 George Cukor (who also directed the 1954 version of *A Star Is Born*). *What Price Hollywood?*

14 In addition to both having made screen appearances as Dolly Levi, both actresses earned Oscars for their film debuts, repeating, incidentally, roles they created on Broadway—Miss Booth for *Come Back, Little Sheba* (1952) and Miss Streisand for *Funny Girl* (1968).

15 Claudette Colbert. *It Happened One Night.*

16 George Chakiris. *West Side Story.*

17 Montgomery Clift. *The Search.*

18 *100 Men and a Girl.*

19 *Porgy and Bess*, *My Fair Lady*, and *Gigi.*

20 *Barefoot in the Park*, *The Chase*, and *The Electric Horseman.*

21 Claire Trevor.

22 Gene Lockhart.

23 Bing Crosby's Father O'Malley in *Going My Way* and *The Bells of St. Mary's* and Al Pacino's Michael Corleone in *The Godfather* and *The Godfather Part II.*

24 Zsa Zsa and Magda Gabor.

25 Robert Ryan, nominated for *Crossfire.*

26 Victor McLaglen.

27 Charles Laughton.

28 Claudette Colbert.

29 John Lithgow.

30 1-b, 2-h, 3-e, 4-o, 5-f, 6-c, 7-m, 8-n, 9-d, 10-g, 11-a, 12-k, 13-i, 14-l, 15-j.

31 Bing Crosby. "Sweet Leilani," "White Christmas," "Swinging on a Star," and "In the Cool, Cool, Cool of the Evening."

32 "When You Wish upon a Star" by Jiminy Cricket.

33 "The Woody Woodpecker Song."

34 Muppet Kermit sang "The Rainbow Connection" from *The Muppet Movie*, 1979.

35 Jack Albertson.

36 George C. Scott.

37 Kim Stanley.

38 Ruth Gordon, Peter Ustinov, and John Houseman.

39 Montgomery Clift.

40 Ronald Reagan and Ann Sheridan; George Raft and Hedy Lamarr.

41 Spencer Tracy.

42 *It Happened One Night* (Clark Gable and Claudette Colbert) and *One Flew over the Cuckoo's Nest* (Jack Nicholson and Louise Fletcher).

43 All have received their only Oscars for directing.

44 All have won Oscars for Best Actor/Actress, and all have directed themselves in films.

45 Cher.

46 Bing Crosby and Walter Brennan.

47 *Finian's Rainbow, One from the Heart* and *Cotton Club.*

48 Audrey Hepburn.

49 *Sleuth* (Laurence Olivier and Michael Caine) and *Give 'em Hell, Harrry* (James Whitmore).

50 Jennifer Jones.

51 All have been nominated for an Oscar in two acting categories in the same year.

52 He was awarded the only Oscar ever given for Title Writing (for *Telling the World*, 1927–28). He was also the first Oscar winner to die.

53 Jeanne Eagles, for *The Letter*, 1928–29.

54 All were nominated for Best Actor after they died. Only Peter Finch won (for *Network*, 1977).

55 All five films had three performers nominated in a single category. *Bounty*: Clark Gable, Charles Laughton, and Franchot Tone for Best Actor; *Waterfront*: Rod Steiger, Lee J. Cobb, Karl Malden for Best Supporting Actor; *Jones*: Diane Cilento, Joyce Redmon, and Edith Evans for Best Supporting Actress; *Godfather*: James Caan, Robert Duvall, and Al Pacino for Best Supporting Actor; and *Godfather II*: Lee Strasberg, Michael V. Gazzo, and Robert De Niro for Best Supporting Actor.

56 Because of the attempt on Ronald Reagan's life.

57 Both won for portraying living people—Jake La Motta and Loretta Lynn—both of whom were in the auditorium that night.

58 Albert R. (Cubby) Broccoli. His grandfather developed the hybrid vegetable that bears his name.

59 Charles Chaplin's score for *Limelight* won twenty years after the film was released.

60 *When My Baby Smiles at Me, Peyton Place, Pillow Talk, Mogambo,* and *The Rose.*

61 *Let It Be.*

62 Jon Voight.

63 John Ford. For *The Informer, The Grapes of Wrath, How Green Was My Valley,* and *The Quiet Man.*

64 *It Happened One Night, Mr. Deeds Goes to Town,* and *You Can't Take It With You.*

65 *The Bitter Tea of General Yen.*

66 *The Bells of St. Mary's.*

67 All have won Oscars in both acting categories—leading and supporting.

68 One, for directing *Reds.*

69 *Internes Can't Take Money.* Joel McCrea.

70 They won Oscars the only times they were nominated.

71 Paramount and RKO, respectively.

72 *Another Part of the Forest.*

73 Liza Minnelli and Ingrid Bergman. Vincente Minnelli.

74 Edmund Gwenn.

75 *Stagecoach.*

76 Hoagy Carmichael, Barbra Steisand, Keith Carradine, Paul Williams, and Irene Cara.

77 Henry Mancini and Johnny Mercer, who wrote "Moon River" in 1961 and "Days of Wine and Roses" in 1962.

78 Irving Berlin, for "White Christmas," in 1942.

79 *The Unsinkable Molly Brown, Saturday Night Fever, Rocky, The Defiant Ones, A Song to Remember,* and *Days of Wine and Roses.*

80 England's King Henry VIII and Queen Elizabeth I—Laughton in *The Private Life of Henry VIII* and *Young Bess*, and Davis in *The Private Lives of Elizabeth and Essex* and *The Virgin Queen.*

Index